MW01130281

Adventures in Special Education and Applied Behavior Analysis

A Practitioner's Guidebook to Understanding and Treating Problem Behaviors in Schools

Merrill Winston, Ph.D. BCBA-D

Professional Crisis Management Association

Sloan Publishing
Cornwall on Hudson, NY 12520
www.sloanpublishing.com/behavior

Library of Congress Cataloging-in-Publication Data

Winston, Merrill.
Adventures in special education and applied behavior analysis : a practical guidebook for understanding and solving behavior problems in school / Merrill Winston, Ph.D., BCBA, Professional
Crisis Management Association.
pages cm. -- (Adventures in special education)
Includes bibliographical references and index.
ISBN 978-1-59738-056-0 (alk. paper)
1. Children with disabilities--Education. 2. Behavior disorders in children--Treatment. I. Title.
LC4015.W56 2015
371.9--dc23
2015016057

Cover design by Amy Rosen, K&M Design, Inc.

Sloan Publishing, LLC
220 Maple Road
Cornwall-on-Hudson, NY 12520

An earlier version of this book was self-published by the author under the title,
"Adventures in Special Education: A Practitioner's Guidebook to Understanding
and Treating Problem Behaviors in Schools" (2012)

Printed in the United States of America

10 9 8 7 6 5 4 3 2

ISBN 13: 978-1-59738-065-2
ISBN 10: 1-59738-065-2

Contents

Acknowledgements

I would like to dedicate this book to the first kid with disabilities I ever worked with, Peter. My professors taught me about behavior analysis, but Peter taught me about behavior, behavior change and how rewarding it can be to see children get better and give parents hope. B. F. Skinner is known for saying the "rat is always right." Well, in this case Peter was always right. Eventually I was never worried about making a clinical error because Peter always corrected me (and typically it wasn't the nicest of corrections).

I would also like to extend my thanks and gratitude to the following individuals who shaped and continue to shape my behavior: Jim Johnston, Hank Pennypacker, Peter Harzem, Raymond Pitts, Dean Williams, M. Christopher Newland, Gerald Shook, Steve Starin, Michael Hemingway, Neal Fleisig, Vincent Carbone, Jim Partington, Patrick McGreevy, Steve Ward, Jeff Kupfer, Ennio Cipani, Glenn Latham, Eb Blakely, Brian Jacobsen, Pamela Tepsic, David Lubin and all of the kids, parents, and teachers that I've worked with over the past 10 years. Oh yes, thanks to visionary Steve Jobs, and all the people at Apple who helped me create some educational materials that are easily accessible, convenient, and engaging. Of course Apple should be thanking me for making you all buy iPads….You're welcome.

A special thanks to my wonderful wife and colleague, Laraine Winston, M.S., BCBA who read this damn thing almost as much as I did and provided me with insightful feedback, the motivation and encouragement to finish the book, and tried to keep me as politically correct as possible (the jury's still out on that one).

Chapter 1

Introduction

1.1   Who is this book for?

First, those of you not reading this on an iPad are really missing out! You can find it in the iTunes bookstore. Okay, now we can start. This book is intended to assist behavior analysts, special educators, and other professionals in their treatment of persons with disabilities who exhibit behavior problems in classroom settings. Now, I realize that I use the phrase *behavior analyst* a lot in the book. This does not mean that if you're a teacher dealing with behavior problems that I am not talking to you as well. Sure, sometimes I'll say something like, "Okay teachers, leave the room now because I just want to talk to behavior analysts and I don't want you to learn all our secret passwords and handshakes," but that doesn't mean it's meant only for behavior analysts. Look, if you're trying to *understand behavior* so that you can learn 1) how *you* can behave differently, 2) how to change the environment, and 3) *how to pick skills to teach*, then this book is for you. Also, as long as we're getting to know one another, I have worked with some of the most awesomely awesome teachers there could ever be. I have defended them, praised them, and listened to them patiently when they were in tears. Now that doesn't mean that I haven't consulted with some teachers who have no business teaching, but the same can be said of behavior analysts. I have the greatest respect for teachers, especially those who work with children with challenging behavior. I'm pretty sure that regardless of how balanced I try to keep things that I am going to burn somebody's biscuits, but that isn't my intention, just an unfortunate side effect of asking people to take a good hard look at *what* they're doing and *why* they're doing it. I personally am not concerned with how "right" I am, but I am very concerned about continually increasing my competency. As I tell parents, I'm happy to be proven wrong if it means that their child gets better and I learn something new and useful.

Regarding parents, although this book is not specifically intended for parents, it doesn't mean that they won't find useful information that might help them understand their own child better and how other professionals are trying to help him or her. So, although this book is intended for behavior analysts and other professionals with *some knowledge* of behavior analysis, parents are encouraged to read it as well as they, as a group, will be mentioned often and can be critically important in the success of their children at school. So, if you are NOT a member of one of the aforementioned groups of individuals, please put this book down immediately and try to get a full refund. I'm quite certain that you've got something good recorded on your DVR, and the sooner you watch it the sooner you can make space for the other 25 shows that you don't have time to watch. Incidentally, sometimes I'll be speaking directly to the behavior analyst, sometimes to the teacher, and sometimes to the parent. Be forewarned, this book contains within its massive pulp a veritable B-52 loaded up with a full compliment of "truth bombs." I'm going to say some stuff that some people are not going to like, and that's okay, but I'm not writing this book to confirm what everyone has been told before. I'm going to be shaking the tree to see what falls loose. It's quite possible, in keeping with the tree-shaking analogy that someone, including me, is going to get hit with a few coconuts. However, if a blow to the head gets people to start thinking critically about what they're told (and that includes what I am saying) then the book will have served one of its functions.

1.2   What is the goal of this book?

This book is the product of over 25 years of experience in the field of behavior analysis and intellectual disabilities, the last 10 of which were spent working with children with a variety of disabilities in public school settings. Although I am a traditional behavior analyst and do use the typical "tools of the trade" in terms of the assessment and treatment of behavior problems I have, like many longtime behavior analysts, developed my own style, methods, and "tricks" for treating behavior problems. I have also developed a particular philosophy that looks at the child in the broader context of how typically developing children (and adults) behave. Although I have written hundreds of recommendations for teachers working with children with behavior problems, this is not a book about how to write programs or how to conduct a functional assessment or even necessarily how to treat a specific topography (physical form) of a behavior e.g., "How do you stop children from throwing things?" or "What do you do with a child who is noncompliant?" Instead, this book will focus on how to *conceptualize* the problem that the child presents.

1.3   Emphasis on the problem

During the last decade of my work as a Behavior Analyst I have begun to focus less on the *behavior* part of the phrase "behavior problem" and more on the *problem* part. Now my major professor, the venerable Dr. James M. Johnston, would be rolling in his grave[1] if I didn't mention that the behavior itself is worthy of study in its own right and is not merely a symptom of some deep underlying psychological cause. Clearly, if a child is hitting her head, the head hitting must be stopped and there are a number of ways to stop the behavior. Some methods might require no analysis whatsoever, and some might require a functional analysis in which we manipulate variables that have been known to produce behavior problems and note the corresponding changes to behavior as a function of different conditions. Still other analyses might go even deeper to try to track down multiple variables in the causal chain, all of which "conspire" to produce the undesirable behavior. We can analyze behavior in various ways by changing from a zoom to a wide-angle lens, if you will.

One way to explain this approach is that for a child exhibiting severe self-injurious behavior, the behavior is most certainly A problem, but it is most definitely not THE problem. Many clinical psychologists have criticized behavior analysts because, according to them, we treat only the symptom (self-injury) and not the underlying cause. Well, I believe that there is a certain grain of truth to that criticism. I would agree that in some ways the behavior is a symptom, but that the variables that give rise to it are not necessarily "underlying" or even "deeply rooted" or any other subterranean metaphor. I believe that there's truly something to be gained by seeing behavior as a symptom, a very serious symptom, of a broader problem or set of interrelated problems. Now, for the behavior analysts in the room, I am not proposing that we forsake the holy grail of modern-day behavioral treatment and give up the functional analysis (Iwata, Dorsey, Slifer, Bauman and Richman, 1994) in

---

[1]Of course Jim would not actually be rolling in his grave because the last I checked he was still alive and well and, as he put it, "not that old." So, he would probably just be rolling in his sleep, but either way, he'd definitely be rolling.

which we assess alone, attention, and demand conditions for their impact on behavior. I am suggesting, however, that such an analysis should be considered just the beginning of our assessment and not by any means the end. Let's take our example of the girl who hits her head. As mentioned above, we could have a significant affect on the self-injurious behavior by using a powerful punisher, or by providing copious amounts of positive reinforcement contingent on the absence of the behavior for a short pre-specified time. These "blind" procedures, as I like to call them, may certainly improve the behavior yet may not be the most complete treatment. I refer to these procedures as blind because the clinician is blind to the reason(s) that the behavior is occurring and yet there is still a chance that the procedures will have a favorable outcome with little or no knowledge of the history of the individual or the development and maintenance of the behavior problem. This is more akin to what people used to refer to as "behavior modification." My father once and forever modified my behavior of playing with a ball indoors (I broke a light fixture) through the single high velocity application of a fashion accessory used to hold up one's pants. He didn't particularly care WHY I was playing ball. He didn't know if I was doing it to fulfill some primal need to visually track small objects, or to avoid work, or to gain his attention or just because I was bored out of my mind. It turns out that it didn't really matter because the behavior never occurred again. Behavior modified. End of story.

Modern-day behavior analysis goes quite a bit further and is arguably more elegant and certainly more analytic than my "father's behavior modification." Today, it is generally considered to be standard practice to look at the immediate consequences that maintain a behavior at its current level to gain insight into "the function" of the behavior or the purpose that it serves in meeting some need of the organism (child). We also look at the antecedents (major players in the causal chain) to help determine not only why the behavior continues day after day, but also what kicks off any particular episode. Once we are reasonably certain of the function(s) of behavior, by conducting an analogue functional analysis (a.k.a. real-time experimental manipulation) or by administering a less powerful functional assessment (taking a guess at function via direct observation and/or staff interview and data review), we try to decide which behavior to teach or strengthen that will serve the same "function" as the problem behavior. The assumption, which is a reasonable one, is that the "replacement" behavior will take over for the naughty behavior and that said naughty behavior will be forever banished to the behavioral equivalent of the Island of Misfit Toys[2]. So for example, let's say that we have determined that self-injurious behavior occurs only under demand situations. If we leave Paula alone, there is no self-injury. If she has been working for 5 minutes, self-injury occurs. The consequence of the self-injury is that the teacher terminates the demand and Paula gets some impromptu "me time." The behavior analyst decides to teach Paula to sign "break" the moment she starts to appear agitated. Paula learns (eventu-

---

[2]Personally, I believe that a water gun that squirts jelly would be sweet, particularly if you happen to like toast. If you have no idea what I'm talking about, then you need to watch the classic Rankin/Bass *Rudolph the Red-Nosed Reindeer* as narrated by Burl Ives. Long live the Bumbles.

ally) to sign "break" unprompted. The self-injurious behavior stops, and now the behavior analyst only has to worry about the much-dreaded generalization and maintenance of the new replacement behavior.

Now this scenario is quite common, and, when successful, will result in the cessation of the problem behavior and the acquisition and (with hope) maintenance and generalization of a new skill. Nonetheless, the overriding problem (not the underlying one) may still remain, and this is one of the main points of my book. The question of what maintained the behavior (escape from demands) has been answered, but other equally important questions may have never been asked. Questions like:

Why does Paula wish to escape?

Does she always want to escape?

Does she hate all work or just certain kinds of work?

Does she hate work or does she hate the person she is working with?

Does she have difficulty with any task that is longer than 5 minutes?

Do other children try to escape from the same task? If not, why not? (very important)

If we don't attempt to ask and then answer these kinds of questions, I believe that our analysis or assessment is not so much *incorrect* as it is *incomplete*. When a behavior analyst explains the premise above to teachers, they will often say "Okay, I get it, she doesn't know how to say she doesn't want to work, so we will teach her the right way to let us know, but what happens when she starts signing "break" all day long? I can't just let her sit on her beanbag chair all day! I have IEP (Individualized Education Program) goals to implement!"

This (highly valid) criticism can be dealt with by explaining to the teacher that we will teach the child (eventually) how to wait after she asks for a break or that she can only get a break 3 times in a row and then she has to work, etc. The problem remains, however, that we have not really addressed the issue of why she is so motivated to escape. In this hypothetical scenario, for our purposes here, the self-injury really isn't the important issue. It's a problem that must be stopped; we can all agree on that. The issue revolves around work and why she wishes to escape. We can certainly teach better ways to escape, but she's in school and we need her to work so that she may learn. It is here, in my humble opinion, where the bulk of our work lies. If we conduct this kind of analysis of problems we will not only rid the individual (and society) of the problem behavior, but we will end up helping her be more successful at school and, dare I say it, happier.

1.4   Organization of the chapters

Although the emphasis of this text will be the assessment and treatment of problem behavior, other school-related topics will be touched on as well including working with the major players (teachers, parents, principals, behavior analysts). Other topics will include issues related to diagnostic labels as well as included classrooms and how they may positively or negatively affect a child's behavior. There will also be a section on the use of restraint and seclusion in classrooms including how they both can be used properly, how they can be abused, the utility of using them at all, and what questions parents should be asking school officials about their usage. Naturally, no book about behavior change could be complete without addressing the issue of punishment, and there is a chapter devoted to that topic as well. The remaining chapters will be devoted to different categories of problems. These categories are:

1. Problems with reinforcers
2. Problems with aversives
3. Problems that are chronic versus intermittent
4. Problems with adults
5. Problems with peers
6. Problems with repertoires
7. Problems with teaching and curriculum

Note that these categories are not organized by function of behavior (to get things/attention, to stop/avoid things, or "automatic reinforcement" (self-stimulation). Neither are they organized by type of behavior (aggression, self-stimulation, self-injury, pica, etc.). For example, we aren't going to look at pica (eating inedible or nonfood items) in terms of "how do you get rid of pica," or "what treatment is good for pica?" but in terms of what kinds of problems does pica reflect? Well, for one it reflects a possible reinforcer problem, that is, the person's behavior is controlled by aberrant (atypical) reinforcers. Chuck likes to eat pencil erasers and he is not supposed to like eating pencil erasers. We can still ask numerous questions about the pica behavior that may help reveal more about the individual and why he eats things that other children do not. Knowing that the pica may serve a so-called "automatic reinforcement" function (they do it because it feels good) will not necessarily help us specify other factors responsible for its occurrence or tell us what to do about it. Furthermore, these seven categories are not necessarily mutually exclusive. That is, reinforcers and aversives can be seen as two sides of the same coin. Also, problems with adults may be related to problems with peers. For example, some children who like inordinate amounts of attention from adults (Category 4: Problems with adults), may also like a special form of attention characterized by angry facial expressions, (Category 1: Problems with reinforcers) and one way to make adults angry is to attack children who are the most defenseless (Category 5: Problems with peers). So it's easy to see that a single behavior problem (hitting peers) could easily cut across several categories of problems. In attempting to see how any single behavior problem can be viewed from different angles and from different distances, it is easy to conclude that we can address not just one, but several problem areas. In addressing the problem from different perspectives we may help create more lasting, meaningful, clinical gains because we are not just trying to stomp out "aggression."

1.5 Discrepancy analysis

Although I'm not sure if she coined the phrase, (I only know that I did not) Dr. Christine MacFarlane at Pacific University has used the term *discrepancy analysis*, and she defined it as "the difference between what is required of a non-disabled peer to succeed independently in a particular setting and the current level of performance demonstrated by the student with severe disabilities" (MacFarlane, 1998). The term is also used in some educational testing instruments (Pearson WIATT-III). The term is generally used to refer to discrepant skills so that it is easier to determine which skills should be taught. Dr. Ennio Cipani, a good friend and colleague of mine has been using the term since the nineties, so he clearly scooped me, but that's okay, he's a good guy to get scooped by. He also used the term "performance discrepancy analysis" (Cipani & Schock, 2007). I will use the term here to help the practitioner ask questions about what a typically developing child would do when exposed to the same kinds of situations as a child with disabilities who engages in problem behavior. For our purposes here, I would like to define a discrepancy analysis as:

> An analysis of the reasons why the child exhibiting behavior problems does not respond in the same (acceptable) ways as a non-disabled peer who is exposed to the same situations.

It's a fairly simple definition, but then again, the idea itself is fairly simple yet useful. When analyzing the reasons why one child behaves one way and another child behaves a different way when confronted with the same problem, we would look at differences in skill levels, the absence of entire repertoires, differences in histories of reinforcement, differences in social environments, etc. My point is that there are typically a number of reasons why a child with a disability displays behavior problems in situations where another typically developing child would not. There may also be several reasons why one student tries to escape from a math-based task and another does not. What I am urging the reader to do is to focus not on a single reason why a behavior problem continues but on a few of the reasons why the problem continues. True, we may never figure out *everything* responsible for a particular behavior problem, but we will most likely be more effective clinicians if we don't stop our analysis at the first most obvious cause.

1.6 Problems

I'll talk about a variety of kids I've worked with to help illustrate problems and the ways to conceptualize solutions to those problems for each category listed. I have purposefully changed the names and/or genders of the children in the examples and have withheld their diagnoses so as not to violate confidentiality. I usually don't want to know their diagnoses anyhow, but that's a discussion left for Chapter 10. Please keep in mind that this text is not intended to be a behavioral "cook book," nor is it a summarization of the current applied research. That's a different book. I will, however, list references as relevant. This text is intended to give guidance and to help practitioners look in places they typically don't look so that they may gain new insights into solutions for behavior problems. Applied Behavior Analysis is, in essence, an exercise in problem solving and, as a group, behavior analysts[1] are pretty good in that regard. That said, I still believe our greatest problem is that we are sometimes not very good at recognizing and then clearly stating the less obvious problems. While reading this book, please try to keep in mind that not all problems are so "high profile" as severe self-injury or aggression. Some problems are much less noticeable; they may not even result in a request for the services of a behavior analyst. Still, some children with disabilities can suffer not only from what they do, but also from what they have not yet learned how to do. Clearly, things that are problems from an adult's perspective are not always problems from the child's perspective, but the opposite is true as well. Incidentally, in case you haven't noticed, some form of the word "problem" has already appeared 54 times and we haven't even gotten past the introduction, which I fear may be problematic (make that 55).

1.7 Diagnosis

The reader (i.e., you) will notice that I am not going to give the diagnosis of the children in the examples I use. Sure, many of them have had the label "autism" bestowed on them, but many have not. *This is not a book about treating autism.* Believe it or not, I'm probably going to lose anywhere between 25 percent and 50 percent in book sales because the word "autism" is not in the title, but that's the price you pay for being noncompliant. If I were really clever, I would have somehow worked autism into the title in a way that didn't undermine the theme of the book like, *Adventures in Special Education That Are Totally Not All About Autism!* At least that way Google searches would pick it up. This book is instead about treating children with behavior problems (of which children who are labeled "autistic" are a subset). It is my firmly held belief that we are not all that different, none of us. We all work the same basic way. We love things, we hate things, we are happy, we are sad, we are indifferent and we are angry. We are, more or less, categorized as different from one another based on what we love, what we hate, what we fear, and what we can and cannot do. No doubt, things are certainly more complex than this, and yes, biological and genetic variables and neurochemistry and neuroanatomy may be more relevant in some cases than others, but on the whole I believe that those characteristics just mentioned make up the bulk of the func-

---

[1]A behavior analyst walks into a bar... I'm just kidding. All the behavior analysts I know would never have left the bar to begin with and, if you've ever been to any behavior analysis conferences, you would realize that this truth is self-evident.

tional differences between developmentally delayed and typically developing individuals. The can of worms that is diagnosis will be opened up (with a mallet) in Chapter 10, but I just wanted to orient everyone and explain the *blatant absence* of diagnostic labels throughout the book. I would like everyone, at least while reading *this* book, to remove their diagnostic glasses and view children as children and not as autistic, ODD, PDD, OCD, ADHD, or any of the other labels ending in "d" with the exception of the label "child."

1.8 What population of special needs kids are we talking about here?

I'm so glad you asked that question! As Jim Johnston likes to say, behavior is behavior. I have worked with all ages of kids functioning at all kinds of levels and having all kinds of diagnoses. Verbal, nonverbal, medically fragile, and multiply handicapped. I still conceptualize problems and solutions the same way. What's the most significant difference between children to me? Language. Some of the strategies in this book require a reasonably sophisticated level of language: that is, the child would be able to have a conversation with you. Only some of the strategies require good language skills. I am confident that, regardless of the population with which you work, you will find something of value here. Some examples involve nonverbal children and others involve those who are verbal. Some examples involve younger children and some involve older children. A thorough understanding of the problems of reinforcers and aversives alone cuts across all levels of functioning. Working with children who are entirely nonverbal has its special challenges, but the same principles apply.

1.9 Curse words

This book is written in a sort of unusual style. Some of it is more pedantic and technical in nature, and some of it is more conversational. The only problem is that when I converse with people I tend to curse a bit now and then (actually, almost always). I'm an emotional person and it's just how I talk sometimes. I don't do it to be offensive; nonetheless, I have been advised by some colleagues that using bad words might be seen as unprofessional and off-putting and might sully my message and/or distract the reader from my main points. One individual suggested that I use the word "diddly" in place of another more vulgar term, yet "diddly" doesn't quite convey the same feelings, emphasis, or sense of exasperation or urgency. To remedy the situation, I have decided to use ampersands, asterisks, exclamation marks, and the "at" sign, etc., to convey to the reader that I'm cursing. That way the reader may insert whichever word he or she is comfortable with and *technically* there will be no foul language in the book. Sure, I may use some phrases that might increase the probability that readers will *think* of a bad word, but only if they had a general inclination to do so in the first place. So, you should most certainly feel free to replace *&^#$ with "diddly" or "squat" or you can even go old-school with "horse feathers" which was also a great Marx Brothers movie. I really don't see what the big &*$%@!^ deal is, but I suppose that my colleagues are correct. What?? I just meant "freaking." Man, you guys are such foul readers!

1.10 Questions

Last, this book is about questioning. I give quite a bit of advice in this book and I think some of it is pretty damn good, but that's just me. I'm not a researcher, I'm a clinician, but I was trained in how to think critically and in proper scientific methodology and I know enough to leave room for doubt in my hypotheses about behavior. This book is not about me telling new behavior analysts or teachers what to do; it's about things that I and others have found useful. I urge the reader to keep an open mind and to question what I have written, then go back and read again and think about it some more. Even after I write something, I'll look at it 3 months later and say, "What the hell was I thinking?" "That was total crap!" It seemed great at the time though. This is not very unlike most scientific endeavors. It's not that we're simply looking for the next best thing, but that we're willing (with hope) to let go of what just might turn out to be the second best thing when something new just makes more sense.

I ask many questions in the book, just like I ask during my consultations. It's good to ask questions. It means we're thinking. I only hope that this book will get all of you to start asking more and better questions and I'm hoping to give you all good question-asking ammunition. Everyone needs to ask more questions. Parents need to ask good questions, but first they need to *have* good questions. Sometimes they know something is not right with their child's education but they don't know what to ask. Sometimes the teacher fundamentally knows the child quite well, but the behavior analyst isn't asking the right questions to bring out the information. I see people who spend a lot more time complaining, demanding, and brandishing the sword of litigation, instead of asking good, productive questions that might lead to some meaningful solutions. If this book helps any of you come up with some better questions in your work with children with special needs, then it will have been well worth the effort. Some people will find this book very helpful and entertaining and they may be very thankful. Some may find it highly irritating, and still others may even find it a complete waste of their time. So to all of you, respectively, I would like to say, you're very welcome, take a Xanax, and no refunds!

— Merrill Winston, Ph.D., BCBA-D

Chapter 2

Problems With Reinforcers

INTRODUCTION

Although many people (including behavior analysts) might lead you to believe that punishment is the true root of all evil, the opposite is actually true. Positive reinforcement, more specifically, certain reinforcers, are responsible for an unimaginable amount of human suffering. Punishment never even stood a chance for the title of "scourge of humanity." Poor punishment, always a bride's maid and never a bride. We'll return to issues with punishment in Chapter 9. Why do I say that positive reinforcers can cause such misery? Well, for one, there is an entire government agency whose sole purpose is to control the use and distribution of some of the most potent reinforcers known to man. Yes, the Department of Alcohol, Tobacco, and Firearms. Three great things that go great together. As a nation, we love our cigarettes, we love our alcohol and we love our AK-47s. Unfortunately, too many people love them in exactly that order. There are entire specialized divisions of law enforcement agencies devoted entirely to the apprehension of criminals who peddle potent, life-destroying reinforcers. The Drug Enforcemenet Agency is another division of law enforcement that "polices" reinforcers that are so insidiously powerful that people are willing to both die and kill for them. Vice divisions of police departments also concern themselves with powerful reinforcers, namely gambling and prostitution. Where is the law enforcement division that handles response-cost, time-out, point-loss, having your gold stars taken away and losing that much-coveted trip to Burger King? Speaking of Burger King, the fast food industry is roughly the equivalent of the Columbian Cartel when it comes to selling the public powerful reinforcers that destroy lives. Admittedly, no one has ever killed anyone over a Value Meal; well perhaps if it were super-sized, it's hard to say for sure. Nonetheless, fast food is another genre of fantastically powerful reinforcers that can contribute to an array of health problems. My point is that reinforcers aren't always so nice-nice like gold stars, praise, goldfish crackers and Skittles, and sometimes they are a little funky. To each their own, until it becomes harmful or illegal or requires the services of a behavior analyst.

Remember, there are no bad kids, just bad reinforcers. There are reinforcers that are "good for you" and then there are those that really aren't good for anybody, especially when it comes to behavior problems. Some of these "bad for you" reinforcers are common, but still problematic. Some of these other "bad" reinforcers are what I like to term "aberrant" or perhaps "atypical," which sounds nicer. The former makes it sound like the person needs ten years of psychotherapy and a trial period of Abilify. At least the label "atypical" just means that, statistically, you're way out at the tails of that bell shaped curve. Atypical reinforcers demonstrate how a traditional functional analysis just does a drive-by in terms of specifying the scope of a behavior problem. Of course, the category of atypical reinforcers is only one of a number of categories of problems with reinforcers. Here are the ones we will examine in detail.

Atypical reinforcers
Intermittent reinforcers

Insufficient reinforcers
Short-lived reinforcers
False reinforcers
No reinforcers
Uncontrolled reinforcers
Low Rate reinforcers
Delayed reinforcers
Reinforcement magnitude problems
Reinforcers contingent on non-behavior

I suppose, for clarity, any discussion of reinforcers has to be preceded by a definition so let's get that out of the way first. Most of you are familiar with the positive/negative reinforcement distinction. Some behavior analysts like Jack Michael (Michael, 1975) question the utility of the distinction, but that discussion is for another book perhaps, and I haven't even finished this one yet.

Positive Reinforcement
A stimulus, such as an object or event, that follows or is presented as a consequence of a response and results in the rate of that response in   creasing   or   maintaining. (Mayer, Sulzer-Azaroff, & Wallace, 2014).

Negative Reinforcement
A behavior that is increased or maintained as a function of the contingent removal or reduction of a stimulus (Mayer, Sulzer-Azaroff, & Wallace, 2014).

For now, we will concern ourselves primarily with positive reinforcement, because we all know that negative reinforcement is evil and should be shot on sight.

SECTION 1:   ATYPICAL REINFORCERS

As mentioned earlier, I am using the term "atypical" because I really hate passing judgment on persons with disabilities. I like to try to see things from the individual's perspective as much as possible. I decided against "aberrant," "detrimental" or "non-socially normed" reinforcers, and I was also discouraged from using my favorite phrase, "#$*@ people shouldn't like" as my wife Laraine told me that it probably would not be seen as very professional, and anyone who knows me knows that I'm all about the decorum. Atypical reinforcers could take many forms, like something that's just kind of unusual for the child's age (Johnny likes caviar and not McNuggets), or something that is unusual for most people (like a young lady who insisted that you open your mouth so she could see all of your teeth), something that is unacceptable/unlawful (like a young man who thought it was hilarious to gently fist bump the breasts of an ample bosomed lady and watch the subsequent mammillary oscillations), or something that is just plain dangerous (jumping off of the tallest point you can find in the immediate environment). Atypical reinforcers in their most dangerous forms may result in sexual assault, battery and even homicide. For the purposes of this book, however, I would like to focus primarily on those atypical reinforcers that are unusual, unacceptable and dangerous.

SECTION 2: UNUSUAL REINFORCERS

2.1 Specific forms of attention

It is very common, like dropped toast landing butter side down common, for a functional assessment to reveal that the behavior in question is at least partly maintained by attention. In most instances, however, attention is treated as an undifferentiated "thing" and it is assumed that all attention is the same from all people. It is equally common that the problem is not simply that the child's behavior is maintained by attention, but that it is maintained by a very particular kind of attention, possibly only from a particular adult or peer. In some cases, the attention giver may appear upset, agitated, concerned or just really angry. I have heard many people refer to such attention as "negative" attention, but I find the term more confusing than useful and see no justification for its use. I think that some children just enjoy making people mad, making them cry, watching that vein in their head pop out or perhaps they just like breathing in the sweet air of desperation billowing out of an exasperated teacher. My point is that children are not *supposed* to like making the teacher angry. They are supposed to like making the teacher smile, but they don't and THAT is the problem, not attention per se. A child like this, when given the type of praise that would cause most children to positively beam with pride, may instead engage in his premier problem behavior. This might happen because the teacher attention wasn't what he had in mind, but this still gives the child an opportunity to access the atypical reinforcer (bulging forehead vein). Unfortunately, behaviors that produce this particular brand of adult attention are typically highly inappropriate at best.

It is a relatively simple matter to see if a child's behavior is reinforced by this "atypical" attention by making angry types of facial expressions contingent on reasonably appropriate behavior and then noting any increase in the frequency. Now it is entirely possible, as some of you may be thinking, that the child's behavior is not necessarily reinforced by anger per se, but that an angry expression is simply more stimulating and interesting than typical grown-up expressions, especially if said grown-up is normally somewhat deficient in their general emotional content. I have conducted numerous probes with children in which I would screw up my face and look like I was in pain contingent on some fairly appropriate play behavior. Children who like to access these forms of attention will typically laugh and show an immediate increase in the behavior that produced my elaborate facial contortions.

Although I am calling this type of attention "atypical," it's really quite common for people to tease their friends to see their faces go crazy for a moment. It becomes a problem, however, in that children with intellectual disabilities don't know "nice" ways to do the kinds of gentle teasing that we might do with a friend. Consequently, the individual may engage in low-level aggression, violate rules, and do things that are generally unpleasant for the adult.

It's easy to start asking additional "why" questions once there is some understanding that a behavior can be reinforced by this particular atypical reinforcer.

Why does the child like to access this particular kind of attention?
Does he seek any other forms of attention that are more typical?
What kinds of appropriate attention-getting behavior does the child display?
Does the child receive any attention at all when he is engaging in productive/prosocial behavior?

These are just a few questions that could be asked. Some readers may be wondering at this point what can be done about someone who reliably tries to access these atypical reinforcers? The simplest procedure, which I frequently recommend, is to act more predictably and robotically after any inappropriate behavior, and act like you've just found out you're being audited by the IRS after any reasonably appropriate behavior. All things being equal, this is a good general strategy even if it has never been demonstrated that a behavior problem is maintained by attention. Now this generic strategy of supplying a reinforcer that is relatively similar to the atypical one is not always possible or even ethical depending on the nature of the atypical reinforcer. Later in this chapter we'll look at the problem of attempting to "shift" reinforcers from less to more appropriate forms.

2.2 Inappropriate self-stimulation

Everyone engages in behavior that is known as "self-stimulatory behavior." It just so happens that we really only worry about it when working with people with disabilities. If there were a prize for the #1 redundant behavioral term, "self-stimulatory behavior" or just "stim" for short, would come home with the blue ribbon. Can anyone engage in any behavior that does not produce stimulation? Anything one does produces auditory, visual, tactile, gustatory, olfactory or kinesthetic stimulation. I think that what we may really mean, but never say, is that the behavior has no obvious use, you know, like watching television. Self-stimulation, often taken as a hallmark of autism, is seen by some practitioners as the bane of their existence.

Before continuing with this discussion, I should try to provide some clarification regarding terminology. The concept of self-stimulation or behavior maintained by "automatic reinforcement" can sometimes be misleading because people may believe that this is some special behavioral phenomenon that is somehow outside the realm of our ability to affect it. Behavior analysts may use the phrase "automatic" to denote that there is no social mediation (no one delivers reinforcement to the child). Of course to make the mechanical analogy complete, any socially-mediated reinforcers should be termed "manual reinforcement." Unfortunately, the terminology may do more harm than good, and ultimately it doesn't tell the practitioner how to behave differently. From a practical point of view, however, these kinds of behaviors may be more difficult to treat because the practitioner cannot control the reinforcer. For example, if someone's scratching behavior is maintained by the stimulation produced in the arm, this stimulation can't be blocked or prevented by another person. Yes, you could block the behavior of scratching, but when the scratching happens, you can't block the resulting stimulation of the arm. Sure, you could argue that it's possible to anesthetize the arm, but this sort of tactic is not always possible or ethical. I think it's safe to say that a strategy of anesthetizing someone's genitals to discourage masturbation would never make it past the local human rights committee.

Perhaps, from a practical point of view, automatic misses the mark. Some behavior analysts I have spoken to use phrases like "engaging in the behavior itself is the reinforcer." This is not likely a very accurate statement. In the case of masturbation, the act of flailing one's hand in the air without touching one's genitals is not likely something that occurs normally unless it is meant to communicate to another person something that is an act of futility. The reinforcer produced during masturbation involves the physical contact, not just the motion of the arm. Similarly, making a scratching motion with your fingers in the air near your mosquito bite is not likely to be reinforced. Certainly, things are more complex than this and one type of behavior could be maintained by several consequences. Does a child hand flap because it results in an increase in visual stimulation or kinesthetic stimulation or because it results in a decrease in the overall level of physiological arousal? It could be any or all of those consequences.

From the behavior analyst's point of view, the reinforcer in these cases might be considered "unblock-able," or at least very difficult to prevent. Please don't start telling everyone that Merrill invented this awesome new category of reinforcement called "un-blockable reinforcement" because Dr. Hank Pennypacker (my very first mentor in behavior analysis) would probably shoot me. I merely wish to point out why these "self-stimulatory" behaviors can be difficult to treat. It is undeniably helpful to demonstrate that a given behavior is not maintained by any social consequences (some form of attention) or even by any socially-mediated consequences (I just want the damn cookie, I don't even like you, but I need you to get the cookie). Unfortunately, this knowledge doesn't necessarily leave the practitioner in any better position strategically.

Now I realize that I more or less just trashed the term "self-stimulation," and, unfortunately, I'm going to continue to use it because so many people already know what I'm talking about. I just wanted everyone to understand that this category of behavior isn't all that special. Furthermore, coming up with a new more accurate but cumbersome phrase like, "Behavior maintained by un-blockable reinforcement" or "Behavior that may produce stimulation of others but wasn't meant to and any additional social stimulation is purely coincidental" would just make the book less readable than it already is.

Regarding the problem of self-stimulation, although many professionals may disagree (it's a free country and they have a right to be wrong), we do not need to eliminate self-stimulation. It's just the wrong goal, a goal that is derived from an inadequate specification of the problem. Hand flapping can most certainly be eliminated. "Self-stimulation," on the other hand, is like the Energizer Bunny: it keeps going, and going, and going. We have to specify the problem. Hand flapping looks funny, and is not very productive (if you value productive children). Incidentally, I love the phrase "hand flapping interferes with _____." You can fill in the blank yourself, go ahead, I'll wait…. This kind of statement is another fine example of the mis-conceptualization of the problem. Hand flapping "interferes" with teaching color matching about as much as watching television "interferes" with paying bills. There are two activities available for you to do. One of them sucks (paying bills) and the other one sucks less (watching T.V., and depending what's on it may suck even more). The hand flapping *does not* interfere with the task. The more accurate statement is that your attempt at teaching is interrupting (or producing) the child's hand flapping! Clearly, there was a conflict because the child had scheduled hand flapping at 9:30 and you scheduled speech. I guess she didn't get your text. Sometimes the hand flapping may occur during brief moments of down time, and because the child does not have her new iPhone 12 to check her email, she may engage in some hand flapping to "pass the time" (please don't get too excited, I don't know if there is an iPhone 12 yet, but by the time you're reading this there might be). Are these the only reasons hand flapping might increase or decrease? No, it certainly could increase or decrease based on current levels of physiological arousal (more on this in Chapter 3 on aversives), but remember, hand flapping is not the problem, it's the symptom. Could hand flapping also help the child avoid work? Sure, that could be an additional function and they all will have to be addressed.

One possible problem is that there may not be any other "appropriate" self-stimulatory behaviors in the child's repertoire. Another way of looking at self-stimulatory behavior is in the context of other freely available activities that can be instantly and consistently accessed. As an extreme example, hand mouthing is a huge problem, especially in persons with more profound disabilities, and those with severely limited motor abilities and/or who are wheelchair bound. This particular behavior, seen in individuals with these characteristics, can be extremely durable in the face of a variety of treatments. One of the reasons that this behavior is particularly intractable is that the hand mouthing is one of the few methods of producing reinforcement that does not require social mediation. It also requires little effort, produces instant reinforcement and is always accessible. Furthermore, the behavior is "appetitive" in nature, i.e., related to eating, which is another possible reason for the persistence of the behavior (Zhou, Goff, and Iwata, 2000). These characteristics of hand mouthing (instantly and constantly available, low effort, non-socially mediated) are the same characteristics associated with many forms of self-stimulatory behavior. Vocal stimulation, body rocking, playing with string, etc., can be difficult to compete with because they may be some of the few things the individual can "access" with no social mediation whatsoever. In essence, the child can start and stop it whenever he likes.

So, if you can never truly get rid of it, what do we do about problems of "self-stimulation?" The ultimate solution is to teach a variety of more appropriate forms of self-stimulation (socially acceptable or those that produce a socially valued product). For example, some forms of self-stimulation produce an outcome that is socially valued. If you are flipping string back and forth, it is seen as odd and undesirable. If you wrap string around sticks in a sequenced manner, we call this knitting and the result may be a sweater or a scarf or a set of ill-fitting socks (depending on one's skills). People who knit are essentially playing with string, they're just very, very good at it, and instead of telling them to stop it, we thank them for it. Sometimes the most difficult thing to do is to "get your foot in the door" with some newer more appropriate means of providing stimulation. Remember, however, that this new behavior must be as easily accessible as the behavior that we wish to discourage, and this is usually where people get tripped up. It might be useful to divide self-stimulation into two basic categories; material-dependent and material-independent (yes, I totally made them up).

Material-dependent means that the person is using some item to help produce stimulation. String flipping is common, playing with paper, spinning things, using toys inappropriately, etc. The great thing about material-dependent self-stimulatory behavior is that you can physically remove the item when needed. That doesn't remove the need for stimulation, but it gives you an opportunity to whip out some Premack principle! (Premack 1959; Premack 1962). Basically, the Premack principle involves low and high probability behaviors. You create a condition whereby access to the high probability behavior (playing with string) is only allowed after engaging in a lower probability behavior (pushing a toy car). If done properly, there is a good chance that there will be an increase in engagement with the new item and, as a bonus, the new item may acquire "conditioned reinforcing properties." This just means that repeated pairings of the new stim item (car) and the old stim item (string) may "enhance" the appeal of the new stim item. You know, like you may hate cats but you move in with someone you love who has a cat and soon you may begin to tolerate the cat. Later on, you may even like the cat. After a year you may even love the cat. Eventually, after many years in the relationship, you can no longer stand the person and then you and the cat live happily ever after. My point is not simply that I like cats, but that we can increase the number of independent self-stim types of behavior. The more enjoyable things the child can do independently, the less the need for *any single form* of stimulation. All things being equal, material dependent stimulation is probably easier to alter through substitutions/additions.

Material-independent is a bit trickier. This means that the child doesn't need anything but her own body, which she has access to all the time. These types of behaviors can be divided into fine motor, gross motor, and vocal. Some of the gross motor is just fine (swinging your leg back and forth while seated) and some of the fine motor is just gross (spitting on your hands and playing with it). The problem with all of them is that you can't take away the person's body parts; consequently this type of self-stimulation is available 24–7. We ALL engage in the same classes of behavior, be they fine motor (drumming your fingers), gross motor (pacing), or vocal (talking to ourselves, humming, singing, and whistling). Of the three categories, I think that fine motor is probably the easiest to work with because it can be stopped and redirected to an alternate form of self-stimulation. It's also easier to prompt behaviors that may be at least partially incompatible with stereotypical hand movements (holding a toy for example). Gross motor behavior is a bit tougher to redirect as it may involving jumping, running or body rocking. For gross motor, it may be necessary to see if there is some other activity that might compete with it, something that might yield potent reinforcers at a fairly high rate. Vocal self-stimulation can be among the most difficult to deal with because you can stop hand flapping physically, and you can prompt a person who is jumping to sit down, but it's quite difficult (and not recommended) to physically stop someone from making sounds. Remember, however, that the problem is not vocal stim per se. It is the volume, the particular sounds and where and when they occur. Even typically developing children will do "scripting" of favorite TV shows, singing and talking to themselves, but they can easily be instructed to do so quietly so that it's not much of a problem. Sometimes we just can't "get rid of" a behavior problem entirely but we may be successful in changing it to a less problematic form. A child who scripts TV shows loudly may be disruptive and the behavior may be inappropriate for certain settings. Children who sing softly to themselves or hum are doing the same basic thing, but it is rarely considered to be a problem. Whatever type of intervention you attempt, it is critically important that any "replacement" behavior (one that is alleged to serve the same function as the problem behavior) is as quickly and easily available and as easy to do as the undesired self-stimulation. If this is not the case, then the person will not likely engage in the alternate behavior, that is, it will not be as functional as the problem behavior. Always try to use a discrepancy analysis to look at the self-stimulatory behavior of typically developing children and then try to determine why the child with disabilities is unwilling or unable to do the same types of self-stimulation. What kinds of self-stimulatory behaviors are seen in typically developing children?

Rocking in chairs
Making noises (like sound effects)
Self-talk, whistling humming
Pencil tapping
Drumming on desks
Mouthing pens/pencils
Playing with hair
Scribbling
Leg swinging
Foot tapping

These are just a few examples, of course. The big difference between typically developing children and those with disabilities, however, is that typically developing children engage in these behaviors *while* they are engaged in functional behaviors, not *in place of them*. So, in some sense, the self-stimulatory behavior may not be the real problem. The real problem may be engaging in self-stimulatory behavior to the exclusion of all else! Remember, the more functional skills we teach, the more things we can redirect individuals to do. It's not that there's only so much room in their repertoire and we are going to try to "crowd out" the undesirable behavior, but that there will be a greater variety of sources of reinforcement besides body rocking. In the next chapter, on problems with aversives, I'll try to address the issue of self-stimulatory behavior that occurs primarily under aversive stimulation (duress).

SECTION 3: UNACCEPTABLE REINFORCERS

Although one might argue that it's usually *the behavior* that is truly unacceptable, sometimes it's the nature of the reinforcer that may be part of the problem. For example, the behavior of putting things into one's mouth and swallowing them is not necessarily a problem. We do it all the time. If that thing happens to be food from the trash, we've got ourselves a problem. That is, sometimes the class of behavior (eating) is not the problem, but the reinforcer that maintains the eating is the problem. My point is that asking why someone eats may not be as important as asking why someone eats a slightly used chicken nugget from the garbage can. Unacceptable reinforcers are sometimes a problem from a socially-normed standpoint, and sometimes the unacceptable part is not so much the behavior, but some inherent quality of the item. To put a new spin on something comedian Ron White says, it's not *that* you're eating, it's *what* you're eating. It's not that you like making sounds, it's that the sounds have to be very loud. Sometimes the unacceptable part is not the behavior itself, but only wanting to do the behavior in certain settings. It's not what you're doing, it's where you keep trying to do it. As an example, masturbation sometimes occurs at school, and there is pretty much a zero tolerance policy on that particular behavior. Often times, however, it's not necessarily the natural reinforcer that maintains the behavior (you guys know what that is), but the shocked expressions on the faces of others that may be the real problem in a school setting. If a functional analysis reveals that the behavior is maintained by a certain kind of attention, then I would argue that shocked expressions is the unacceptable reinforcer and this reinforcer can be accessed in a variety of inappropriate ways, not just by dropping one's trousers and gettin' busy. My point is that if the child didn't seek these particular reinforcers there really wouldn't be any problems at all. So, sometimes the unacceptability lies mostly with the reinforcer itself when the consequence is not socially-mediated (eating pencil erasers) and sometimes the reinforcer in and of itself is not so terrible, (shocked faces) but this "kind" of reinforcer can only be accessed by engaging in really bad behaviors (stripping). It's not that taking your clothes off is inherently bad, but it is this interaction between the behavior and the kind of consequence (reinforcer) that is the problem. Regardless of the specific behavior that the child comes up with, wanting to see shocked, frantic, embarrassed faces may be the real problem. Is it possible that masturbation is just masturbation and the child doesn't really care about anyone's reaction and just doesn't know any better? Sure, but then this would not be a reinforcer problem, but more of a skills problem (knowing where you are allowed to do those things).

As mentioned, another unacceptable reinforcer may be food on the floor or in the trash that prompts eating (a mild form of pica). Yes, I know all about the "five-second rule" for food on the floor, but I'm not certain of the medical research to back up that particular rule. Also, when it comes to some atypical, unacceptable reinforcers, there is simply never a good time or place to access them (playing with whatever was deposited into the toilet). The best bet is to attempt an analysis of the variables that lead to seeking these particular reinforcers and eliminating any motivators to the greatest extent possible while simultaneously providing alternatives. If everyone involved is reasonably certain that the behavior serves to access a particular non-socially-mediated reinforcer and not the attention of others, then the strategies described in the previous section on self-stimulatory behaviors should prove just as valuable for these unacceptable reinforcers. However, everyone should remember this...

If it comes out of a child's body, it's going to get some attention!

It doesn't matter whether the behavior happened for reasons completely unrelated to attention; it's going to produce it anyway. Will the subsequent attention make it worse? You must investigate that on a case-by-case basis, but if the child in question is known to seek a tremendous amount of attention, you can expect the behavior to increase over time if the reaction is large.

3.1 Dangerous Reinforcers

Some reinforcers, as mentioned in the beginning of this chapter, are themselves dangerous or can occasion dangerous behavior. Some children seek out bodies of water and subsequently may drown. Some may engage in life-threatening pica behavior, which can go far beyond just eating food off the floor. They may also eat nonfood items, items that cannot be digested, cannot be chewed and those that may get lodged somewhere in the digestive tract. These nonfood items can even cause esophageal tears and/or bowel perforations. The quality of these reinforcers makes them dangerous. On the other hand, some children like to be chased by adults (not dangerous in and of itself) but may run with no regard for their own safety. In this case, what the child wants is not dangerous per se (seeing things burn) but *what the child wants* occasions dangerous behaviors (running without attending to traffic).

Let's talk about how to conduct a discrepancy analysis for a child who "bolts" under the assumption that the reinforcer is being chased (a form of attention). Again everyone should understand that running might serve other functions or even several functions, but for our exercise here we will stick with the attention maintained variety. Is wanting to be chased a problem for a typically developing child? Not really, but the child probably knows:

How to ask to be chased
When running is allowed
Where they can and cannot go while running
How to stop when the adult says, "Stop!"
How to come back when the adult says, "Come back!"

Now, if you have "a runner" (and it really should be "a child who runs") how does his or her behavior stack up regarding the description above? I would say that most of the children I see who like to be chased are capable of exactly zero of the steps above. Well, that's one reason why "being chased" as a reinforcer is problematic and in some cases life-threatening. Many parents are scared out of their wits to take their children into the community because they display this type of behavior and lack the five skills just outlined. Let's go a bit further in our analysis. Given that the behavior isn't maintained by escape, why would a child suddenly want to run? Would she want to run if she were already engaged in an activity that produced numerous reinforcers, including but not limited to teacher attention? B.F. Skinner used to say, "The rat is always right" (Skinner is generally regarded as the father of behavior analysis). We have to listen to the child's behavior because that tells us everything. A child who suddenly just "up an' runs" is telling us that this is the most reliable means of producing some quick action around here. The reinforcement world for a child (and for the rest of us) is an "economy" and it's all about supply and demand. If the supply of "exciting things" is low, demand increases (deprivation). In this case, the child demands a specialized form of attention and may access that attention by bolting. Also, running without permission gets reinforced and the child becomes increasingly stealthy in her ability to breach the classroom perimeter. I have had dozens of teachers tell me, "I just let her go, and don't chase her, but I keep an eye on her and she looks back at me to see if I'm chasing. When she realizes I'm not chasing, she stops." Now sometimes you can use this strategy, but sometimes you can't. In a closed hallway that doesn't lead to the outside, it may not be a problem, but some children will keep on running whether you chase them or not. Depending on the circumstances it can be a risky strategy. Running that is reinforced by chasing is like many types of "play" behavior. The question is, what type of play can the child access as *easily and reliably* as the "chase me" game? I knew a wonderful teacher who would play "monster" with a child as a form of reinforcement. He wasn't really a "runner" per se, but engaged in a great deal of inappropriate attention seeking. She would pretend to be a monster and say, "I'm gonna get you!" and he would squeal and run to the other side of the room. He clearly loved it and would frequently ask to play "monster." Would runners still be running if they had access to monster time? I don't know, but it could be worth a try, especially for a child who is deprived of this simple adult interaction. Now let's ask some "why" questions about the running.

Why does the child run? He likes to be chased.
Why does he like to be chased? Because it's more fun than what's going on now.
Why isn't there anything fun going on now? Because it's work time.
Why is the child not engaged during work time? Because running allows him to escape the task, and produces bigger, faster reinforcers and he can get these reinforcers (being chased) more easily.
Why is the child so motivated to escape the task?

These five questions, (and you could certainly ask more) are the underpinnings of what is known as a "root cause analysis." Originally used to get to the root cause (the first link in a chain reaction) of sentinel events (catastrophes), the root cause analysis forces us to go deep to the source of the problem by asking at least five "why" questions. If we stop short in our analysis we may only be putting a Band-Aid on things. As an example, what if we stopped short at step one? The child runs because he likes to be chased. Conducting a functional analysis might reveal this. One possible treatment might be to use an "extinction" procedure in which we withhold the reinforcer i.e., we wouldn't chase the child (assuming you could do that safely). Theoretically, the running would stop, but what about the greater problems specified in steps 2 through 5? Certainly, the running would be replaced with something else because we never got to the root cause. As mentioned above, we could go further than five steps and perhaps get an even more thorough treatment plan. Take a look at questions 6–10 here:

> Why can't the child tolerate more than a couple of minutes of work? Because he gets the same amount of reinforcement whether he works for one minute or five minutes.

> Why does he need so much reinforcement to do this task? Because he hates this particular task the most.

> Why does he hate this task the most? Because he makes many errors.

> Why does he make many errors? Because he is missing some critical skills that would allow him to do the task well.

> Why is he attempting this task even though he is missing critical skills? Because of improper assessment and improper goals.

I stopped at ten because ten is a nice round number and I think that I might have already lost half of you at six…. I think I've made my point, however. The five "why" questions may seem somewhat arbitrary, but asking them forces people to do more than just a surface level analysis of the problem. When you really understand the problem, on several levels, the possible solutions just sort of start bubbling up to the surface. I think this is why we sometimes get stuck while trying to treat behavior problems. This sense of being stuck can happen to the best behavior analysts. The answers we end up with after asking our five "why" questions not only help us converge on the problem(s), but also sometimes suggest solutions, and a detailed specification of the problem is not much help without solutions.

What are some other *dangerous reinforcers*? There may be certain reinforcers that are produced by aggressive acts. Dr. Eb Blakely refers to these as *Signs of Damage* (SOD). You can find the reference at www.fitaba.com. Some of these reinforcers may be unconditioned (like food and sex), or they become conditioned reinforcers by being paired with other primary reinforcers, but individuals may engage in highly aggressive behavior until the behavior produces some of these signs of damage. You can find the powerpoint of Dr. Blakely's presentation by following the previous link. You can also download references that support the idea of signs of damage from his website and some of them are referenced in this book.

SOD could also figure into some cases of more severe self-injurious behavior (SIB). These very dangerous (possible) reinforcers may range from significant destruction of property to pulling out hair, tearing clothes, causing emotional facial expressions and drawing blood. These signs of damage typically do not function as reinforcers *except under certain conditions*, which is pretty much true of just about any reinforcer. That is, a child may only seek signs of damage when exposed to a significant aversive event. For example, being scolded, losing a reinforcer, being attacked by another student first, and being stopped from obtaining a reinforcer (blocked access), etc., can all be aversive events. Just to make this seem a bit more normal, have you ever been really angry and just wanted to break something? It's not that uncommon. If you got mad and wanted to snap your pencil, would you be more mad if it broke or more mad if it *wouldn't break*? To me, it's just more satisfying if it breaks (Snap!). On the other hand, if *you weren't angry*, and if you *accidentally* broke your pencil (same result), instead of feeling better you might get so mad about accidentally breaking your pencil that you might purposely start breaking more pencils! Oh the humanity! I'm sure that many readers are wondering about what to do when the dangerous reinforcer may be a sign of damage. Well, it certainly isn't as simple as teaching the child the "right way" to get to see blood or the right way to break windows and make someone scream and cry. Those are very bad reinforcers. The way to approach treatment is, again, by performing a discrepancy analysis. We get mad, we get physiologically aroused too, and we may even feel like breaking things or hurting people (physically or verbally). Why don't we? Well, the answer is that sometimes we do, and we usually regret it, but when we don't, what keeps us from doing it? In short? The answer is that we have mad skills. I'm referring to *self-control skills* and *coping skills,* which we will talk about more in Chapter 7, so remind me when we get there, okay?

Remember, there are no bad kids… just bad reinforcers!

Aggression, be it against property, against others, or even in some cases against one's self can be a tricky thing to treat. Most people tend to forget that aggression is part of who we are as human beings. It is adaptive in many circumstances. Unfortunately, as we come across it in school settings, aggression is primarily "maladaptive" as they say (at least from our perspective and that of the victim). One thing to understand is that aggression is not a single thing. It is generally accepted among animal ethologists that there are two different kinds of aggression, affective (sometimes referred to as retaliatory) and instrumental (Behar 1990). In behavior analysis lingo we might say affective is a bit *more like* respondent behavior (like a reflex) and instrumental is *more like* operant (purposeful behavior). It isn't quite that simple, however. I am not implying that the act of punching is a reflex, that is, babies don't punch really well, and there is some learning that goes on. In fact, some persons with disabilities don't even make a fist when they hit, instead they use an open hand. Although punching or kicking someone is in all likelihood not a true reflex (like the Babinski reflex seen in infants or the knee jerk elicited by a tap on the patellar tendon), the physiological arousal that often precedes aggression is a different story.

I love cats. Not only are they great pets, but they're also great to talk about if you want to illustrate affective versus instrumental aggression. If a cat is in any way frightened or startled you will often see the classic "Halloween cat" pose complete with the arched back, hissing, and piloerection of the hair. I'm sure you all have a pretty good mental image. If you get scratched during that display, you have been a victim of "affective" aggression. Now, if you've ever seen a cat stalk and kill a bird or lizard (which it thoughtfully leaves for you at the bottom of the stairs), you have witnessed "instrumental" aggression. The cat didn't make noise or freak out, it didn't look excited (although cats aren't much in the facial expression department to begin with) and appeared to be very focused as though it had just received its morning dose of Kitty Ritalin. This form of aggression is typically quick, stealthy and highly targeted. The human equivalent would be the boxer. Children can behave the same way. Incidentally, we make these two seemingly distinct categories, but it doesn't mean that those categories truly exist in nature. In other words, we're making a division between the two so that we can talk about them, but that doesn't mean that they're completely separate from each other. I'm not entirely convinced that Mike Tyson's aggression was completely instrumental when he bit off a piece of Evander Holyfield's ear! Why is this discussion so important when it comes to treating behavior problems? For the simple reason that it is best to understand the problem as thoroughly as possible. For example, a child who engages in instrumental aggression (hits because of a history of getting a toy from her peer), may benefit more from learning a functional communication skill than the child who hits as a direct result of being attacked by another child. No doubt there still is some level of physiological arousal, even with instrumental aggression like boxing, and it is common for boxers to "lose their cool," which is really a reference to physiological arousal overpowering, if you will, the instrumental aggression (hence the ear biting). Coming back for a moment to signs of damage, my best guess at this point is that we are looking at behavior that is more instrumental in nature. It may be like what we call revenge. You don't just walk around exacting revenge on people. It doesn't work that way. Someone has to do something to you first (or at least you think they did, which is another behavior problem). After you've taken out your revenge on said person, you usually feel a bit better (maybe guilty, too). My point is that I don't believe that most people just walk around seeking to produce signs of damage, but that there are critical events that momentarily establish signs of damage as a reinforcer (we'll talk about motivating operations later). We will come back to aggression in the chapter on problems with aversives, as one of the primary causes of aggression is aversive stimulation.

3.2   Shifting reinforcers

Jet Blue is my new favorite airline! Dunkin' Donuts coffee on the plane? Outstanding! Now I don't like Delta anymore. Sorry, I've written at least half of this book on airplanes, so even the little things excite me now. Before leaving this section, I must address what the practitioner can do when faced with a naughty, naughty reinforcer. There has to be a discussion of what I'll call "shifting" reinforcers (from bad ones to good ones). This means that a person stops seeking one type of reinforcer and begins to seek a different one; hence it is the person that shifts, not so much the reinforcer. This happens naturally all the time, we just don't really stop to think about it, and it happens for a variety of reasons. Perhaps earlier in your life you might have dated a certain type of person, but later in your life you no longer sought out that type of person. You may have had a favorite food that you used to eat all the time, and now you eat it only once in a while. Children stop playing with stuffed toys and want to play with race cars or action figures.

Why do some reinforcers stop being reinforcers? There are, I believe, a number of factors that determine whether some item or event continues to function as a reinforcer over long periods of time. Some of this information on factors that affect the "potency" of a reinforcer comes directly from applied research (Zhou et al., 2000) and some comes from the animal literature (Courtney and Perone, 1992). We truly owe quite a bit to rats, pigeons and monkeys. It turns out that they have far more use than just eating holes in your baseboards, defecating on statues, and throwing their poop (Rhesus monkeys do this a lot, and trust me, Reese's Pieces are much nicer than Rhesus feces). In my opinion, some of the greatest determinants of reinforcer shifting are 1) the availability of the current (problem) reinforcer versus the availability of appropriate competing reinforcers; 2) the amount of effort required to obtain the reinforcer; and 3) reinforcer attenuation (making it less powerful, smaller, weaker). Please don't take this as an exhaustive list of factors. I know that it can't be because I just wrote it down in like five seconds. These seem to me, however, to be some of the most salient factors that we may be able to manipulate most easily. Let's take them one at a time and I will provide examples.

1. *Availability of the current problem reinforcer versus appropriate competing reinforcers.* As Mick Jagger says, you can't always get what you want. Luckily, we are fairly resilient organisms: we adjust. As a testament to this fact, my stepson Weston, when he was very young, had to occasionally receive some mildly unpleasant consequences for his behavior (or lack thereof). He was essentially a pretty good kid, and is now a fine young man, but now and then there would be some school-related problems. I remember one time in particular that he lost television privileges. He adjusted. Then he lost his music privileges. He adjusted. He then lost his "Harry Potter" book privileges. He adjusted. I believe that by the end of all our abortive attempts to motivate him, he was spending much of his spare time drawing. To this day I am convinced that had we taken away his notepad he would have undoubtedly used up all the toilet paper. Weston was one of those few kids who could adjust to almost anything and seek out other available reinforcers. Don't worry—he's doing quite well now and is becoming a responsible adult. I believe he's even had his television privileges reinstated, but he spends most of his time working, sleeping, and going to school. The ability to adjust to reinforcers is both a blessing and a burden. If you can always get used to being without certain things, then you will tend to be less disappointed on the whole. The down side of a child who displays this ultra-adaptability is that it may be difficult to motivate him because you may have nothing he wants badly enough to do what you want him to do! On the other hand, if a child can't adjust at all to the unavailability of a reinforcer then he is going to be very miserable (and he won't be the only one).

As another example, I would like to tell a "Tale of Two Italian Ices." One of them is called "Lindy's" and it will represent the bad reinforcer. The other is "Luigi's" and will represent the appropriate competing reinforcer that we hope will eventually be accepted. I used to just love Lindy's Italian Ices. I found their taste, texture and variety of flavors to be far superior to Luigi's Italian Ices, which I surmised, must be Lindy's fiercest competitor and longtime Italian Ice rival. I used to drive all the way to a Walmart many miles from my home to get them because the local supermarket didn't carry them. One ill-fated day while perusing the ice-cream novelty aisle I noticed they weren't where they should have been. Neither were they anywhere else. After the initial wave of panic subsided, further investigation and subsequent conversation with the stock manager revealed that this particular store wasn't carrying Lindy's anymore and I was advised that perhaps other locations might have it. Naturally I drove all over checking the other stores, but to no avail. Perhaps it was time for the ice-cream novelty 12-step program. Luigi's Italian Ices remained, of course, but I refused to buy them (I refused to shift) until I had exhausted every possibility. I was certain that there was some sort of international conspiracy and that the Italian Ice crime syndicate was behind the sudden scarcity of my favorite treat, yet I could prove nothing. Eventually, I just stopped looking for them and (slowly) began to accept Luigi's instead. They're still not my favorite, but they're better than nothing (marginally).

I know that many of you are wondering if the last paragraph is destined to become a movie because of the suspense, mystery and international intrigue, but I wrote it just to make a point. And that point is… I really like Italian Ices. Just kidding. The point is that children will still seek out the "naughty" reinforcer, even if it isn't present, as long as there are signs (discriminative stimuli) that it might still be available, and that they might go to considerable trouble to gain access to it, even when reasonable alternatives are also present. In fact, one way to determine the strength of a reinforcer is to see if it still maintains responding in the presence of other potential reinforcers. That is, how does it stack up to the competition? Allow me to illustrate.

I used to work with a woman with a developmental disability who engaged in pica (eating non-edible objects). Let's call her Justine. Justine would eat things off the floor, and she didn't go by the five-second rule, it was more like the five-day rule. Really there was no rule, and the items on the floor weren't always food. She searched for food on the floor almost constantly. She was blind, but would bend over and feel for floor snacks with her hand and then eat the items she found. Now, this was a problem reinforcer if ever there was one. After finding out that she really loved eating, we tried a probe in which we got her a fanny pack, filled it with puffed rice (to keep calories low) and then secured the zipper so that it would only open up enough to allow Justine to put in a couple of fingers to pull out a few small pieces of puffed rice. Yes, I know it seems like a mean trick to play on a person with disabilities, but we were trying to prevent pica and make her happy at the same time.

To make a short story longer, the pica stopped completely…. Yes you are correct, providing that she was wearing the fanny pack. Did we "cure" Justine's pica? No, we did not, it was mainly a stopgap measure to make her safe, but it was a damn good stopgap measure. Incidentally, Justine was happier than a pig in Rhesus feces. The fanny pack had to be refilled twice a day on average, and it was worn mostly when staff couldn't be right next to her. This illustrates quite nicely how you can battle bad reinforcers with appropriate competing reinforcers. This sort of tactic doesn't teach skills, but not every intervention demands it. *Her quality of life and safety both improved dramatically.* One problem in natural settings like schools, however, is that in many instances there are no competing reinforcers and the bad reinforcers run rampant. This can make it very difficult to stop children from seeking them at every opportunity. Just something to think about....

2. *Effort.*   Some behavior analysts use the phrase "response cost" to refer to the effort it takes to produce reinforcement, but others use it to denote the loss of some portion of a reinforcer that is in your possession (fines) contingent on naughty behavior (Siegel, Lenske, & Broen 1969). To avoid confusion I just decided to stick with "effort." In keeping with the Italian Ice example, I was willing to drive thirty minutes each way to get my beloved frozen fix. Would I have gone sixty minutes? Maybe. Ninety minutes? No way. Interestingly enough, during my travels I did find them one day at a Walmart in Marianna, Florida. I bought them and ate all of them immediately and was certain that I was suffering from hypothermia of the tongue. In reality my tongue appeared oxygen deprived because I bought the blue-raspberry flavor, but I was worried there for a moment. Now, I live in South Florida. Would I purchase a round-trip airline ticket, fly up to Marianna to get Italian Ices and then bring them back in one of those organ donor coolers? No. The effort would simply be too great, that and the airline would most likely lose the cooler.[1]

Allow me to illustrate how this concept of effort applies to a child with a "funky" reinforcer. I saw one child with two diagnoses, and possibly even a third one because the psychiatrist was running a special (pay for two and your third one is free). This cute kid had a peculiar behavior of holding up two items of different sizes (like a block and a paperclip) and then asking the adult "bigger or littler?" If you tried to ignore him he would escalate quickly. He engaged in this kind of behavior at a fairly high rate and wouldn't stop until you answered him. I decided to try to slightly increase the effort it took for him to get his reinforcer (which was an answer from the listener as to which was bigger). The very next time he asked me, I told him, "I'll tell you, but first, what's this?" and I held up a toy cow. He replied, "Cow." Then I asked him, "What does a cow say?" He replied, "Moo." I then told him, "This one is bigger!" and he was satisfied. Each time he asked, I added a few more questions. Within a few minutes he just stopped asking me the obsessive-compulsive disorder-like question. Furthermore, I made certain I complied immediately with any other appropriate question he had (very little effort on his part). No, I didn't "cure" his OCD-like behavior, but I demonstrated how increasing effort could alter reinforcer efficacy. Essentially, I spoiled a good thing by making him "work" for it. For this manipulation to work,

---

[1]Little did I know, but Winn Dixie had been carrying Lindy's Italian Ices during the entire Italian Ice Crisis of 2009 and I was none-the-wiser. Oh well. I have plenty of them now. In fact, that's another behavior I have to get under control.

the effort has to be increased *very slowly*, and other competing reinforcers must be super easy to get. That is, you can't take the effort from 0 to 100, where 0 is an immediate answer every time for "free" and 100 means he has to re-shingle the roof before you answer him. From a practical standpoint, requiring too much effort when trying to "ruin" a reinforcer is equivalent to withholding the reinforcer and it will produce the same undesirable results. "Daddy, can I have a pony?" "Yes sweetie! Right after you rebuild Daddy's transmission!" How does response effort relate to our friend Justine with the pica problem? She had to bend over and feel around for her floor snacks remember? It was very, very easy for her to get out a piece of puffed rice from her fanny pack, and it worked every time for her. Feeling around on the floor was sort of hit and miss. Justine's rate of reinforcement shot up, and her response effort plummeted. This phenomenon has been demonstrated in the literature (Piazza, 2002).

3. *Reinforcer attenuation.*   Okay, so this all makes sense so far, mostly to me, but I'm hoping that my readers are still on board. What about situations where the (naughty) reinforcer is just so much more potent than anything else you have available? You can try to attenuate it, which literally means to reduce the force, effect or value of something. Well, we kind of got a jump on that with the section on effort, because increased effort will reduce the value of something, but what if the child is very sensitive to increased effort and becomes aggressive? Then we can look at the possibility of changing the quality of the reinforcer itself. If you've ever had free drinks at the casinos in Vegas, then you know what reinforcer attenuation is. Yes, there is nothing worse than watered-down drinks, except for really expensive watered-down drinks. If they put enough water in them, you don't even want them anymore. This example gets at the magnitude of reinforcement issue. Magnitude is not merely size, but you might also think of it as "good," "better," and "best." If a child likes to tear clothing (perhaps a sign of damage), it may not be quite so satisfying if you are wearing your leather jacket. The child can still grab you, but can't really destroy the jacket. It's like a watered-down drink. Earlier in the chapter on the section covering atypical forms of attention, acting like a "robot" after problem behavior is a form of reinforcer attenuation. You really can't turn it off completely, but you can turn it way down. I recently worked with a young man who just loved to flip over chairs. Not really dangerous, but certainly not appropriate. He seemed to get particularly excited when the back of the chair hit the floor, because right at that moment he would scream. The resource teacher who was accompanying me suggested that perhaps the hardback chairs could be replaced with lighter chairs and that we might have maintenance attach a foam strip to the backs of the chairs in the classroom. It was fairly cheap, and easy to do, and I thought it to be a great idea. I'm not certain if it helped or not as I was not called in for a follow-up consult, but I am fairly certain it helped. That particular strategy was by no means a complete answer to the chair-flipping problem, but it may have made it easier for the child to switch over to a more appropriate plaything by potentially reducing the "wow" factor when he toppled the furniture. Remember, one of the aims of this book is to provide a number of vantage points from which to view a problem,

so that the practitioner can write a behavioral intervention that attempts to address all the child's problems, and not just the most obvious one.

SECTION 4:   INTERMITTENT REINFORCERS

Intermittent reinforcement is not by itself a problem. In fact, it's usually a goal to maintain desirable behavior under intermittent reinforcement for several reasons. One of those reasons is that we want children to be able to work independently without the constant need for some form of praise or tangible reinforcer. If a child requires high rates of praise, then it will be very difficult—if not impossible—to get her to work independently. Also, intermittent reinforcement makes behavior more resistant to extinction. This just means that you will continue to "persevere" even though there is no immediate payoff on the horizon (kind of like going to graduate school). We want behavior to be resistant to extinction so that children will "endure" even some very difficult tasks without any encouragement for long stretches of time. All types of intermittent reinforcement are not created equal, however. Fixed-ratio schedules allow for the delivery of the reinforcer after a certain number of responses, but these do not generate the greatest resistance to extinction. Furthermore, if the ratio is too high or increased too rapidly and the reinforcer too small (one hundred math problems for one Skittle) you get "ratio strain" and the person gives up in the middle of working (and may get really mad in the process). In the animal literature you may also see what is known as schedule-induced aggression or "adjunctive behavior" (Kupfer, Allen, & Malagodi, 2008). Adjunctive behavior occurs not in the middle of working, but *right after the reinforcer is delivered*. Other adjunctive behaviors in animals include self-injury, hyperphagia (overeating) and polydipsia (drinking too much, and not the Mardi Gras drinking too much). So under certain very long fixed-ratio schedules, a pigeon might attack another pigeon right after it earns food. My take on it is that the pigeon has to do a tremendous amount of work to get food and it likes getting the food, but the paltry food delivery also "signals" that he needs to get ready for another long, difficult pecking task. It's like you may like Sunday night because you can relax and watch television, but at the same time, you hate it because it also means that tomorrow is Monday and you have to start the work week all over again. Schedules of reinforcement in applied settings can be incredibly complex and may occur in sequence or be superimposed on one another. For our purposes, it's only important to understand that some behaviors can continue for a long time without any obvious reinforcement depending on how often reinforcement occurs and the magnitude (size) of the reinforcer.

Intermittent reinforcement is the thing that keeps us going in the face of adversity. That and some of the small conditioned reinforcers that arise from the work we do, like completing a book chapter! Intermittent reinforcement is also the thing that makes Las Vegas casino owners inordinate amounts of money. The people who program slot machines probably know more about human behavior than most behavior analysts, because when they're wrong the casinos stand to lose quite a bit of income and casinos don't like losing income. Slots are programmed according to the ratio of bets to payouts (on average) and the amount of the payout. Frequency of payouts can affect behavior, but so can the size. Usually slot machines pay out on some form of a variable-ratio schedule. That is, after two pulls, after ten, after three, after nine, after thirteen, after one, etc. The ratios are calculated using a random number generator, but the number averages around a mean. You really never know when your machine might "hit." Now throw into this mix, if you will, that the magnitude of reinforcement changes as well. You can imagine that a person who is starting to get discouraged after a few too many losing pulls might be highly motivated after hitting a larger than usual payout. A very small payout after the same number of pulls might cause the individual to move on to a different machine. Add to these factors that you can win more by betting more money, which might be seen as an increased effort or greater response cost. If a machine almost never pays out after twenty pulls, many people might just move on to another machine or stop playing altogether. The trick for casino owners, is to pay out as little as possible but still keep the person playing as long as possible. Do you see why they would want to do this? Those bastards! Not to mention that they water down those damn free drinks! This balancing act is really no different in other settings with other behaviors. Organisms (including school children) are constantly trying to maximize their reinforcement and minimize their efforts. We can't blame them for that, as all organisms do it. It's just what we do. The problem is that programmed reinforcers may take too much effort and may be too predictable. Different amounts of effort often result in the same level of reinforcement, and working faster won't necessarily get reinforcement faster. It doesn't have to be this way but it often is.

For example, James has to complete twenty math problems every morning. They are difficult for him but he does them. After he completes twenty problems, he gets five minutes of computer time. The problems are of varying difficulty, and no matter how hard or easy the problems are, the reinforcer is always five minutes of computer time. After he gets his computer time, if he wants more, it will take another twenty math problems to earn it. Now, for the sake of argument, let's say that James has to do twenty problems within ten minutes and wait for the timer to go off before he can access his computer time. So, not only does his effort have no relation to reinforcer magnitude (it's always five minutes of computer time), but how quickly he works doesn't matter either because the reinforcer is only available at the end of the 10 minute interval when everyone changes stations.

What would this classroom reinforcement do to our gambler in Vegas? Well, lets see, now the gambler always has to pull twenty times to get a payout, and the payout is always the same and it's a relatively small amount of money, in fact it's only fifteen dollars and our guy bets a dollar with each pull of the lever, so he's really losing five dollars every twenty pulls. Now let's add a delay to being able to claim the winnings. How fast our gambler places his bets has nothing to do with the rate of payment. That is, the machine pays only after ten minutes like in the classroom example. That means that no matter how fast our gambler pumps money into the machine, he still won't win anything until the ten-minute interval is up. But wait, it gets worse. No matter how large a bet he places, one, two, or five dollars, the machine pays the same amount, fifteen dollars. Our gambler knows he's losing money, he knows larger bets do nothing, and he knows how fast he plays in no way changes how quickly he gets paid. I know that "What happens in Vegas stays in Vegas," but if this were the way gambling worked, no one would go to Vegas in the first place.

Is it any wonder that sometimes we can't get kids to work even for things identified as "reinforcers?" What if things in the classroom were more like Vegas? No, we can't give children free watered-down alcoholic beverages and tickets to see Carrot Top (a well-known Las Vegas performer). Letting them see Carrot Top would be unethical. We can, however, make the contingencies for reinforcement more like they are in Vegas. James might get five minutes of computer time after two problems, then after ten problems, then after four problems than after one problem, etc. James would also be able to access computer time the moment the allotted number of problems has been completed. Finally, any time James had to do more difficult problems, he would get ten minutes of computer time instead of five. Now, just like the Vegas casino, the teacher has to find the "sweet spot" as well. If James gets ten minutes of computer time after every math problem, there won't be enough hours in the school day for him to "cash in" all his time.

What does all this have to do with behavior problems? Remember how our Vegas gambler would move to a different machine if the current one didn't hit regularly enough? It's the same way for the child in the classroom; only the different machine is called the "Wheel of Misfortune!" Like many unplanned behaviors, problem behaviors are almost never reinforced on a strict schedule. Reinforcement is usually intermittent, true, but it's not like the teacher *decides* to give attention after every fifth chair the child throws; that is, it isn't completely predictable. Also, the faster the child throws chairs, (typically) the faster the adult intervenes. Furthermore, problem behaviors may start out small and get bigger (require more effort). Finally, the reaction given may be larger for more effortful responding by the child. Sure, the reinforcers in our two examples are different (computer time versus teacher reaction), but which scenario is more like Vegas? Which scenario is more "wild and crazy?" The inappropriate behavior produces unpredictable consequences, and the teacher attention (the reinforcer) changes dynamically as a function of how fast the child responds and the effort he or she puts into the problem behavior. "Payouts" are sort of unpredictable and sometimes they are huge! Sometimes there is very little delay between the problem behavior and the teacher attention. In fact, in most cases, the more severe the behavior the faster the attention. It's generally a lot more like Vegas and a lot more exciting. Behavior that is reinforced (like in the example here) is much more resistant to extinction (a condition in which a reinforcer is withheld) than behavior that is reinforced on a strict, predictable schedule. Also, because bigger, more effortful behavior may produce bigger reinforcers it's very easy to unwittingly differentially reinforce (select for) more severe problem behavior.

This analysis makes a good case for arranging things so that productive behaviors produce reinforcement that is more "Vegas Style" and problem behaviors produce small, predictable reinforcers. What? Reinforce problem behaviors? Surely, that must be a typo. No, *thiss* is a typo. True, you can try to ignore a problem behavior, or as we say in the biz, "Put it on extinction." The one caveat is that behavior under extinction typically gets worse before it gets better. The behavior will often increase in magnitude and frequency and become more variable (and not in a good way). The question is always one of how bad the behavior will get at its peak before subsiding. As my friend Steve Ward likes to say, an "extinction haircut[2]" is never fashionable. Using an extinction procedure is fine if you can be reasonably certain that the behavior will not get too bad, and you can completely stop the reinforcer from being delivered. In applied settings like classrooms, however, this can truly be more difficult than one might think. If you are not fairly confident in your ability to cut off all sources of reinforcement, then you may be better off giving very (small) controlled amounts of reinforcement consistently and immediately after the *very start* of a behavior problem before it has gotten bad (Athens and Vollmer, 2010; Carter 2010).

As an example, you have a child who seeks the "naughty" type of adult attention in which adults get angry. If the child sometimes starts his chain of behaviors by making fart noises you can immediately approach the child and ask him (as if you didn't even hear the fart noises) if he needs any help getting started on his task. True, the fart noises produced some immediate attention, but it was very low-key and there was no discussion of farting noises. As long as your attention is: 1) given quickly, and consistently; 2) the level of your attention is always the same after the inappropriate behavior; and 3) it is a very small amount of attention, then it should be less Vegas-style and less exciting. Typically, what actually happens is that a teacher may hope that the inappropriate behavior goes away on its own, so he ignores it (puts it on extinction), and the child continues making the noises. The teacher may intervene after 3, 5, 8, 2, or 12 instances of inappropriate behavior. The child learns to persist until there is a payout. Also, teacher attention may start small for mild behavior problems then grow as the problem grows. This is what must be avoided. On the other hand, if a very small payout is given at the first sign of trouble, then there should be less need for the child to "kick it up a notch."

Giving small, boring, consistent reinforcers for the start of inappropriate behaviors is not sufficient, however. There must be exciting Vegas-style reinforcer programming for low effort (initially) academic tasks or other adaptive behavior. Naturally, we also have to address the variables that motivate the child to engage in the problem behavior to begin with. Another good thing about tiny reinforcers for every occurrence of the start of problem behavior (beside the point that it is no longer being reinforced haphazardly) is that the behavior will become much less resistant to extinction when you finally decide to just ignore it. This is

[2]Actually Steve uses the phrase "escape-extinction haircut" and this is when you purposefully cut your hair very short so that little kids won't pull it out when you won't let them escape from a task.

something you might consider after appropriate responding has become much stronger in the child's repertoire.

SECTION 5:   INSUFFICIENT REINFORCERS

God bless 'em, some people just don't need or want very much. They're content with always doing the same thing. It isn't necessarily only a characteristic of persons with disabilities, but can be a trait shown by just about anyone. Some children in classroom settings are quite similar. There isn't very much that they want. Typically, but not exclusively, these individuals are functioning at a much lower level than the typical child. As mentioned earlier in the chapter, they may engage in material-dependent or material independent self-stimulatory behavior. They may have very limited interests in adults, other children, toys, videos, computers, or edibles. Another problem arises when potent reinforcers are only available at home. Good luck getting someone to stay at a table and work with you if they only like swimming or jumping on a trampoline (yes, if you get creative the child may accept water play at the sink, or a "mini-tramp"). For many children like these, work is negatively reinforced. That is, they work to make the teacher go away. Perhaps this describes the relationship between you and your boss. This is especially true of individuals who engage heavily in self-stimulatory behavior (especially the material-independent variety), as you have nothing they want.

I recall working with a young man early in my career, and it was my job to get him to acquire some simple skills, but there really wasn't very much that he wanted. He really did like doing self-stimulatory hand flipping. He would roll his hand at the wrist while simultaneously opening and closing it while he looked at it. He did this primarily with his left hand. Not knowing what else to do, I scooted his chair in so that his hand was under the table to help prevent him from seeing it. I would ask him to perform a very short simple task and then, as the reinforcer, I would scoot his chair back and let him "stim" for thirty seconds to a minute, then we started again. This worked quite well, but in my opinion was not an ideal solution.

A person with severely limited reinforcers is a disaster just waiting to happen. Disappointment is just part of life, for every appointment you make, there can also be a corresponding dis-appointment. Remember my stepson Weston from the section on availability of reinforcers? He was easily able to jump from one reinforcer to another as his options were slowly curtailed, but what about someone with very few powerful reinforcers to begin with? I knew of an individual who loved having a shoelace to whip around. If he didn't have that shoelace he was miserable, as there was nothing else he wanted to play with. People were terrified that the shoelace might go missing and that he might become terribly aggressive if they could not find another one. When everyone started wearing Crocs he probably went into crisis. Some children only eat Chicken McNuggets and French fries. One kid I saw only ate Doritos at school, I swear, only Doritos! This is not just a problem because these kids are all going to need triple bypasses by the age of nine, but because something very bad may happen when there are no Chicken McNuggets or French fries to be had.

None of us were born liking everything we like now, hence the phrase "it's an acquired taste." If, the first time you drank whiskey, it were necessary to like it for you to continue to drink it, who would still be drinking it? At first it's nasty. Don't believe me? Give a shot-glass full to a three-year-old and let me know if she says, "More please!"[3] One of the greatest things you can do for children is to increase their range of interests. It creates more for them to do, and gives them "back-up" reinforcers if something is no longer available. How do you create interest in other things? In much the same way you increase the child's repertoire of self-stimulatory behaviors. If the new potential reinforcer is an object that can be manipulated, you can prompt the individual to touch/use it and then immediately give him or her access to the "default" reinforcer. Sometimes just a simple pairing will help an item acquire conditioned reinforcing properties. The taste of whisky is initially pretty nasty, but it's paired with the effects of alcohol, and in many instances a tremendous amount of social reinforcers from one's drinking buddies.

In a less hedonistic example, let's say that a child only likes "Barney" videos (you know, the oxygen-deprived purple dinosaur). Which reminds me, nothing better illustrates that one man's reinforcer is another man's punisher than Barney. If my only two reinforcers were string and Barney, I would use the string to hang myself. If you want to get the child to play with a toy, but she won't even touch it, you could just plop the toy down on the floor next to her just a few seconds before you start the Barney video. She doesn't even have to touch it. Also, you would take the toy away just before you stop the Barney video. There are no guarantees, but you might find that after a number of pairings like this that the presence of the toy alone might get the child a little bit excited. Also remember, *the right amount of effort can really ruin a good thing.* So anytime you are trying to introduce a new reinforcer, make sure that there is at least a tiny amount of effort needed to get the usual reinforcer (the effort should be gradually increased over time). You must also ensure that any new potential reinforcer is "free." Why do you think companies spend millions of dollars giving out free samples? They want you to give up your current reinforcer and switch over to theirs. Are they going to charge you twice as much and make it hard to get, or make it easily available and free? These strategies of making things free or selling them at low, low introductory prices (low effort) and pairing them with other powerful reinforcers have been used in advertising for years. These approaches are usually highly effective because, like casinos, large corporations lose big money if they're wrong. Why do you think they always show these young, ripped, glistening hot bodies demonstrating the new AB-Exploder 5000! It's practically exercise porn. If they show some hairy, sweaty, guy with a beer-belly exercising in a stained tank top and torn sweat pants how are you going to keep down those two shots of whisky you just had?

---

[3]My attorneys have informed me that I must explain that the statement above is for entertainment purposes only and that I do not advocate the consumption of alcohol by minors, although I highly recommend it for miners.

Expanding someone's range of food interests is quite a bit more difficult because many children (and I'm not just talking about children with disabilities) won't even sample the food. With some children, it's not even possible to get them to look at or touch the food. Personally, I don't even like to see mayonnaise being put on a sandwich, even though it isn't my sandwich! Sometimes the only answer is to fade these new foods in slowly, very slowly and to avoid forcing them on the child. Some of these kids are so tough that you can't even change the brand of chicken nuggets, so you might have to get the kid to accept the current nuggets cut into pieces and sneak in a couple of cut up pieces of the other brand. If you are dealing with a child with a serious eating problem, however, you will really need to recruit someone who has some expertise with feeding disorders.

SECTION 6: SHORT-LIVED, FALSE, AND NO REINFORCERS

Let's get some things straight first (sort of)....

Very often, when I'm consulting, I will hear from teachers that they can get a child to work for a particular item or activity, but that the child will not work for it consistently. These "reinforcers" may last a day or so, then the child loses interest and they can no longer be used as reinforcers. One problem is that reinforcers are, by their very nature, fickle things. Our own interest in pursuing things varies as well and we get tired of certain items/ activities/foods just like some children. Typically, you might find that children with fewer skills (those who can't really operate toys or computers or games) will be interested in the same thing day in and day out, just like very young children who are non-disabled. Most of us have witnessed a child's wide-eyed delight with a toy on Christmas morning quickly turn to indifference by New Year's Day or sooner.

In other instances, I will hear from the teachers that they can find no reinforcers at all and they can't even get the child to approach, let alone complete a task. For one child in particular, Jeremy, it wasn't that there weren't things he was interested in, because he most certainly was interested in playing with things, especially balls and bubbles. The problem was that the moment he smelled a work contingency (do this and then get that) he completely lost interest in the item (a.k.a. take this ball and shove it). Despite their best efforts, the teachers didn't have anything that he wanted badly enough to even come to the table and sit down.

This problem exemplifies a fundamental misunderstanding about reinforcers. Reinforcers are not static things. They are dynamic "living" things and in the land of reinforcement, context is King. We call "things" (stimuli) reinforcers because they have been known to strengthen certain behaviors, or because we suspect that they might be able to. The question "What are Joeys reinforcers?" is a very misleading question indeed. A better question would be, "What things have been shown to maintain working on math problems for twenty minutes on days when Joey hasn't been able to play with anything all day?" That's kind of a mouthful to say the least, but it's far more accurate. Saying, "There are no reinforcers" doesn't really make sense without the context of what Joey is being asked to do. Most reinforcer assessments don't apply this acid test of looking for changes in behavior over time depending on the task: instead, they're usually based on the number of times an item is chosen from a lineup, or they're based on how a child distributes his or her time interacting with various items (Piazza, Fisher, Hagopian, & Toole, 1998). These are encouraging indications that the items "may" function as reinforcers for certain levels of effort, but you really won't know until you try. Another consideration is that there are also slightly different ways to see a reinforcement effect.

Keep in mind that some effects of positive reinforcement are seen instantaneously through an immediate increase in the frequency of a response. On the other hand, some of the effects can only be detected over hours or days. For example, a child raises her arms to indicate a desire to be picked up and she is subsequently picked up and spun around while the adult utters the obligatory "wheeeee!" After lightly touching down again she immediately throws her arms up and says, "Again!" The cycle repeats several times, usually to the point that you start wondering if there are any good chiropractors in the area. This is the "classic" reinforcement effect. This kind of effect typically happens when the delivery of the reinforcer doesn't totally crush the motivation to engage in the behavior that produces it. Honestly, the first reinforcer delivery often increases the motivation above the initial level just before the reinforcer was delivered. You could see it as being a little bit of a motivating operation (MO, which I'll talk about shortly). My own feeling is that our definitional divisions of positive reinforcement and MOs might not be all that clean and tidy in nature. For example, my dog, Ginger, never wants chicken more than when she has just had her first piece of chicken. She wasn't thinking about chicken, she wasn't looking for chicken, but after getting some chicken, acquiring another piece of chicken seems like a fantastically good idea. Some people call this "reinforcer sampling." So, reinforcers of the right size (magnitude) not only don't kill motivation but also may, in some instances, actually increase it temporarily (like appetizers, mmm).

Another way to see a reinforcement effect is to observe an increase in the probability of a response at some later time. This is often seen with the delivery of reinforcers that are large enough to crush any subsequent motivation, at least temporarily. This is why it really isn't a good idea to give children a one-pound bag of Skittles after the completion of a task, not to mention that you're going to get a particularly nasty letter from the Juvenile Diabetes Foundation. Sure they'll be really happy, but they probably won't be very motivated to work again anytime soon. However, if you looked at the probability of responding under the same conditions (same task, same need for Skittles) on subsequent days, you might find that the probability is very high compared to the non-Skittle condition. The point is that you can't tell on the first day if Skittle delivery acts as a reinforcer for task completion because you would need to know the baseline probability of task completion over several days (the child only attempted the task 1 out of 10 days) and then compare that probability over several more days under the "giant bag o' Skittles" condition (the child attempted the task on eight out of ten days). The moral of the story is that just because you don't see an *immediate increase* in behavior, it doesn't necessarily follow that you don't have a useable reinforcer. The insightful Dr. Peter Harzem, one of my mentors whom I miss very much, and who was one of the most brilliant and clear thinkers I have ever met, used to point out that people would throw the word "reinforcer" around like a Frisbee. Some would say things like, "Getting married was a very big reinforcer for me!" To which Peter would say, then why didn't you just run out and get married again right after the reception? As always, Peter made a good point, that people were using the term incorrectly. First, you would have to specify what behavior was reinforced. Walking down the aisle? Buying the ring? Spending $5,000 for the flowers? The other part, the increase in the probability, could only be seen if you are in a condition where you can get married again and you choose to engage in all those behaviors again, you know, like Elizabeth Taylor. Hell, she married Richard Burton twice!

Some things can influence how effective a reinforcer is going to be or they can alter the probability that we will engage in a certain behavior that has been reinforced in the past. That is, some things can make us engage in a "whole lotta" behavior initially, but it doesn't mean that we will do those things again. Wait, it gets worse....

Jack Michael referred to this altering of behavior as the "evocative effect" of a Motivating Operation. A Motivating Operation (MO) is something that can happen naturally or can be programmed (just like reinforcement), and is said to serve two purposes or functions. It can momentarily increase the chances that a given thing (stimulus) will function as a reinforcer, or it can serve an evocative function and produce an increase in behaviors that have led to reinforcement in the past. If you'd like to get further confused, let me suggest a great article, "Motivating operations and terms to describe them: Some further refinements" (Laraway, Snycerski, Michael, & Poling, 2003). To further complicate matters, you can have MOs that require no learning history called unconditioned motivating operations (UCMOs) or MOs that require a learning history (CMOs). Your local tavern knows about the power of UCMOs, which is why you get free snacks. Salty snacks. Very, very salty snacks. It raises the chances that drinks will function as reinforcers for the behavior that precedes them, but the snacks may also produce (evoke) behaviors that have resulted in drinks in the past. Sometimes just seeing a potential reinforcer will be sufficient to produce behaviors that have led to reinforcement in the past even though just a moment earlier you did not feel particularly deprived of anything. For example, you're sitting on the couch and not feeling particularly "car deprived." No one has withheld your car and you may even like your car very much. Then you see a commercial for the new Chevy Camaro along with some disclaimer that says you shouldn't drive the car like you see it being driven because you're not a professional driver on a closed course, and suddenly you feel *very* car deprived. I believe this is what Michael would refer to as a CMO. Babies do nothing when they see the commercial, well maybe the E-Trade Baby, but no other babies. You, on the other hand, begin to engage in behaviors that have produced cars in the past, which may include checking the Internet, reviewing your finances, reading reviews, going to dealers, and arguing with your spouse about why you absolutely *must* have this car. Behavior analysts did not discover the concept of the motivating operation. Madison Avenue advertising executives beat us to it. We just gave the thing a name.

Now, this Chevy Camaro may evoke a great deal of behavior, but it ultimately may not be enough to increase the frequency or future probability of the behavior of buying Camaros over time. That is, right after you buy the Camaro you don't go out and buy another Camaro, unless you're Jay Leno. Furthermore, if the Camaro turned out to be a big piece of crap, then the next time you need a new car you will not buy a Camaro. If you see a commercial on television for the Camaro again it will no longer be a CMO. It will just make you really mad. Think of all the things you've ever bought that you were *just dying to get*, but once you got them you were severely disappointed. Clearly, you can be motivated to get something, but it does not necessarily mean that you will be motivated to keep it or to get it again at some later time when the conditions are similar.

Star Trek explains a lot.

If you haven't seen the original *Star Trek*, 1) I'm not your friend anymore and 2) go out and buy the boxed set of the original series right now or you will never be a good behavior analyst. The book can wait. Seriously. Go right now and get it and watch them all. All done? Great, now we can move on. Remember that *Star Trek* episode called Amok Time? Of course you do, you just finished watching the entire series. Spock got all hot and bothered and decided that it was time to go back to the planet Vulcan to fulfill his obligation in a prearranged marriage to T'pring (his betrothed). In essence, Spock was really hot to trot, and he was challenged by another suitor, Stonn, but somehow got logically cornered into fighting Captain Kirk to the death (don't worry—Kirk didn't really die). After Spock realized that he had killed his Captain, yet won the hand of T'pring, he suddenly didn't desire her so much and that was that. What Spock said afterwards, however, has great bearing on our discussion. After relinquishing T'pring to the other suitor, Stonn, he told him...

> After a time, you may find that having is not so pleasing a thing after all as wanting. It is not logical, but it is often true....

What Spock meant to say was that T'Pring was a UCMO but once he believed that he killed Kirk, it crushed the motivation to marry her (known as an Abolishing Operation). Apparently T'Pring took Jack Michael's course on MOs. Now Spock went to a hell of a lot of trouble to get T'Pring, but his fighting behavior was not necessarily reinforced. We really wouldn't know for sure until Spock got motivated again and then started beating the crap out of Kirk. Remember, it's not just the alleged power of the reinforcer, but ultimately it is the ability of that stimulus to strengthen a particular behavior that matters most. In other words, a handful of Skittles is just that, a handful of Skittles. They are not reinforcers until you observe their effect on some particular behavior. This relationship makes things greatly confusing in applied settings, however, so allow me to lay out a (somewhat arbitrary) hierarchy of indications of the potential strength of any alleged tangible reinforcers. This is by no means exhaustive, and I have not conducted empirical research on the matter. It's just to help give an idea of how likely something is to function as a reinforcer. This hierarchy is well suited to someone who is nonverbal as it's based on nonverbal behavior. It could work fine for people who can talk as well. Remember, just because someone says they want something doesn't mean it will function as a reinforcer for a given behavior right? When presented with a tangible item:

1. The child will look at it
2. The child will approach it
3. The child will stay near it
4. The child will try to touch it/pick it up (but might put it down again)
5. The child will manipulate it for perhaps a few minutes, but will give it up easily when asked
6. The child does not want to give it up when you ask him to
7. The child becomes agitated when you try to remove it (getting warmer)
8. The child will follow you to a place where there are tasks as long as you bring the item
9. The child will begin a task as long as the item is close by
10. The child will actually finish the task that was started in step 9
11. The child still wants to access the item after the task is done
12. After accessing the item the child complies again with subsequent requests either immediately, or when the conditions are the same again (e.g., the next day) when prompted
13. After accessing the item, the child immediately engages in the behavior that produced the item (unprompted) OR when conditions are the same again (the next day), the probability of the child complying with the same request is higher than in baseline
14. The child demonstrates 9 through 13 with all sorts of different tasks of varying difficulty levels
15. The child willingly accompanies you to a Rosie O'Donnell Film Festival[4] to earn the reinforcer. Now that there's a powerful reinforcer, I don't care who you are!

The reason that I mentioned the behavior might be prompted or unprompted in levels 12 and 13 is that (typically) with a very strong reinforcer, the child will emit the behavior that

---

[4]Of course I'm only kidding. Bringing a child to a Rosie O'Donnell Film Festival is classified as a universal punisher and requires the approval of your local human rights advocacy committee.

produced the reinforcer without any prompting at all (like the child who says, "Do it again!" after being given an airplane ride.)

Now in our *Star Trek* example, Spock never really made it past level 3. Sorry T'pring, that's the way it goes, but she really wanted Stonn anyhow. So clearly, you can like things, but not everything you like will "work" as a reinforcer for a given task. You'll see this problem with edibles too. A child may take what you give him and eat it, but that doesn't mean that it will reinforce the completion of thirty math problems. As mentioned earlier, a reinforcer is a contextual critter. For the most part, there must be a balance between the strength of the reinforcer and the difficulty of the task. If the balance is off, the motivation to escape from or avoid the task increases. We will talk more about that in Chapter 3 on problems with aversives.

6.1: Short-lived reinforcers?

First, it's important to take a good hard look at the alleged reinforcer (soft looks are for wimps). The preceding discussion should allow a more critical examination of what *appears* to be a reinforcer, But this possible reinforcer may (ultimately) do little to establish and maintain productive behavior. Regarding short-lived reinforcers, it's important to specify how short. Is Tyrone interested in earning it over a period of five minutes? One hour? Will he work for it all day long? I find it helpful to have three levels of these potential reinforcers defined by their "staying power." *Brief* (maintains interest for a few minutes), *moderate* (maintains interest for thirty minutes or more) and *extended* (maintains interest throughout the day). Yeah, yeah, I know, "Maintains interest" is not very accurate terminology, and it may only correspond to the levels 1–5 in the 14-step rating scale in the last section. We don't know if these things will function as reinforcers for any given behavior (doing math, reading, naming animals), but if they don't at least maintain interest, they are not likely to work.

It can also be useful to divide the possible reinforcers into food-based, tangible (toys, items you can hold and carry around), activity-based (computer, television, video games, drawing), movement-based (running around, jumping, spinning, bouncing on a balance ball), and social (fun interactions with adults or peers). It may also be helpful to divide tasks into high, medium, and low probability categories. They are arbitrary distinctions, but it makes it easier to see how different reinforcers stack up against tasks of varying difficulty.

High probability	Tasks the student is very familiar with and can finish easily
Medium probability	Tasks the student will try to escape from at least half the time and require quite a bit of prompting to finish
Low probability	Tasks that the student almost never complies with, and when she does it's only with great difficulty and the task may also generate some problem behaviors.

If an alleged reinforcer won't even motivate a child to begin the high probability tasks, do you really even need to try the others? Really? It can also be helpful, in the case of tangible reinforcers, to have a large "reinforcer pool" that the child does not have access to, and then use a smaller pool from which the child may choose an item. I knew one particularly clever teacher who had a bucket of about 100 different small toys and she would pull out 10 of them and place them in a smaller bucket from which the child would choose something. The next day those toys were retired and 10 new toys were in the choice bucket. She would cycle through them every day to keep things fresh. Clever, no? Don't forget that you can always take a page from the Madison Avenue executive's handbook and try to manipulate motivating operations to "make" the student want something more. I can't tell you how many times I've seen a child who couldn't care less about an item until another child started playing with it, especially if the other child appeared to be having a great time. You may find that you have to create some "buzz" around an object to increase the chances that it will function as a reinforcer. Hell, I've even seen this happen with dogs! One dog isn't playing with his squeaky chew toy, the other dog grabs it, all of a sudden the first dog wants his chew toy! I guess that in this instance CMO stands for "Canine Motivating Operation."

6.2: False reinforcers

I define a false reinforcer as something that the child simply likes, but isn't necessarily willing to work for; that is, you don't really have a functional reinforcer for the task at hand. Sometimes the only behavior that a cookie can reinforce is the behavior of asking for it! Now, if you're conducting mand training (teaching a child how to request items), then the cookie is likely a perfect reinforcer. On the other hand, if you need a child to sit in circle time for twenty minutes and participate, a cookie may have little or no effect. I don't care how much a child talks about and asks about an item or activity, until you see what it does to prompt the initial behavior (MO) and whether it causes an increase in the frequency or probability of subsequent behavior (reinforcement effect), all you know is that the child "likes" it, and that's about it. Remember, just because the item/activity is powerful enough for a child to start the task, it doesn't mean that it will actually strengthen the behavior that you want it to.

6.3: No reinforcers

What about no reinforcers? Well, it's not very likely that there are absolutely no reinforcers operating at any given moment. If there are no reinforcers, people don't move. Usually it means they're dead, but sometimes it just means they are very, very unmotivated. This is one characteristic of depression. People who become very depressed may not even want to get out of bed, may not want to eat, go out, participate in activities they usually love, and tend not to move as much. Regarding a claim of "no reinforcers" all you may know for certain is that there are no motivators strong enough to produce academic behaviors. The young man,

Jeremy, mentioned at the beginning of this section, spent much of his day moving around the classroom looking for things to get. He was certainly motivated enough to look for things to do, but the things he found were barely strong enough to get the smallest amount of work out of him. Furthermore, he seemed quite content to just roam around the classroom looking for stuff to get. The problem of "no reinforcers" can easily be re-conceptualized as *uncontrolled reinforcers*, which is our next topic.

SECTION 7: UNCONTROLLED, LOW-RATE, AND NO REINFORCERS

7.1: Uncontrolled reinforcers

Poorly controlled reinforcers is, hands down, one of the single greatest problems in applied settings. In the experimental analysis of behavior (EAB), reinforcers are incredibly tightly controlled. Pigeons are typically food-deprived to 80 percent of their free feeding weight and kept there for the duration of an experiment to ensure that the motivation to respond is fairly high. The pigeons don't get any extra snacks on the way to the experimental session. They don't break into the grain cabinet at 2 a.m. and steal a whole bunch of it. Their moms don't stop at Dunkin' Donuts to get them some pre-session bear claws. It just doesn't happen. In applied settings, however, especially in schools, it can be very difficult to completely control some reinforcers and impossible to control others.

What are the easiest things to control? The most likely things would be edibles, and access to special items/activities (television and computer). Unfortunately, I have seen children get unauthorized access to edibles and/or computers and videos. Typically these things are not under lock and key. Another problem is that the average classroom, especially at the elementary and pre-k levels, looks like a Toys "R" Us exploded (I couldn't make the "R" backwards, besides it sets a really bad example for young minds). Books, toys, games, puzzles, blocks, paper, are just out in the open, free for the taking. If you cannot control reinforcers, it is still possible to control the child, but your options become more limited. The late great Dr. Glenn Latham wrote a wonderful book, *The Power of Positive Parenting: A Wonderful Way to Raise Children* (Latham, 1994). Glenn laid out three types of control that we use with children (and everyone else for that matter). The first is Direct Control. That is why we must sometimes physically intervene (yes even with restraint) to stop children from doing dangerous things to themselves or others. There is an entire chapter devoted to the topic of restraint, so I'll just stop here. The second type of control is Indirect Control. You don't physically make the person stop some behaviors and start other behaviors, but you simply control the consequences of their behavior (reinforcers and punishers). You control the person by controlling her environment. This is why we have governments, rules, and laws (and attorneys). Last, there is Influence. Influence is the last bastion between the child and the horrible consequences that lay ahead in the real world. This is what you end up using with teenagers much of the time because, as they get older, you control fewer of their reinforcers (Godspeed to you, parents of teens). Influence relies on the power of your positive relationship with the child to gently nudge them in the correct direction when they begin to veer off course and is most appropriate with children who have good verbal skills. Glenn summed up these methods of beneficial control very nicely. What I see everywhere I travel (whether in a school or other type of facility) is that people who do not control the reinforcers adequately enough find themselves in the position of coercing (forcing) individuals into doing things that they do not wish to do. Sometimes I see teachers trying to use their influence on children (which is a good thing to do) and sometimes it's effective and sometimes it isn't, but if you control the reinforcers, influence is not as necessary. Of course that doesn't mean you can't use your influence all the time to gently move behavior in the direction you want.

I strongly suggest to teachers that they eliminate as many "loose" reinforcers as possible if they are having difficulty motivating particular children. Yes, I realize that the other children may suffer because they don't have free access, but quite honestly no one should have free access to certain reinforcers. It's public school, it's not the child's bedroom. When you go to any public place you can't just start grabbing things like you own them unless you're in a library and I can't even remember what those look like. This becomes unbelievably important if you are going to teach a child with no language how to mand (ask) for things. I remember doing a consult with a colleague regarding a young girl with whom they were trying to conduct mand training. They were not being successful. I asked what kinds of things she had free access to at home. My colleague, exasperated, replied "everything!" Not good. The parents positively bristled at the idea that their child had to "work" to get things that she normally was allowed to have for free. This is not an uncommon problem when trying to teach mands. If you are a parent reading this right now, I'm going to get all righteous on you and bust out the phrase that has been used on children since the dawn of parenting "it's for your own good!" This phrase is second only of course to "this hurts me more than it does you!" but we'll save that for the punishment chapter. To get children to the point of independence, we must sometimes first make them heavily dependent! Yes, later on we'll make them independent again, after they learn what they need to learn. Kids who can get what they want, when they want it, don't need you! Neither do they need to do the work you want them to do. I think we can agree that it can be difficult, yet still possible, to control tangible and edible reinforcers. What about other reinforcers like attention? You may want to sit down for this one.

Imagine that the attention you command in the classroom is an unlimited bag of Skittles, and said Skittles have been shown to be powerful reinforcers for a variety of behaviors. Now, envision yourself walking around with this bag of Skittles that, unbeknownst to you, has a hole in the bottom. Every time you turn around Skittles go flying from the bag, but you don't notice them. This is exactly how well attention is controlled. To make matters worse, there are as many types of attention as there are flavors of Skittles, so the analogy holds. Maybe it's their favorite flavor and maybe it isn't but it's still a Skittle. (FYI, there are anywhere between 5 and 8 different flavors of Skittles per pack and there are currently about 6 different varieties on the market. Do the math and maybe I'll give you some). Recall in the section on intermittent reinforcement that it is sometimes advisable to purposefully continue to reinforce low-level inappropriate behavior with a very small amount of attention (assuming the behavior is attention maintained), so that the behavior does not contact highly intermittent and highly variable levels of attention. If you are reasonably certain that such a child is going to end up getting a Skittle anyhow, it should be small, stale, and maybe licorice flavored (they actually made them in Europe). You must also be proactive and be certain to give more and better quality Skittles after the desired target behaviors. Incidentally, peers are another source of uncontrolled attention, but we'll cover that problem in Chapter 6.

What about other uncontrolled reinforcers? As mentioned in the beginning of this chapter, many pages ago, there are many self-stimulatory behaviors that cannot be controlled very well. Kids can pretty much get up and move around any time they want. You can bring them back to their seats, true, but legally, it's almost impossible to keep them from getting up in the first place and I don't think that forcing them to stay seated is the answer. Sometimes the best you can do is to reduce the child's motivation to engage in these behaviors by making sure that things are as interesting and stimulating as possible. You might also have to capitalize on a child's motivation to move around by rescheduling activities so that her desire to move can be accommodated (unless she is simply trying to escape).

At this point, you may be asking, "What if I control everything in the classroom, but the kid gets whatever he wants at home?" First, who are you talking to? You know I can't hear you right? You're reading a book. Second, okay parents, I told you we'd be talking about you, so here it comes. For children with greater verbal skills who understand long-term contingencies like "earn five stars in school and get one hour of video games at home," parent participation can mean everything. Communication between teacher and parent, allowing them to work together, presenting a unified front to the child, can work wonders. Is it more work for the parents? Undeniably, but as I say to the teachers I work with, you're always going to be doing significant amounts of work if you're trying to help a child with significant behavior problems. You may as well choose the work you are going to do (productive work). Hopefully, that work won't simply get you through the day, but it will contribute to the child's long-term treatment gains and that's really the name of the game.

In summary, can you perfectly control reinforcers? In some cases no, however, in all cases you should be able to do a significantly better job, and it may take some classroom management changes. Also, just because you tightly control reinforcers doesn't mean that they have to be difficult to get, they just have to be contingent on pre-specified behaviors. Even if the behavior is just saying, "May I have _____ ?" If you have good reinforcers (for that person) and you clearly specify how he or she gets the reinforcer (which we'll talk about shortly), you'll be head and shoulders above everyone else (notice how I resisted the urge to make a dandruff reference).

7.2   Low rate reinforcers

Once again, pigeons to the rescue! As mentioned earlier, they can be of greater utility than just ruining the finish on your new Camaro or graciously accepting food from old men on park benches. There is a concept in behavior analysis known as the "Matching Law." In essence, the Matching Law states that when pigeons are able to respond to two separate but simultaneously available (concurrent) schedules of reinforcement that they will allocate responses in accordance to the actual rate of reinforcement available on each key they peck (they figure out how to get the best deal possible). The "keys" are just little plastic discs in the wall of the experimental (operant) chamber mounted on micro-switches and are just right for pecking. Herrnstein developed a formula to describe the relationship, and I could have put it here, but many of you, upon seeing it, would just run screaming for your *Star Trek* DVDs. The two different schedules didn't produce the same rates of reinforcement and the pigeons would peck accordingly. So, if 80 percent of the reinforcers were available on one key and 20 percent on the other, the Pigeons' responses were distributed across keys at the same (matching) percentage. Animals try to get as much reinforcement as they can. It's not that we're all greedy; it's just something we do. Children "allocate responses" as well and you can't blame them for it. Dr. Bruce Abbott at Indiana University-Purdue University gives a very nice summary of Herrnstein's work (http://users.ipfw.edu/abbott/314/MatchingLaw.html). For our purposes, the most striking thing is how Dr. Abbott summarized Herrnstein's single-key formula of the matching law. Simply put, you could look at how a pigeon allocates its pecks to two different keys, or how it allocates its *time* between pecking on a single key and doing other "pigeon stuff" (walking around the experimental chamber, looking for a stray piece of grain, preening, wondering if there are any good statues around to crap on, etc.). The rate of the pigeon's responding depends on what other pigeon stuff is available for the pigeon to do. It all comes back to competing reinforcers. Some of you may be skeptical about the applicability of the matching law, as kids are very different from pigeons. Correct you are, pigeons crap *on your car*, kids crap *in your car*. All right, that's not the only difference.

A reasonable analogy is that children in the classroom have a "key" too, if you will. Their key is the task you are trying to get them to do. The problem is that they have a lot more "kid stuff" they can do when they are not responding to the task in front of them. It has been my general observation that some children are exquisitely sensitive to changes in the rate of reinforcement for the current task/situation. When these rates of reinforcement are insufficient (by the child's standards, not ours) the kids start to seek out other sources and voila! The next thing you know, little Joshua has left circle-time and he's climbing the bookcase.

Recall for a moment, our earlier discussion about slot machines and "Vegas-style" intermittent reinforcement. Often times, reinforcers are only earned after students have completed an entire assignment, not after each sentence they write, shape they name or word they spell. Very frequently, behavior problems generate reinforcers at a much higher rate than doing worksheets. Also, if the reinforcer is social interaction of some kind, it's very common for a child to work well with an adult next to him, giving prompts and praise, but when the adult leaves, the child's rate of reinforcement drops too low too quickly and he stops working altogether and starts doing something he shouldn't. This is very true of some children who work well with an adult in a one-on-one situation, but when you bring those children to a circle-time activity, they quickly fall apart. This most likely occurs because the rate of reinforcement in circle-time has dropped significantly. In fact, a child has to wait for an opportunity to be called on before she can even have a chance of obtaining reinforcement. In a one-on-one situation, however, the child has multiple opportunities in a row to answer questions and participate, and the overall rate of reinforcement is generally much higher. It's not just that the child has one-on-one attention, but more specifically, that the rate of reinforcement is much higher. If you could lower the rate of reinforcement in the one-on-one setting and then raise it in circle-time, you might find that the child's behavior changes accordingly. This is why many children have difficulty waiting. When you wait, your rate of reinforcement typically drops (depending on what you are doing while waiting). Also, the number and magnitude of reinforcers may be much lower while waiting. The clearest signs that a child's rate of reinforcement is dropping too low, too quickly is that her self-stimulatory behavior may increase, she may require more prompting, make more errors, show more "off-task" behaviors (looking around the room, asking irrelevant questions, etc.) and she may show some other indications of impending bad behaviors.

7.3: Delayed reinforcers

God I hate waiting for things. So does just about everyone else. The more technology evolves, the more we can't tolerate delayed reinforcers because technology gets better and cooler and faster. I went to graduate school with an absolutely brilliant young man named Rich DeGrandpre and he wrote an outstanding book entitled *Ritalin Nation: Rapid Fire Culture and the Transformation of Human Consciousness*. (DeGrandpre, 2000) One of the themes Rich touched on was a "transformation of consciousness" that has led us to become a nation of impatient people who can't tolerate delays and need to be constantly stimulated. As the speed with which things happen increases, our tolerance grows weaker and weaker. Remember modems? You know, those little boxes that used to let you log on to AOL, made weird noises (sssshhhh....waaaaaahhhhhhh....eeeeee-ahhhhhhh) and let you connect at a blazing 14 kbps? For those of you not up on your Internet jargon, 14 kbps is approximately the speed at which Congress moves. Today, if a web page doesn't pop up in about .25 milliseconds, like me, you most likely find yourself drumming your fingers on the desk and cursing the day that you failed to listen to that Best Buy geek who told you to upgrade to more ram and a faster processor. Although everyone can improve in their ability to tolerate reinforcer delays, no one truly likes it, and if by chance someone tells you that he does, then you can take your sweet time paying back that twenty bucks you owe him. If a reinforcer is delayed too long, you don't even get a reinforcement effect (strengthening of behavior).

Q: What do you get if you deliver food five seconds after a pigeon pecks a key?
A: A really confused pigeon.

Whether the student is verbal, nonverbal, typically developing, or disabled in some manner, sooner is better. Consumer behavior explains a lot.

There used to be a furniture company in Miami called "Modernage." If you shopped at Modernage you gave them a bunch of money and *maybe* you got your new couch six to eight weeks later. Big effort, big delay. One day, along came a company called "Rooms To Go." Rooms To Go used to offer financing with no interest and no penalties if paid off in time. They used to have ads that would say, "Take your furniture home today and don't pay any interest until the year 2012!" and that was in 2009. People reacted like it was practically free. No delay whatsoever and no money down and small monthly payments (very little effort). Modernage has been out of business for some time now. Rooms To Go is now the number one independent furniture company in the U.S.A. As further evidence of the power of *now*, people who win the lottery almost never take the full amount of their winnings distributed in yearly payments over twenty years. They typically give up about one half of their winnings to get one lump-sum payment immediately. That is, they give up MILLIONS of dollars to get it all as quickly as possible. What is the scientific significance of this and the implications for applied behavior analysis and treatment? Simply put, immediate reinforcement kicks-@$$! There I go again with the decorum. It really does however sum things up quite nicely. To be more accurate, from an experimental point of view (you know like pigeons and rats and labs and stuff like that), the phrase "immediate reinforcement" is redundant, because a significantly delayed stimulus (more than a few seconds or so) will not function as a reinforcer at all. Remember the confused pigeon? Just in case the pigeon isn't the only one who's confused, allow me to explain. Reinforcement as a procedure means you give the alleged reinforcer, a Skittle, immediately after the behavior. We also tend to call the Skittle "the reinforcer." Remember sometimes a Skittle is just a Skittle. Read on….

There are numerous implications regarding the importance of immediacy. First let's talk about the importance for individuals who are primarily nonverbal. It is critical that alleged reinforcers are delivered almost immediately after a behavior to have their maximum effectiveness. As discussed earlier, reinforcers (eventually) do not have to be given after each instance of behavior, although initially you might have to use continuous reinforcement. That reinforcers may occur intermittently does not mean that there has to be a delay between the response and the reinforcer. It's fine if every response doesn't contact reinforcement, but when you're *deciding to reinforce a response* it should still be within a couple of seconds of the one you choose to reinforce.

All too often, the scenario is that naturally occurring reinforcers (accidental attention, or allowing escape, etc.) may be delivered immediately after a particularly severe behavior. Unfortunately, there are often delays when appropriate behavior occurs. As a quick example, I have witnessed children hold their hands up for more than a minute in a classroom and not be acknowledged by the teacher, but another student who pushes his book off the desk, or curses gets *immediate* attention. The classroom is most certainly not the only place this occurs; you can see it all around you wherever you go. Not only does the "squeaky wheel" get the grease, it gets it much faster than the quiet wheels (especially when the squeaky wheel is getting on your last nerve). I always tell teachers working with so-called attention-maintained behavior to attend to the chosen appropriate response as though the child is on fire, as this is often how they respond to a three-alarm behavior problem.

I know that most of you understand the importance of providing immediate reinforcement for children who are nonverbal, but what about children with *good verbal skills*? Often times, teachers feel that these children can tolerate delays better because they have verbal skills that can "bridge the gap" between the appropriate behavior and the somewhat distant reinforcer. This is not technically what is happening, however. Remember, we can get people to do things even before they get the reinforcer (motivating operations). Motivating someone to do something, then reinforcing that something are two different things. There are many ways to get people to start doing things even though no reinforcer is given for some time. Many times there are conditioned reinforcers that arise as a product of just doing work. Perhaps there is really good instructional control by the teacher and when he or she asks the students to start reading, they read. Perhaps the child likes what she is doing and doesn't really need the so-called "extrinsic" reinforcers to strengthen each academic behavior. I know that good teachers aren't thinking about the money they are earning each time they help a student solve a problem. Typically, a student's smiling face is enough of a reinforcer but that smile doesn't occur a week after the teacher helps, it occurs *right now*. This reinforcement business is far more complex than most people can appreciate, and I'm only briefly touching on some of the nuances. Think about this statement for a moment:

I am writing this book because I know I am going to get money for it.

I cannot possibly be writing this book because I will get paid, because that is an event that has not yet happened. It is a metaphysical and a physical impossibility. (Thank-you Dr. Steve Starin!) It ain't happnin'. I am writing this book for many reasons, that is, there are many motivators. I said to someone the other day that I was thinking about writing this book and she said, "That's a great idea Merrill, I'm sure it will be fantastic!" I actually told many friends, and they all said the same thing, in other words, all my friends are liars. Not true, but part of my motivation is that I don't want to incur the wrath of all the people that have given me encouragement. I really don't want to hear, "Hey Merrill, uh, I thought you were supposed to be writing this fantastic book that will save the world, what the hell happened?" Of course my behavior cannot be motivated by future bad things either, for they also have not yet happened. It is our histories, some might say, and the current contingencies that move us forward. For example, someone might say, "Hey Merrill, how's the book coming?" and I'm like (&@!$), "I haven't worked on it lately, but I'm going to start tomorrow!" Also, notice that if you forget to do something really important, and then you happen to *glance at the calendar* and realize how much time has gone by, THIS is the event that gets you working again. This event coupled with what you remember (your promise to finish the book) and the history of consequences for turning things in late, motivates you. So your work behavior is controlled by *what has happened* and *what is happening now,* not by events that have yet to occur. I'd love to work in a Back to the Future reference but I'm afraid that I might affect my future self in ways that I couldn't possibly imagine!

Social motivation is, of course, not the only reason that I am now pecking on the keyboard like a food-deprived pigeon. There are also *conditioned reinforcers*, available immediately in real time, like reading about a point that I've made (if I think it was particularly well stated), seeing how many pages I've accumulated, and getting closer to the end of a chapter. The same things happen with children in school, but this typically doesn't take place until they begin to gain a certain degree of competence. The key concept to bring away from this example, is that the reinforcer that comes after a long chain of behavior becomes less critical when the person is highly motivated to begin with. Many children with behavior problems in school are not highly motivated to do school work or comply with teacher requests for many reasons. Those children tend to initially need more "contrived" reinforcers (Skittles, points, tokens, bouncing on the mini-tramp) until they become competent. I'm sure that many of the teachers reading this text are familiar with many students who will do certain academic tasks without even being asked to because they *like* them and are *good* at them. For those who still need praise, hugs, food, gold stars, and five minutes on the balance ball, make sure the delay is as short as possible. You can also reinforce a "chain" of behaviors by giving the reinforcer at the end. We try to reinforce "links" in the chain by supplying a constant stream of conditioned reinforcers like praise and feedback ("Good work!" "Almost done!" "Just one more!"). Still, the reinforcer at the end of the chain should come immediately after the last link! Okay, I do believe this particular dead horse has stopped moving. We may now proceed,… (no dead horses were actually harmed during the writing of this section. Live ones weren't harmed, either).

SECTION 8: REINFORCER MAGNITUDE PROBLEMS

Magnitude and immediacy are probably the two most critical dimensions of reinforcement. Sometimes magnitude is more important, and sometimes immediacy wins out. In the lottery example, in which most people give up about half of their winnings for a lump sum payment, it appears that immediacy wins out over magnitude, but there is quite a balancing act going on that most people are unaware of. Just like casinos and advertisers, states that have lotteries stand to lose large amounts of money if they don't understand how people behave.

Most people will accept an *overall* lower magnitude of reinforcement (and I am using the term reinforcement loosely here) to gain a larger *immediate* magnitude. In other words, if they win $100 million, they would immediately get about $5 million and then another $5 million per year for about twenty years (not accounting for taxes). If they take the lump sum, instead of getting an immediate $5 million, they get about $50 million. It's more now, but less overall. So in some sense the magnitude is greater. Now certainly, the decision may be affected by other factors (taxes, interest earned on a lump sum, life expectancy, the ability to pass winnings on to one's children, etc.), but at certain extremes immediacy will lose. Say for example that you win $100 million to be given in 20-year installments, but this time a lump sum payout is only $6 million, not $50 million. That is, if you take it over twenty years, it's $5 million per year. If you take the lump sum it is $6 million once, a difference of only $1 million more. Are you going to give up $94 million over twenty years to get $6 million now? Maybe if you are homeless or 92 years old, or you've run up a huge tab on the home shopping network. The people who put together the rules about the lump sum payment have presumably found the "sweet spot" that most people will go for, and they know that most people will go for it because if they are wrong they stand to lose quite a bit of money. This way states can advertise an amount of money that, in all probability, no one will ever go for. Brilliant! How does this translate to kids in classrooms? If you want to teach a child to tolerate a delay in reinforcement, you can create a condition in which the immediate reinforcer is two pretzels, but if the child can wait 10 seconds (have him count slowly) he can get 10 pretzels. It's a good way to get your foot in the door when you want to teach someone how to wait without freaking out. By the way, when delaying the primary reinforcer, you have to give immediate conditioned reinforcers to "bridge the gap," e.g., "doing great, almost time!"

In applied settings it's very important to pay attention to the magnitude of reinforcement. All things being equal, it needs to be greater for better quality/more effortful behavior. *Differential Reinforcement* usually refers to the complete reinforcement of one behavior and the total non-reinforcement of another to differentially "select" the behavior you want. However it doesn't *have* to be an all-or-none affair. You can differentially reinforce according to magnitude as well. If there is no differential reinforcement, there is no reason to try harder because it doesn't get you anywhere. Having worked for the state for nine years, I can tell you with absolute certainty that job performance never resulted in more money or less money at the end of a pay period. That is, some pay periods required more work than others. We didn't get less money on easier weeks and more money on tougher weeks, but this is exactly what we need to do with our students who are struggling.

Most of you have probably heard of the phrase "prompt dependence." It refers to a problem in which the student waits to be prompted every time and the teacher can't seem to wean the student off of the prompts. Now there are many things that lead to and maintain prompt dependence, but one of them is that there is absolutely no differential reinforcement. I have watched some sessions in which the children were heavily prompted, or barely prompted at all, and received the same magnitude of reinforcement. If we assume that Travis's behavior can be reinforced by Skittles, if he gets one Skittle for performing a task with verbal prompts only, and one Skittle for performing the same task needing full physical prompting, why on Earth would Travis want to strain his brain to figure things out when he could just wait for the teacher to help him? He gets the same magnitude of reinforcement no matter what he does. It's like having a salaried job where you are paid the same amount during fast times and slow. On the other hand, in real estate sales, if you sell more houses you get mo' money. We need to give children a damn good reason to try as hard as they can. We also need to find as many of these damn good reasons as possible. One reason to try harder is because you get more; more Skittles, more time on the computer, and more enthusiastic praise with a wider smile!

Magnitude can be a tricky thing, especially when it comes to finding the "sweet spot." Too big and you kill the motivation for subsequent work for the time being. Too small and you can cause agitation. Ask any server at a restaurant who has felt that he or she had been tipped too little. What's worse than leaving no tip? Leaving a nickel on a $50 tab. Not tipping at all could be seen as an oversight. Tipping a nickel is a clear slap in the face. Magnitude must also be balanced with satiation, which is defined as getting so much of a reinforcer that it temporarily loses its effectiveness and may even become aversive, like eating too much of a particular food (remember, reinforcers are not static). Satiation "crushes motivation," so it is also known as an "abolishing operation" which we'll talk about more in Chapter 4.

In battling the problems of satiation, praise should be the number one horse in your stable of reinforcers. Praise is so wonderful because it's zero calorie, gluten free (don't get me started) limitless, and some children never seem to tire of it. It can be very helpful to find reinforcers like praise because you can avoid satiation problems. Many children can sit on the computer all day, but you can only eat so many Skittles before your jaw begins to hurt from chewing (I have firsthand experience in the matter). Good teachers can vary the magnitude of their praise in very obvious ways or in very subtle ways depending on the sophistication of the child and the demands of the situation. Saying, "I like the way you have nice, quiet hands!" in the same way, every time, is a motivational death sentence. Wield magnitude expertly, regardless of the type of reinforcer (praise, tangibles, activities) and you will get much faster behavior change.

Reinforcers that are more powerful than Superman, Batman, Spiderman, and The Incredible Hulk put together

Other than being a blatant *Family Guy*[5] reference, this problem also falls under the category of magnitude problems. The fact is that I completely forgot about this problem until I

---

[5]The actual *Family Guy* Episode was "Fish Our of Water," Season 3 Episode 10 and the title of the section was named after Peter Griffin's Boat. Perhaps you can run out and buy that season when you're done with those old *Star Trek* episodes?

was writing Chapter 6 on problems with peers when I suddenly realized that I really needed to address this issue, so here we are. Some reinforcers are so incredibly powerful that teachers just don't want to use them, and when you see some of the problems that happen as a result of these "über-reinforcers" you realize that you can't blame the teachers for not wanting to use them. It's great that the kid has some powerful reinforcers: in reality it's a much better problem than few, weak reinforcers. However, just as Uncle Ben said to Peter Parker in the first *Spiderman* movie, "With great power comes great responsibility." The problem of these über reinforcers is that they can generate many problems if not handled properly. I was in one classroom doing a consult and I noticed there was no television in the class, and almost all the classes I visit have some kind of television or LCD projector or something for displaying movies and other media. I asked the teacher why he didn't have one and he said that the child I was seeing, Clifford, was constantly trying to access the television and, when prevented from watching, he would go into crisis. If Clifford did get to watch television, he would go into crisis when it had to be stopped. As there was no longer any television in the room, Clifford had no more television-related problem… in the classroom. When Clifford ventured outside his classroom, however, to transition to a different activity like fine arts, he would often bolt to the next available room, run inside, run to the television, snatch videotapes and start shoving them in to the VCR. You do remember VCRs don't you? Those things that looked like a once-slice horizontal toaster that you couldn't program to record your shows because you could never figure out how to set the time? So the problem with the super-reinforcer wasn't really solved, it was just redistributed across the entire school.

What then do we do about extremely strong reinforcers? Do we just give up on them? I suppose that you could, but I really hate looking a gift reinforcer in the mouth. I believe that it's better to teach the child how to access these powerful reinforcers *responsibly*. That means learning how to wait to get them and learning how to give them up and learning how to accept reasonable alternatives until they become available again. Yes, it's much faster and easier to just get rid of them, and maybe it's a reasonable solution to temporarily improve a difficult situation, but this is not how a child's world expands—it's how it collapses in on him. If you keep on removing reinforcers the child can't handle, where does it stop? I have, many times, heard people say, "Don't give attention to Jimmy! That's just gonna make him want more!" Jimmy! You greedy little bastard! How dare you keep on wanting attention after it's been stopped?! Really? Is this what we're going to do to children with disabilities? Are we going to take away things they love because it causes problems for us? Not on my watch, and I have a really big watch. We can teach children how to give up reinforcers, we can teach them to wait, we can teach them to accept alternatives, and we can even teach them how to handle disappointment, but that's going to be work for us and that's okay. All of that teaching will make them much more well-adjusted people who are more prepared for the real world outside of their homes and classrooms.

SECTION 9: REINFORCERS CONTINGENT ON NON-BEHAVIOR

As pet peeves go, this is easily my favorite pet, the one I would keep in my lap and stroke while contemplating new ways to take over the world. Much of our lives is based on the following simple, but time-tested concept. Don't screw up, and you'll get good stuff. The other concept is, don't screw up, and *we won't screw you up worse!* We are constantly surrounded by these kinds of contingencies. Good things happen based on the absence of bad behavior. Even one of the most beloved Christmas songs is based on this concept, "Oh you better not pout, you better not cry, you better not shout, I'm telling you why." I believe you know who's coming and why you shouldn't screw up. Incidentally, that whole "he sees you when you're sleeping" thing still creeps me out a little. Has this Santa guy had a background check? Where was I? Right—other examples of non-behavior. If you go without having any infractions on your driver's license for a minimum amount of time (usually a few years), your auto-insurance provider may bestow upon you the label of "safe driver." The scientific term for this of course is "bull&@!$." All your insurance company knows is that you have not had any speeding tickets or accidents, but they don't know why. I have a motorcycle and it's very fast and very dangerous if you are not careful. I accelerate very hard and I usually speed and sometimes I have to put on the brakes really hard. I've come very close to getting a speeding ticket, but not quite. Once or twice I've had to slam on the brakes so hard that my back tire skidded. Guess what? I have a safe driver discount and so do thousands and thousands of other drivers who almost hit somebody every day. That guy who was tailgating you this morning and weaving in and out of traffic, he's a safe driver too. Are you a safe driver or a lucky driver? Perhaps you are a little bit of both, or perhaps you truly are a safe driver who never speeds, always maintains one car length for each 10 miles per hour and signals 200 feet before you intend to turn. It doesn't really matter as far as your insurance company is concerned because they are basing their decisions on "non-behavior."

No discussion of non-behavior would be complete without bringing up the "Dead Man Test." Many behavior analysts have never heard of this test, but it's a great one and it's easy to apply to any situation. The Dead Man Test is credited to Dr. Ogden Lindsley circa 1965. Essentially, if a dead man can do it, it isn't behavior. So clearly, decomposing is not something that someone "does." If we are going to do a good job of eliminating behavior problems we have to specify exactly what we want people to do. Granted, not every behavioral intervention may require the so called "replacement behavior," but in many instances it is necessary. Sometimes, just limiting reinforcement for inappropriate behaviors is sufficient. Many simple behavior analysis interventions are indeed "behavioral," but not very "analytic." For example, many people use some variation of Differential Reinforcement of Other Behavior or just DRO. It is often used in conjunction with other procedures, but I have seen many behavior plans in which it was the primary intervention. Essentially, in a DRO, reinforcement is delivered as long as the behavior in question has not occurred for some minimum amount of time. The reinforcer is allegedly delivered contingent on any other behavior, but this is rarely the case. That is, if Johnny hasn't punched anybody for 5 minutes he gets candy, or praise, or a hug, or what have you. Truly, no behavior in particular is being selected. The teacher just makes certain that the bad behavior doesn't contact reinforcement. For higher functioning children, this DRO can be taken to the extreme and the child may be required to "not screw up" for a week. Dr. Tim Vollmer (Vollmer, Iwata, Zarcone, Smith, & Mazaleski, 1993) found that a Fixed-time (FT) schedule of reinforcement is just as effective as a DRO and avoids some of its pitfalls. FT is even easier to use because (unlike Santa) you don't have to figure out if the person was naughty or nice.

The way the FT schedule works is that the person gets what you believe is maintaining their behavior, e.g., attention, every three minutes. It doesn't matter what they are doing at the time or what they have just done; reinforcement gets delivered anyhow. They just finished a task? Reinforcement. They just punched someone? Reinforcement. They just robbed a bank? Reinforcement. It doesn't matter. Sometimes schedules like these are referred to as non-contingent reinforcement (NCR). NCR is without question the premier behavioral oxymoron (Vollmer, 1999). There must be a contingency, a clear functional relationship, between the behavior and the reinforcer. Otherwise the behavior never gets selected or strengthened. So NCR really isn't reinforcement at all. It cannot be. Reinforcement requires both contiguity (immediacy) and a contingency (an if-then causal relation). That is, if on occasion a reinforcer falls out of the sky it may happen right after some behavior. If there is no contingency related to that particular behavior, then that particular behavior will not be selected from the pool of all current behaviors in the repertoire. Essentially, if there is no contingency and no contiguity there is no reinforcement effect. The one caveat might be what Skinner referred to as "superstitious behavior" (Skinner, 1948). With superstitious behavior there is allegedly contiguity (immediacy) but there really is no contingency, i.e., "Dumb luck." I believe that the continuance of these kinds of behaviors has more to do with rule-following than with a one-time dumb luck "reinforcer." In other words, you won't get the same persistence in babies as they don't have a long history of rule-following. For example, you put on a new shirt, the phone rings and someone tells you that you've won the lottery. Now it's your "lucky shirt!" If you put a new shirt on a baby and then plop down a new toy (and you do this just once) the baby will not likely seek out that particular shirt well into adulthood (besides, it won't fit). My point is that conditioned reinforcement and our own verbal behavior about random occurrences (winning the lottery) are probably far more important than the occurrence itself in the long-term maintenance of behavior (wearing your lucky shirt whenever you need luck). Think about it and get back to me.

Back to NCR. NCR, more accurately described, would be "the non-contingent delivery of a stimulus which, under certain conditions, has been known to function as a reinforcer for certain behaviors." Quite a mouthful, but technically more correct. In essence, schedules of stimulus delivery like these reduce the motivation to engage in behavior that normally produces such stimuli. In other words, if you bang your head about every five minutes to get attention, and we give you attention every three minutes, why the hell do you need to bang your head? You've got everything you need.

Procedures like those listed above have been shown in the applied literature to have a positive effect on behavior problems. There's no question about it. It's just that from a standpoint of trying to figure out the nature and scope of the problem, these procedures merely scratch the surface. A discrepancy analysis together with a root-cause analysis would go much further in helping us to design a more comprehensive treatment. For example:

Why don't typically developing children bang their heads for attention?
     They know a variety of ways to get attention
Why does this child bang his head?
     He knows very few appropriate ways to get attention
Why doesn't he use the few appropriate behaviors that he can do?
     Adults fail to reinforce the appropriate attempts because they are busy.
Why are they so busy?
     Because they are dealing with seven other children with behavior problems!
Why do they attend to the head banging?
     Because they *have* to attend to head banging!

We can't simply tell a child what not to do, we must also tell the child *what to do* and we must be specific. Let's take the highly popular rule "Keep your hands to yourself." Another great one I hear is the phrase "Quiet Hands!" What the hell does that even mean? We want aggression to stop because it's too loud? I fully understand that, "Quiet hands" is a way to say, "Stop hitting me" without talking about the bad behavior. Now, without a doubt, this is better than saying, "Don't hit," but "quiet hands" doesn't address the function of behavior: it's more of a prompt to engage in a self-control behavior. Now don't get me wrong—learning self-control is fantastic, but it's typically much harder than teaching a replacement behavior that gets the child's needs met. Also, "Hands in your lap" or "Hands in your pockets" would be much clearer than "Quiet hands." I've also heard the phrase, "Quiet Feet!" presumably because one child hired an attorney who found a loophole in the quiet hands ordinance. Phrases like, "Keep your hands to yourself!" and "Quiet hands!" can only be understood in terms of the context in which the adult utters the phrase. If a child is shoving someone, "Keep your hands to yourself" means don't shove. If the child is in a china shop, it means don't touch anything. Is keeping one's hands to one's self behavior? No, dead men are highly adept at keeping their hands to themselves, and if you don't believe me, just ask dead women!

Instead of telling a child who punches to keep his hands to himself, how about (God forbid) we figure out why he is punching people (the problem) and teach him how to solve his problem? If one child is teasing another, what do we do to help the victim? Can we teach the child what to do when he is teased, what to say, where to go? Can we discover why the teaser is teasing? Can we prompt the teaser to engage in pro-social, cooperative behaviors with the teasee? Can we arrange powerful reinforcers for both children when they work together? Aren't these better solutions than just telling a child not to do things? I think they are, but I will also acknowledge that they will, initially, take more work. We tell people, "Don't screw up" because it is the easiest thing to do. We tell our children, "Be good in school today." When they get home we ask them, "Were you good in school today?" We seldom, however, specify exactly what good *means*. Invariably, if you ask your own child, "Were you good in school today?" he will tell you "yes," which means he's probably lying to you. Just for the sake of argument, let's say that he is telling the truth. After he tells you that he was good, ask this zinger, "What did you do that was good?" Typically, children will scratch their heads a bit and then come up with something that is the equivalent of not screwing up, e.g., "The teacher didn't have to write my name on the board." Try it with your kids as it can be very revealing about their understanding of school-related expectations.

Returning for a moment to the DRO schedule, one reason that these "treatments" should not be expected to work very well is that the child is never told what to do: therefore it's unlikely that appropriate behavior will ever be reinforced. As an example, if little Jimmy punches Mary every day of the week, as though it's in his job description, someone may arrange a "behavior program" whereby Jimmy gets to have pizza in the cafeteria with the teacher of his choice if there is no hitting for one week. These kinds of programs are very common, like a family-values-politician-cheating-on-his-spouse common. Even the common housefly is not as common as these kinds of programs. Let's say that Jimmy hits Mary every day as sure as the sun rises. He does this because she teases him. Jimmy is put on a one week DRO that specifies no hitting. To everyone's surprise, Jimmy makes it a week with no hitting. However, the reason he showed no hitting is that Mary was picking on some other unlucky new student and she just never provoked Jimmy. Jimmy, because he satisfied the conditions of the weeklong DRO (no hitting), gets pizza. What behavior, exactly, is getting reinforced? Jimmy showed no "self-control." Jimmy didn't turn the other cheek. He didn't even get hit on the first cheek. In fact, there were no cheeks involved at all. Dead men didn't punch Mary either. So where is their pizza??!

Whenever a child is about to do something really bad, there is something else that they (theoretically) should be doing instead. To really make a lasting, meaningful change in behavior, we should be teaching children, ahead of time, what they *should* do at the very moment they're highly motivated to do the wrong thing. Then we need evidence that not only didn't they punch, but that at a time when they wanted to punch, they turned around and walked away from the confrontation (which Dead Men cannot do). Then when we give pizza, we can say, "Hey Jimmy, nice job walking away from Mary when she teased you! You did the right thing!" Yes?

Some teachers already understand this concept of specifying not only what they don't want to see, but also what they want the child to do. I know one great teacher who had a creative technique for correcting the behavior of children who called out and interrupted the class. When a student would start to answer a question without asking permission, the teacher would tell the child "take that thought, and put it into your hand and hold onto it tightly until I can call on you. The child would make a fist and hold it next to his head to most efficiently transfer his thoughts. Genius. Pure genius. This teacher didn't even have to tell the child "don't call out!" She clearly stated what the child should do (make a fist containing the thought), and she stated when reinforcement would be available (she would call on the child). The main point is that this tactic gave the child something to do while waiting to be called on, namely make a fist and think about transferring his thoughts to his fist and to then remember the thoughts that were contained within his tightly coiled little mitt. It worked well (I believe) because the child didn't have to hold up his arm all day (effort) and because the teacher could look for the student with the balled up fist as a way of remembering to call on him.

Many times, children don't know what to do because *no one has told them what to do*!

Very often, children want to "be good," but no one has specified how they should accomplish this elusive goal. Avoid politically correct vagaries like "be respectful" when what you really mean is "don't curse at people." Furthermore, instead of saying, "Don't curse" it would be better to try to understand what leads to cursing and specify (set expectations) what you wish the child to say instead. I know that giving instructions that describe what children should not do can be a hard habit to break because these kinds of proscriptive instructions are rampant. Admittedly, it's more of a pain in the butt to figure out what children *should* do, but it is, I believe, ultimately more effective. You'll get really good at it if you keep practicing, I promise. Remember, *understand it*, *specify it*, *prompt it*, and *reinforce it*!

Chapter 3

Problems With Aversives

SECTION 1: INTRODUCTION

As outlined in the previous chapter, there are clearly many things that can go astray when using reinforcers, and problems with reinforcers can absolutely cause and maintain numerous behavior problems. Aversives can be seen as the *yin* to the reinforcer's *yang*, or vice-versa. I'm not entirely certain which paisley is the male (evil) one, the white one with the black dot in it or the black one with the white dot in it, which reminds me of another *Star Trek* episode, but we'll save that for another time. It's interesting that I used the yin-yang example because, as I just mentioned, the yin's got a little yang in it and the yang's got a little yin in it. Reinforcers and aversives have the same sort of relationship. Before pressing on, let's start with a definition. An aversive is defined in much the same way as a reinforcer.

> A stimulus is aversive if its contingent removal, prevention, or postponement maintains behavior—that constitutes negative reinforcement—or if its contingent presentation suppresses behavior—punishment. (Perone 2003)

So, like positive reinforcement, we again have this idea that events (stimuli) are defined not by how they appear or how other people may feel about them. Instead, we define events (reinforcers or aversives) in terms of their functional effects on behavior. What does this mean? It means that just like positive reinforcers, aversives are, in many instances, not what you think they are. Things that may function as aversives in some situations may not be in others. Things that may function as aversives for some people may not for others. Conversely, things that are in no way aversive for some people may be very strong aversives for others. Furthermore, as mentioned in Chapter 2, one man's reinforcer can be another man's aversive (Barney the Dinosaur). Essentially, everything that is true for reinforcers is true for aversives.

We are dynamic organisms living in a dynamic world. It makes no more sense to say, "demands are aversive" than it does to say "M&Ms are reinforcers." Demands to perform what? M&Ms used to reinforce which behavior? It is critically important to break away from any preconceived notions of good, bad, painful, unpleasant, etc. That's not how we define aversive, and of course when I say, "We" I mean behavior analysts. There are numerous federal, state, and local laws and rules defining what some people have decided to call "aversives." These definitions of aversive are typically based on the perception that certain things are universally unpleasant or because they were *intended* to be used as punishers. What kinds of things are we talking about? Some examples are water mist, electric shock, noxious stimuli (ammonia smell, lemon juice, and Listerine) and other things that some people used to suppress severe problem behavior. True, we don't want to subject people with disabilities to these kinds of things if not necessary, and these kinds of things are almost never used anymore. In this discussion, however, I am trying to stick to clear language and clear definitions so that those of you working in applied settings can better understand how various events are truly functioning to affect a child's behavior. Is contingent water mist in the face aversive? If you're in Michigan, outside in the middle of winter, quite possibly. What about in Tallahassee, Florida in the middle of summer after you've been standing in the noonday sun for 30 minutes? Context, context, context.

Allow me to give another example. Is tabasco sauce an aversive? Well, it depends on whom you ask and how it is applied. I only find it aversive if it ends up in my eye. I can safely say that I will actively avoid getting tabasco in my eye, and if it does get in my eye I will try to terminate the sensation immediately. Tabasco in my eye; aversive. Tabasco in my mouth with a taco; delicious. As Mike Perone so eloquently explained, (Perone, 2003) "aversive" is not an inherent property of a stimulus. I'll explain what that means.

I know a behavior analyst who used to use aversives to attempt to decrease severe self-injury back in the days when it was much more common to do so. Keep in mind that this was done before functional analysis in applied settings had been developed (Iwata et al., 1994). This particular behavior analyst (no, it wasn't me) would administer, (orally, not ocularly), a small dose of tabasco contingent on head banging. After the first instance of head banging, tabasco was placed in the individual's mouth. Head banging stopped for perhaps a few seconds to a minute. After the second instance of head banging, the same result followed. After the third instance of head banging, the client opened his mouth and stuck his tongue out and seemed to be waiting for the tabasco to be administered. Not only was the tabasco shown to have only fleeting efficacy as a punisher, but the client quickly learned to appreciate the hearty piquant flavor. It turns out that, like whiskey, sometimes things can grow on you. How many times in your life have you heard someone say, "I used to hate _____ but now I love it!" Granted, there may be some things that manage to retain their aversive qualities no matter what, but this is clearly not always the case.

One big difference between aversives and reinforcers is that alleged reinforcers may have no effect at all depending on your current level of deprivation. Aversive stimuli, however, do not necessarily require that the organism be in "in the mood" for them. That is, if a pigeon's key pecks are reinforced by food, and if you run an experimental session with a pigeon who just got back from the "All U Can Eat" grain buffet, you'll get very little if any responding. On the other hand, if key pecks terminate very high levels of shock, you can bet your next paycheck that you'll see pecking every time. On a more human level, you're not always in the mood for pizza[1], but you're always in the mood to *not get audited* by the IRS! This is one reason why so many people's lives are dominated by avoiding bad things. Dr. Jack Michael is known for saying, "Aversives make the world go around," and I don't know that he's wrong. We will discuss more of these issues in the chapter on punishment. Stimuli that act as punishers are by definition aversive, but not all aversives act as punishers.

---

[1] It is an incontrovertible fact, that I am always in the mood for pizza, even right after having pizza, as long as it's good pizza. In fact, I wouldn't mind having some right now.

Finally, it is critically important to understand that just as things you love may not reinforce a particular behavior, things you hate may not be aversive enough to motivate one particular behavior or punish another. Really, it depends on how much you hate it. That is, we might say that we "hate" some things, but those things aren't truly aversive unless they actually change behavior. Have you ever been watching television and there was a show on that you hated, but you couldn't find the remote? Instead of looking for the damn remote you just lay there, helpless, and watch the stupid show. Now if it were your most hated show, then you would get your butt up off the sofa and start searching for the remote or, God forbid, walk all the way over to the television and change the channel directly. Okay, now we've got ourselves an aversive because it *motivated us to do something*. We categorize things based on their *ability to change behavior*, not based on what we say about them. Are painful things aversive? The definitive answer is: It depends. Not all things that are aversive can be characterized as painful, and not all painful things can be characterized as aversive! What? I'll explain.

I do my very best to avoid speeding tickets. If I get one, my speeding behavior is usually suppressed for quite some time, but not permanently. Are tickets truly painful? No, of course not. Sure they hurt your wallet, but that's about it. When I lift weights, near the end of my sets when I experience muscle failure, it hurts like hell! Does it cause me to avoid weight lifting? No, because I understand that the pain means that the muscles will get stronger. "Feel the burn, man!" I don't like the pain. I don't look forward to the pain. I *tolerate* the pain because I know what it has accomplished in the past. Is it possible that this pain might function as an aversive for some people? Absolutely! It's one reason why some people never go to the gym again after they begin their New Year's Day membership. The word "aversive" clearly carries too much baggage. I hope that I've unpacked those bags or at least made them a bit lighter, so that we may continue.

I gave a definition of negative reinforcement earlier in Chapter 2, and touched on it in Perone's definition of an aversive (removal of a stimulus). Many refer to the aversive as THE negative reinforcer. It strengthens behavior too, just like Skittles, but the removal is what strengthens behavior rather than the presentation. Just as positive reinforcement can occur naturally (like with self-taught skills), so can negative reinforcement. We engage in many behaviors every day that keep bad things from happening. Furthermore, these bad things are not necessarily done to us by anyone. If there is a crackling noise in your stereo speaker you might jiggle the wire to make the crackling noise go away. In the future, when you hear the crackling noise again, you may immediately start jiggling the wire. Boom, negative reinforcement.

Typically, most people like to say that they only use positive approaches, and although we may not actively decide to program aversive events, they occur with or without our consent. Aversive events have their own agenda. Aversives are all around us every day in every possible form. Some of them are barely even noticeable, like our clothes catching us in the wrong way, or that itch that you just can't scratch (at least not in public). Others are much more obvious like catching your fingers in a three-ring binder because you weren't paying attention. Some aversives come from people (teasing), and some come from the natural environment and have nothing to do with our behavior or the behavior of others (hot or cold temperatures). Some aversives come from our own bodies (headache, toothache), and some come from the results of our own behavior that is not yet well developed (hitting your thumb with a hammer, crashing your bicycle, falling when you are learning to walk, or getting a math problem wrong). It may be helpful to have different categories of aversives, because there may be some very different ways of solving these various problems. Keep these categories in mind as we look at some typical aversives as children experience them in school settings. This is certainly not a complete listing of possible categories, but I think that it covers quite a bit of the aversive landscape.

Some Categories of Aversives

Socially-mediated aversives (someone else delivered the aversive)

Naturally occurring non socially-mediated aversives (unplanned, unrelated to the individual or the behavior of anyone else, e.g., you get stung by a bee)

Private aversives (pain, discomfort, physiological arousal, hunger, thirst, etc.)

Response-produced aversives (inefficient, ineffective, incorrect behavior)

SECTION 2:   COMMON AVERSIVES: TASKS

When I say, "Common" aversives, I simply mean things that have been known to function as aversives for many people. Naturally these things have to be taken on a case-by-case basis, like positive reinforcers, but even for those there are some common ones as well. Before embarking on this section, I have to emphasize that, in many instances, aversives of a particular magnitude will produce significant levels of physiological arousal, and I'm not referring to the good kind (nudge-nudge, wink-wink, say no more). This is also the case with positive reinforcers. If you don't believe in the power of an impending positive reinforcer, just turn on *The Price is Right* and watch what people do when the announcer calls their name and says, "Come on Down! You're the next contestant on *The Price is Right*!" They positively freak out. The same is true with high-magnitude aversives, except that the physiological arousal takes us to the "dark side." This physiological arousal can also produce increases in motor activity, and if the person tends to engage in highly repetitive "self-stimulatory" behavior you will often see an increase in such behaviors. I have seen these increases in frequency when the person was excited and (apparently) happy, as well as when the person was extremely agitated. You've got to admit, it's kind of difficult to stay still when your central nervous system is doing the Macarena.

2.1 Tasks

Tasks fall under the category of socially-mediated aversives. I'm making a distinction between *tasks* and *demands* because I think that sometimes there are different problems going on. I'll talk about demands in general as a category of aversives in Chapter 5 on problems with adults. Demands can be a problem irrespective of any tasks. That is, the kid may not mind doing tasks per se, but has a problem with being *told* to do tasks. In other cases, demands aren't truly the problem (come here, sit down, give me the ball, and get out your math worksheet) but it's certain tasks that have aversive qualities. Whenever I'm working with a child and there is some evidence that he or she engages in frequent escape/avoidance behavior, I'm not only thinking of appropriate ways for the child to escape (although this is a standard treatment option), I'm also thinking of *why* the child wants to escape from the task. This is when I start asking several questions about tasks, questions like:

Does the child avoid all tasks or only academic tasks? Some children love to be helpful, and they will help with a special task (erase the board), but won't do something they are *supposed* to do. Does the child escape from *anything* that may involve some effort or only things they are "supposed" to do, like academic assignments? Children who don't shy away from tasks that require some effort are usually easier to work with than those who do. Now what about those who avoid academic tasks? Maybe they're good at nonacademic tasks but lack the skills they need to be successful at academic ones. We can also be reasonably certain that it isn't necessarily a problem with demands from adults but is something more specific to typical academic tasks. I've often seen children who are not so much avoiding a specific task, but simply anything that looks like work. That is, a child may do what you ask when you are playing with him on the floor, but make a similar request at a desk and you'd better make sure you're wearing your denim jacket! I worked with one young man who was a task avoidance juggernaut. We will call him Brian. Brian not only hated academic types of tasks, he hated anything associated with them including the sing-song "teaching voice." Brian so hated academic tasks that when I used the "teaching voice" to tell him to eat some Skittles (which he loved), he started to have a meltdown. "Eat SKIT-tles! They're YUM-my! Taste the RAIN-bow!" If you tried to get him to do a simple "put in" task (in this case putting a gift wrap bow into a bowl) he absolutely refused to do it and started having a fit if you were at the table. If you were playing with him on the floor and put the bow in the bowl yourself using a regular conversational voice and making silly noises, he would put the bow in without even being prompted to do so! He didn't have a bow-aversion. He wasn't traumatized by bows when he was a baby. He wasn't suffering from Opp-bow-sitional Defiant Disorder. He just hated anything to do with traditional academic stuff. This is someone who really needed to have everybody back way up and start from square one. For some kids we simply need to establish the basics of liking adults, then liking to do things for adults, and then slowly working our way forward towards academics.

Does the child avoid certain academic tasks but enjoys or doesn't mind others? This is quite different from the case with Brian. Many children just love certain academic tasks, but they avoid others just like you avoid that chatty person at work who still hasn't figured out that when you say, "Anyway..." that they are supposed to stop talking, say goodbye, and leave. If you know that the child can work well in one academic area (reading) but another area is a battle every time (math), then you have a different (and better) problem on your hands. Now you can start asking questions about why the child doesn't like math. Does she hate all math or just the new math that she isn't good at yet? Does she hate that she's working on math that is two grade levels below what her classmates are doing? Does she hate tasks that involve writing, but loves those that involve reading and speaking? Many kids just hate writing! Hell, if I had to write this book with a pencil I would have had a nervous breakdown by now. Right? Does the child hate several tasks with certain commonalities or only one specific task or subject? The premier question to answer is, "What is the aversive nature of the task?" Then you must ask follow-up questions. You just have to keep asking questions until you understand the fundamental problem. If you dig deep enough and long enough you will strike oil.

Which factors contribute to the overall aversive nature of the tasks? There are some tasks that may acquire their aversive properties because of a single problem (they involve writing and the child hates writing) and there are those that are aversive because of a number of factors that work together. The following is a list of six *potential* factors that could each act individually or work in concert to create the perfect storm for escape motivated behavior. Here we go...

1) Task-related skill deficits:

Does the child have the prerequisite skills to be successful with the current task? It's fair to say that people like to do things they're good at and avoid subjects in which they fail to excel. You may as well get used to reading about this concept as I'll mention it quite a bit. If the phrase weren't so damn long I'd have it made into bumper stickers. Yes, there are exceptions to this concept, those who love a good challenge don't mind that they are bad at doing something temporarily, but those individuals usually have an extensive history of going out and kicking some major butt in just about any arena. The rest of us stick with things that we can do well. A child who's a poor reader typically avoids it like politicians avoid yes or no questions. Which support skills is he lacking? How do we increase those skills? Is he working on a level that is too difficult given his current skills? Was he advanced too quickly? These are all important questions. It may be necessary to perform a task analysis of the skills the child needs to be successful for a given academic task and then see how the child's skills compare to those identified as critical.

2) Errors:

Most people aren't very fond of making mistakes. If you make numerous mistakes you can get discouraged and frustrated. Many children exhibit tremendous behavior problems in response to multiple errors in a row. These are those "response-produced" aversives I mentioned at the beginning of the chapter. For many children, if you analyze why errors are being made and can reduce or prevent most of them, the task becomes much less aversive. Sometimes we only need to increase our level of prompting so that the individual can be successful and then figure out how to lower our prompt level once the error rate comes under control.

3) Rate of Reinforcement/Magnitude of Reinforcement:

What if you get a little positive feedback for every response you make? Like on a computer program where every time you select a correct answer you get a "ding!" or a point or something? Now what if the nature of the task requires you to work continuously for many minutes, like writing three paragraphs. You don't cop any reinforcers after each sentence, and you might only get feedback after you have completed the entire assignment. Now, what if you complete the entire assignment and it's wrong? Then there is no reinforcement at all. Many children cannot tolerate long periods of effort with little or no reinforcement. Even if the big reinforcer comes at the end of the task, are there any conditioned reinforcers given along the way at regular intervals or after certain portions of the task to keep motivation high? Also, the reinforcer may not be big enough given the difficulty of the task. To properly match the magnitude of reinforcement with the task difficulty you really have to know how difficult the task is from the child's perspective.

4) Task Duration:

The duration of a task can add to its overall aversiveness and contributes to low rates of reinforcement if the reinforcer is given at the end of the task. I know some teachers working with higher functioning students who will not schedule 50 minute lesson plans. They do 20 minute lesson plans that rotate quickly. For some children, 10 minutes of "circle-time" may not be aversive at all. After 30 minutes, however, someone needs to call in the crisis team. It's a good idea to increase the rate of reinforcement as the task duration increases to enhance the child's ability to tolerate longer tasks.

5) Does the task make sense from a developmental standpoint?

I run into this one quite a bit. This is where a discrepancy analysis comes into play. I have seen children who were working on money-handling skills when they couldn't even communicate their needs very effectively. If you're nonverbal and you aren't getting an allowance and don't use vending machines, and aren't running to the store to get milk and bread for mommy, why are you being taught to discriminate between nickels, dimes, and quarters? What's the point? Where are we going with this? I can guarantee you that everyone reading this book could talk up a storm before any of you ever needed to know money handling skills. You all were able to have a lovely chat with mommy and daddy before learning how to write your names.

Why do children end up working on these kinds of skills? There's probably a number of reasons. Some have to do with inclusion gone awry, and some have to do with the parents who feel the need for their child to come away with something from school, even if perhaps that "something" isn't particularly functional. Still other reasons may have to do with improper assessment of the child's needs. Frankly, in Florida anyhow, I'm surprised anyone learns to write her name as it isn't tested on the FCAT! There are many skills that typically developing children have mastered well before they attempt traditional academics. For some children with disabilities, however, those skills (social, communication, cooperation) may have never been learned. Consequently, traditional academics may prove too difficult and may not be very meaningful to the child.

6) Does the task "make sense" to the child?

If you are thinking that this section doesn't sound particularly behavior analytic, you're correct. I'll try to explain myself. Have you ever had a job, and during your employment you were asked to do things that made absolutely no sense to you? If you're like most people, then you probably have experienced this at one point or another. Some of you are probably shouting right now *"That's my entire position description!"* How did you feel when you were asked to do things that you thought were a waste of time? Did you find those tasks aversive by chance? Even though you were getting paid? As we've talked about in Chapter 2, there may be a variety of conditioned reinforcers produced by any task you do. When you are asked to do things that don't make sense to you, there may not be many conditioned reinforcers involved in the task, and there may be many aversives. Now let's take the example of teaching name writing for a child who is essentially nonverbal. Does he understand the significance of learning to write his name? Does he understand what it will enable him to do? Well, if you can write your name, you can write your name on your things so that no one else tries to take them and that's pretty damn cool! How are you supposed to understand that if you can't talk? Could you teach someone how to do it anyway with enough reinforcement? I suppose, but how did you feel about doing stupid things at work that made no sense to you even though you were well compensated? I don't know about you, but I can't stand it and neither can my wife Laraine. We can't be alone in this regard. Doing things you hate, just because you get "paid" for it can often lead to a whole lot of agitation, and do we really want angry learners? I don't. We'll come back to this notion in the section about the aversive properties of reinforcers.

Some may bring up the point that typically developing children do all sorts of things that don't make sense to them and they learn that they just *have* to do it. This is true, however, these children also have different histories and many, many more skills than most people with disabilities. Typically developing children also have much better self-control and very little if any problem behavior. My point is that the greater the disability, and the more restricted the learner's repertoire of functional skills, the more important it is for the task to "make sense" to the individual. Now my question is, did all of that make sense to you?

SECTION 3: COMMON AVERSIVES: CONTINUED

3.1 Extinction Conditions

As mentioned briefly in Chapter 2, extinction is a procedure in which a reinforcer is simply withheld at a time when it is normally delivered. If you say, "Hello" to someone who usually greets you and smiles, and they just look right past you and keep going, it's fairly unsettling. You did what you usually do, but the usual result (smiling back and waving) did not occur. This example illustrates extinction. Eventually, you won't even say, "Hello" to that person any more because it no longer produces reinforcement; that is, saying, "Hello" gets extinguished. Extinction can cause some very severe behavior problems that occur in what most call the "extinction burst." Behavior analysts are well aware of this term, as are many non-behavior analysts. As a reminder, the behavior may get worse before it gets better and may become more variable and you may see the reappearance of behaviors that you thought were long gone. Extinction conditions can be socially-mediated, or they can occur naturally. When you turn the key in your ignition one morning and you just hear click-click-click-click, it's not a good morning. For me it usually means at least ten seconds of cursing. How do we know extinction conditions could be aversive? Easy. If you knew, in advance, that someone was going to give you the cold shoulder, would you willingly walk up to the person and say, "Hello!" or would you avoid them? I thought so.

I worked with a really cute little girl, we'll call her Sheila. Sheila was minimally verbal, and slowly doing better with her mands (requests) but she still needed quite a bit of help. Sheila wasn't really good at handling extinction conditions. She loved playing on the computer, but when the Internet was slow and webpages didn't load fast enough, it constituted an extinction condition for her. Apple couldn't manufacture mice fast enough to replace the mangled, tangled heaps of shattered plastic that found their way to the ancient mouse burial grounds. When she clicked the mouse but nothing happened, Sheila would slam the mouse down on the desk as hard as she could. That didn't fix the computer but it permanently unfixed the mouse. It also recruited help quite quickly. Something had to be done and it had to be done soon. She was killing so many mice that PETA was about to get involved. Many of you may be thinking that they should have taught her to ask for help, which is generally a good idea. The problem, however, is that the computer malfunctions happened without warning, which is a much more difficult problem from a teaching perspective. The real answer is to contrive or simulate a broken computer repeatedly in a systematic fashion so that we can be prepared to prompt asking for help and thereby prevent senseless mouse-abuse. Typically, in cases like Sheila's, I would sabotage the computer by unplugging the mouse without the child's awareness (I'm such a bastard). I would then watch carefully for signs of distress, and before errors occur (smashing something), I would give a prompt to request help. After a request for help I would give a prompt to wait, fix the mouse, and the student is once again happily using Google to search for *Toy Story* pictures. Incidentally, when you give a prompt to wait, you initially want to follow it with many conditioned reinforcers so the kid doesn't freak out on you. Say things like, "Almost there!" or "I'm gonna fix it right now!" Also model calm behaviors, smile, and maybe use a gesture to get the child to stay where she is. Sheila's problem was a good example of naturally-occurring "environmental" extinction that we turned into programmed socially-mediated extinction so that we could control it. This basic strategy can be used with all types of extinction-related problems. Regarding socially-mediated extinction, in which the extinction condition is planned, deciding to completely withhold a reinforcer can be a bit dicey. You have to be able to "read" the kid you're working with to know the right time to jump in and prompt the appropriate behavior (asking for help for example) that will terminate the planned extinction condition.

3.2 Blocked Access to Reinforcement

If you think extinction is a real pain, in the immortal words of Bachman Turner Overdrive, "You ain't seen nothin' yet!" Extinction is kind of like when you go to a restaurant and say "I'll have the ribs," like you always do, and they say "I'm very sorry but we ran out at lunchtime." The ribs just aren't there, and now you're just sitting around with a bunch of moist towelettes and nothing to wipe. *Blocked access*, which really isn't a separate behavioral phenomenon, but more like a clinical term, is best exemplified by the bag of peanut M&M's that is hopelessly caught in the coil of the vending machine. Even though the coil is turning, they just won't drop. It's much worse than no M&M's at all. Why? The sight of the M&M's coupled with their proximity and the presentation of numerous conditioned reinforcers (money going in, lights confirming your selection, coil rotating, etc.) are all one big fat motivating operation that may increase the effectiveness of M&Ms as a reinforcer. I don't think that it's *fundamentally* different from a typical extinction condition, but blocked access is like extinction on steroids. I just described environmental blocked access, which could create a very angry person. Socially-mediated blocked access can sometimes result in people being attacked. This is when you verbally or physically get between the individual and their beloved reinforcer. If you're going to attempt this you may want to put on your denim jacket first.

I have a fresh example of blocked access to reinforcement. It just so happens that only moments ago, I finished a phone consultation with someone in the United Kingdom. I'm not kidding—it happened just as I was about to write this section. Not only is the example fresh, but it's also imported, and therefore more expensive. A very large, very strong, 12-year-old girl had some big problems with blocked access to reinforcement. She had some rudimentary verbal skills, but only one- or two-word utterances, and, like many people, when she gets upset all the words go out the window and the problem behaviors abound. This particular girl, we'll call her Becky, engaged in very high frequency self-injury which was biting a large callous on her arm. Like many individuals who are veteran "biters" she rarely broke the skin and she always bit in the same place. Whenever she was told "no" or that she couldn't have something that she just asked for, she immediately started biting. Is the problem biting? Like so many behaviors, it's a problem but not the only one. In one sense, if she hadn't bitten her arm I never would have gotten the phone call. Also, getting agitated because you can't get something isn't really a problem. It's what you do when you get agitated and the level of your agitation that's the problem. So, Becky had several problems. One of them was that blocked access (physically blocked, or verbally blocked) was far more aversive for her than for the other children in her class. Also, Becky didn't know what to do when faced with blocked access conditions. What skills do typically developing children have that Becky did not that allows them to deal with blocked access? Well, for one thing, they can ask lots of questions, too many if you ask me. For example:

Student: Can I go on the computer now?

Teacher: No, it isn't time yet.

Student: When will it be time?

Teacher: At 12:00.

Student: What time is it now?

Teacher: 11:50.

Student: It's just 10 minutes! C'mon can't I just go now?

Teacher: Everyone has to wait.

Student: Joey didn't wait, he got to go early!

Teacher: Joey did extra work.

Student: Can I do extra work too?

Teacher: Okay, Three more problems and you can go early.

Student: Oh yeah!

The hypothetical student in this example can do many things and understands many things that Becky could not possibly do or understand. Also, this hypothetical student wasn't happy that he couldn't get onto the computer immediately, but neither was he in a rage. So you can look at Becky's problems as: 1) super-sensitivity to blocked access conditions, coupled with; 2) not knowing what to do to end the blocked access condition; and 3) not knowing what to do while waiting for a reinforcer. You could also add: 4) Becky doesn't know how to calm herself when she is agitated. How would you approach this problem from a treatment perspective? Like our friend Sheila, the malevolent mouse-murderer, we need to contrive blocked access conditions instead of letting them occur haphazardly when we're not prepared to handle the behavioral fallout. We could easily handle items one, two and three above in an intervention. Here's what it might look like:

1. Wait for Becky to mand (ask) for something she typically asks for.
2. Be prepared to give it to her.
3. Delay giving it for only seconds, you might even say, "No it's not ready yet."
4. Prompt her to say, "Ready yet?" or "Ready?"
5. When she complies, say, "Yes all ready!" and give her the item.

Now, don't run out and paste this into your behavior plan or I will be very disappointed. It's just an example of what treatment *might* look like. Also, depending on how severe the problem, uttering the word "no" with just a 3-second delay may be enough to produce self-injury, and we'd like to avoid that. Some people are so exquisitely sensitive to the word "no" that you would have to, over many trials, fade that word into the phrase that indicates a blocked access condition. *By contriving conditions, it puts us in the driver's seat, not the student.* Also, by doing this frequently, the child can acclimate (habituate) to the blocked access condition and this should somewhat decrease her super-sensitivity.

Regarding sensitivity to the word "no," a great strategy that many people use is the "yes but" strategy a.k.a. the "Yes as soon as" strategy which can be used for children with decent verbal skills. I use this strategy quite often, and I believe that there 3 very important tips to follow: 1) you have to be "upbeat" about whatever you say or you'll crash and burn; 2) you have to specify where, when, and how the child will get what she wants; and 3) you have to lace your verbalizations with words that have great conditioned reinforcing power. So, for the first tip, you have to smile when you are denying something someone wants. You have to look and act like they are totally going to get it (they're going to, but not until certain other things have taken place). For the second tip, when you fill them in on the details, don't leave things too vague. For the third tip, you have to use as many "encouraging" words as possible ,but you mustn't lie to the child. Here are some examples:

Student: Can I have computer time?

Teacher: Absolutely! Which assignment would you like to complete first? Math or spelling?

Student: Can I have juice?

Teacher: Of course! As soon as the timer goes off everyone will get juice. Which will you want, apple or grape?

Student: I want to feed the classroom hamster!

Teacher: Wow, that sounds like fun! No problem! After Timmy gives him a carrot, you can feed him too. Which do you want to give him, carrots or nuts?

In all of the examples, the children aren't getting anything immediately. However, everything that normally occurs when they are about to gain access *is* happening... except actually gaining access. It's a bit of a conditioned reinforcer trick[2]. However, you can't pull it off if you look and sound like a big sourpuss. If you look indignant because someone dared to ask you for something when it wasn't time, then you have already lost. We see indignant faces when our requests are about to be shot down. The teacher must model happy, excited behavior and talk about where and when things will happen and what it will look like. You can talk about the reinforcer too. You can ask the person questions about the reinforcer. Still, they aren't getting it yet. One more thing, you must be careful to avoid getting sarcastic...

Student: Can we watch movies today and do no work?

Teacher: Sure! When Hell freezes over we will have movie day!

Some may make the point that children need to be able to hear "NO!" I don't disagree. Eventually, they *should* be able to handle what I like to term a "hard no." That is, when they ask you for something it would be nice if you could just say, "No we don't have any." However, they may not be ready for a hard no at the moment. You can always work your way up to that, but first you have to be successful with a "soft no." Once they can accept "soft" blocked access conditions you can start to sneak in the more abrupt ones so that *they will be successful no matter where they go*.

3.3   Reinforcer Removal

Reinforcer removal is what some refer to as "negative punishment" because it gains its aversive power through the removal of a reinforcer. We are not really discussing punishment as a behavior change procedure in this chapter, but we will discuss reinforcer removal because sometimes people have to give things up. You may not be doing it to attempt to punish anything. It's part of life and certainly part of being in school. Children have to learn to share and how to give up things and leave things and accept other things. Bobby can't stay on the computer for five hours. Jessica can't play with the water in the bathroom sink all day. Sometimes you're not so much removing the reinforcer from the kid, but the kid from the reinforcer (you can't pull the sink out of the wall). Either way, eventually, somebody is going to have a fit.

I commonly hear things like, "Peter has problems with transitions!" If I had $1,000 for every time I heard that, I could retire tomorrow (hackneyed phrase adjusted for inflation). In many instances, the problem is transitioning from a potent reinforcer to a "known" aversive or just having to give up the current reinforcer regardless of what the child is going to do next. True, for some children, the act of being forced to stop something before it is complet-

---

[2]It's kind of like the "Jedi mind trick" that Obi-wan used on the Imperial storm troopers when he and Luke were trying to escape from Tatooine in *Episode IV*. Sure, this trick won't work on every kid all the time, but at least they don't have blasters. Good luck, and may the rein-FORCE-er be with you...

ed may constitute an aversive event. Even if what they are doing isn't their favorite thing. The real test of transitioning problems is to see what kind of difficulty the child has when transitioning from something she hates to something she loves the most. If the child still has a major meltdown, then we may be dealing with an atypical aversive (I hate leaving things before I'm done) or we could even be looking at an atypical reinforcer (I love ticking off my teacher anytime I have an opportunity). I believe that you will find that few people (disabled or not) transition well from something they like to almost any other activity unless that new activity is considerably better than what they were just doing.

So, we can take kids from their reinforcers or take reinforcers from the kids. Either scenario may produce behavior problems. First let's start with reinforcer removal using something tangible. Sometimes (read always) it's a good idea to "get into the kid's head" to gain a better perspective. For children who are nonverbal, or whose verbal skills are not very sophisticated, they often have absolutely no idea of how, when, or *if* they will ever get something back once it has been removed. Again, it becomes necessary to contrive conditions for reinforcer removal. That is, take it away when you have every intention of giving it back immediately. Typically, we have to remove things at a time when we cannot possibly give them back again immediately and this is why the problem can be difficult to address. Say for example that the item is a small toy the child is holding. I would just say something like "wow that's cool, can I see it?" Naturally, I wouldn't really ask permission, I'd just snatch it, but I'd also give it back to the child within a nanosecond. When you try this, you must (at first) give the item back immediately. Also, you can't look like you're upset or anything. After you've done this a few times in a row, children will typically start to relax. The first couple of times they'll probably start whining almost immediately, but once they realize that the toy isn't disappearing forever, they start to calm down. That is, they begin to acclimate (habituation).

Once you can remove the item and give it back quickly without any major meltdowns, it's time to prompt the individual to say or do something to get the item back. If the child can echo, then you can prompt him by saying, "Can I have it" or "it's mine" or whatever is appropriate. If he can't echo, you can just prompt him to hold out his hand as a mand to get it back again. I have even used this particular strategy with a person with a profound developmental delay who was also blind. Once the child stops freaking out and can somehow mand to get the item back, we can work on introducing a delay by requiring some type of academic behavior (answering a question, manipulating an object, pointing to something when asked, etc.). This tactic addresses several problems at once. We can eliminate the potential problem of aggression or self-injury becoming reinforced by occasionally producing the item that was taken, we allow the person to acclimate to having objects removed, we teach individuals the proper way to get objects back again, and we teach them how to tolerate a delay by doing something that fills the "delay void." Finally, children may learn that the way to get things back again is to do a small amount of work and then ask for what they want. That's a whole lot of behavioral goodness in one package! I should also mention that this basic technique might be used when a child won't work for something. That is, the child hates doing work so much that it crushes the motivation to get a particular reinforcer. I will very often start with the reinforcer and then use this reinforcer removal/interruption technique to sneak in a quick task and then let the child resume her activity. It works quite well because the child is usually eager to get back to what she was doing, but you have to (initially) be quick about it or you'll have a tantrum on your hands. The moral of the story is that *earning something that you never had is very different from earning the privilege to get it back again when you weren't quite finished enjoying it.* What's worse than no ice cream? Ice cream that falls off the cone and lands on the floor after only two licks. It's not just that you couldn't get your reinforcer, but that you lost it just as you were starting to really get into it!

Regarding problems with transitions, they can sometimes be eased by starting with multiple brief transitions (again, contrived), at a time when you can immediately go back to what the child was already doing. You can start by having the child transition to a different task without moving from the one she is already doing. Sometimes the problem in transitioning is the interruption of an activity, but sometimes it may be the physical movement away from what the child was doing. Sometimes I will just present another task in the middle of an activity and let the person resume the activity immediately. It's more or less a "fading" procedure. Once the child can tolerate a brief change-up in the activities, you can start having him physically move to the other activity and then back again.

Another tactic is to structure a child's activities so that he is constantly moving toward more preferred tasks. This, of course, requires the teacher to construct a hierarchy of tasks going from least to most preferred. One more tool for your toolbox is to establish moving from Point A to Point B as something that is seen as a good thing. I worked with one child (Sean) who seemed to have difficulty complying with any request to go somewhere else. For example, even though he liked *being* on the playground, he would often refuse to go. Once his teachers got him to the playground he was fine, but getting him there was hell. Sound familiar? Skittles to the rescue! After discovering that he liked Skittles, I grabbed the bag and started taking Sean around the room. Every time we got where we were going, he got a Skittle. He wasn't asked to do anything at all; I was just pairing arriving at a new location with a Skittle. Then we went outside the classroom and he got a Skittle, then we went back inside and he got a Skittle, then to the end of the hall—Skittle—then outside the building—Skittle—then back inside—Skittle, etc. When it was time to go to the playground, no problem whatsoever. We arrived at the playground—Skittle. No, Skittles will not be required forever; they can always be changed over to an intermittent schedule of reinforcement. This manipulation broke the routine in which going somewhere meant that bad things were about to happen.

The key to many of these strategies is that the aversive events *must* be contrived. We control when they happen, we control when the events are over, and we control what happens after the events are over. Good teaching involves much repetition, and to get this repetition we have to *purposefully*, *carefully*, and *systematically* bring children into contact with the things that upset them. Do we have to do this for all upsetting things? No, absolutely not. *Making* people get used to things they don't like always poses ethical issues. The same would be true of any behavior change procedure.

3.4 Words associated with reinforcer loss

This is kind of an interesting category of aversives. I have included it because for children with good verbal repertoires, being informed about something that they have lost or being told of something that they *will lose* can often generate problem behaviors. In Chapter 2, I talked about problems with behaviors not passing the "Dead Man Test." I then gave the example of DRO schedules (differential reinforcement of other behavior) as an example of things that don't really pass the Dead Man Test. It's noteworthy, that in a true DRO schedule, you do not "notify" the organisms of their impending reinforcer loss. That is, if one were conducting an experiment with pigeons and they were responding on a DRO 1 Min Schedule (there must be no pecks for 1 minute to get food), they do not get notified that they have "lost" an opportunity to eat grain. They just don't get any. It's not as though the experimenter opens up the experimental chamber and tells the pigeon, "What happened? You were doing so well and then you had to go and peck the key! You *know* you're not supposed to peck it, but you did it anyway! Why can't you be like the other birds?" Then the pigeon would fold its wings and roll its little pigeon eyes and look all "whatever." With people, however, some teachers and parents feel compelled to tell children what they have lost when they violate the conditions of the daylong or weeklong schedule. The real kicker is that the child is being informed that they have lost something that they never really had to begin with. "Sorry Joey, you just lost your outing!" I know some kids who have lost things they never had so often that they just stopped even caring about them anymore. Although this kind of reinforcement schedule is not considered "aversive," *verbalizing the violation of the contingency* and the subsequent "virtual loss" of what you never had will often be enough to produce aggression. Now remember, nothing is really being removed, instead, words are *presented*. The child, however, may act as though someone has just ripped something out of his hands. I have seen instances in which the child engaged in a moderately bad behavior (cursing) and then, on being informed of the loss of something he never had, began throwing chairs.

Sometimes there may be words that signal an impending loss of a tangible reinforcer as opposed to the loss of a field trip. These too can function as aversive events. Sometimes a child will begin to exhibit behavior problems even if he is informed, in a reasonably friendly way, that he will soon have to stop using the computer so someone else can use it. Some children will also exhibit behavior problems if they simply don't meet the criterion for reinforcement. As Perone says, "Whenever a reinforcer is contingent on behavior, it must be denied in the absence of that behavior." (Perone, 2003 p. 7). This is made even worse when the child believes that he met the criterion. If a child needed ten gold stars to attend the pizza party at the end of the week but only had nine, being informed that he is one star short may be enough to produce aggression. To some extent, it's possible to minimize these problems by choosing your words carefully and setting the expectations before the individual attempts to access the reinforcer. That is, all through the week you can gently remind the child of how many stars he has and how many he needs and what he can do if he can't attend the pizza party. You might even describe what he might receive if he can remain calm even though he did not get to attend the party. There *must* be a good reason for him to handle it. Regarding giving up a reinforcer that is being enjoyed right now (computer time), it may be necessary to use frequent reminders of when the reinforcer must be relinquished and *how it can be obtained again*. Some teachers are very successful in using a neutral party like a timer, preferably one that is tamperproof. In so doing, it's not the teacher who says, "Time's up!" it's the timer.

For children with good verbal skills, the wording of a failure to meet contingencies can make a huge difference. Glenn Latham used specific phrases that took the focus off of the parent as the reason for reinforcer denial. For example, some people might say, "Bobby, I'm not giving you computer time because you were goofing off when you should have been working!" This phrase emphasizes that the *teacher* is doing something to the *student*. It makes the denial seem personal. Latham preferred to use the word "choice." I have seen many good teachers do the same. Some will even use an apologetic tone as in the example below:

Teacher: Bobby, I'm very sorry that you chose to socialize with your friends instead of choosing to do your work, but can you tell me how we're supposed to earn playground time?

Student: We are supposed to finish all our assignments, but it's not fair!

Teacher: That's right, Bobby. I'm glad you remembered how to earn playground time. I'm sorry you didn't earn it today but I'm sure you will make a good choice tomorrow.

Now, our friend Bobby still might be very unhappy, but this is probably the best possible way to give him bad news. It's not a guarantee that there will be no behavior problems, but it takes the power away from the teacher and shows children that they can control their reinforcers based on their choices. Dr. Latham was not only one of the kindest people I have ever met, but he was a genius, plain and simple. He learned how to strip away all the excess baggage that often accompanies the enforcement of a rule or the delivery of bad news to preserve his status as a well-liked person. As Tony Sporano would have said, "It's just business, not personal."

3.5   Aversive properties of positive reinforcement

In Dr. Michael Perone's paper entitled "The Negative Effects of Positive Reinforcement" (Perone, 2003, which I reference repeatedly because it is a totally awesome paper), Dr. Perone argued that the whole good or bad thing about reinforcement and aversives is largely illusory. As I've discussed in the previous sections, there are many reinforcement procedures that have aversive properties "embedded" in them as Perone would say. I don't embed them, and you don't embed them. They're just there. Like I keep saying, you can be as nice and as sweet as you like, but if Bobby is working for computer time, and there is nothing punitive" in your proedure, and it's all nice-nice and positive and smiley faces, he still won't be able to get on the computer if he hasn't *earned* it. If he hasn't earned it, then it *must be denied*. Unfortunately, even if bad news is given gently, there just might be hell to pay.

The moral of the story is that you can say you don't use time-out, and you can say you don't take away privileges, and you can say you don't use a point loss system in your token economy. You can't, however, claim that you don't expose your kids to aversives. Because if you aren't, you're not exposing them to reinforcers, either. The good news is that it's okay. Aversives aren't bad things. Now, pretending that they're not naturally occurring all around us and firmly embedded in the fabric of society? That's a bad thing. We'll chat more in Chapter 9 on punishment.

SECTION 4: OTHER AVERSIVES

4.1 Private aversives (PAs)

Some behavior analysts commonly refer to things inside the person, things that cannot be observed as "private events" (Friman, Wilson, & Hayes, 1998; Skinner 1984). Private events can really be anything (remembering something, figuring out a problem without talking, experiencing pain, etc.). I'm just going to talk about those private events that cause the child some sort of distress, so I've decided to use the term "private aversive" or "PA." Now private aversives are really just MOs (which we've talked about), but these kinds of MOs pose a special problem because you may not be able to identify them as such and, unlike seeing someone fall down and hurt their knee, you weren't there to witness their onset. PAs are no special thing—I'm just using the label as a convenience so we can talk about a subset of MOs that are hidden to us. That's totally clear now, right? Hello? Is this thing on?

So far, most of what has been covered in this chapter falls under the category of socially-mediated aversives and the occasional environmental aversive. Some things, however, follow the child to school and have nothing to do with the classroom or the teacher. Painful stimulation, particularly with nonverbal children, can be extremely problematic. I won't limit private aversives to things that are painful per se, but will include any kind of condition that is present right now that you or I would want to terminate. Pain and/or discomfort occur with everyone, but we all handle these conditions differently. Children with disabilities usually have more difficulty with these conditions than most of us. We'll come back to this topic in Chapter 4 where I'll attempt to tackle intermittent behavior problems.

Some of the big PAs are hunger, pain, illness, and sleepiness. Pain stands out as one of the most difficult conditions to diagnose if the child is nonverbal, unless there is an obvious observable condition that correlates with pain (redness, swelling, cuts, bruises, etc.). Also, a tremendous number of children are receiving psychotropic medications, all of which can cause side effects that even you and I would not be able to tolerate. Children, on the other hand, have little choice in the matter. I'm not saying people are evil for giving children medications, but I'm saying that some people give them irresponsibly. Some side effects, particularly those experienced with antipsychotic medications, are so pronounced that they require additional medication just to control their occurrence. Remember, even children who have decent verbal skills may not be sophisticated enough to explain which side effects they are experiencing, yet their behavior may still be affected. If private aversives are missed or ignored, behavior problems will typically persist. Some of the biggest and fastest changes in behavior I've ever seen were because an astute teacher or staff member picked up on a problem that was ultimately resolved through a medical intervention. We'll talk more about these important issues in detail in Chapter 4.

4.2 Response-produced aversives

This is a really interesting category; at least it is to me. This is the stuff that falls under that category "you did it to yourself!" Sometimes, as they say, "&@!$ happens!" Sometimes we bring the &@!$ on ourselves. Either way, we're not very happy with the odiferous outcome. A really awesome example of a response-produced aversive happened to me just the other day. I was on my motorcycle waiting to get into my gated community. I was behind someone who just didn't know what he was doing and I was feeling kind of impatient. In other words, it was me being normal. The dude in front of me wasn't able to get in, and he was holding me up, so I figured I could sneak up on the sidewalk between some hedges and a post by the arm that moves up and down to let cars in. Well, me and the motorcycle fit through just fine. My hard sided, expensive saddlebags did not. It may be only rumor, but I hear that a cat knows whether or not it can fit through a hole because if its whiskers can make it through, so can its body. My motorcycle, on the other hand, has no whiskers but I'm seriously considering installing some. My left saddlebag snapped off like a toothpick and I fell over like a preschooler who had just had his training wheels removed, only my bike was 750 pounds. Major cursing. Two hundred and fifty dollars later for a new saddlebag lock assembly and permanent scratches on both saddlebags, I can safely say that I will NEVER try that maneuver again. Update! I have *still* not tried it again….

Response-produced aversives can be subdivided into responses that are erroneous (behavior goes in… bad things come out) ineffective (behavior goes in… nothing comes out), and inefficient (a whole lot of behavior goes in… relatively little comes out). I could be wrong, but I believe that people will try to escape from all of these conditions, which, if true, would make these conditions *aversive*. My motorcycle mishap easily falls under the *errone-*

ous category (motorcycle goes in… saddlebags snap off). Children do the same things, only when the aversive happens it may produce behavior problems. Some children have difficulty with the erroneous category and they are very sensitive to making mistakes and being told "no." I have both seen and heard of many instances in which some children, after making a mistake, would completely tear up their assignments. It wasn't necessarily that they were trying to escape from doing work. They actually did quite a bit of work, and near the end they screwed up a problem and just "lost it."

Sometimes the child's behavior is *ineffective* and because they are doing something wrong, they essentially create their own extinction condition. This happens to anyone who has ever used a computer. You think that you are doing what you normally do, but you've done something wrong, and as a consequence of your behavior the printer doesn't print! After speaking with technical support for three hours, you must come to accept the horrible truth. User error. Ineffective behavior can be extremely exasperating, not just for the individual, but also for the people around him (just ask my wife).

Behavior can also be *inefficient*, which can lead to a task being harder than it has to be, and this may slow down the rate of reinforcement and/or the amount (magnitude). The child may be able to do the task, but it becomes more effortful and takes longer than when performed by someone with better skills. For example, many children can *technically* read, but they cannot *functionally* read because they read too slowly and stumble on difficult words. If your behavior is terribly inefficient the task may become highly aversive. In essence, it's like a super hard job that pays poorly. This problem can usually be addressed with a proper analysis of skill deficits and remedial teaching.

4.3   Atypical aversives

Just as with reinforcers, there can be atypical aversives. Things that are not aversive for most people may be highly aversive for others. Many of us fear or hate certain things that don't create problems for anyone else, but it doesn't necessarily mean that we have a disorder. I knew a woman in graduate school who was deathly afraid of kittens. She was probably afraid of cats too, but she described a fear of kittens. People have been afraid of weirder things, but still, kittens? Although children who are given the label "autistic" may be known to have unusual aversives (noises, touch, textures of food, clothing, etc.), they by no means have the exclusive rights to those aversives. I know people with absolutely no developmental disorder of any kind who don't like certain kinds of clothing, don't like people touching them, and can't stand sounds that most people tolerate just fine. I, for instance, hate tiny sounds that many people would not notice. If something is making a sound that it shouldn't make, something uncharacteristic, I try to figure out what it is so I can stop it. It's aversive, plain and simple. I do not, however, freak out; I just don't like it and want it to stop.   Some children find certain words aversive, one kid I know of will go off if you use the word "hello." Some children find changes in their environment aversive, changes in the way people wear their hair, or if they are wearing glasses. These children often have the label "autism" or "OCD," but just about everyone finds certain kinds of change aversive. If one of my coworkers does her hair differently, I might say, "I liked it better the old way," but I don't start breaking chairs and scratching my arms until they bleed.

Sometimes, aversives are atypical in the sense that they just don't bother many people. That is, a very small percentage of the population finds this particular thing aversive. For example, when you tri-fold an 8.5 x 11 sheet of paper to fit into an envelope, if each folded section isn't precisely 3.66 inches long, you get so upset that you tear up the letter. Most people are okay as long as the damn letter fits. Some aversives are things you may be afraid of, and perhaps some others are things you just hate, but you will try to terminate or avoid all of them. Typically, things you fear fall under the category of "phobias" and things that drive you crazy if they aren't just so, are referred to as "obsessions." The behavior that you must do to terminate the aversive is called a "compulsion." Nonetheless, all of these things are aversive if you are motivated to avoid them or make them go away.

Sometimes aversives are atypical because of the magnitude of the response they generate. If there is a small tag or irregularity in my clothing, I notice it, and I don't like it. Sometimes I will cut the tag off. I will not, however, tear up my shirt and start hitting my head. Some individuals with disabilities also don't like certain aspects of their clothing, but they get much more severely agitated. If I had to take a guess, I would say that most of the atypical aversives fall into this second category. Most children with disabilities dislike the same things that we dislike. They are just (at times) far more sensitive to these events and have much larger reactions. No one would blame you if you yelled, screamed, cursed, and kicked your car if it broke down when you were late for the most important job interview of your life. Similarly, no one would blame you if you started kicking, scratching, and punching someone who had just attacked your small child. What about if you engaged in those behaviors, but you displayed them because someone did her hair differently one day? It's okay to be upset about things, but sometimes it's *what you do when you get upset that is the problem*. I don't get called to do a consult at a school because a child hates it when the chairs aren't exactly straight. I get called because when the chairs aren't straight, the child punches people. Punching isn't always a problem. If you're a boxer, you're *supposed* to punch. If you're being attacked, you're supposed to punch. If a police officer writes you a speeding ticket, you are NOT supposed to punch. Sometimes it's okay to get mad, but you have to be able to handle getting mad, and in that regard, many children with disabilities need to improve their skills.

This issue of what you do when you encounter an aversive is where a discrepancy analysis comes in handy. Why don't I totally tear up my shirt when the tag bothers me? Well, I know how to use scissors, and I know what to cut off, and I can even decide to wear a different shirt in the morning because no one makes me wear a particular shirt. I also have become very good at tolerating things that are annoying at mild to moderate levels. Many persons with disabilities can't even tolerate things that are mildly annoying. Why else don't

I tear up my shirt? I will have to buy another, which costs money, and I know the value of money. Furthermore, I don't like walking around half-clothed. I would also worry about what people would think and/or say (it would be aversive to me). I know children with disabilities that will run buck naked down the hallway of the school. They don't appear to find that to be aversive at all. Many of us, on the other hand, have nightmares that we're still in school and wearing only our underwear (not me of course, but I didn't want the rest of you to feel alone). So you see, there are many reasons why I don't tear up my shirt, not just one. I didn't even do the most thorough discrepancy analysis possible because I was not comparing my own skills, reinforcers, and aversives to any particular child. I was merely generating some ideas. It's easy to see how this sort of analysis can lead to a treatment with numerous components that could help a child in a number of areas of his life.

4.4 Non-aversives that should be aversive

What? Okay, this Winston guy has finally lost it, I could see it coming in the end of Chapter 2, but this confirms it! This is really the mirror image of the problem with reinforcers, you remember, "&@!$ people shouldn't like." This is, admittedly, kind of a weird issue to talk about, but it's a very real problem. Many children (adults too), don't find certain things aversive that *should absolutely be aversive*. I'm not just talking about children with disabilities either. Throughout our lives, that which is aversive to us changes. Let's look at things we're afraid of as examples of aversives that change. True, this only addresses one kind of aversive, but it's fine for this particular exercise. As you should know, not all aversives cause fear (one kind of physiological arousal). Some just make us really mad (another kind of physiological arousal) and still others we would just rather avoid (little or no physiological arousal).

Allow me to elaborate on how aversives can change over a lifetime. You and I may be afraid of snakes, but infants are not afraid of snakes. Don't believe me? Go ahead, throw a fake snake on your coworker. He or she will probably freak out and then want to kill you. Now, go throw a fake snake on an infant and see if he freaks out. Most likely, he will attempt to put the rubber reptile in his mouth, as he probably would with a real one. *You have to learn to be afraid of snakes.*[3] Incidentally, whose bright idea was it to give babies rattles? If they ever come across an actual rattlesnake they will no doubt try to pick it up and shake it. Bad idea. Infants are afraid of almost nothing, because they know almost nothing. Conditioned aversives mean nothing to them because there hasn't been much time yet to condition anything. Infants will crawl off tables, aggressively grab the ears of unfamiliar dogs, lick wall outlets, drink poison, eat paint chips, and wear a Dallas Cowboys jersey to a Philadelphia Eagles game. What would you expect? They're babies. When children get a bit older and

[3]"Little Albert" was reportedly just fine with bunnies until John B. Watson got ahold of him. Soon he was fearful of bunnies, hammers, steel bars, and experimenters who apparently didn't need Internal Review Board approval to scare babies.

have been hurt a few times, some of them become afraid of almost everything, including things that they shouldn't be afraid of. Hell, I was afraid of Jell-O until I was six, Jell-O! Unfortunately, children become teenagers and all of a sudden it's like they're infants all over again because now they are afraid of nothing! What the hell happened? I thought they were done being afraid of nothing at 18 months? Once teens become adults they become increasingly afraid of newer and different things (bills, health insurance, the national deficit, the future of their children's children). The range of things we become afraid of and try to avoid is truly astounding. There's a big, complex world out there and there's a lot you can find aversive. As you reach retirement age, you start to be afraid of your ultimate demise, second only to your fear of the imminent collapse of Social Security. Then, in your twilight years, you reluctantly accept that your visa to remain on the planet will soon expire, at which point, like the infant, you are no longer afraid of anything anymore (which is why seniors say and do whatever the hell they please and damn the consequences).

What did that discussion have to do with anything? Well, aversives can change; therefore, it is possible for things that *should* be aversive to eventually serve that function. Some behavior problems continue to occur, in part or completely, because there are events that should function as aversives that fail to do so. For example, it bothers me if I make someone cry. I don't like it and I feel bad that I made the person cry. I do what I can to make amends and make the person feel better. I don't even like it if someone else made the person cry, I still feel bad. There are some things that you should feel afraid of, and some that should make you feel bad, and some that you should dislike just enough to avoid them. The point is, that if you fail to act accordingly to things that *should bother you,* you may develop some very big problems somewhere down the line. Children who don't see busy traffic as something to be avoided are more likely to run into the street with a complete disregard for their safety. A child who doesn't care if another child cries may be more likely to hurt that child when there is a disagreement. A child who doesn't care about being sent to the principal's office or being suspended may be less likely to exhibit self-control. I will touch on the issue of these "non-aversives" in Chapter 9 on punishment and how they can help to explain why traditional "punishers" are ineffective for many children.

Many schools are currently struggling with bullying and they're making greater efforts to reverse a dangerous trend. One of the aims of most anti-bullying programs, whether they explain it this way or not, is to try to reduce the reinforcing efficacy of bullying, and try to sensitize children to the feelings of others. If children value the feelings of others they will tend to avoid bullying. If seeing people crying or otherwise hurt is aversive, a child may tend to assist instead of bully the person. This explanation does not take into account everything that produces bullying, but it highlights an important point. Bad things can happen when the suffering of others is "neutral" to us. I think that Edmund Burke said it better, however, when he wrote, "All that is necessary for the triumph of evil is that good men do nothing." I think you could "behavioralize" this famous phrase by saying that some non-aversives *should* be aversive. At least they need to be aversive enough to move us to action.

SECTION 5: HANDLING PROBLEMS WITH AVERSIVES: THE SIX "ATES"

To help the practitioner generate solutions to problems of aversives, I am suggesting six categories of tactics that may create a path for treatment options, and they all end with the suffix "ate," hence the "Six Ates." They are: 1) Procrastinate; 2) Eliminate; 3) Terminate; 4) Compensate; 5) Acclimate; and 6) Tolerate. You can use the acronym PET-CAT. Some of these categories are not mutually exclusive—that is, they can be used together for greater effect. I didn't really "invent" anything; I'm just laying them all out so that practitioners can more easily see their options when there is a problem with aversives.

1. *Procrastinate.* Why not? We do it all the time. Some aversives just can't be completely avoided,. With this tactic, we teach the child to delay or put things off. They aren't escaping from a current task, but *delaying the onset*. Being able to put off doing things is very valuable to people, and it generates quite a bit of behavior. Do you have a line of credit by chance? Ah yes, there's nothing quite like putting off paying for things. Of course you want to teach responsible procrastination (if there is such a thing), meaning that you want to teach the child that there are limits to delays that they can request. Certainly you don't want Billy to delay doing math until the next school year, but perhaps allowing him to delay it twice in a row, or even three times is reasonable. You can even get creative with children who possess good verbal skills and explain contingencies that are more like what you and I are exposed to. That is, you can tell a child that she may delay a task, but that she will earn slightly less computer time (there is a cost, just like with your credit card). I fully understand that certain things cannot be delayed if a teacher is to keep the class on schedule, but typically some amount of individualization is permissible. Furthermore, delays don't always have to be very large to have some value. Even small delays *may* have value. For example, sometimes I ask for a delay so that I can finish reading an interesting article on the web before complying with my wife's request to empty the dishwasher.

The great thing about teaching appropriate procrastination is that it gives the child the control that everyone is always saying that they are trying to get. I love it when I'm conducting a functional assessment interview and someone tells me "he does it for control!" I believe that the scientific rejoinder to such a description is, "Well duh!" If by control, one means producing some discernible change in one's environment, then every operant behavior (as opposed to reflexes) falls under the shade of the control umbrella. Being able to control things occasionally is a common part of life, and a valuable part of life, so we may as well teach children to do it appropriately and responsibly. Makes sense, no?

2. *Eliminate.* This is easily the most overused and abused tactic. Trying to eliminate all aversives is a road you don't want to travel. It's poorly lit, filled with potholes, and it gets narrower the further you go. So many individuals attempt to go this route because it can rapidly result in the immediate reduction of problem behavior. Parents who don't have

the necessary resources and training often resort to extreme forms of elimination to produce stable behavior in their children. Food has to be served a certain way, you can't say certain words or phrases, you can't change your hairstyle, you can't change your schedule, and you can't change your mind without producing behavior problems. Many refer to this as "walking on eggshells." This sort of extreme elimination of aversives only creates the *illusion* of improvement in behavior. The problem behavior, of course, remains fully intact but lies dormant. The moment something is amiss, the child will have significant problems. Soon the child's environment is so hopelessly and highly customized that he cannot successfully venture outside of these detrimentally detailed parameters. For children living in these specialized environments, their chances of success in the real world actually *decrease* as their environment becomes *increasingly* specialized.

Clearly, trying to eliminate all aversives is counterproductive, unrealistic, and in some ways, immoral. Aversives are a part of life; they make the good things we experience that much better. This is not to say that there should be needless suffering. Generally that's considered a bad thing. Adversity, however, is a necessary part of life if one expects to grow and mature. Some of the greatest figures in history became great because they overcame adversity. Denying individuals the opportunity to overcome aversives is to deny them a real life. On the other hand, if your entire life is dominated by aversives, big ones, all day long, every day, you will be miserable. There must be a balance. The question is, I believe, which aversives do we try to eliminate and which do we try to help the child overcome? A child with a disability may not be able to cope with the same things as appropriately or effectively as a typically developing peer. We certainly may need to adjust our expectations. I would suggest by starting to eliminate those things that we ourselves would not tolerate or tolerate only with great difficulty. None of us wants to be scolded, yelled at, embarrassed, humiliated, or coerced into doing things we don't want to do. Like many of you, I have witnessed interactions between teachers and children, parents and children, and children and their peers that I personally would not have tolerated very well. It is reasonable to attempt to reduce or eliminate "nasty" interactions between people on the whole. What about all the other aversives we experience every day? What about changes in routine, aches and pains, sickness, disappointments, making mistakes, consequences for rule violation, and the much dreaded "not being able to get your way?" Can you always get your way? Are you happy when you don't get your way?

The tricky thing about eliminating aversives is parceling out reasonable and unreasonable aversives. Who says what is reasonable and unreasonable? True, it can be somewhat subjective, and it may be necessary to come together as a team to try to figure out how to support a child and make reasonable accommodations that may produce rapid behavior change. Still, we must remember that we don't want to adversely affect the ability of the child to be successful regarding long-term treatment gains. For example, if a child starts to self-injure when she hears another child screaming, is it reasonable to try to eliminate the screaming, especially when it is the only event that produces self-injury? Can I get a "Hell yes!" from the congregation? Even I become extremely agitated when I am subjected to loud screaming for long periods of time, and I don't know very many people who would feel any differently. That is, we don't want to find ourselves in a situation where we're being asked to teach children to *tolerate the intolerable*. On the other hand, what about the child who starts to eye-gouge when he hears another child cough? Do we buy a case of Robitussin for the entire classroom? I hope you all said, "No." I know one teacher who avoids playing any kind of board game with one of her students because he might have an explosive outburst if he loses. How is this kid ever going to enjoy himself when he goes to Vegas? I guess he'll have to avoid the casinos and just stick to the shows. Elimination is a great tactic to gain quick control over a problem, just try not to go crazy with it and do your best to slowly, reintroduce some of the more reasonable aversives using some of the other "Ates."

3. *Terminate.*   Sometimes we cannot possibly eliminate the aversive that bothers the child, yet it's reasonable for the child to want to terminate the event. The classic example is the functional communication replacement behavior, which involves teaching the child to ask for a break to end the current task. Under normal conditions, the child's scratching may terminate demands, so instead the child may be taught to signal "break" either by signing or speaking or otherwise communicating her needs. A child may be seeking to terminate an interaction with an adult or with a peer. She may also wish to stop a condition, like circle-time or being in a room other than her homeroom. Just as with reinforcement, sometimes the termination of the event can be done directly by the child (like turning off music they don't like or covering their ears), and sometimes it may be socially-mediated (like asking an adult for a break). In some cases, children just don't know how to terminate aversive events in any manner, and just become agitated. In other cases, a child may know how to terminate an event but the behavior is inappropriate (swiping everything off the table). Either way, it's quite acceptable and standard to teach individuals how to appropriately terminate what is bothering them. One of the biggest problems encountered in applied settings is resistance from teachers whose job it is to ensure that children meet their IEP goals. "He can't just ask for a break all day long, he won't get any work done!" The teacher is absolutely right; the child can't sit around on break all day. So we eventually have to teach the child that a request for a break will only be honored after a certain duration of work, or that breaks only last for a short time. Initially, you might honor every request until the behavior is fluent, then, as with any other behavior, you might switch to some sort of intermittent reinforcement sched-ule. Learning to terminate certain aversives without resorting to aggression or self-injury is vitally important to anyone. The only difficulty is in determining what we will let the child continually terminate. At times it may be necessary to teach the child how to terminate pri-vate aversives, but it's necessary to know what pain or discomfort the child is experiencing.

4. *Compensate.*   Nothing makes a bad thing better quite like big-time reinforcers. Have you ever had a job that you really didn't like, but they started to pay you more money so you stayed? My friend, Dr. Dean Williams, used to work for the state and he referred to that

condition as "the golden handcuffs." I think the United States Mint's new slogan should be "Money, it makes things suck less!" The tendency to try to escape from things that are aversive can often be offset by the introduction of reinforcement. My friend Dean didn't suddenly love his job. None of the bad things went away when he got paid more, but his job was no longer so aversive that he wanted to escape. Remember, aversive stimuli are defined by their function. Stuff you like isn't always going to function as a reinforcer for hard work and stuff you hate isn't always going to function as an aversive that will generate escape behavior. If your salary is cut back severely, you may find yourself looking for new work, even if you like your job. Similarly, powerful reinforcers can shift the balance of the reinforcer/aversive seesaw, which can decrease the motivation to escape. Incidentally, you don't always have to deliver reinforcers after the aversive event is over, (a spoonful of sugar helps the medicine go down). Sometimes you just provide the alleged reinforcer *during* the aversive event. Why do you think they have crayons for kids at restaurants? We can offset aversive conditions (waiting for food to come) by providing non-contingent access (it's free) to preferred activities during those conditions. This isn't always possible or desirable because the activities themselves will disrupt what we are trying to accomplish. You can't let the child color *while* he's doing math. You could, however, rapidly alternate math-coloring-math-coloring throughout the math lesson until the child's behavior becomes stable. Incidentally, this method has been shown to work for increasing the chances of engaging in a low probability behavior (Hanley, Iwata, Roscoe, Thompson, &Lindberg, 2003), so it's possible that increased non-contingent reinforcement might offset the motivation to escape from a mild aversive.

Will you always be able to compensate for aversives with reinforcement? Well, what is the reinforcer and what is the aversive? Money is valuable to most of us, but not many people will do anything for money, no matter what the amount. It's important to understand that I'm not saying that gummy bears and Skittles and computer time will make children love to read. That isn't the goal of these things. With hope, children will love to read because they will be able to do things that they previously couldn't do, and for all the other reasons that other people love to read. We would try to use compensation to "get them to the table" and, with hope, keep them there with a minimum of difficulty. Furthermore, this doesn't have to be a tactic that must be kept in place forever. This should be true of all behavioral interventions. Eventually, we want the more natural reinforcers to take over.

5. *Acclimate.* "Habituation" is the process whereby a stimulus, because of its repeated presentation or presence, no longer controls behavior. That is, we adjust to it to the point that we "don't respond to it." You know that little logo in the bottom right hand corner of your TV screen on most networks? You know, the little translucent one that says, "HBO" or "FOX" or whatever. When you first see them they're kind of annoying and distracting. After five minutes of watching the program you don't even know they're there unless you are looking for them. *That* is habituation. I used acclimate because it helps make the acronym PET-CAT and it's a more common word. As I said in Chapter 2, people are remarkably adaptable

organisms. We can get used to quite a bit and in some ways it's adaptive and in some ways maladaptive. It all depends on the event you're getting used to. I was watching the show "Hoarders" and I was astonished to see the level of filth, debris, and odor that one woman had become accustomed to; it didn't even appear to bother her. She was a food hoarder and there were unimaginable amounts of rotting food in her home. The people helping her had to wear respirators because of the stench. The woman, however, acclimated quite nicely. Keep in mind that she had gotten accustomed to these conditions slowly over many years.

To a certain degree, children with disabilities can also acclimate or habituate to a variety of aversive conditions. However, if people only use the eliminate tactic, how can anyone ever acclimate to anything? Now, acclimate doesn't mean that we're teaching the child to put up with something they don't like—that's the final "Ate," Tolerate. Acclimate just means that it no longer bothers the child very much. The great thing about this tactic is that the child doesn't really have to *do* much of anything. Acclimation happens all by itself. We do, however, have to present the aversive event repeatedly in a programmed fashion. Also, if the event is just too upsetting—that is the child begins to scream, attack, and self-injure the moment the task is put on the table, we may need to introduce a "muted" version of the aversive event. For example, if the child gets agitated when you put a book on the desk, just put a small card with two words on it for them to read. If the card bothers them too much, put it off to the side while the child plays with a toy and slowly move it closer while the child is playing so that it no longer bothers him. There are all sorts of clever things you can come up with to slowly introduce aversives regularly so that children can acclimate. For example, some kids positively can't stand the fire alarm, and fire alarms are one of those things where the eliminate tactic would be inappropriate. You can, however, record the fire alarm with your smart phone or download the "school fire alarm ring-tone" or what have you. Then you can play the digital recording back at steadily increasing volumes. You may have to hook it up to an amplifier to approximate the volume of the actual alarm, but that will probably come later after the person has acclimated somewhat to the lower decibel sound. You can also enhance acclimation by using compensation. You might pair the fire-alarm sound with powerful positive reinforcers that cannot otherwise be accessed.

In the section on reinforcer removal I described how I sometimes remove a toy and quickly give it back over and over until the child stops freaking out about having the toy removed. The child acclimates to having the toy removed. Sure, I was changing what toy removal meant to the child. Instead of losing it indefinitely, the child only lost it for a few seconds. Still, the child's initial reactions were not good. Eventually, toy removal was fairly neutral as an event. The key to successful acclimation lies in creating predictable (the student gets a heads up), controllable (can be stopped immediately), and modifiable (can be altered in form or magnitude) aversives. Finally, it's not necessary for the event in question to become completely and totally neutralized, but if its aversive qualities can be reduced to the point where the child only whines to escape (instead of biting to escape), then the result may be sufficient from a treatment perspective.

6. *Tolerate.*   I'm afraid that this one may be the toughest of the bunch. When I say tolerate, I mean that the aversive in question has not faded into the background, like a mild, dull headache when you close your eyes. Instead, the event is causing significant increasing physiological arousal—that is, it's very bad. Tolerating means that you can't terminate it, you can't completely acclimate to it, and no amount of reinforcement (compensate) is going to make it okay. This is when we start talking about coping skills. I view tolerating as something that we may need to do for short periods of time. That is, a child shouldn't be expected to tolerate screaming from another student all day, but it would be *very helpful* if she could tolerate screaming long enough for the teacher to remove the screaming child from the room. Think of tolerating as a commodity that gets used up. Like when people say, "My patience is wearing thin," they're referring to their own diminished capacity to tolerate something. Even the best of us can get worn down by too many cumulative, successive stressors or a single sustained one. "You're on my last nerve," "I'm at the end of my rope," "that was the straw that broke the camel's back," or Popeye's favorite "That's all I can stands and I can't stands no more!" You get the picture. First you open up a can of spinach, then you open up a can of whoop-@$$.

How do we teach children with disabilities to tolerate? Well, for one, we have to teach them what to do during the aversive in question. Time for a discrepancy analysis. What do *you do* when something is bothering you tremendously and you "can't stands no more?" We do many things. Maybe you go to your "happy place," or you clench your teeth, which my dentist tells me is very bad for me, but it turns out that I mostly clench them when I see his bill. I like to take a huge breath, then purse my lips and blow it out slowly. Anyone who knows me knows that it means I'm really angry and I'm about to open up a can of spinach. Some people physically cover their own mouths as an act of self-control. Sometimes we tighten up to literally inhibit muscle movement—you know, like how you're supposed to resist the urge to strangle people. The better thing, in my opinion, is to loosen up and relax, which can be a very tall order for any child, let alone a child with disabilities. My friend Steve Ward uses a very clever technique to teach tolerating, which he calls a "calm count." Of course counting to ten has been around forever as a means of calming one's self, but his approach is simple yet very systematic. You can find out more about it by going to his website www.wholechildconsulting.com. There you can find a Downloads section and a presentation called "calming." If it isn't there I'm certain you could contact Steve and inquire about calm counts. Essentially, Steve introduces the stressor (aversive) and prompts the child to count while providing support and modeling calm behavior and then he removes the stressor when the count is completed. You could also teach progressive muscle relaxation or deep breathing (Jacobson, 1964). As mentioned previously, I cannot overemphasize the importance of contriving situations or at least role-playing, if the child is capable, to increase the chances that the child will be able to tolerate events. I view tolerating as a skill. Some of us are good at it, some of us are bad at it, and some people have the patience of Job. However, everyone can improve, even if only a little. Being able to tolerate things is *critically impor-*

tant if we want children to be successful and reasonably independent adults. It isn't even something a person needs to do every day, but being able to tolerate things, even for short durations plays a critical role in medical and dental treatment. Imagine how difficult this is for children who can't tolerate being touched? You can most likely increase the success of any program for teaching tolerating by pulling from the categories of *acclimate* and *compensate*. There are numerous texts available to assist teaching persons with disabilities to relax, as it is not my intent to outline a detailed procedure. I simply want the reader to understand the importance of tolerating and the role of learning to stay calm in the face of aversives. If children can't manage to stay calm, they may be able to learn to relax when upset, even if only a little bit and for a short while.

Remember! PET-CAT!
Procrastinate-Eliminate-Terminate-Compensate-Acclimate-Tolerate

SECTION 6: ANTIPSYCHOTICS AND AVERSIVES

Certain medications can affect our reactions to what are known as "conditioned aversives." As mentioned earlier in the chapter, conditioned aversives are those things that have been paired with primary aversives so often that these new stimuli now control behavior. Most of what controls our collective behavior as a society are conditioned aversives. Laws, rules, fines, warnings, traffic signs, letters from attorneys to cease and desist, you name it, we're controlled by it. Children with disabilities can also show behavior problems when exposed to conditioned aversives, like being informed of a point loss. The words alone may be enough to cause aggression even though nothing was actually physically removed from the child. This doesn't mean that the child is sensitive to *all* forms of conditioned aversives. Remember that some conditioned aversives are just unpleasant consequences that happen to us, like losing points, getting speeding tickets, and receiving an "F" on a term paper. Other conditioned aversives actually *warn us of impending danger and require that we take some action* (or avoid doing some action). Like stepping on the brakes when the light turns red. That is, many children do not respond appropriately to warning stimuli, e.g., "You better straighten up or you'll lose all your points!" If the kids we worked with responded properly to these warning stimuli (that help them avoid the actual aversive), we wouldn't have so many behavior problems. Well, that and making certain the we have functional aversives in the first place.

Certain psychotropic medications known as antipsychotics (formerly major tranquilizers) may actually make it *harder* for children to respond appropriately to warning stimuli. First, what are these drugs? We're talking about Haldol, Thorazine, Mellaril, (the older antipsychotics) and Risperdal, Seroquel, Clozapine, Geodone, and Abilify (the newer antipsychotics). How do these drugs become classed as antipsychotics? That's a good question with an interesting answer. Once again, rats to the rescue. Behavioral pharmacologists use various experimental protocols for testing new drugs so they can figure out how to classify them. The standard protocol for classifying a new substance as an anti-psychotic is called the CAR model, which stands for conditioned avoidance response. This is how all antipsychotics are classified, because they all disrupt conditioned avoidance responding in rats (Li He & Mead, 2009). This is really cool. Rats are taught how to terminate a foot-shock (unconditioned stimulus [UCS]) that is delivered through an electrified grid that they stand on. They terminate this shock by pressing a bar in the experimental chamber. So, rats deal with their stressors by pressing a bar, and we deal with ours by walking into one.... Once the rats have acquired a reliable shock terminating response, a warning stimulus is produced that is paired with the foot-shock and the rat eventually learns to avoid the foot-shock altogether by hitting the bar as soon as the warning stimulus comes on (the conditioned aversive stimulus [CAS]). Don't worry, the warning stimulus comes on maybe a few seconds before the shock, so the rat still has plenty of time to press the bar so that it can avoid being shocked. It's the rat equivalent of you giving your credit card number over the phone when getting called by the electric company (CAS) to avoid having your power turned off. In some experiments the CAS is white noise and the rat just runs to the safe compartment of a two compartment chamber to avoid the shock, but it's essentially the same protocol.

When rats are given the proper doses of antipsychotics they will typically either lose any conditioned avoidance responding or fail to develop it altogether. That is, in the case where the rat has learned to avoid the shock by taking some action after the CAS (pressing a bar or running to the other end of a shuttle box) the antipsychotic medication will cause the rat to essentially not give a $#!& about the shock. The rat can still detect the CAS, but the rat is like, "Whatever" and it gets shocked. Of course the rat will still try to escape the actual shock (UCS) but it will no longer *avoid* it, at least not reliably. What are the implications of this protocol for special needs children? Well, most children with significant behavior problems are also taking psychotropic medications and *many* of those are classed as antipsychotics. Many if not most children with behavior problems, and children as a group, are not very good at demonstrating self-control behaviors. Recall that I spoke about non-aversives that *should* be aversive? If a child receives some sort of warning from an adult, "Stop!" (CAS) just before the child does something dangerous like touch a hot stove (UCS), it is *quite possible* that a child taking antipsychotics will never learn to stop before experiencing dangerous things. If these medications do in fact disrupt or prevent responding appropriately to warnings, how will children with behavior problems learn to avoid potentially dangerous consequences of their behavior? My point is that the very drugs we give to control some behavior (aggression) may make other behaviors (self-control) difficult to learn.

'To appreciate the problem on a more personal level, have you or a friend ever been way too drunk and then gotten into big trouble? What happens when people get too drunk? They might find that they don't respond very well to warning stimuli. If a friend warns you that you're too drunk to drive, you may completely disregard the warning and drive anyhow. Dangerous. Taking this analogy back to kids, they already have poor judgement and poor self-control and they're not even drunk. Generally speaking, the younger the child the poorer the judgment and the poorer the self-control. Additionally, children with various intellectual disabilities usually have poorer judgment and self-control than their typically developing peers. Finally, those children may be taking antipsychotic medications which disrupt conditioned avoidance responding. See any potential problems?

Let me relate a story from a marvelous book called *Blaming the Brain* by Elliot Valenstein (Valenstein, 1998). In this book, Valenstein recounts the birth and subsequent proliferation of antipsychotic medications. The first one, Thorazine (chlorpromazine) got its trade name from the Greek god of thunder, Thor. I suppose it was named after Thor because taking a big enough dose left you "Thunderstruck!" Before the drug was given as an antipsychotic, it was given to relieve preoperative anxiety in patients going into surgery. It was also intended for use as an antihistamine. One man who received the drug as an antihistamine was pulled over for running a red light. When the officer asked the man why he ran the red light, the man replied that he *just didn't care enough to stop.* This story is consistent with our friends the rats and their foot shocks.

My point is that many people believe that drugs will either help, or hurt, or do nothing at all. Most people don't stop to think that a drug may improve one problem but cause others as well. Psychotropic medications don't simply affect a single behavior or class of behaviors and leave all others untouched. They do many things, and in many cases they do so unpredictably. You can't weigh the risks and benefits of various drugs if you don't know what they are. I'm always concerned with how various drugs might affect the learning process in children. Most people are only concerned about snuffing out bad behavior. We need good learners to deal with behavior problems because most problems reflect a skills deficit. How would you know if a drug were affecting a child's ability to learn if you didn't have a good baseline before giving the drug? As always, I don't have all the answers about behavior, and I don't claim to have all the answers regarding medications either, but I do hope that I have at least raised some good questions. We'll talk some more about medications in Chapter 4 and more about self-control in Chapter 7.

Chapter 4

Chronic vs. Intermittent Problems

SECTION ONE: INTRODUCTION

I included this chapter because the frequency and regularity of a behavior problem can sometimes be clues to some complex and/or poorly understood variables that may contribute to that problem. The frequency of a behavior, in many instances, can tell us a lot about the nature of the problem. For example, someone who hits her head five times per minute for five minutes at a time, throughout the day, is a very motivated individual. That's a lot of work. Someone who only hits her head once a month has got some very different stuff going on, to say the least. Not just the frequency of behavior, but its *regularity* also gives us some very good information. A child who is aggressive every Monday morning, but fine the rest of the days of the week presents a very different problem than a child who has the same overall frequency of aggression (1/week), but shows no patterns across hours of the day or days per week.

When conducting an initial interview, if there are no graphed data,[1] I will just ask the teacher if the behavior of concern happens hourly, daily, weekly, or monthly, then I start the stopwatch in my head to see how long she takes to answer and whether or not the response is strong (eye rolling, eyebrow raising, head-shaking, or crushing and snorting a valium). I use the same inner stopwatch technique when I'm asking parents if a medication has helped their child. If they both answer immediately and say, "Oh, it's a night and day difference" I feel more confident that it's actually helping. If ten seconds elapse and they are both looking at each other with that kind of "what do you think?" look, then I'm not too confident in the drug's ability to change behavior. Let me add a bit more detail about this "frequency guesstimate." I tell the interviewee that each time division means that the behavior of concern occurs at least once during that interval. For example, if the person answers that the behavior happens hourly, then it must occur, on average, at least once per hour. Once the person has chosen an interval I will try to narrow it down a bit. So if the teacher answers "hourly" I will ask if the behavior occurs every 5, 15, or 30 minutes. If she answers "weekly" I'll ask if it happens 1 or 3 times per week. The teacher may or may not know exactly, and her estimate may be off, but I'm just trying to get an idea of the overall frequency. It's not meant to replace traditional data collection—I use it when there is no formal system. Again, this is not touted as "best practice," I just ask these questions as a narrowing down process so I know which questions to ask later.

---

[1]Yes, believe it or not, sometimes there are no data collected or graphed. Should there be? Yes. Does it mean we can do nothing if there are no graphed data? No. If you can teach a pig how to sing, you don't need data. Well I don't know, maybe you need baseline levels of pig singing first if you want to get a publication out of it. Still, unless the information giver is either delusional or flat-out lying, there is no reason to believe that he or she can't give a reasonable estimate just to help rule out some initial hypotheses. Based on the response, you may be able to figure out what kind of data you need to collect, which could be even more helpful in your analysis. Am I proposing we stop collecting data? No. I'm just saying that it doesn't always mean that nothing can be done until data are collected.

When I use the terms *chronic* and *intermittent*, I am defining them differently than most individuals probably would. By *chronic* I mean that rarely (if ever) does a day go by that the child doesn't exhibit the behavior. I will use the term *intermittent* to denote that the child can go at least one day without exhibiting the behavior, and the behavior is not regular. That is, if the child shows the behavior only on Wednesdays, I don't call that intermittent. That's more like a low-rate predictable pattern. To help narrow things down, I will often ask the teacher/parent/caregiver to describe the longest interval he or she has seen where there were no behavior problems (e.g., one day, two weeks, etc.). After that I may ask how often those intervals have happened, e.g., three times, five times, etc. If the interviewees have absolutely no idea, or sound highly uncertain, then I will usually request some simple data collection. I have to use these interview strategies, because, as I mentioned, in school settings not everyone takes data all the time (or at all), and even when data exist, they may be the wrong kind, recorded improperly, or the definitions of the problem behavior may be too broad to be useful, e.g., "number of bad days" (for the student, not the teacher...).

1.1   Chronic behavior problems

These problems are typically high frequency, occurring many times per day or per hour. If the chronic behavior problem occurs with everyone in all settings and if it appears to be multiply maintained (attention, access to tangibles, escape/avoidance, "automatic") I call that problem "insidious." Very often a child uses these insidious behaviors, like high frequency SIB, to navigate his or her day. That is, the child has needs all day long that are not being met (from his point of view) and the behavior is being used in much the same way that you and I use language. This is the so-called "communicative intent" of behavior (more on this later). Although it's not exclusive by any means, you will often see this kind of behavior problem exhibited by children with very restricted repertoires. These kids are essentially "one-trick ponies." They have one main "go-to" behavior whenever there is any kind of problem. Can't get food? Aggression. No one is giving you attention? Aggression. You don't like this task? Aggression. An adult is trying to play with you, but Santa didn't leave you any playtime skills under the tree? Aggression. Some of you may be thinking, "OMG he must have met Darryl!" No, I didn't meet Darryl, at least I'm pretty sure of it. However, I've met many children like Darryl and they fit this same profile of an individual who is functioning at a lower level, has impoverished communication and social repertoires and very high-frequency chronic behavior problems. Incidentally, "self-stimulatory" behavior will usually fall under the chronic category (nobody takes a week off from hand flapping because they're skiing in Aspen, although you've got to admit that skiing would probably be incompatible with hand flapping).

Let's say that you're working with a "Darryl." Does it make sense that Darryl would just give up on his behavior problem for a full week, or even a couple of days? If Darryl is clearly using his behavior to get his needs met in every way throughout the day, and then suddenly just stops showing the problem for one day or several days, then there are *at least* four possible reasons. The *first* possibility is that Darryl suddenly has no more needs. He's fine just sitting, he doesn't even move. Maybe he's depressed, or sick, or just incredibly tired and he's sleeping. You'll notice that people who are pretty content don't tend to show their behavior problems very much if at all. The *second* possibility is that a key aversive just wasn't present for a short time (one or two days) and this resulted in a temporary cessation of any behavior problems. The *third* possibility is that Darryl still has the same needs he had yesterday, but everyone around him has become acutely aware of his needs and provides him with what he wants (almost before he even knows what he wants), and his behaviors are therefore, at least temporarily, unnecessary. This anticipation of needs might include eliminating any aversives that have been known to cause problems. Many parents, for example, have become so highly attuned to their child's needs that the child shows almost no behavior problems at home. The child doesn't need to communicate anything because he or she either has free access to any and everything, or because his parents ensure that no need goes unmet for very long, including the need to escape from or avoid aversives. The *fourth* possibility is that the behavior is somehow being suppressed through a powerful punisher or the threat of a powerful punisher. Could there be a fifth and a sixth reason? Sure, why not, but I believe that these four reasons cover quite a bit of analytical territory.

These chronic, insidious problems are quite honestly my favorite problems in many ways. There just isn't much detective work involved. The child's problem behavior is like the American Express card; she never leaves home without it. The silver lining to this particular cloud is that because the child is motivated throughout the day to engage in the behavior, there are many opportunities to conduct probes to test your hypotheses and try to teach appropriate replacement behaviors. I know that these chronic problems may seem like a handful, because it appears that we get no respite from the behavior, but it is *highly preferable* to being caught off guard because you haven't seen the behavior problem for a few days. I don't know about you, but I don't want to come to work every day with my fingers crossed hoping that the good behavior streak continues for another day. Interestingly enough, these chronic, insidious problems are the meat and potatoes of the traditional functional analysis. Many clinicians lament that the functional analysis is more problematic with low frequency, high magnitude behaviors that occur intermittently, which is exactly what I'll address now.

1.2   Intermittent behavior problems

As a consultant, intermittent behavior problems are my personal bête noire. For those of you who don't speak French, like me, that means "&@!$ I can't stand." All too often I have gone into a classroom to see a kid with challenging behavior and I'm wondering if someone paid him to make a liar out of the teacher. You know, like when you bring your car into the mechanic and it just won't make that whirring/buzzing/clanking sound? Not only does the kid not show out, but he's so good you start wondering if he's running for class president or something. Although not always a cakewalk, many people can figure out what to do when presented with chronic problems. It's a whole different story when you need to figure out what to do with behavior that stops for a week at a time, happens for two days straight, stops for three, happens for one, etc.

When I see intermittent problems, I start asking different questions based on the characteristics of the child. For example, it can make a big difference if the child is high-functioning with many skills (verbal, social, academic, play, etc.) or if the child is functioning at a much lower level like the mythical "Darryl" described in the first section on chronic problems. For a child who is higher functioning with really good verbal skills, I start trying to determine if he "needs" his inappropriate behavior to get through the day. Let's say I'm working with such a child. We'll call him Kyle. I might ask his teacher the following kinds of questions to get an idea of how he handles the curve balls life throws at him. I might ask:

1. What does he do when he has to do an assignment he doesn't like?
2. What does he do if he can't have a desired item?
3. What does he do if another child bothers him?
4. What does he do when he's having difficulty with an assignment?
5. What does he do if he needs to get your attention?

If the teacher gives answers that indicate that Kyle knows what to do under these conditions, and that he typically demonstrates the appropriate behavior, (e.g., asks for a different task, asks *when* he can get a reinforcer, calls an adult when bothered, asks for help during tasks, and calls the teacher by name to get attention), I start to get the impression that we are dealing with an *intermittent problem* based on some sort of unknown motivating operation. This MO decreases the probability that Kyle will engage in the appropriate response that he usually shows, and increases the likelihood of problem behaviors.

What about the Darryls of the world? Can they show intermittent behavior problems as well? Absolutely, but things are trickier because, unlike our friend Kyle, these children typically have problems getting their needs met appropriately. If our other friend Darryl only wants to escape from tasks on occasion, but the rest of the time doesn't mind doing tasks, then it's even more difficult to teach him how to escape appropriately (sign "break") because he doesn't want to escape very often. If he wanted to escape all day long, every day, you could easily have dozens of trials of mand training every day.

Although I'm sure that you could slice things up differently, I believe that it's useful to talk about two broad categories of intermittent problems. Those that are caused by private aversives that are *present* when behavior problems occur and those more distant kinds of motivating operations that have occurred *at some time in the recent past*, and are still increasing the chances of problem behaviors in the present. *Back to the Future!* In the sections that follow I'll talk about some different kinds of motivators that may cause intermittent problem behaviors including medical/medication variables, deprivation, and discrete events I call "bombs," which are over quickly perhaps, but still create quite a bit of behavioral fallout.

SECTION 2: MOTIVATORS THAT CAUSE INTERMITTENT PROBLEMS

2.1   Private Aversives (PAs)

I'm going to reserve the term PA for those unobservable events that are occurring *right now* and that may *also* contribute to behavior problems. An example would be painful stimulation or discomfort as discussed in Chapter 3. What kinds of painful stimulation are we talking about? Headaches, toothaches, stomach aches, essentially all the aches and anything else you can think of that hurts or causes discomfort. For our discussion about intermittent behavior problems, the key thing is that the problem is happening *right now*. These PAs, like any motivating operation, can easily decrease reinforcer efficacy, or increase the efficacy of an aversive (Laraway, et. al 2003).

For example, I like to play video games. On most evenings, maybe I'll play for a half-hour or so. If my stomach is bothering me, I DO NOT want to play video games! Furthermore, if my stomach is bothering me and I have to pay some bills, and I don't know about you, but I'm *not normally wild about* paying bills, then I REALLY DON'T WANT TO PAY BILLS! So it's pretty easy to see how a PA (private aversive stimulation occurring right now) could render some reinforcers useless and create giant aversives out of tiny ones. Now depending on their magnitude (level) some PAs could greatly increase the efficacy of the "opportunity to be aggressive" or signs of damage as a reinforcer. That is, even if no one places a demand on a child or blocks his access to reinforcement, the child may attack the first person who comes near him. There is compelling experimental literature indicating that animals subjected to aversive stimulation will work to gain access to a "target" on which they can focus an attack (Azrin, Hutchinson and McLaughlin, 1965).

2.2   Short-range and long-range behavior bombs

What the hell does that mean? There goes Merrill, making &@!$ up again. Hey, if you can't make &@!$ up what's the use of writing a book, right? I only invent these phrases (not new concepts) so that I can quickly communicate a scenario without having to keep writing long paragraphs (there are enough of those already). *Please* don't think that these are "special" behavioral phenomenon, because they ain't. I'm just using them to make our discussion easier. For our purposes here, I'm going to talk about "bombs" as events that happen to a child that can result in behavior problems for some time after the bomb has been "dropped." That is, bombs involve aversive events that happen and then they are over, done, kaput. These aversive events ARE motivating operations that contribute to behavior problems later on, even though the events themselves are over and done. These events or "bombs" can continue to have their effects (fallout) for different amounts of time depending on a number of factors. Unlike PAs, however, the initial aversive event itself is long-gone at the time of the actual behavior problem.

A *short-range* behavior bomb might only affect the individual for minutes after the event. As an example, let's say that you have a nonverbal child and it's necessary to take away a toy. You may get some initial agitation when taking the toy away, even if there is no behavior problem per se. You may find, however, that any subsequent demand placed on the child may immediately cause escape behavior until the child has calmed down (which normally happens with the passage of time). Even though the "bomb" itself was very brief (toy removal), the potential for behavior problems may remain for several minutes, because even reasonable requests may be (temporarily) highly aversive. However, that same reasonable request, given ten minutes later, may produce no problems at all. This is an example of a "short-range" behavior bomb. These probably happen more often when the bombs are small, or with individuals who are either nonverbal, very young, forget about things easily, or are otherwise easily distracted.

Long-range behavior bombs are not fundamentally different from the short-range variety (an MO is an MO). However, their "blast radius" is much more far-reaching, affecting more things for a longer duration. Allow me to illustrate. A verbally competent child is being subjected to a behavior program whereby any misbehavior (say aggression) will put the kibosh on access to the "treasure box" at the end of the day. The child violates the terms of the program and the teacher informs him that he will no longer qualify for the much coveted treasure box. Bombs away. Not only might this event cause an initial act of aggression, but it *may* also reduce the efficacy of other lesser reinforcers and/or increase the aversiveness of any school-related tasks. Children who are highly verbal may continue to ruminate[2] on their misfortune for the rest of the day even if no one mentions "treasure box" again. They may bring up the event to everyone they see and they may even engage in self-talk about the event, keeping themselves "pumped up" for hours. Even a child whose verbal skills are not as well developed, or who isn't as good at rehearsing events privately or publicly may continue to have problems throughout the day by merely *seeing* the treasure box. The sight of the treasure box, or even hearing someone talk about it, may be enough to cause problems when demands are presented. For higher functioning kids, it's not entirely uncommon for them to show up to school the next day, talking about the previous day's bomb.

Now in the case of the "treasure box that never was," the bomb wasn't physically painful, and, as mentioned in Chapter 3, nothing was actually taken from the child. The bomb was nothing more than words (conditioned aversive stimuli) that described an impending blocked-access condition. Remember, the future condition doesn't control behavior (it didn't happen yet): it's *words spoken to the child* that causes the problem. Furthermore, in this instance the teacher knew what the bomb was because she was the one flying the B-52

---

[2] I mean ruminate in the sense of thinking about something over and over, and not the act of regurgitating food into your mouth and re-swallowing it as do bovine farm animals. This is unfortunately also common in persons with more severe intellectual disabilities. This is what can happen when you're done with dinner and can't ask for "seconds." It is also highly likely that I've counted more ruminations than any other human on the planet; an unglamorous distinction at best.

that dropped it! What about unknown bombs? Do these happen as well? Oh yes. Parents who communicate well with teachers may give an update from the front lines describing how many bombs were dropped and when. At least this way the teacher knows what to expect when the child arrives. In some cases, however, the only way of discovering that a bomb has been dropped is that the child displays behavior problems under conditions that are typically incident-free. That is, sometimes behaviors are intermittent because the bombs themselves are intermittent and behavioral outbursts may seem mysterious because the bombing happened at home. Now remember, guys, these bombs don't have to be dropped on purpose, but the subsequent behavior problems can be just as bad. I'll talk about the treatment implications for these one-hit wonders in section 4 of this chapter. There are a number of things that can be done to deal with the fallout from behavior bombs and they may differ based on the level of functioning of the child, the size of the bomb (megatons), and whether or not it was the short or long-range variety.

One other thing to think about is that smaller "cluster bombs" don't necessarily produce immediate behavior problems but several of these in a short period may act in concert to increase the potency of subsequent existing aversive events. This is why we have the phrase, "That was the straw that broke the camel's back." That last straw produces behavior problems only because of the cumulative effects of all those other straws. I strongly suspect that some behaviors that seem intermittent and/or out of the blue may be a result of these cluster bombs that we don't even notice because each bomb by itself fails to produce any observable behavior problems but, as they accumulate, become a form of stealth motivating operation. I should mention, before moving on, that not all bombs have to be aversive in nature. Let's say that a child's behavior is maintained by attention. There could be a bomb that serves as an MO to *seek attention.* Similarly, there could be a bomb that is an MO to seek tangible reinforcers as well, just like the commercial you see that makes you want to buy a Camaro. I don't honestly know, but I suspect that these kinds of bombs occur less frequently—that is, many severe behavior problems are probably more related to sudden aversive stimulation, which we just talked about, and *deprivation,* which we will turn to now.

2.3 Deprivation

Deprivation is another motivator that can be responsible for intermittent problems, but instead of the *presence* of some event or setting, it is the *absence of something for a particular duration* that causes the problem. You might feel very on edge if you've started a new diet and you are feeling hungry all the time. Being deprived of just about anything can be a huge motivator. As mentioned earlier, a chronic behavior problem may become masked because the parents or teachers ensure that the child's needs are constantly met. The moment the child is deprived of attention, food, stimulation, etc., long enough, the behavior problem occurs in full force. Essentially, the child's perfect world has been tilted off axis. This is why I am wary of behavioral treatments that rely too heavily on antecedent manipulations and excessive supports. These are essentially some well-meaning attempts to eliminate all aversives, which would presumably include various states of deprivation. *The only real way to make clinical progress is to deal with this wolf in sheep's clothing as a chronic problem and not as something that only happens when the child is exposed to infrequent/unusual conditions.* As an example, if a child shows behavior problems that are maintained by attention, and she also has a one-on-one staff member, occasionally that person will be unavailable. You can expect behavior problems during the staff member's absence because the child is not going to receive the same level of attention (they are deprived).

One sneaky thing about deprivation that makes behavior problems seem more *mysterious* is that it is almost exclusively a time-based, and not an event-based, phenomenon. That is, when we're analyzing behavior we typically focus on *events*. What triggered the behavior? What did you say to him? What did you do to him? Who walked in? What task was presented? What did you take away from him? What noise triggered it? These are ALL event-based phenomenon. Unlike behavior-bombs, that are discrete motivators (boom, and they're done), deprivation happens *continuously* over time. Yep, deprivation is a sneaky little bastard. It's not that Bobby doesn't have attention and it's not simply that Bobby lost attention. It's that Bobby lost attention for *seven minutes*. Like deprivation, some aversives become MOs not because of their onset, but because of their *duration*. That is, like cluster bombs, the duration of an aversive can also be a "stealth" MO. The child isn't bothered by his classmate's initial screaming, it's *ten minutes* of screaming. If we start looking for the causes of intermittent behavior problems with time-based phenomenon (duration from the onset of work, or duration *since* the termination of attention) we may uncover variables that could help us design an intervention. Very cool, right?

2.4 Medical problems

PAs can be the result of not just the occasional aches, pains, and discomfort, but may reflect specific medical problems or conditions. These medical problems can profoundly affect behavior. Understatement of the year, I know, but it had to be said. These problems can be chronic in the sense of ever-present but also in the sense of regularly recurrent problems that last for days such as seasonal allergies or menstruation. Medications can be considered to fall under medical problems as well because some of them that are intended to improve problem behavior actually cause medical problems, sometimes serious ones, but we'll cover them in the next section. I find it useful to divide medical problems into three categories (at this point in the book you know that I be lovin' me some categories) and these are: 1) Undiagnosed, 2) Unresolved, and 3) Managed.

By far, undiagnosed problems are the worst. They can easily cause us to misinterpret the efficacy of medication or a behavior program and they may render any functional assessment of behavior inconsistent or inconclusive. Worst of all, the child may be suffering needlessly. Undiagnosed medical problems are typically more problematic for nonverbal individuals as they can't tell us what is bothering them. However, even children with better verbal skills may not be very good at localizing and accurately describing unpleasant internal stimulation. Some children can communicate most of their basic needs, but they still may not say that their tummy or head hurts, that they feel nauseated or that their muscles are sore. Of course not all medical problems involve pain or discomfort, but a vast majority do. As mentioned in the previous section, it's quite common for people to become highly agitated and possibly aggressive when subjected to painful stimulation, regardless of the source.

Some medical problems have observable correlates (a runny nose with a cold) and some do not (headaches). Problems that often afflict infants are usually first detected by parents because of crying, changes in mood and/or changes in eating/sleeping habits. Unfortunately, there are a multitude of medical problems that have no particular observable behavioral correlates, as some of these behaviors must be learned. For example, you may know that someone has a bad headache because she is rubbing her temples, but you have to *learn* how to do that. Babies don't rub their temples when their head hurts, they just scream. Older children may never have learned to rub their heads or tummies when they hurt, but now not only can they scream, they can also throw chairs across the room. Big problem. All too often, for a child with a history of intermittent behavior problems, an unexplained recurrence of behavior is just seen as "something that Jimmy does." That is, "It's the autism." I have heard phrases exactly like that from physicians (not very thorough ones) when staff were trying to explain that a medical issue might be contributing to behavior problems. This is one very big problem with labels. The label becomes the reason for all bad behavior and we stop looking for other possible explanations. This bears repeating:

"The label becomes the reason for all bad behavior, and we stop looking for other possible explanations."

I'll come back to this point, resplendent in my full battle regalia, in Chapter 10 on problems with diagnoses. What if the head banging isn't "the autism?" What if it's a tumor? What if it's an ear infection? What if it's migraines, a toothache or a bowel obstruction? Sure, we all know that some children may use their problem behavior to control things, but that doesn't mean it's the only reason they engage in the behavior. Not everything a child does is for attention in all circumstances. A single behavior problem can be occasioned by multiple stimuli and strengthened by multiple consequences. Remember when I referred to the kind of child who is a behavioral "one-trick pony?" Ah yes, it seems like only pages ago. It makes the diagnosis of problems more difficult because the child engages in the problem behavior for all sorts of reasons, not just one or two. You really have to play detective when looking at the possibility of an undiagnosed medical problem, and just because one doctor can't find anything wrong doesn't mean that another one won't. This is why we get second opinions.

Unresolved problems are much better problems if you ask me. At least everyone is aware that there is some chronic/recurring problem that we are trying to address. At least if everyone can identify *when the medical problem is present*, proper preventive measures can be put into place that may temporarily reduce behavior problems. So if everyone *knows* that Nancy is constipated because she hasn't had a bowel movement for five days, it might be a good idea to alter her schedule or change the kind of work she is doing, or decrease her requirements for time on task. The problem still exists, and maybe we can't predict *when* it will occur and perhaps we don't know *why* it occurs or how long until it subsides. We may, however, recognize it when we see it and have a plan for what to do to make the best out of a bad thing. Ultimately, unresolved problems must get resolved if the child is going to make real progress.

Managed problems are still problems, but they're arguably the best. Sometimes medical problems can never be eliminated despite everyone's best efforts. With managed problems, there may be occasional rough patches, but they may be rare. Children with diabetes may never have perfect blood sugar, and they may occasionally get agitated or sleepy if it gets too far out of range, but if the medical issue is well managed, everyone knows what to do to prevent it and what to do when it occurs and when it is most and least likely to happen. Special safeguards and procedures may have to be put in place, and it's possible that they may have to remain in place forever, but such is the nature of some types of medical issues. Finally, the child can be taught new skills that may help him cope with these recurrent managed problems.

SECTION 3: MEDICATIONS, SIDE-EFFECTS, UNSTABLE REGIMENS

3.1   Medications

Don't get me started. Whoops too late. Psychotropic medications; the behavior analyst's kryptonite. Do I mean that we hate psychotropic medications because they will put us all out of business? No, there is no chance of that happening any time in the near or even distant future, and If I'm proven wrong you can feel free to send a strongly worded email to my corpse from your smart phone. I'm not against the judicious use of medications to improve severe behavior problems. As much as I hate to admit it, there are times when medications can help to alleviate behavior problems more quickly, more inexpensively, and more easily than behavioral interventions. I believe that they are, unfortunately, not used as carefully, thoughtfully, and systematically as they should be. That was me being politically correct. Enough said. The two biggest problems I've seen are undiagnosed side effects and unstable medication regimens (substitutions/additions/deletions/dosage manipulations, and inconsistent administration).

3.2   Side effects

Do you know the difference between a main effect and a side effect? Well, one of them you expect and the other one you hope never happens. Sure, allegedly the main effect is experienced more than the side effects, but it's very hard to predict who will experience what.

Sadly, many individuals experience a medication's side effect as the main effect. How do you think Viagra was discovered? Viagra (Sildenafil Citrate) was originally developed as another treatment for hypertension. Apparently some men were experiencing the side effect as the main effect.

The effectiveness of psychotropic medications is highly dependent on the person who is receiving them. Similarly, some people may experience few if any side effects and some may experience many side effects or just a single side effect at a much greater intensity than other people. Side effects are commonly referred to as "adverse reactions" and may be categorized as either *common* or *serious*. As an example, let's look at Abilify (aripiprazole), which is given for schizophrenia, bipolar disorder, and autism.

First let's look at all the serious and then the common adverse reactions.

Abilify: Serious Reactions[3]

1. Neuroleptic Malignant Syndrome (NMS) (This is rare but can be lethal if not caught in time)
2. Extrapyramidal Symptoms (EPS) (These can be rapid regular tremors, like six cycles per second, almost like Parkinson's disease)
3. Tardive Dyskinesia (TD) (Involuntary movements of the eyes, lips, facial muscles, tongue, fingers, neck, trunk, feet and toes and these movements are sometimes permanent even after discontinuation of the drug; really nasty)
4. Dystonia (twisting repetitive movements and unusual posturing)
5. Stroke
6. TIA (Transient Ischemic Attack, stroke-like symptoms for 1-2 hours)
7. Syncope (fainting)
8. Hypotension (low blood pressure)
9. Seizures
10. Hyperglycemia (high blood sugar)
11. Diabetes Mellitus
12. Dysphagia (trouble swallowing)
13. Hyperthermia (over heating)
14. HTN (Hypertension)
15. Tachycardia/Bradycardia (racing pulse, slow pulse)

---

[3]Don't you just love those psychotropic medication commercials that manage to work in those **lethal side effects** using that hyper-articulating nonchalant soothing voice as though they're referring to a runny nose? This product may cause trouble swallowing, diarrhea, migraines, muscle pain and upset stomach. Some side effects may prove lethal. Consult with your doctor to see if you're allergic to lethal side effects. If lethal side effects occur, please discontinue use and consult with a medical professional immediately…

16. Hemorrhage

17. Intestinal Obstruction

18. Cholecystitis (gall bladder inflammation)

19. Pancreatitis (Pancreas inflammation)

20. Blood Dyscrasias (part of the blood is not present in normal supply)

21. Leukopenia (decrease in the number of white blood cells)

22. Neutropenia (number of neutrophils [most common white blood cells] in the blood are too low)

23. Agranulocytosis (Severe and dangerous Leukopenia)

24. Hypokalemia (lower than normal potassium in the blood, symptoms are abnormal heart rhythms, constipation, fatigue, muscle weakness paralysis and breakdown of muscle fibers)

25. Hyperkalemia (higher than normal potassium in the blood, often there are no symptoms but may include irregular heartbeat, nausea, slow/weak/absent pulse)

26. Rhabdomyolysis (breakdown of muscle fibers)

27. Suicidality

28. Depression, worsening

Sure, those are quite a few possible serious reactions, but in defense of Abilify, other than those 28 horrible things, not much can go wrong.... Of course, if you're lucky you may simply experience one or more of the ***common*** reactions.

Abilify: Common Reactions

1. Headache

2. Weight Gain

3. Anxiety

4. Insomnia

5. Nausea/Vomiting

6. Lightheadedness

7. Dizziness

8. Somnolence (sleepiness)

9. Sedation

10. Akathisia (a.k.a. restless leg syndrome, individuals are highly motivated to keep moving and become extremely uncomfortable if made to sit still for even short periods of time; this is reportedly really nasty)

11. Constipation

12. Incontinence

13. Blurred Vision

14. Tremor

15. Dry Mouth

16. Cough

17. Restlessness

18. Fatigue

19. Arthralgia/Myalgia (joint pain/muscle pain)

20. Sialorrhea (excess saliva, drooling)

21. Diarrhea

22. Pyrexia (fever)

23. Appetite Increase

Clearly, those were a much nicer bunch of side effects. Yep, if I have to choose a side effect, I'm choosing from column B. Sadly, physicians may mention only a few of these, if any. You've got to admit, if a physician described every one of the common and severe reactions of any psychotropic drug, it might give parents pause to more carefully consider the potential risks versus benefits. Sometimes physicians may only explain those common or serious reactions that they have personally seen. This doesn't mean that any particular child won't experience the side effects. How does your physician know if *you* are experiencing a side effect of any medication? Quite often, you have to report it. What about a child with some sort of developmental disability who is either nonverbal or not very sophisticated in their verbalizations? What then? I find it helpful to divide the discovery of side effects into three categories:

Patient-Dependent
Patient-Independent
Physician-Dependent

With patient-dependent side effects, we must rely on report from the child to identify the presence of these side effects. Unfortunately, there may be no easy way to detect the presence of those side effects apart from verbal report. For a child who cannot communicate at all, or who cannot communicate the presence of various internal painful, uncomfortable, or unfamiliar stimuli, one may only notice changes in behavior (problem behavior or adaptive behavior). As mentioned earlier, we have the same kinds of problems with infants but infants aren't taking Abilify and their kinds of problems are usually more predictable. Also, if an infant cries excessively, we don't all just say, "Oh that's just their behavior problem," or "Oh that's just their HID [Human Infant Disorder] acting up again." Instead we believe that there *must be something wrong with the infant.* If you have a long history of aggression, however, parents, teachers, and others may just interpret any increase in aggression as an expression of the child's diagnosis and/or just another of the child's many bad days. Regarding the side effects listed previously, how would we know if a child were experiencing headaches, anxiety, muscle or joint soreness, lightheadedness, dizziness, nausea (without vomiting), or blurred vision? Could these possible side effects alter the frequency or magnitude of behavior problems? Is it possible that a worsening of behavior might prompt a parent, physician, or psychiatrist to increase the dose? How would we be able to detect the presence of these patient-dependent side effects? It could be very difficult, especially if the child doesn't even point to or rub the site of pain, and very few nonverbal children will do that. To detect the possible presence of these side effects, we might have to ask ourselves how a child might behave differently if experiencing dizziness or joint pain. However, if we never knew that the child could experience these things, how could we possibly interpret her behavior change correctly?

Patient-independent side effects are those reactions that could be readily observed by anyone who knows the child and spends many hours per day with the child (which could be a parent or teacher). Back to the possible Abilify fallout, we could readily observe weight gain, insomnia, somnolence, sedation, constipation, incontinence, tremor, dry mouth, cough, restlessness, fatigue, drooling, diarrhea, fever, and appetite increase. Akathisia is a bit tricky (the inability to stay still for very long), because if you don't know about the disorder, you would easily attribute the symptoms to the child's diagnosis or just explain it away by saying that the child is "hyper" because of difficulty staying seated. Theoretically, we *should* be able to detect possible akathisia by noting the child's ability to sit still before and after starting a medication. Again, like other side effects, you still have to know of the existence of this common reaction.

Physician-dependent side effects are those adverse reactions that would require diagnosis by a physician either through an explanation of (seemingly unrelated) symptoms by a caregiver, direct observation of the child, or the use of medical equipment or lab tests. Many of the more serious reactions fall into this category. Tardive Dyskinesia, for example, is typically only diagnosed if the symptoms are very severe or the medical professional has specific training in diagnosing the disorder. The untrained person will sometimes miss a diagnosis of TD because the child may already engage in highly stereotyped movements (stim) and the physician may believe that this new movement is nothing more than a new type of self-stimulatory behavior that is a hallmark of autism and other similar disorders.

In summary, side effects may contribute to intermittent behavior problems and their presence may not be easily detected until medications are either adjusted, swapped or discontinued entirely. I always recommend that parents completely familiarize themselves with ALL possible side effects and not simply those that the physician may mention. We must constantly ask ourselves, "Could this change in behavior be due to the medication?" Very often, side effects may be transitory and the body adjusts over days or weeks. It's also possible, however, that the side effects could be delayed for weeks, months or even years as in the case of TD (tardive [late onset] dyskinesia). Some effects, like withdrawal dyskinesias or neuroleptic discontinuation syndrome would not happen until the medicine is stopped completely (Tranter and Healy, 1998). Knowing what these effects may be and how they may affect a child are *critically important* in using medications as safely and effectively as possible.

3.3 Unstable medication regimens (substitutions/additions/deletions/dosage manipulations and inconsistent administration)

There is a new disorder that I want to add to the DSM-V! I'm calling it "Physician by Proxy." Parents hear of a medication that is touted as the new wonder drug, then they rush to the physician and ask for it and, in many instances, the physician complies (especially if he or she has numerous free samples lying around). I know that parents are acting in good faith when they request a trial of a certain medication, but I find it curious that they wouldn't suggest which antibiotic to use for strep throat. Why do parents make requests for medication trials? One reason is that they are *told to do so* by all the drug commercials. These ads show someone unhappy without Prozac, then they show the same person happy with Prozac, then they say, "Ask your doctor if a trial of Prozac is right for you!" Don't worry, if your doctor says it isn't, there are probably 10 others who will say it is. There are many, many problems that frequently occur in medication administration. They all can result in the same outcome; too many changes too quickly with little or no objective evaluation of the effects. Sometimes medications are switched suddenly, and sometimes the physician/psychiatrist will recommend a cross-taper (slowly decrease one and increase another). Sometimes one medication is added to another one, which is known as polypharmacy. Typically, even a single medication is not truly evaluated properly (graphed data of proper target behaviors showing the medication start and any dosage changes), but when you add a second one to the mix, things become more complicated. If there were a resulting change to behavior, was it because of the actions of both medications together or simply the addition of the new one? Some children may be taking several medications at once. Thankfully, younger children do not typically take the three to seven medications that you will find some adults taking. Still, polypharmacy is a huge problem. The sudden discontinuation of a medication can also wreak havoc, as can dosages that are almost constantly changing. Typically, the communication between home and school is less than stellar and, in many instances, not only is the school staff unaware that there have been medication changes, they may not even know if the child is taking any medication at all. Another problem is that the parents may not consistently give the medications. They may give it on the weekdays, but not the weekends or they may give it only a few times per week.

I don't typically approve of medications for behavior control, but at times they can work. However, if one is going to use medications, they must be given a chance to work. Granted, some may take more time to gain effectiveness than others and some may require "tweaking" by a competent physician/neurologist/psychiatrist, but some children never really get a chance to get accustomed to a medication before something is changed, often because of a particularly severe behavioral episode. Between starting new medications, stopping old ones, adding medications together and changing doses, I strongly suspect that some children *never* achieve any neurochemical stability whatsoever. Imagine if you would, having your body in a constant state of physiological flux. Now add to that a significant disability. Now add to that a possible inability to communicate pain, discomfort, or just plain being "weirded out" by unusual new feelings. How can this child's behavior stabilize? How can we evaluate our treatment efforts? In my opinion, these "flying blind" medication changes make a difficult task nearly impossible.

SECTION 4: TREATMENT DIRECTIONS

What are treatment options?

4.1 Medication/Medical PAs

For medical/medication problems, I think that first it's really necessary to stabilize the child's condition and/or stabilize the medication regime. At least with medications we can (ostensibly) hold the medications constant to evaluate side effects better and perhaps even teach the child how to cope with the side effects. You and I may have a number of things we do to cope with intermittent medical/medication problems. The question is, which of these strategies can be taught successfully to a person with a given disability? First, one has to specify the problem caused by the illness/medication, and then it's necessary to determine how non-disabled individuals would adapt to the problem, and finally we must determine if a child with a disability can be taught the same or similar skill. My father gets dizzy from his heart medication, but he has the option of walking with a cane if he feels particularly dizzy. In his case however he can verbalize the dizziness and can compensate for it.

For children with disabilities, there are two big questions. First, can they verbalize some type of internal painful stimulation/discomfort and second, can they be taught how to use a coping skill to deal with the problem? As with any behavior problem, we may do things for the individual or we can teach skills to the individual. If the child can at least verbalize the presence of internal problems, then he should be able to learn some adaptive skills that might help him cope with the pain/discomfort. The bigger problem lies with children who cannot verbalize/localize the source of painful stimulation and cannot easily learn adaptive skills. For these individuals, an adult may be able to alleviate the problem somewhat by providing access to items or conditions that might make the child feel better. The adult might provide a quiet place to lie down or access to something that provides competing stimulation, which might make the discomfort more tolerable (music, vibration, heat, cooling, etc.). This is essentially what we must do with infants. The most difficult condition, of course, is an undiagnosed medical/medication problem. With unresolved or managed problems at least we can focus our efforts based on knowledge of the source of the PA. That is, if we know the child suffers from headaches or stomach aches we might be able to give medication. This option is largely unavailable for undiagnosed (but suspected) problems.

One thing about these medical PAs, however, is that you can almost never eliminate them immediately. There are, of course, exceptions, like if the PA is terrible itchiness, you can apply a topical anesthetic. Unfortunately, things like cramps, headaches, nausea, and muscle pain just can't be turned off. To summarize, for PAs like medically related pain/discomfort or medication side effects, here are some steps that you might go through if the issues *have not* been resolved:

1. Eliminate, to the greatest extent possible, those events that are temporarily aversive (because of presumed PAs), like tasks, demands, movement from one place to another, etc.
2. If indicated, provide alternate forms of stimulation that might mitigate pain and/or comfort the individual.
3. Reduce other sources of stimulation if possible (excessive sound/light/temperatures).
4. Teach relaxation skills if the individual is capable of learning a skill that is functional. These should be taught initially in the absence of PAs and prompted during their onset if possible.
5. Attempt to eliminate any potential targets for aggression (other children, other adults, property).

This is about the best you can hope to do for a medical problem that is essentially undiagnosed or not well managed. The ultimate goal of course is the proper diagnosis and treatment in the case of medical disorders and the alteration/discontinuation of medications in the case of side effects. Often times, new medications are prescribed to combat the effects of existing medications and even *those new medications* will have side effects. For example, benztropine (Cogentin) is often given to alleviate some of the side effects of antipsychotic medications, but carries its own potential side effects such as psychosis, dry mouth, constipation, nausea, dizziness and headaches just to name a few.

4.2   Short range behavior bombs

Behavior bombs are quite different from PAs even though both are motivators. The great thing about behavior bombs is that *unlike* PAs you can crush their motivating effects in a number of ways. Something that can crush an MO is known as an Abolishing Operation (AO) (Laraway, et. al 2003). Because behavior bombs are discrete events that have typically ended well before behavior problems occur, children may react very differently to typical reinforcers and aversives, but they are not typically experiencing any *actual* continuous painful stimulation. Like if your boss chews you out, it's upsetting, and you may be agitated, upset, or just have the ever-popular stick up your butt, but you're not in *pain* (it is a metaphorical stick, right?). Depending on the size of the bomb, the motivation caused can sometimes be easily crushed by (gently) prompting a high probability behavior or routine that the child typically doesn't mind doing (some might call this a distraction). What you can get the child to do, however, will most likely be limited by exactly how aroused she is at the moment. A highly agitated child will not likely follow instructions well, even if it is to access something she normally likes. For clarification, I'm NOT talking about letting a child do her favorite activity as a consequence of bad behavior. I'm suggesting to prompt someone to do something that she does frequently and can do well (bring the attendance roll to the office) to crush the motivating effects of the behavior bomb. There hasn't been a behavior problem at this point, it's just that the child is primed for a behavior problem.

One of the easiest things to do for the short-range behavior bomb is to simply *stop interactions* with the child for a few minutes. I don't mean ignore the child, I just mean that you don't necessarily have to try to be helpful. For some individuals, until they calm down a bit, the less said the better. If there is no actual behavior problem, just agitation, or moodiness or what have you, waiting a while before doing anything will typically do no harm and *may* result in a rapid dissipation of the MO. One of the biggest mistakes people make is to talk to individuals or make requests of them while they are agitated. One thing I like to try, as a probe, is to arrange for the availability of a preferred activity near the individual, but I avoid making a specific request for engagement. That is, if the child likes to play ball, you don't necessarily want to say, "C'mon, let's play ball, you'll feel better!" You *can* however start playing ball with *someone else* in the child's vicinity so that he can see you doing it. I would rather have a calmer child approach me independently than bring over a potential reinforcer to a child who is not very stable at the moment. A child *who approaches you*, independently, is generally going to be more stable than one who is off by themselves pouting or sulking.

4.3 Long-range behavior bombs

These are a bit different. Recall that these are typically going to happen more in higher functioning individuls who can keep the motivation going by self-talk and talk with others. These children will probably not be distracted so easily. Just like if you come home from work really bent out of shape, a request for you to engage in a preferred activity or other suggestion may be met with quite a bit of hostility. Remember, when people have had a sizable bomb dropped on them, even the most well-meaning suggestion could function as an aversive event. Under these conditions, a better goal might be to allow the individual to calm down *slightly* (enough to listen or respond better to prompts) and *then* prompt a routine. It's also easier to give the person information that might further crush any current motivation. Have you ever been really ticked-off at someone, I mean steamed, and then someone gave you a small piece of information like, "Didn't you hear? He just found out that his grandfather passed away." Unless you're completely heartless, you will, like most people, suddenly feel sorry for the person. The motivation to do or say bad things to the person is suddenly crushed, hard. The only problem with this tactic is that you often have to say *exactly* the right thing and the child has to be very sophisticated verbally. Some potentially helpful tactics for shortening the duration of this "behavior bomb" fallout is to:

1. Try to discover the source of the original bomb, i.e., what happened to upset the individual. This will help determine what to say to the person. Knowing what to say will help determine whether your conversation will be an effective AO. As an example, If you don't know a child was teased, you can't create an AO by saying, "I used to get teased too, but I knew that the other boy had a terrible family life and I felt sorry for him."

2. Try to be careful about making verbalizations worse by giving too strong a reaction. If a child is talking about the behavior bomb to everyone, you don't want to say anything while the individual is in the middle of reliving the event. Even strategy number 1 above can backfire if the kid is still too hot. In that case it would be far better to give a brief, but sincere empathy statement (a la Glenn Latham) followed by a gentle redirection. "I'm sorry you missed the field trip, it must be hard. I need to turn in the attendance sheets. Would you care to come with me?"

3. Try to establish a different routine if there has been a bomb. For example, if you know riding the bus can be a bomb (as opposed to riding in a car, which the child usually does), you can avoid going directly to the classroom and instead go to a novel/neutral area, *especially* if the child is known to engage in aggression. I have seen teachers bring a "hot" kid directly into the classroom and that might not always be the best thing to do until they cool off a bit.

4. Following up on number 3, try to establish *probes* you can do to test for any residual fallout from the bomb. You could ask the individual if he would like to engage in a particular activity that he normally doesn't mind doing. If the response is very negative, it's probably a good idea to continue to avoid the normal routine.

5. Try to look for signs that the child is beginning to stabilize again (starting to smile more, talk more, breathe more normally, move in a more relaxed manner, start to talk about favorite reinforcers, etc.). When a child begins to talk about or seek out typical reinforcers again, it's usually a good indication that the fallout has diminished considerably. It's critical that *everyone* knows what the child looks like and acts like when he is starting to come around. These signs may be obvious for some kids but somewhat cryptic for others.

6. As a more *proactive*, preventive measure, if the bomb is a reliable one (typical aversives like failing to earn reinforcers, being teased, losing a game, being disappointed) then you can look at *contriving* small bombs that the person is prepared to deal with ahead of time instead of "hoping" that the individual remembers what to do when one of these

more powerful motivators occurs naturally. Recall the six Ates from Chapter 3. You can especially make use of the CAT part of PETCAT (compensate, acclimate, and tolerate). The worst bombs are the ones that no one sees coming and the ones that no one knows were dropped!

4.4 Deprivation

In cases where deprivation causes behavior problems by acting as an MO (a hungry child becomes aggressive when asked to do work), the obvious solution would be to address the deprivation directly by supplying food, water, stimulation (which could include attention), cold, heat, or sleep. Perhaps the most important thing is to supply what the child needs *at a time when they are more stable* and *not* in the middle of a behavior problem. Like any other kind of problem, there are two main areas of concern; how do we fix the problem that exists at this moment, and how do we prevent it from occurring again in the future?

I can't think of a real solid way to fix an existing deprivation problem without supplying *at least som*e of what the child needs. If the child is hungry, it may be necessary to give some small amount of food just to "take the edge off" (reduce the current motivation to engage in problem behaviors) This could help you gain just a small amount of cooperation. The biggest error people make is that they attempt to reduce the level of deprivation ONLY after a behavior problem has occurred which, because of the current motivation, can greatly strengthen the problem behavior. Appropriate access behaviors can very likely be prompted and reinforced *before the level of deprivation gets too high*. All too often, a child indicates a need based on deprivation, but his requests are denied. Consequently, the motivation builds to the point that behavior problems occur and THEN the deprivation is addressed. Sound familiar? Time for a discrepancy analysis. How is it that we address *our own* deprivation problems? We usually start by telling others about our current state of deprivation, "Man I'm hungry!" and we often start the moment we feel even slightly deprived. We also know a variety of things to do to address our own deprivation problems (how and where to get food). We also have long histories of *tolerating* all sorts of demands and delays during high levels of deprivation, but this can be a daunting task for a child with disabilities. That is, it may be difficult enough for a child to wait for a snack even when he isn't extremely hungry. What chance does that child have of being successful under more severe deprivation conditions? What if the child is *also* faced with a task?

So we can, as with any other aversive, deal with deprivation on the front end by making sure a child eats every two hours, (give a man a fish) or we can deal with deprivation in the middle, by teaching a child how to ask to get food when he is already *slightly hungry* (teach a man how to fish), or we can supply food on the back end when the person is just about ready to go into crisis (throw down the fish and then run like hell). I feel that the second option, when possible, is the most viable long-term solution. Fortunately, deprivation-based intermittent problems, like behavior bombs, can be contrived for teaching purposes. The same cannot be said of medical conditions. We just can't schedule a headache whenever we want at whatever magnitude to teach a child how to handle a headache. Even if you could, I think you would have difficulty getting it past the local human rights committee. If you decide to contrive a deprivation condition, you would have to know (on average) how long it takes for the MO to build to a level that causes the child to show signs of a problem. You would then need to catch him when he is still "workable." For example, if a child reliably starts to misbehave after 10 minutes with no attention, I would start prompting appropriate attention-getting behaviors around minute five or six. Also remember that conditioned reinforcers may stave off the effects of deprivation just long enough to give the child what he needs. As an example, I know that if I'm in a restaurant and I'm very hungry I will be much less upset if a server at least drops by the table and says, "I'm going to get you some bread and I'll be right back to take your order." Naturally, I'm no less hungry because I wasn't given anything to eat. What *was* I given? Hope, and sometimes hope can tide you over until somebody delivers the goods.

Chapter 5

Problems with Adults

What's Inside:

SECTION 1:   INTRODUCTION

When I'm getting a feel for a behavior problem, when first talking to a teacher, I typically ask if the behavior occurs primarily in situations with adults, situations with students, or both equally. I'm not so much trying to discover if the behavior is maintained by attention as I am just trying to narrow the field a little bit. I would strongly recommend to anyone assessing the function of behavior to leave the door open on your conclusions. This is the way science *should* work. Always leave some room for doubt and for questioning. I question my own conclusions constantly. At some times I'm more certain than others, but I always leave a little room for doubt. Anyhow, anytime I'm narrowing things down I like to think of putting other hypotheses on the back burner. I'm increasingly confident that I've nailed the problem when a probe is repeated successfully. This leaving room for doubt business is not any different from how things are done in medicine. There's a lot of ruling out to be done in some cases and sometimes this is accomplished by trying reasonable treatments. Even an analogue (real-time experimental) functional analysis can turn up goose eggs.

So, why do I narrow the field by asking about adults versus peers? Well, sometimes I get fast, conclusive answers from the teacher one way or the other, like, "Oh it's definitely only a problem with adults. They never bother with the other children" or "Oh, he loves adults. He only has a problem with peers, and it's one peer in particular." These kinds of answers aren't necessarily conclusive either, but they are encouraging.

Okay, so what if the teacher answers that it's only a problem with peers? I'll address that in Chapter 6. What if he answers that it's only a problem with adults? Then you're in the right chapter. Well, what if he answers that it happens everywhere with everyone? That means you have quite a bit more narrowing down to do. For this chapter, however, let's assume that the problem is either exclusively or at least *primarily* with adults. Why would a behavior problem be focused around adults? There are many possible reasons, but I'll stick with the most frequently recurring ones that I've seen.

1. Adults will often give a bigger and more varied reaction to behavior problems than peers (this would cover the "naughty" kind of attention).
2. Adults typically mediate most of the powerful reinforcers, therefore they (at times) must also remove, block access to, or withhold powerful reinforcers.
3. Adults require children to do things that they don't want to do (this may feel like most of your job).
4. Adult attention can generally be a tremendous reinforcer for a variety of behaviors (this refers to the "nice" kind of attention).

In essence, the teacher is very often the nexus of highly powerful reinforcers and aversives. In this regard, they are like the child's parents. Unfortunately, problems with the parents can become problems with all adults. It's noteworthy, however, that you will see instances where a child reportedly shows none of the problems that he shows with his own parents while in the presence of the teacher. There are other instances in which a child shows problems with the teacher that he allegedly never shows while at home with the parents. I have seen parents become angry because the child is showing problems only at school, and I have seen parents become angry when the child only shows his behavior problems at home. If I had to guess why the parents get so upset about this, I'd say it's because they either don't understand what the teacher is doing wrong or what *they* are doing wrong and what the teacher is doing right. I imagine that it could be very frustrating. Additionally, I would say that there are quite often more demands at school, and more free access to reinforcers at home, and this could cause more behavior problems at school. There may be several reasons why you might see more problems at home. There may be only one parent to provide attention (as opposed to several adults at school), there may be additional stressors at home (siblings), or it may be that the teacher has a different history than the parents and/or reacts differently to behavior problems. Some children quickly learn that they need to behave differently in different settings to minimize aversives and maximize reinforcers, just like we do. You wouldn't do some of the nasty bad behaviors you do at home while at work would you? No, you're like the rest of us. You wait until you get home and *then* have a meltdown. For the present chapter, we will assume that the child is presenting problems specifically relating to the teacher, regardless of the existence of problems in the home.

SECTION 2   ATTENTION FOR PROBLEM BEHAVIOR

We touched on atypical reinforcers in Chapter 2, and although it's true that sometimes a child is *trying* to push the teacher's buttons, sometimes behavior problems can be reinforced by *any response* the teacher makes. It may not matter if the teacher looks happy, sad, mad, or neutral. Anything we do, *anything*, as a consequence of inappropriate behavior *could* act as a reinforcer. Sometimes the teacher is the primary source of this attention because the other students in the classroom, depending on their level of functioning, may not really care what the child does as long as it isn't bothering them. Many behaviors that children display don't bother other children, but they bother adults. Even if the behavior doesn't truly bother the adult, he or she still has to interrupt certain behaviors.

It can be helpful to try to determine if the child appears to be looking for a particular kind of reaction from the teacher, or if any attention at all is sufficient to maintain the problem. A situation in which the student is trying to get the teacher's goat can be a huge problem as no one likes to let his goat be gotten (besides, what is the child supposed to do with the ill-gotten goat?). It's a problem. Teacher button-pushing is a bit of a double-edged sword. On the one hand, it's good to know that the child's behavior is under the control of a specific "brand" of attention. All we have to do is make that sort of attention unavailable while increasing the availability of more appropriate attention. Easy, right? Sometimes, once teachers know that their big reactions are the problem, they can learn to react more calmly. For an easily agitated teacher, however, a PEZ dispenser filled with Valium wouldn't prevent that vein in his head from popping out. Don't get me wrong, I'm not *blaming* the teacher; it is what it is. Handling a classroom full of children, all of whom have special needs, sometimes without the proper support, can be very difficult and stressful, even for the best of teachers. I've never had an entire classroom myself, but I've consulted with my share of stressed-out teachers, and faulting them isn't going to help anyone. We just want to help them the best that we can. For the rest of the section, let's focus on two categories of attention problems. Those maintained by button-pushing, and those maintained by *any change* in teacher behavior.

2.1 Button-pushing

Button-pushing occurs with both verbal and nonverbal children. Seeing adults suffer can be fun for all ages and developmental levels. Maybe it's because our range of expressions is much more sophisticated than the average child. I haven't seen many kids look *consternated*. You've got to admit, you've got to be on the planet for a while to master a really good "hopeless" or "beaten down" look. Kids don't get exasperated: that's what they do to us. They are the exasperaters. As I mentioned in Chapter 3, when dealing with aversives (a kid pushing your buttons) you've got two ways to go. One is to hold it in and the other is to stay relaxed as best you can. The problem of holding it in, is that people can get visibly tense and that may be enough to maintain a behavior problem. It's one thing to explain the importance of staying calm, and the teacher may acknowledge this, but staying calm is primarily a performance issue, not a knowledge issue.

Once the teacher understands that losing his cool makes things worse, you've only got two problems left; the teacher's motivation to keep his cool and his skill level. If the teacher is sufficiently motivated to try to maintain his composure, he may still find it difficult depending on what the child is doing. Staying cool when a younger child is being silly and flopping on the ground may be much easier than when an older or more verbally sophisticated child is telling you to "go %&!@ yourself." I knew a very good teacher, one of the best I've ever consulted with, and the little boy in her class cursed at her so badly, and said such personal, terrible, hurtful things, she eventually lost her ability to remain rational. She didn't do anything terrible; she just reacted. My point is that staying calm when someone is specifically trying to get you going isn't always so easy and the behavior analyst needs to take this into consideration. Everyone has his or her limits. Everyone.

When working with children who like button-pushing, one has to look at the entire range of adult attention in a classroom. That is, we have to look at the "attention economy." Are appropriate interactions occurring in equal amounts with confrontational/corrective kinds of attention? Many times this is far from the case. Remember that simply ignoring button-pushing behavior may not reduce it; not without also making other competing reinforcers (Chapter 2) readily available. The teacher should provide not just *any* attention, but the kind that may compete with the variety that results from button-pushing. Another critical factor is that *all adults* have to minimize reactions to button-pushing and maximize all other reactions. If only one of the teaching staff does a good job, the child will zero in on the next available adult who gives the kind of reaction that he likes.

When working with these kinds of problems, I always recommend that the adults all decide what they will say to the child when he or she pushes their buttons, that is, the buttons all have to make the same "noises." Many higher functioning children will try to argue with the teachers or lure them into an argument. I knew one child who would purposefully negate what ever the teacher said to produce an argument. I call it "confrontation seeking." Confrontation seeking is a form of button-pushing, but instead of just looking for any reaction, the child is looking for an *argument*. That is, it's a more severe form of button-pushing. For example, he would ask the teacher, "Where is my folder?" and she would say, "It's where it always is, on the wall" to which he would reply "No it isn't!" Of course the folder was there. What could she say instead of arguing? Stating a clear expectation usually does the trick. If you are certain that the child knows the answer, you can just say, "Let me know when you're ready to begin work." Verbal confrontation-seeking is very common with children who possess good verbal skills. I always find it interesting that many nonverbal children may just haul off and whack you, but more sophisticated children will often try to create some problem to justify an argument that then results in aggression. Incidentally, this is by no means specific to children with disabilities, or children labeled as "oppositional-defiant." Angry drunk guys in bars don't typically just start punching people. They seek confrontations. The classic "what are YOU looking at?" is a fine example. No matter what you're looking at, or what you say, there's going to be a problem. That's why it's usually best to decide that you have an urgent engagement that is somewhere outside the drinking establishment.

Before leaving this discussion about button-pushing, it's very important to understand that most individuals are not constantly operating in button-pushing mode. Often times there has been a behavior bomb at some point or some cluster bombs (Chapter 4) which may increase the probability of button-pushing/confrontation seeking. Sometimes it may be a form of counter-control after a child has been coerced into doing something. Sometimes it could be because the child's rate of reinforcement is too low and they are trying to kick it up a notch. Could button-pushing even serve an escape function? Anything's possible. Certainly, if a student starts to button-push in the middle of a task and that results in a task delay or termination, then the child might be more motivated by escape than attention. Typically, button-pushers are seeking attention. When trying to assess the motivators for button-pushing, it's helpful to see if there are some people that are almost never targets and observe their style of interaction for clues that may lead to better interventions.

2.2 Any change in teacher behavior

There may be times when problem behavior is maintained by any change in adult attention. That is, the child may not be trying to produce any specific result, but just any result at all. This can be more problematic because the behavior may have to be stopped, or at least redirected. Even looking in the direction of a child may be sufficient. However, trying to manage every facial expression or body position can be nearly impossible. Fortunately, unless you're attempting to produce an extinction condition, you don't have to eliminate all attention—you just have to make sure it isn't as good as the attention produced by other more appropriate behavior.

Attention usually consists of looking at someone and/or speaking to someone, and even just a glance can be very powerful. In some cases, however, it may not be attention per se;

it may just be any *social stimulus change*. That is, if you're already looking at a child, and the child says or does something inappropriate, and you look away, the child controlled your behavior of looking away. Even if that isn't the most desirable of all outcomes, it is nonetheless an outcome. This is when some teachers will tell me "It's all a big game to Joey!" Sometimes they are right. It's not a very good game, but at least it's something. I hit myself, and you look away. Every time I hit myself you look away. Perhaps not what I was looking for, but it'll do. Even changes in your proximity, as a result of a problem behavior could be enough to reinforce it. Even if you aren't looking at or talking to the person while you move closer. It's still a consequence (a response-produced change in the environment), and if you, the teacher, have any reinforcing value at all, then the source of reinforcement just got closer.

Now, I certainly don't expect teachers to freeze like Han Solo stuck in carbonite (*The Empire Strikes Back*). I just want everyone to be aware that an easily observed change in teacher behavior can serve as a reinforcer, even if only a mild one. The key is to *modulate* your attention and *minimize* changes in your behavior. How can you modulate your attention? You could avoid eye contact, lower your voice volume, use fewer, less descriptive words, avoid moving closer if possible and flatten your affect a bit. Relax, relax, relax. What about minimizing behavior change? Don't re-act, *act slowly and deliberately and as quietly as possible*. If you have to redirect the child, verbally set a behavioral expectation, or just stop inappropriate behavior; you can do it, but do it in a matter-of-fact manner. Even slightly more appropriate behaviors should produce the exact opposite. If you can master the basics of modifying your attention, it will work wonders for children who engage in frequent attention-seeking. Remember when we talked about shifting reinforcers and reinforcer attenuation in Chapter 2? This is what we're talking about here.

If you do find it necessary to approach a student to prompt him, it can be useful to use another student as the reason for your approach. I will walk past the child with the problem behavior and interact with the child next to her, but I won't make eye contact with the target child. If the target child then stabilizes even slightly, I will begin to interact with him or her. You can also use what we call in our crisis management training course a "pivot praise" (Fleisig, 2005) in which we praise the appropriate behavior of one student with the hope that the child with the problem behavior will imitate the appropriate behavior. Pivots are somewhat limited in application to those individuals who are paying attention to the interactions of other children with adults. Also the child in question must be able to imitate what she sees others do and it must be something that she doesn't absolutely hate. In the natural environment, this sort of thing happens even when the teacher has not planned it. Charles sees Whitney get a lot of attention for cleaning her desk and he shouts out "I'm cleaning mine too!" Unfortunately, the same thing happens with inappropriate behavior so be on the lookout for the "accidental naughty pivot." This is when the child sees another child get attention after head banging and then starts head banging until an adult approaches. Well, the good news is that the child has pretty good gross motor imitation!

Incidentally, the pivot can be used not only with attention as the reinforcer but with any tangible reinforcer. I have seen great teachers grab a handful of Hershey's Kisses and start making the rounds as a means to get a target child back to work. They just find each child doing work, describe what the child is doing (e.g., "nice handwriting!"), plop a kiss down on the table and move on to the next child. If the target child likes chocolate, she may begin working immediately. It depends on a number of factors including the work difficulty and the power of the Hershey's Kiss. Of course, like any single *tactic*, you don't want it to become your treatment. Although in using a pivot you are not giving the reinforcer until the target behavior has been demonstrated, the thing that started this whole pivot business was *inappropriate behavior*. This can result in a chain of; 1) make noises, 2) teacher pivots, 3) do a small amount of work, and 4) get Hershey's Kiss. You always have to be on the lookout for this chaining of behavior. How can you escape from the pivot trap? Easy. Why isn't the child working to begin with? Doh! You'll have to do some analysis to figure out what's going on so that you don't have to use a pivot 89 times a day. That's a lot of chocolate.

SECTION 3: OVER DEPENDENCE, BLOCKED ACCESS AND DEMANDS

3.1 Over dependence on adult attention

A very common problem with children of all ages, regardless of their level of functioning, is an over dependence on adult attention. For example, the child is great in a "one-on-one" scenario, but falls apart the moment the adult attention is diverted for more than a few seconds or the adult moves away more than a few feet. This problem prevents the teacher from being effective with the entire class and/or requires the use of a devoted paraprofessional. There are two primary factors that contribute to this problem. The first is that the child may have few or no skills that she can demonstrate independently. This is more often a problem found with younger children and those functioning at a lower level. The second factor is that adult behavior may be the most powerful reinforcer in the environment. The first problem can be addressed through the development of skills that can be performed independently (leisure, academic, play) and we'll talk more about this in Chapter 7 on repertoire problems.

Regarding the second problem, in which the adult is the only game in town, the adult attention has to be used carefully to reinforce independent task completion. So let's say you're working with a child who can, with adult supervision (not prompting, but supervision), complete some simple academic tasks. However, when the student is left for even a moment she stops the task and begins to display inappropriate attention seeking. This kind of problem isn't just common, it's rampant. This is where attention modulation comes back into play. The problem is that the child is accustomed to getting high levels of attention while the adult is next to her and when the adult leaves, she ends up recruiting attention through inappropriate behavior. The trick is to reduce the amount of attention a few minutes before leaving to create a large contrast between the quality of attention the child gets when she works with the adult next to her and the quality of attention she will get when she completes a task independently. The behavior we want to reinforce is *independent task completion*. It doesn't matter if it's only the last minute of a ten-minute task, as long as the child is alone when she completes it. Ideally, we want the child to complete the very last part of the task independently, and then call the adult over who can then review the completed work and give praise. For individuals with decent verbal skills, I will give the instruction "I'm going to help someone else for a minute, can you finish this last part and call me when you're done because I want to see it, okay?" If the student completes the last part independently (you don't have to be very far away, just not right next to him), when he calls you over you must be very enthusiastic and your interactions must be much better when compared to your interactions just a few minutes before leaving the child. This can effectively break the chain of teacher leaves—problem behavior occurs—teacher returns.

This tactic can even work with children who are nonverbal, you just have to be watching them to see that they have completed something and then run over to them the moment they complete the task so that *task completion brings you back and not problem behavior*. All we're trying to do here is emulate what typically developing children already know how to do. A typical child will raise his hand and say "I'm finished, come look at what I did!" This is precisely what we're shooting for, a chain of (work) behavior that ends with a "summoning response" as I call it. Even if a child won't start work independently, if he or she can at least complete a task independently it is a *huge* step in the right direction. It's also a good idea to talk about what the child completed, and to ask questions about what he did and how he did it to provide more opportunities to praise his academic behavior.

3.2 Adults block access to reinforcers

If you're a child, adults are *great* because they give you good stuff that your peers can't give you. On the other hand, adults *suck* because they also stop you from getting what you want. Damn! Why do you think kids love their grandparents so much? They give them everything and don't stop them from getting a damn thing! You want to go to Disney World? Okay, let's go! What? You want to stay up until midnight and eat a gallon of ice cream? No problem! Of course when the kid gets back from Grandma's house everything sucks again. Very similar problems can happen in school as well. Some (not all) parents can only control their children by essentially letting them do whatever they want. I'm not *blaming* the parents, because for some of them it may be the only sane and safe thing that they can do. Sometimes it's just unavoidable, but it's not very healthy in the long run. Teachers will often find themselves in a position of having to block access to a child's reinforcers. There are certain things you just can't do at school. You can't sit in the sink naked while the water runs (yes this actually happened). It's not great to do that at home either, but it's really a problem at school. For some teachers, it seems like half of their job description is blocking access to reinforcers. Consequently, they end up getting attacked a lot.

There are two main categories of blocking access. There are things that the child is never allowed to access, and things that the child just can't access right now. For example, a child is *never* allowed to take food off of someone else's plate or stand up on the table in the cafeteria. Some children also have dietary restrictions like gluten free diets and they can't have what the other children are having.

When faced with having to block things that a child is not allowed to have access to, the best tactic is to try to arrange for reasonable replacements so that at least you can redirect the child. For example, I knew a teacher who was conducting a cooking module and the kids were baking cookies. One child couldn't have the cookies because his parents believed they would make his autism worse (for me they just make my pants fit worse). To prevent major problems, his teacher made sure that he had his "special" (read crappy tasting) cookies available when all the other children were eating their delicious, hot, gooey cookies.[4]

If the child has good verbal skills and the problem is a predictable one, you can often use pre-correction techniques (Lewis, Colvin, & Sugai, 2000) to prepare the child, in advance, so that she understands what she will and won't be able to access. I ran into this problem with an individual who wasn't supposed to go to the token store. If the teacher had regularly reviewed with the student that he wasn't going to the token store that day, because he hadn't earned any points, it most likely would not have been a problem. However, the student wasn't reminded of this fact until he was already in line to get something and at the last second he was pulled out of line and told that he hadn't earned any points today. Big problem. It was an error because the student never should have been allowed to get in line to begin with, but these things happen. The moral of the story is that if you can give an advanced (gentle) reminder, the student won't be blindsided with a blocked access condition. The reminder should not be given in a threatening tone (e.g., "Remember, no token store for you!"). It's better to ask a question to check for understanding (e.g., "do you remember our talk about when you can go to the token store?").

Regarding things that the child *can* have, but can't have right now, there are a few tactics you can use based on whether the item/activity just isn't there, or it's there, but it isn't the right time or place. You can use the "yes, but" or "yes as soon as" strategy discussed in Chapter 3. Another tactic for items/activities that are present is to temporarily remove an item so that it is more like a plain old extinction condition instead of blocked access. Here is an example: The child is trying to get a toy flashlight from the cabinet, so you lock the cabinet. You've already explained to the child when and how he can get it, but it isn't working (as it sometimes won't). As even very young infants have already passed Piaget's stage of object permanence (Baillargeon & DeVos, 2008), he knows that the flashlight is only

[4]I firmly believe that being denied a freshly baked chocolate-chip cookie may be a civil-rights violation and I am working with Congress to add, as the 28th amendment, (A.K.A. the Tollhouse amendment) "No unreasonable refusal and/or seizure of the occasional baked good."

inches away on the other side of the locked cabinet door and he starts crying and pounding on the door (remember the bag of M&Ms caught in the vending machine?). If the child can be distracted for a moment, you can get the flashlight, leave the room, and come back with no flashlight. You may then leave the cabinet door unlocked so that the child sees that the flashlight just isn't there. The child may still be unhappy, but there are no longer any stimuli (locked cabinet door) that signal the presence of the flashlight and hopefully the phrase "out of sight, out of mind" will hold true. Sometimes this works and sometimes it doesn't, but it makes sense and it's worth a try.

A final tactic comes from a book called *How To Talk So Kids Will Listen & Listen So Kids Will Talk* (Faber & Mazlish 1980), and is called "giving them their wishes in fantasy." Now before you get all "where is the empirical basis for this?" on me, let me just say that I don't know of any research confirming this tactic but I will attempt to explain the process in behavior analytic terms and I believe it to be an easily explainable phenomenon. Clearly, this tactic would only be appropriate for verbally fluent individuals, but I have used it many times and, if you're a good actor, it can be very effective for situations where something is temporarily unavailable. Essentially, this is another "Jedi mind trick." Words are very powerful, but if you've ever studied martial arts you quickly learned that the pen is not in fact mightier than the sword. No one ever ran screaming from a pen-wielding Samurai. Words, however, can be very powerful conditioned reinforcers (or aversives). Words are not the things we love (unless you're a wordsmith), but they remind us of the things we love. The child says, "I want Goldfish!" The teacher says, "I'm sorry sweetie, but we have to wait to get Goldfish, we just ran out." The child will not suddenly adopt a British accent then say, "Well then, that's quite dreadful. I suppose that me carrying on about it won't make it happen any faster now will it?" Instead, they keep on crying and whining as children will do. What do you do? You have to look kind of mysterious like you have a secret to tell. Then you go into storytelling mode. You're not going to lie, you're going to fantasize out loud. Here is an example:

> I'm sorry, I can't get the Goldfish crackers right now and I know you're hungry (empathy), but you know what I'd do if I could? I would drive a giant dump truck to the Goldfish factory and I would fill up the back with Goldfish crackers and then I would empty out a swimming pool and dump all the Goldfish crackers into the pool and you could go swimming in the crackers! Do you think you could dive down into them? Would you need a mask? Could you eat your way clear through to the bottom?

Some of you may be skeptical, or think that this tactic only works with very young children, but I actually use this procedure with non-disabled adults! I sometimes conduct very long trainings that last four days. By the end of the fourth day everyone is getting a little cranky, including me. If my participants are begging to get out early, instead of getting all nasty and saying, "Too bad! You should have read the course outline!" I say the following:

I'm real sorry guys, no one likes staying late on a Friday, (empathy) but you know, if I could...I would get you guys a couple of kegs of beer, some hot wings, a do it yourself taco bar and I would let you drink and eat while we finish up the training!

They almost always laugh and get excited and go, "Oh yeah, that's what I'm talkin' bout!" Guess what? They got nothing. No beer, no hot wings, no taco bar and they didn't get out early. All they got were words, just words, and no one was upset. Pretty damn powerful. Naturally, this tactic will not work all the time and you have to try to catch people before they get too physiologically aroused, but it's certainly worth a try.

Before moving on, I feel that I have to address this whole "empathy statement" thing. I've also referred to this kind of statement in Chapter 4. Glenn Latham talked about it as well in his teachings. I know the empathy statement doesn't appear to be very behavior analytic. I also don't believe that there's any empirical research about looking empathetic and saying, "I'm sorry about _____." I suspect that what's going on, when it is effective, is that the empathy statement *may* accomplish a couple of things. It could be an AO (abolishing operation) for an earlier MO. Why is it that when my wife says she had a hard day and I say, "I'm sorry about that. I know that _____ is part of your job you don't like very much" she feels better? I'm not sure why. I could speculate, but speculation is all it would be. I suspect it's because those kinds of statements used to be said to us by our parents when we were young, and they also may have hugged us (unconditioned reinforcer). Under the assumption that some good ole' unconditioned reinforcement may serve as an AO (e.g., comfort food), it's not surprising that an empathy statement might serve to crush any current MO. The empathy statement may also be a means of providing a very specific response to a particular behavior and this may prevent problems of intermittent reinforcement and changes in magnitude of reinforcement across staff members (they all say and do the same kind of thing). Now you might ask, "Couldn't an empathy statement reinforce problem behaviors because it provides attention? The answer is yes it could, depending on the level of deprivation. So, if a child almost *never* gets any attention, then an empathy statement could backfire. Remember though, I am talking about giving that statement when someone is faced with a blocked access condition. This is not the same as walking up to a child who has just hit her head 17 times and saying, "I'm sorry that you feel like you have to hurt yourself! It must be very upsetting to see other kids get cookies when you can't have any!" That is a *totally* different scenario. The long and short of it is that I am *convinced* that using these kinds of statements *can* be very beneficial. I would caution the reader, however, by saying that under certain conditions these kinds of statements could just make problems worse. Either way, some research on the matter is in order but I don't think that it would be difficult to see some sort of beneficial effects under some conditions. Let me just end this section with this: If a child, who normally gets plenty of attention, falls and hurts her knee and she's crying because it really hurts, should you avoid hugging her because it *might* reinforce crying, or will you hug her because she might feel better quickly and stop crying? Hmmm. Maybe we need to do some research. Yes people, I'm being sarcastic. C'mon—it's been five chapters, you know me better than that! Of course I'd hug the child!

3.3 Adults as a source of demands

"Demands" just sounds, well, so demanding. I could have used the more neutral "instructions" instead, but I'm just accustomed to talking about demands. When using the phrase "demand" I don't mean that the teacher is saying, "Do your math right now, Mister!" For the present discussion, I am using the phrase "demands" in the sense of *reasonable requests to do work*. Sometimes it is claimed that the child has a problem with demands, but like other things, demands always have a context. A demand to eat ice cream (assuming the child likes ice cream) is not likely to produce behavior problems, but a demand to trace letters (which may be difficult for that child) may produce tremendous escape behavior. So in the case of ice cream versus letter tracing, does the child have a problem with demands? I would say no. Don't get me wrong—some children have such terrible experiences in education that if they even smell a demand of any kind they start showing signs of an impending meltdown, but those are the more extreme cases.

Unfortunately, there's no way around it. If you're a teacher in charge of a classroom, a large part of your job is getting children to do things that they don't want to do. Sometimes you're trying to get the child to do something that *you* don't even want to do, like working on an IEP goal that makes about as much sense as instructions in Braille on the drive-thru ATM. Very often, a teacher will tell me that the child doesn't always have a problem with demands and that it depends on the child's mood, and what he or she is being asked to do. Some people like to use the phrase "noncompliant" to describe a child whose sole purpose in life is to refuse things that adults ask him to do. I prefer to avoid the use of this term because noncompliance isn't behavior. Remember our dead man? He's very noncompliant. You just can't count on dead men to get things done. In that regard they're sometimes like live men. Saying "No," on the other hand, or throwing the educational materials across the room, is *definitely* behavior. An overwhelming number of behavior problems are produced by demands and may be reinforced by the termination of those demands. For particularly intractable cases, even approaching a child with that "here comes work" look in your eye may be enough to cause escape.

In one particular case, a very young child, Harry, was notorious for having huge problems with demands. He was about six years old in a specialized kindergarten classroom. A cute little tyke was he. Harry was seated on the floor playing with some little beanbags of some sort. I sat down next to him and started playing with a truck but I didn't say anything to him, I was just kind of hangin' out. Harry threw the beanbag up in the air a few times and caught it. I said, rather nonchalantly, "Nice catch." To which he replied, "$&@! you!" many times. Bob Dylan was right—"The Times, They Are a-Changin'." I didn't even *hear* that phrase until I was at least 10, let alone say it to my teacher. After the cursing tirade, Harry Potty-mouth's teacher looked at me with a simultaneous sympathetic and "I told you so" look, which is sort of hard to pull off, but she managed. OMG, I thought (because I think in texting), this little kid really hates praise! As a follow up to my profanity probe, I joined the class when they went out to the playground. Harry was running around the playground area in a big circle and I thought I would try the praise statement again. I said "Nice running!" I then waited for the flood of obscenities that would surely follow. Instead, he looked right at me and flashed a broad smile and continued running. After cocking my head the way my dog Ginger does when I ask her if she wants to go for a walk, I realized that he didn't have a problem with praise per se. No, it wasn't that Harry's heart grew three sizes that day[5], no it was something much, much more. Harry had a problem with anything that might predict an impending task. Clearly, there are no educational materials on the playground and praise out there is different from praise in the classroom. For Harry, most adult interactions in the classroom meant work. For him, praise statements (in the classroom) were his version of the "teaching voice" I talked about in Chapter 3.

How then can we counteract these problems with demands? Problems with demands can be greatly reduced through balancing out interactions and moving the child's attention from what they have to do to what they will be able to earn. Regarding the first strategy of balancing out interactions, it is vitally important that the teacher is seen as someone who not only asks the child to do things they don't want to do, but also as someone who can be fun to be around. Think about bosses you've had in the past. If your boss only showed up at your desk when there was a new assignment, or to chew you out over something you didn't do, you would probably hide under your desk when she approached. What if, on the other hand, sometimes your boss just stopped by to shoot the breeze or asked you if you liked your new car, or wanted to know how your children are doing? No demands, not even necessarily praise for a job well-done, just a regular interaction like you might have with one of your friends. These kinds of interactions help cast the individual in a different light. You start seeing your boss as a person and not just a source of aversives. I remember the first time I saw my elementary school teacher outside of school, in the supermarket, doing regular person stuff. My first thought was "what the hell are you doing here?" Teachers should only be in school, how could they exist outside the bounds of public education?

I have seen some really great teachers who could have a great quick chat with the class, ask students what they did over the weekend, what movies they saw, and what they were going to do on vacation. This teacher could then go right into teaching mode. It was nice because her interactions with her students were balanced. She was friendly and personal, but then she could also get down to business. Remember "Vegas style" reinforcement from Chapter 2 that's kind of unpredictable? Does it make sense that students would see a teacher more favorably if sometimes when she approaches it's just for a friendly little chat and not

---

[5]The Grinch's heart grew three sizes that day not because he suddenly realized the true meaning of Christmas, but because of his chronic high blood pressure, a byproduct of hating the Whos for years, which led to the development of Acute Left Ventricular Hypertrophy. It's currently well controlled through diet and a beta-blocker. Fah who for-aze! Dah who dor-aze!

another request to get busy? It doesn't take much time or effort to balance out your interactions a little bit and it really can make a big difference in the way that someone will respond to a prompt to begin working.

What if your interactions are already pretty effective? What then? You can try to refocus and re-conceptualize the problem. Noncompliance isn't the problem. The problem is a poorly motivated learner. Do you have to be called by your employer, every day, to come in to work? Could it be that you're motivated enough to come into work every day without prompting? Remember, even typically developing children have to be prompted to stop goofing off and get to work, but children with special needs usually have much more difficulty and may have different motivators. When I was a kid, I was highly motivated because I liked praise, I liked some subjects (because I was competent) and feared getting chewed out at home if I did poorly in school. The teacher didn't really have to figure out how to motivate me. This is not often the case with children who have special needs. Assuming that the task is not inherently too difficult (which was discussed in detail in Chapter 3) you have to determine if the child is motivated to work *right now*. Sometimes, if you're lucky, you can get rid of demand-related problems by no longer asking the child to start working and instead asking the child what he wants to earn. So, instead of asking a child to get his work out when he steps into the room, try asking him "what would you like to work for today?" This is where everything should begin. If the child replies "I don't want anything! School is stupid!" you've got your work cut out for you. By far, the biggest problem I've seen in classrooms is students who didn't appear to want anything. Some students, especially older, higher functioning students, don't want to be at school at all and they will tell you so. Why would you tell someone to get to work, when he or she has *no good reason* to work? Then the child would only be complying either because she wanted to please you or wanted to get you out of her face. Although it does happen, ideally we don't want children to work so that we will leave them alone. The big challenge is to figure out how to motivate a child.

For avoiding, reducing, or eliminating demand-produced behavior problems, the fastest thing to do is stop issuing demands and start telling students how they can earn reinforcers. If there appears to be nothing the child wants, then you can only rely on your attention as a motivator or the activity itself. If the child likes you enough, you may be able to use your relationship to encourage her to attempt work. If you coerce (force) the child to work, you will most likely produce aggression, self-injury, or property destruction. Even if coercion produces work, it usually produces some sort of behavioral fallout during the work or after the work is over. You can force a small child to leave a room, sit in a chair, or draw using hand over hand assistance, but even that may prove difficult.

What about an older, stronger, higher functioning child? Could you force him to do long division or verbally answer a question? You could try, but it won't work. When fresh out of graduate school, I began working in a large institution for adults with disabilities. At the time we had some difficulty getting some of the residents up to the work area of our campus. In a heated discussion I was informed that it was my job to make the residents go to work. To which I replied, "No, it's my job to get the residents to think that going to work is a *good idea*." Similarly, for teachers, it's not your job to *make* students participate in their education. It's your job (or at least part of it) to try to create conditions that make the student "feel like" participating, which is not always such an easy task. If the focus is more on motivation and less on compliance, you will generally end up with happier learners. If it proves too difficult to come up with the so-called "extrinsic" motivators (food, praise, points, toys, special privileges, etc.) the last hope is to come up with a curriculum that the child finds interesting, stimulating and motivating. Sometimes, neither of these things works and the teacher finds herself coercing the student into participating. This seldom ends up being a good solution for anyone. I'll address the issues of curriculum/teaching and how they relate to the motivation to participate in Chapter 8.

Chapter 6

Problems with Peers

What's Inside:

SECTION 1: INTRODUCTION

Just as some problems are primarily related to adults, some problems are primarily related to peers, and it doesn't necessarily mean that the child's classmates did anything to him. I mentioned in the last chapter that sometimes the child's problem occurs equally with children or adults. I don't mean that the problem simply occurs in the presence of children and adults (like self-stimulation) but that the problem is related to interactions with both children and adults. You may have already noticed that some children are great with adults; they just love 'em. That's great, but sometimes they love them too much and that creates problems as well. However, those children may want absolutely nothing to do with their peers. There are also instances in which the child in question really wants to be around other children, but he or she is rejected because of the presence of behavior problems and/or the absence of social skills. Subsequently, the child may resort to additional inappropriate behavior. I'll address this issue (and it is often a big one) in Chapter 7 on repertoire problems.

There are several ways that peers can cause or at least contribute to behavior problems. Please keep in mind that sometimes it's the peer who is truly the source of the problem and the child in question is behaving badly (primarily) because of the unreasonable/unacceptable behavior of his classmate. In cases such as these, we need to turn our attention to the peer to determine the causes for her behavior. Peers can be problematic in several ways. They can be the source of aversives, their attention can be a potential uncontrolled reinforcer, they can be competitors for adult attention and other reinforcers, models for inappropriate behavior, and one peer may be the target of aggression so that another child can gain adult attention. We'll examine all these potential problems for the rest of the chapter.

1.1   Peers as a source of aversives

"Stop touching me!" "I'm not touching you!" "Mom! She's touching me!" If you've ever taken your kids on a trip by car this should sound familiar. It should at least sound familiar if you had brothers or sisters. There are at least three immutable laws of nature; 1) The line you pick to stand in will take the longest; 2) your car will break down at the exact moment that you need it the most; and 3) kids are going to bother each other. It has nothing to do with disabilities. Kids bother each other. In fairness, adults bother each other too, but kids are usually worse, hence the phrases "Stop acting so childishly!" and "Grow up!" What are some of the big aversives that peers can generate? Aggression, teasing, reinforcer removal, and signaling an impending reinforcer loss are probably the biggest of the bunch. Except for signaling a loss of reinforcement, these peer behaviors are "instrumental." That is, the behavior is a means to an end. Signaling the loss of reinforcement is not something one peer does to another, it's just that when a peer shows up, a particular child may start getting less attention. I'll talk more about this problem later. There can also be some behaviors that a peer may engage in that are not really targeting the child in question. Some children make repetitive noises that other children can't stand. In some instances, the peer may simply be in the way of the child with the behavior problem (accidental blocked access). It could even be something as simple as the peer standing or sitting too closely to the child with the behavior problem. Let's start first with the "purposeful" behavior.

Peer to peer aggression is very common in schools. Like most acts of aggression, it is typically either a "first strike" or retaliatory in nature. Remember that in Chapter 2 on problems with reinforcers, I mentioned instrumental and affective aggression (the cat example). Sometimes a child may be attacked because he was in the wrong place at the wrong time. The peer was agitated; the child was nearby, and ka-pow! In other cases the behavior of the peer is more instrumental and can occur for all the same reasons as any other behavior (to get something, to stop something, etc.). If Elroy has the behavior problem of aggression, but he *only attacks* when another child punches him first, who's problem is it? I'd have to say it's primarily the problem of the peer. Certainly we would want to teach Elroy, if we could, what to do when someone punches him, but the primary problem in this example is the behavior of the peer. Think for a moment of the main reasons why children attack each other. Finished? There really aren't that many reasons. Some of them are based on a certain history and some of them are based on an immediate motivation. Kids will become aggressive because of name calling, because they were hit first, because someone took their stuff, and because another child blocked their access to reinforcement. These are probably the biggest categories. Also remember that certain other aversives can momentarily establish aggression as a reinforcer (act as an MO for aggression) and a child may attack one of his peers even though the peer did nothing to him.

What do we do in these cases? If children have good verbal skills (can understand rules and can follow if-then instructions) then we can teach them what to do when teased, when punched, or when someone takes their stuff. For children who are nonverbal, this can be much more challenging as they will not be able to follow rules. Still, even for nonverbal children, we really need to teach some form of communication so they can recruit the help of an adult when they are wronged by another kid. Typically developing children will usually recruit the help of an adult without even being specifically taught, but this is not always the case. Think about your own children, if you have children. How did you first know that there was even a problem? Someone started crying. Then you showed up and started asking what happened—who did what to whom, and then when you decided that you couldn't figure out how it truly started, you just punished both parties! Way to go, King Solomon. For children with good verbal skills, however, we can focus on teaching them what to do when their peers "do unto them" in a particularly nasty manner. As an example, when my children were very young, they were playing a video game, and one of them got whacked with a controller. This happened some years ago when video game controllers were wired; hence you could twirl it over your head like a bola and attain considerable RPMs before striking. I heard crying, and asked what happened. Weston said, "He hit me!" I asked Daniel why, to which he replied, "Weston hit me first" (problem number 1). I asked Weston, "Why did you hit him?" Weston replied, "Daniel cheated—he paused the game when he was losing" (problem number 2). Furthermore, Daniel couldn't handle it when he was starting to lose (problem number 3). I solved the problem with a single general rule. The rule was "if your brother does anything to you that you think is wrong, come and get me." I stated the rule clearly to each boy, and then had each one say it back to me. Not five minutes later I received a report from the front lines. Weston reported that Daniel cheated, *I thanked him for coming to get me*, and then we both went back and tried to resolve the issue. After that there was no more hitting.

To do a more thorough job, however, I should have also taught Daniel how to be a good loser, which is why the whole thing started. My point is that we have to help children solve their problems. Someone who is being aggressive has a problem(s). It's just that it gets more complicated when there are two parties involved. We can't simply tell children "no hitting." That won't do it. It never solves the child's problem, but it might just solve the adult's problem.

So, with peer-to-peer aggression, it's kind of important as to who started it. From a practical standpoint, the question is, which child would be able to learn the appropriate behavior more quickly? That is, let's say that you're working with Robert and Alvin. Robert tends to attack Alvin, who is playing with a toy that he wants. One tactic is to teach Robert to ask an adult for help. The question is, can Alvin (the one playing with the toy) be taught some skills as well? If someone tries to take your toy are you supposed to pull it away violently? Not really. Then the focus should be on the kinds of skills the two kids have relative to each other. There are some cases where I work primarily on the behavior of the victim if he generally learns faster than the aggressor. It's not *the* problem but working on the behavior of the victim could be part of the solution.

Peers may also be the source of aversives because of what they say or do, even though their behavior is not necessarily directed at the child with behavior problems. As mentioned in Chapter 3, sometimes children make noises or say things that just bother other children. I knew one child, Jacob, who would consistently try to hit another child, Peter, whenever he started to whine or cry. Other than this crying game, they were actually pretty friendly with each other. This sort of problem can be attacked on two fronts. The first is to work on the behavior of the inadvertent instigator. Why is Peter moaning and crying, and what can be done to eliminate or minimize that behavior? The second is (naturally) to teach Jacob, the aggressive child, what to do when he hears moaning/crying from Peter, like cover his ears, leave the room, listen to music or possibly even help Peter if applicable. When grappling with the problem of whose behavior should get top billing, you might try using the following guidelines as illustrated in the "Grid of Acceptability!"

The Grid of Acceptability!

Behavior/Situation	Unacceptable	Unreasonable	Reasonable
Reasonable	1		
Unreasonable		2	
Unacceptable			3

Let's say that the problem behavior is mild aggression that is occurring in one of three situations. The child's problem behavior may be:

1. A reasonable reaction to an unacceptable situation (you wouldn't tolerate it either).

2. An unacceptable reaction to an unreasonable situation (unreasonable means "not nice" but something that *could* be tolerated).

3. An unacceptable reaction to a reasonable situation.

Now, regarding number 1, I fully understand that in schools children are never supposed to hit each other under any conditions (zero tolerance), but, quite frankly, this does not mirror the laws of society on the whole. We are allowed to use "reasonable force" to defend ourselves. If someone attacks *my child*, and if he can't get away and/or can't get help from an adult, then I *absolutely* want him to be aggressive. That is, if a child were being attacked, aggression could be, under certain circumstances, a *reasonable reaction*. I would argue, however, that number 1 in the "Grid of Acceptability" is not the most typical kind of peer-to-peer aggression. That is, you don't usually see a behavior goal that states, "Joey becomes aggressive and will kick, scratch, bite, and punch whenever another student begins to totally kick his butt!" As a reminder, in Chapter 2 on problems with aversives, I mentioned that I've seen numerous situations where students were being expected to *tolerate the intolerable* and to respond in a reasonable manner when many adults would be unable to do so. When planning an intervention, it may be wise to reconsider the need for behavior change (and consider environmental changes) when a child is faced with an event that might be too much to handle, even for persons with no disabilities.

Regarding number 2, *an unacceptable reaction to an unreasonable situation*, I think you'll find that many peer-to-peer problems fall into this category. For example, José is playing with a toy and Gabriel snatches it away from him, after which José commandeers the closest fire truck and clocks Gabriel in the head. Gabriel's toy snatching was *unreasonable*, true, but José's aggression was *unacceptable* for the situation. Naturally, we want to teach Gabriel to ask permission when he wants something and we want to teach José to recruit help from a teacher when someone takes his things. Incidentally, I am well aware that solving this particular problem is not rocket science and that good teachers are most likely already doing this. Still, sometimes people miss the obvious, so there you are.

Number 3, *an unacceptable reaction to a reasonable situation*, depicts the more difficult behavior problem that lies *exclusively* with the aggressor. So in this case, Gabriel *asks nicely* to play with the car and José becomes enraged because Gabriel had the unmitigated gall to even think about having a turn with his favorite toy and José whacks him. Another classic example of number 3, typically seen with older, higher functioning students, is when one student attacks another one because, "That kid was eyeballing me!" Hey, no one likes being eyeballed, and true enough it can get you into a fight in the real world of adults (especially at drinking establishments), but this is still a pretty unacceptable reaction to a reasonable situation. In many instances, the victim may not have been truly "eyeballing" anyone but was simply looking in the direction of the aggressive child. In this case, we really only need to be working on the behavior of the child who is super-easily agitated. What does that mean? It means that seemingly innocuous things (to the rest of us) function as high-level aversives for this particular student. How do we cope with aversives? Think about the 6 "Ates." Remember, focus on the overall problem, not just the hitting. Hitting is *a* problem, but not *the* problem. As an example, If Jimmy really liked and cooperated with Chris, and copped a lot of reinforcement by working with Chris, do you believe that Jimmy would still misinterpret glances from Chris? Do you really need a good reason to go all "Dark Knight" on a person who you already can't stand? Think about it. Typically the problem for these kids is that they already have a poor relationship with the other student or with all peers.

SECTION 2: TEASING AND UNCONTROLLED REINFORCERS

I've given a couple of examples of aggression and reinforcer removal (toy snatching), but what about teasing? Again, like eyeballing, this is typically a problem with higher functioning, more verbally skilled children. Teasing, taunting, flipping the bird, name-calling, threatening, and making faces can all produce tremendous behavior problems and are responsible for many fights between peers. In fact, I am convinced that this is one reason that some children prefer to hang out with adults. With hope, adults do not taunt, tease, or engage in name-calling. Teasing is a big, big problem in schools, whether it's regular or special education. What is to be done about teasing? Who gets treated—the teasee or the teaser? No matter what, you're going to have to tell the child what to do when being teased—that is, how to handle it. I'm not saying that the intervention shouldn't involve other students in the class. It most certainly should, but the child will not always be in this class and all sorts of people in all sorts of places might tease him.

The first thing to do is to teach the child how to cope with being teased (tolerate). This involves staying calm, giving a non-reactive response to the other student, and/or walking or moving away when possible. The child can be taught how to handle button-pushing in the same manner as the teacher (Chapter 4). It may be necessary to do an analysis of why the child is getting teased to begin with. For example, one student I saw, Benny, was teased regularly by several students in his classroom because (quite frankly) his personal hygiene was abysmal and he was old enough to do a much better job. Did Benny deserve to be teased? Absolutely not. Nonetheless, had his hygiene been better and his clothes cleaner, more children would have accepted him. Sometimes the child does nothing to provoke the teasing, and sometimes he does. Teasing is never deserved but it's still a good idea to do everything you can to decrease the motivation for other children to tease. What about those other rapscallions? Should they be allowed to tease with impunity? Again, absolutely not. Those individuals may be seeking reactions (attention) from either the victim or their peers. Incidentally, I fully realize that teasing could be multiply maintained and that some individuals may tease others because in the past it has resulted in a disruption of the lesson (escape), but it's been my experience that most teasing is access-motivated as opposed to escape/avoidance-motivated. I hope that makes sense. Teasing cannot only be reinforced by attention from victims and peers, but it can also be reinforced by teacher attention, as many times the teacher gives an immediate, highly reactive response to the teaser.

You can attack teasing on several levels:

1. Arrange reinforcers for the rest of the class for staying on task when there is teasing. Children who continue working or continue looking at the teacher when someone is teased, can earn extra privileges (I have seen many clever teachers use this contingency).
2. The teacher reduces his or her attention to the peer who is teasing.
3. The teacher can analyze the conditions under which the teaser teases (when bored, when he can't do the assignment, when he has to wait too long to participate, whenever he is bothered by another student, whenever he hasn't gotten enough attention, when he wants to delay the lesson, etc.). After investigating the variables responsible for the teasing, the teacher can prompt appropriate replacement behaviors for those situations.

If all the MOs for teasing are removed (or at least minimized) and the sources of social reinforcement for teasing are sharply reduced, there should also be a marked decrease in teasing.

2.1 Peers as a source of uncontrolled reinforcement

As in the case of teasing, peers can be very good mediators of social reinforcement such as looking, laughing, pointing, and pretty much doing anything as a consequence of a student's inappropriate behavior. For children who are not very social, this is not much of a problem. For students who regularly interact with and enjoy the company of their peers, these uncontrolled social reinforcers can be a huge problem; in fact in some classrooms it's the number one problem. There are two general subcategories in this section. The first is when a child is seeking a reaction from a particular individual. The perfect example is teasing or eyeballing. We can call this "Peer-Specific Attention Seeking." The second category is when a child is seeking a reaction from any peers for behavior that wasn't specifically targeting anyone. We can call this "Peer-Group Attention Seeking." For example, a child starts making fart noises with his mouth (hopefully it's his mouth), and several other children start giggling. Perhaps he was looking for a reaction from the teacher (perhaps not), but the other children's laughter will typically strengthen the behavior. The double-whammy is when one child provokes another in some manner (teasing) and his behavior is reinforced both by the target of teasing and all the other children in the classroom. It's one reason why teasing can be a very tough behavior to eliminate.

Another problem with uncontrolled peer attention is that you can get an "off-task chain reaction" whereby one child can disrupt the entire class. So if there are eight children, and seven of them are working, one child can start pulling other children off-task by attention seeking. The moment even two children begin interacting with each other, the rate of uncontrolled reinforcers starts rising rapidly, and pretty soon everyone is pulled off-task. The big problem here is that the child can access this social reinforcement party whenever he likes. Often times, the immediate reinforcers gained through the attention of other children easily outweigh those delayed reinforcers earned for work completion. This can be tough competition for the alleged scheduled reinforcer. What can you do to limit this type of uncontrolled reinforcement? As mentioned briefly before, you can sometimes use rules and group contingencies to discourage individuals from attending to the inappropriate behavior of a particular child, for example:

> Teacher to her class: "If someone is trying to be funny I expect everyone else to keep working. Those of you who can keep working will earn an extra five minutes of computer time."

For children in higher grade level lecture style classrooms there are, I believe, two main scenarios for attention seeking and they may have to be handled slightly differently. There is *group instruction* and *independent work*. During group instruction, children who tend to seek attention from peers need to be engaged in the lesson. To do that, they have to have some competence (be able to answer questions) and they need to have a high rate of social reinforcement. If the student can't answer questions or is bored or otherwise under stimulated, the motivation to seek attention will likely rise quickly. I know of one student who was much smarter than his peers, but his rate of reinforcement was still too low because the teacher didn't want to call on him for every question. She eventually decided to allow him to prompt students who were struggling to come up with the correct answer when they were called on. When he was helping other students he tended to stay on task. The higher the rate of reinforcement during group instruction, the lower the chances of attention seeking from peers. What about independent work? This is a problem as well, but in this case there is little if any reinforcement from the teacher. To minimize attention seeking during independent work, you have to make sure that each child's work is not too difficult and there has to be a really good reason to do *continuous* work and to do it *quickly*. I just can't overemphasize the importance of continuous, quick work. Typically, children cop some reinforcement by just completing a task. Sorry, but that may not be good enough. What if the student completes it slowly? What if he stops working 17 times in a 15 minute interval? What if he has to be prompted to resume his work many times? If a student gets bigger and better reinforcers for completing work quickly, without stopping, he may be less likely to seek attention. This would be especially true if most students are too busy working to supply attention. You can easily try a contingency like this by starting with very short work intervals (two to five minutes). You could even start a timer and announce the contingency:

> "Everyone has to solve as many math problems as they can without stopping. Everyone who can work without stopping gets five extra minutes during recess."

Remember, there must be *good reasons* to keep working and not look up and laugh when someone makes a funny remark.

Another way to reduce the motivation for attention seeking is to physically separate children and provide visual barriers (screens). Some children can do better when working in their own personal spaces with dividers that eliminate eye contact with other students. It's a lot more tempting to "start up" with a kid you can see who is just two feet away from you. You could also limit unauthorized social interactions by providing a time when children can have free access to interact with their peers contingent on some small amount of work. Kids may not have enough time to interact with each other freely and this may cause them to seek these interactions at inappropriate times (deprivation may be high). Keep in mind that if you can't control a child's reinforcers it can be very difficult to control the child's behavior, and typically peer-to-peer reinforcement is a free-for-all.

SECTION 3: PEERS AS COMPETITION FOR ATTENTION

It's a fact. Some kids, particularly those whose behavior is maintained by attention, are just perfect when receiving one-on-one attention from an adult but become very difficult around other children. Now this is a very common problem, so common that it happens more often than men forgetting to put the toilet seat back down after they urinate, and I should know. Now fortunately, this is an easy problem to fix—the man just has to sit down when he pees. Problem solved. Now about the competition for attention, that's a bit more difficult. Remember, attention is more or less a limited commodity. There's only so much to go around at any time. I believe that what sometimes happens, from the child's point of view, is that other children become what some might call an S– (S minus) or S_Δ (S delta). It can be seen as a stimulus that is correlated with an impending loss of reinforcement or an extinction condition, and it's essentially the opposite of an Sd, (discriminative stimulus) which is a stimulus that is correlated with the availability of reinforcement. Thomas Woods (Woods 1987) wrote a nice philosophical paper on the meaning of S_Δ and you can find it at this URL: http://www.ncbi.nlm.nih.gov/pmc/articles/PMC2748454/. Essentially, the presence of other children means that things are going to start to suck more in 3…2…1. Sometimes this will get so bad that the attention-starved child will attack other children for even getting near "her" adult. There are two big categories of problems regarding peer competition for attention. The first is when Cynthia is already receiving adult attention and, because of the appearance of Emily, either loses the attention entirely or at the very least experiences a decreased rate of interactions with the adult. The second category is when Cynthia is receiving no attention whatsoever, is fine with that, but then sees attention being doled out to Emily and subsequently engages in problem behaviors that may be reinforced by turning the attention back to her. It may be that Cynthia doesn't so much need attention; it's just that seeing Emily receive attention constitutes an aversive event. The other possibility is that Cynthia doesn't just want Emily to lose the attention (terminate an aversive), but she also wants to gain attention herself. This is presumably because seeing Emily get attention was an MO that temporarily made attention seem like a good thing to get. In other words, Cynthia can get two good results in one fell swoop. By falling out of her chair she can make the teacher stop interacting with Emily, her sworn enemy, *and* she can bring the teacher closer and gain attention.

3.1 Attention loss

Hell hath no fury like attention loss. Naturally, the adult might be terminating his or her attention to briefly chat with another adult, which is sometimes a problem as well, but typically the problem is peers. The usual scenario is that the adult is interacting with the child and another peer requires attention, so the adult turns away from or leaves the child. This may occur for just a few seconds or minutes. Some children can't even tolerate losing attention for a few seconds. The child who loses attention typically does not know how to get it back again appropriately. He or she will often attack the peer who is receiving attention (or possibly the adult) or begin to engage in inappropriate attention seeking (aggression, property destruction, SIB). On occasion, you may see the child use a different peer as a "hostage" (the child runs across the room and starts to attack the most defenseless child) which is almost guaranteed to attract the attention of an adult. You can see the attention competition problem when a child goes from individual instruction to a small group, or individual instruction to the much dreaded "circle time." Remember, in circle time the child's rate of reinforcement (attention) is going to plummet because the teacher has to interact with everyone and there is also an increase in wait time.

When working with a child who has difficulty when a peer diverts the teacher's attention, it's best to focus on proactively programming the divided attention while simultaneously showing the child how to regain the attention. You can even use the reinforcement of task completion that we talked about in Chapter 5. The child could also be prompted to tap the teacher on the shoulder if he is still next to the child or call the teacher's name if he isn't right next to the child any longer. If the child has good verbal skills, I will tell the child "I'm going over to help Joey, keep working though and call me when you're done, I'll be right over here (pointing)." Then I'll ask the child to restate what she should work on and what to do when finished. Initially, for very sensitive kids, you may find it necessary to stay where you are and only divert your attention, as very sensitive kids will decompensate rapidly if you physically move away from them to interact with a peer. As the child becomes better at tolerating the brief, predictable loss of attention, you may begin to increase your distance from the child when interacting with other children. As mentioned in Chapter 5, if you can bump up the level of your interactions when returning to the well-behaved child, it can make the momentary loss of attention more tolerable. The key is that you *must* initially program these interruptions; they cannot be random and unpredictable until the child can tolerate the loss of attention and has become good at regaining the attention appropriately.

3.2 Attention party

What about the second category of peer-related attention problems? In this case there is an *attention party*, and unfortunately for the child with the behavior problem, her invitation must have gotten lost in the mail. This attention party *could be* an aversive event, and we know what can happen when aversives are present. You either want to escape from them or terminate them, and sometimes they may produce agitation/aggression. The attention party could *also* serve as an MO that momentarily increases the value of attention as a reinforcer. Furthermore, who's to say the attention party couldn't function as both an aversive and as an MO that will increase the efficacy of attention as a reinforcer. Allow me to illustrate with what Dr. Andy Lattal once referred to as an "animalogue" (animal analogue).

My dog, Ginger, is lying down on her bed. She isn't seeking attention; she's just lying there. My wife comes up to me and gives me a hug (presumably because I remembered to put the toilet seat back down), and now Ginger is barking and excited. The barking translates roughly to "Hey, what am I? Chopped liver?" Seeing the attention being given out might be an MO that causes Ginger to seek attention. Typically, if we stop hugging, she stops barking and goes back to lying down. Two videos showing this interaction are available at www.sloanpublishing.com/merrill_dog. As you can seee, when the first video starts, it's morning time and she's pretty mellow. She doesn't bark, but hugging still motivates approach behavior. She clearly wasn't in the mood for attention. We *made her* be in the mood for attention. Now, in the second video, you can see that she is quite jazzed up because we just got home, but it's easy to see that when we hug she just goes crazy. She also calms down again a little bit when we separate and then starts barking again immediately when we hug. You might say that I have a very jealous dog, and you would be correct. Now, those of you still paying attention might be wondering if Ginger normally stops barking because 1) the event (hugging) was aversive and was terminated after barking, or 2) because the motivation to seek attention decreased when the hugging stopped, or 3) some combination of 1 and 2. Damn good questions, glad you thought of them! I think you'd have to tease it out experimentally by creating a condition where Ginger could step on one switch to make the hugging stop (no attention given), or press on another switch that would both make the interaction stop *and* provide her with a brief period of attention (petting). Now, if Ginger eventually comes to only press the "stop interaction" button, I would tend to think that we have a basic aversive event that is being terminated. If all of her responses were allocated to the stop interaction/give attention button, then I would suspect that hugging is just an MO to seek attention. I would tend to think that Ginger really just wants attention because she is wagging her tail and looks excited. Now some dogs will actually become aggressive and snarl and growl and flatten their ears. I suspect that for *those* dogs the hugging interaction might just be a huge aversive. My point is that I don't have a nasty dog. My other point is that it's easy to see how you could determine the function of the problem behavior.

As with Ginger, some children will engage in behavior that has produced attention in the past when they see it being doled out, but even worse, sometimes seeing other children get attention is not just a motivator for seeking attention, but it also has aversive properties. Some children will run over and whack the child who his receiving the much coveted attention. Also, like Ginger, sometimes the child will stop misbehaving when the peer attention has stopped. So it's as though the child is saying, "I don't care if you don't give me attention, just don't give it to anyone else either!" What do typically developing children do when confronted with the same situation? They usually look at what the other child did to get attention and then they emulate the behavior. So if the peer built a castle out of Legos, the child might say, "Hey! Look at MY castle! It's even better than Joshua's!" This child too, might not like the interaction he is witnessing, but the difference is that he *knows what to do* that can both effectively terminate the teacher's interaction with the peer and gain her full attention.

The treatment for a child with this particular problem would focus on scheduling interactions with other children while keeping a very close eye on the child who wasn't invited to the attention party. Before the child has a problem, another adult can prompt the child to call the teacher over in some manner (a summoning response). This has to be repeated until the child can independently summon the adult. The child also has to know what to do when the adult comes over to keep that attention for a little while. Children who can both summon adults and learn to wait for the adults generally don't have this problem with peers. It's also helpful if the child can imitate the behavior of the peer who is gaining the attention of the adult (as long as they are imitating good behavior).

SECTION 4:   PEER PRESENCE IS A PROBLEM

Sometimes, presumably because of a bad history, the mere presence of a peer (he walks into the room) or the proximity of a peer (regardless of their interactions with adults) will produce behavior problems. It could be because the peer is mean to the child, or because he is competition for attention or for other reinforcers. Remember, peers usually *do not* mediate powerful reinforcers; that's typically done by the adult. It's not that peers *never* mediate powerful reinforcers. Sometimes they do. However, many children in special education classrooms already have behavior problems and in many instances these children simply do not have the social skills to ingratiate themselves with their classmates. You can frequently see this situation in homes between brothers and sisters and it is often referred to as "sibling rivalry." It's basically the same thing in the classroom. Sometimes the biggest problem in a classroom is the problem between two students. How can you remedy this problem? As I mentioned, from the child's point of view, the appearance of the peer means that things are imminently going to begin to get worse, and we have to reverse this association. There are several tactics you can use to accomplish this.

TACTIC 1   One thing I like to do is to arrange conditions so that the appearance of the peer now increases attention for the child in question. So for example, Jake (the child with behavior problems) doesn't like Bobby because when Bobby shows up Jake gets less attention. I will create a condition in which I am not interacting very much with Jake, but when Bobby approaches I will casually move closer to Jake and start interacting with him more. When Bobby leaves, I will move further away from Jake and interact with him less. It doesn't mean that I completely ignore Jake, I just interact with him less. This is essentially a reversal of what typically happens. If done properly, Bobby will not only stop being an S-, he'll become an Sd and possibly a conditioned reinforcer as well. Who knows, maybe Jake and Bobby would even become friends.

TACTIC 2   A second tactic is to arrange for a very powerful reinforcer that is only available when both Jake and Bobby are *doing something together*. If the reinforcer is a very strong one, and the task is short and easy, you may find that Jake will start to get happy when Bobby approaches because now Bobby's approach has a new meaning (yummy gummy bears are coming soon).

TACTIC 3   A third tactic I will use is to have the less liked peer (Bobby) mediate the reinforcer that is typically only mediated by the adult. I have seen many clever teachers capitalize on this idea. For example, instead of handing out the snack herself, the teacher might choose Bobby to start handing out the snacks and doing other nice things for Jake. Again, Bobby's presence may start to gain new meaning and Jake might start to look forward to interacting with him.

TACTIC 4   A fourth tactic is to provide large amounts of enthusiastic praise/attention to Jake when he is helpful to Bobby. Remember, normally Jake's only interactions with Bobby may be very inappropriate. We need to turn this around. If Jake normally *loses* reinforcement because Bobby shows up, now he can produce *more reinforcement* by helping Bobby. This is perhaps not so easy to accomplish at first, but if you can get it working it's a fantastic way to turn things around.

If you combine these four tactics, it can result in a noticeable turnaround in the relationship between the two kids. It may take some work and some planning, but it will be worthwhile if one child no longer causes behavior problems in the other child. These four tactics, naturally, are not exhaustive, but they demonstrate some different angles of attack for this particular kind of problem.

SECTION 5: KEYSTONE KIDS

There are times when just one student can single-handedly bring the classroom to its knees, and that's a lot of dirty knees. I call these students "Keystone Kids" because if you pull them out, the house of bad behavior comes crashing down. I have seen numerous classrooms that were almost a complete wreck, behaviorally speaking, and on follow-up visits I was shocked to see how calm and quiet these classrooms had become. In one instance, when I asked a teacher about the miraculous transformation, she said "Oh, Joey has moved on to middle school this year." Sometimes you can see the same effect because the Keystone Kid just isn't there for the day. It's quite easy to witness some natural replications based on student absences. How do these kids have such a tremendous effect on the classroom? Classrooms are their own little behavioral ecosystems and the dynamics between just two children can really stir things up. Naturally, the kinds of problems you see might vary with the number of children in the class, whether they are very social, their level of functioning, how well they imitate, and how easily upset they become when subjected to noise/commotion.

Some Keystone Kids cause commotion because they are bad-behavior role models. They come to a classroom bringing with them a wealth of behavior problems that other children may have only heard about in legend and folklore but have never seen before with their own eyes. I hear it all the time. "Ralphie was doing fine until Neal joined our class, now Ralphie is banging his head for attention too!" Surely you remember the "accidental naughty pivot" from Chapter 5? How silly of me, of course you do, it was just one chapter ago. What if you have children who are reasonably well behaved now, but may have a history of violence? What if you get a new student who is very aggressive? It won't take long before you get some behavioral resurgence. Remember, even when we eliminate a behavior problem, it isn't as though it has been surgically removed from the bad-behavior center of the child's brain; they just don't have a *current need* for it so it goes into a sort of behavioral hibernation. It's still there, like a slumbering bear, just waiting to be poked with a bad-behavior stick.

In other instances, the Keystone Kid is causing problems because he takes an inordinate amount of teacher attention to keep him stable, or because the teacher constantly has to stop interacting with other students to de-escalate the child. This has a more indirect effect on the other children. They may not be imitating the behavior of the Keystone Kid, but they suffer from a decreased rate of interactions with the adults. Consequently, other children may start to display attention-related behavior problems. Having to provide all that attention can also be quite taxing on teachers and they will often comment that they feel badly because, irrespective of behavior problems, the education of the other children may suffer.

In some classrooms with higher functioning children, in which the teacher uses a lecture format, one child might disrupt the entire lesson by making snide remarks that cause other children to start laughing and/or making their own remarks. No particular behavior is dangerous, but all education comes to a screeching halt. All too often, this type of behavior results in the child being removed from the class, which can create its own problems (including crisis). This problem typically occurs because the child is uninterested in the lesson and/or doesn't have the skills to participate in a meaningful way. If you add to this uncontrolled reinforcement from peers, it becomes pretty easy to lose control of the classroom.

One of the biggest problems I've seen occurs with higher functioning, older children who want absolutely nothing to do with school. They come to class, why I'm not sure, but it seems that their number one goal is to disrupt the educational experience for everyone else. It's often a motivation problem coupled with a skills deficit problem. These children, quite often, are not very good with academics and they have no real motivation for participating. Sometimes, because they may not be as skilled as other children, the only way they can interact effectively is by relying on their large repertoire of disruptive behaviors. As I'm so fond of saying, people tend to like doing those things that they can do well. This is why it can be so difficult to turn these children around. If you can't answer the question that the teacher is asking, at least you can still crack wise. I believe that for these children the only real solution is *skill building*, and that will require some *motivation* and a *good relationship* with the teacher.

Regardless of the exact nature of the problem being caused by a Keystone Kid, the faster his or her behavior is brought under control, the faster the classroom can be stabilized. Sometimes it's easier to work directly on the behavior of the Keystone Kid, and sometimes it's just easier to arrange contingencies for the rest of the classroom to keep them from reinforcing the Keystone Kid's problem behavior. Please remember that the solution is not simply to keep this child outside the classroom as much as possible. That's a short-term management solution, but not a viable long-term solution. There really aren't any "special" procedures for Keystone Kids that won't work for any other child. The point is that the behavior of these individuals might have to be addressed first and they may also (initially) use up most of your resources until their behavior can be improved. The good news is that helping these kids will help your entire classroom.

Chapter 7

Repertoire Problems

SECTION 1: INTRODUCTION

If ever there were a French word that had tremendous significance for behavior analysis treatment and assessment, "croissant" would not be it. However I'm really hungry right now and a croissant sounds more appetizing than "repertoire." You can usually trace behavior problems back to repertoire problems. In fact, I like to view behavior problems as primarily a problem of a skills deficit. If you can decide on, and then teach the proper skill or skill sets to fluency,[6] the child is usually well on her way to doing better. It's not as though skill development is the only thing that's needed in treatment, but it's overwhelmingly important and underwhelmingly addressed.

Anyhow, choosing what to teach can be very difficult and can be affected by many factors. More often than not, I find that the skills children are taught in the name of treatment grossly miss the mark when it comes to addressing problem behaviors. Now I'm not going to provide an inventory of skills that children should learn, as I only have about 50 years left on the planet (assuming I live to be 100) and that's just not how I want to spend my time. Besides, there are some really fantastic inventories out there. A couple of the verbal behavior curricula cover not only language acquisition, but other useful skills that when learned may lead to a general improvement in behavior problems. These skills may also improve the child's ability to learn independently. Jim Partington's ABLLS and Mark Sundberg's VBMAPP are two great resources, particularly for those with language impairments. Two others that I really like are the Inventory of Good Learner Repertoires (IGLR) by Steve Ward and Theresa Grimes, and Pat McGreevy's assessment guide called "Essential for Living." Steve and Terry's assessment is really great because it focuses specifically on skills that will help someone be a better student, and includes things like self-calming, approaching adults when asked, staying near adults when walking, and a variety of other skills that can help prevent many problems. Pat McGreevy's manual is really great because it's incredibly broad in scope and, like Steve and Terry's assessment, isn't primarily focused on language. In particular, Dr. McGreevy uses categories of skills that are based on the relative importance of various types of skills. He divides things into *must* know, *should* know, *good* to know and *nice* to know. For example, learning how to ask for things you want (manding) is absolutely a "must" know. *Making your bed* on the other hand, would only be "nice" to know. The utility of the assessments is that they outline skills that may never have occurred to some practitioners or teachers. Part of what I'm hoping to accomplish in this book is to do the same—that is, point out things that practitioners may not have thought about so that their repertoires may broaden as well.

Regarding the students we work with, to use Dr. McGreevy's analogy, I'm going to focus more on the kinds of repertoires that are a "must" know if we are going to improve *behavior*

---

[6]Fluency has been defined by Binder (Binder, 1996) as a combination of accuracy plus speed that characterizes competent performance. Some regard latency to responding as part of fluency as well. Basically, the performance is quick, easy and contains few errors (yes, not every one of these footnotes is something silly).

problems. I mentioned the concept of "replacement" behaviors in earlier chapters several times and how they are intended to serve the same function as the problem behavior. Some repertoires will fall under this category, but some won't. That is, some skills don't necessarily *replace* the inappropriate behavior, but may lead to all sorts of consequences (good ones) that make the behavior problem less likely to occur. For example, someone who hits for attention might be taught to use his words to gain attention. That would be a replacement behavior in the strictest sense. Some repertoires or individual behaviors may be "keystone" behaviors that allow a variety of other consequences to take place. Rosales-Ruiz and Baer have called these "behavioral cusps" (Rosales-Ruiz & Baer 1997). Others have talked about using these cusps as a means of selecting target behaviors (Bosch & Fuqua 2001). For example, if a child has poor hygiene and social skills, but loves attention, other children may be somewhat reluctant to interact with him. Consequently, that child may have learned to behave inappropriately to both get and keep attention. If the child were taught to employ the occasional breath mint, not to mention compliment people, tell jokes, learn how to maintain a conversation, etc., other children might be more inclined to approach and hang out with the child. In this case, the problem will most likely not be solved by teaching a single behavior, but by teaching several interrelated skills (a cusp repertoire if you will) that together allow for a significant outcome. Many children with behavior problems aren't just missing one behavior here or there. Instead there are very often gaping holes in a variety of repertoires that we all take for granted. Very often these are the same skills that non-disabled children just pick up with no formal teaching. The sections for this chapter will cover the repertoire problems of the general presence or absence of repertoires, weak repertoires, communication repertoires, independent repertoires (play, academic), social repertoires with adults, social repertoires with children, academic repertoires, and finally coping/self-control repertoires.

SECTION 2: THE PRESENCE AND ABSENCE OF REPERTOIRES

2.1 The presence of repertoires as a problem

Repertoire problems are not simply characterized by the lack of key adaptive repertoires, but by the presence of other problem behavior repertoires that exist in great variety and at great strength. Some children really just have one or two problem behaviors, but others have multiple categories of problems and each one has multiple forms of behavior within each category. So, for example, a child's problem behaviors may be maintained by attention, but she may have developed a very large repertoire of those behaviors. In fact, some of them may even lie dormant and you might not even see them until you start to use an extinction procedure (withhold a reinforcer). The problem with well-developed repertoires of problem behavior is that it becomes more difficult to do good treatment if you are only teaching a *single* replacement behavior instead of *an entire class* of behaviors. So, if a child loves attention and has multiple ways to get that attention (bolting, punching other children, making disruptive vocalizations, destroying property, etc.) and the behavior analyst chooses to teach "waving hello," then it isn't very likely to be effective. The exception would be that waving "hello" produces a highly potent attention-based reinforcer that out-reinforces those that are available for all the inappropriate behaviors. Also keep in mind that a child with a bag full of bad-behavior tricks can quickly and easily pull out another one when the first one fails to produce attention. What about saying, "Hello?" What is the child likely to do when that fails to produce reinforcement or produces very little or the wrong type of reinforcement? What then? As you might guess, the child will fall back on her extensive repertoire of problem behaviors. It is for this reason that it is vitally important that we place more emphasis on *classes* of behavior and not just single replacements. Everyone should have a back-up plan, no matter what you're planning. Things go wrong, and we need to be ready with alternate responses. The same is true for replacement behaviors. We need to teach multiple replacements that range in variety as widely as the problem behaviors. If replacement behavior A doesn't work, maybe B, C, or D will. Sure, it may not be possible or desirable to teach all the replacements at once, but they should most certainly be added as soon as possible. Even if there is only a single identifiable form of the behavior problem, you can't go wrong teaching multiple back-up replacements.

Another concern with extensive repertoires of problem behavior is that they may be an indication that the child is only good at performing those kinds of behaviors. Thankfully, this isn't always the case. Sometimes you will see a well-developed repertoire of problem behaviors, but they occur in the context of an even larger repertoire of appropriate behaviors. For example, you might know a high-functioning student who is horrible with peers but remarkably well behaved with adults. This is partly because there is a well-developed repertoire of appropriate behavior that is quite strong (resistant to extinction) and fluent. The child can easily "switch" from one mode to another depending on the circumstances. A child with these characteristics usually poses less of a challenge because, quite frankly, he has a lot more to work with. A child with the same well-developed repertoire of problem behaviors but very few other skills is going to present a much greater challenge.

I hear that some people really hate to repeat themselves. Sadly, I'm not a member of that particular group. People tend to like doing things that they can do competently and will avoid doing things that are difficult or unfamiliar. Do you know many people who really love golf, but are really awful at it? I mean they're really bad, like hooking-the-ball-into-the-trees-seven-out-of-ten-swings bad. We tend to like to continue to do things that we can do *competently*. Sure there's no shortage of people who continue to do things terribly yet still don't care and that's why there are TV shows like *Dancing With the Stars*, *The Celebrity Apprentice*, and any other show that begins with "celebrity" or ends with "stars," just take your pick. In most cases, people stick with tasks that they know and which play to their strengths. Think about your own life and see if you can come up with situations in which you were having difficulty with something new and dropped it in favor of something that you could do more competently. It happens all the time, and this includes children who fall back on extensive repertoires of problem behavior.

We can't simply teach one new behavior. We have to teach many and, just as important, we need to make children *more competent* at many things. I strongly suspect that an extensive repertoire of inappropriate behaviors can only be overcome by creating an even larger repertoire of competing behaviors. I don't think it can be expressed as a mathematical word problem like, "Bobby has twelve bad behaviors, and he's been doing them five times per day for seven years. How many new behaviors will you have to teach him before he stops hitting everybody? Please show all your work." Remember, one behavior doesn't truly replace another in the physical sense of shoving that particular collection of neurons deep into the recesses of the cerebellum where it can never be found again (although as I age I'm starting to wonder if that's not exactly what's happening). Generally, more competence at more things means more ways to get more reinforcement and more kinds of reinforcers from more people and objects. We must foster the development of multiple repertoires that, in concert, will produce reinforcers that can adequately compete with those that are produced by the child's problem behaviors. It's a tall order, but if that order is filled the results will speak for themselves. Finally, keep in mind that when teaching new repertoires, not only will people prefer to use old ones, but they may fight you over learning the new ones. Even if you're the best teacher on the planet, a student who is learning new skills is going to make at least some errors while struggling at least a little bit. That's a lot to ask of some children. It may be necessary to arrange for some big-time reinforcement to get the ball rolling. Additionally, these new repertoires had better be pretty damn functional or the child will turn back to his standby method of interacting with the world. When teaching new repertoires, you will always have to be hyper vigilant to ensure that old, naughty, bad repertoires are producing as little reinforcement as possible. Remember that those repertoires are stronger and more resistant to extinction. Consequently, it may not take much to maintain those old repertoires despite teaching a host of newer, more appropriate skills.

2.2   The absence of appropriate repertoires as a problem

For individuals with the most severe behavior problems, very often they are not simply missing one keystone behavior, which, when discovered, will suddenly transform the worst behavior problem into lollipops and rainbows (which would be pretty but not particularly useful). Many children have significant and widespread repertoire deficits that should be addressed systematically. Although there are numerous assessments that can reveal repertoire gaps, they may not always highlight those repertoires that are the most relevant for a given behavior problem. All too often, behavior problems are seen as an expression of the disorder that has been attributed to the child. I prefer to see them (in part) as reflecting a skills deficit or a lack of quality in certain skills. Unquestionably, there are things that we can do that many children with disabilities cannot. I'm not just talking about complex academic skills like algebra, but the kinds of skills that most of us just pick up naturally, the ones we tend to take for granted. Everyone has things that they can and cannot do. Sometimes we eventually do learn things that are difficult for us, and sometimes we may never learn certain things despite our best efforts. For example, according to my father, I never learned to put things back where I found them. As I recall, he always wanted to know the timeline for my mastery of this particular skill because he never stopped asking me, "When will you learn to put things back where they belong?" Of course, I had no idea when I would learn it, but as a child I was quite certain that it would be no time soon. I did eventually master this difficult organizational feat, but only after I had developed a need for that particular skill (I kept losing my damn tools). Fortunately, my skill deficit did not earn me a diagnostic label, but the same cannot be said for many children with repertoire deficits. All too often I see professionals attempt to rectify behavior problems without truly understanding the skills that the child is lacking and how this lack of skills relates to the perpetuation of the problem behavior. Again, the *discrepancy analysis* comes in very handy. We can ask ourselves, "What do I know how to do that this child cannot do, and how does my particular skill set decrease my motivation for engaging in problem behavior?" That is, we all experience the same feelings as children with disabilities. We all get mad, we all get frustrated, and we all want to escape and avoid things and access things. We all may feel like engaging in some of the inappropriate behaviors that we see on a day-to-day basis. There are a multitude of reasons why we don't, like current contingencies of reinforcement and punishment. However one of the biggest reasons that we keep from displaying these problem behaviors is that we possess a veritable library of skills that the child does not. We all want to get out of doing work sometimes, but we have extensive multitiered repertoires of shirking our responsibilities! I have worked with some people in my career who must have received their Ph.D.'s in work avoidance. They seem to be able to come up with a limitless supply of excuses, distractions, rationales and redirections. If one tactic doesn't work, they can seamlessly shift to another one. What about the child who bites you to escape from work? What can he resort to if biting doesn't work? How many ways can you avoid work and how many ways can the child avoid work? Is it possible to teach the child what you might do? If not, is it possible that the child could learn a modified version? These are the important questions to ask to help determine how to expand the child's repertoire. As mentioned already, there are some marvelous assessment tools out there (and I'll give links in Chapter 8), but you don't necessarily need to have one of these tools to make immediate use of some of the strategies that I've just outlined. Anyone can perform a discrepancy analysis, not just behavior analysts and teaching professionals. Keep in mind that everything works much better if you carefully specify the problem. This allows for better decision making when it comes to which sets of skills we should be teaching.

SECTION 3: WEAK REPERTOIRES

In some cases, there is a complete lack of the appropriate repertoire, but in other cases the repertoire exists but is *weak*. Weak is definitely not a particularly scientific term, so some explanation is in order. I use "weak" to denote that the skills exist, but that they're sub-optimal along certain dimensions. Other behavior analysts use this term as well, which is probably why I like them. There could be several reasons why a repertoire may be weak. One reason is that skills in the repertoire were learned a long time ago and they have not been used regularly (like having to go through the "learning curve" again for some complex computer software that you haven't used for a while). You might also call a repertoire weak because it's relatively new and the behaviors in the repertoire haven't contacted many rein-forcers yet, which also means that they could easily be extinguished (the person may give up quickly). Regardless of *why* a repertoire is weak, we still need to get things up to speed so that the child's skills may become fluent and functional. In which ways can a repertoire be weak? The skills that make up the repertoire may occur *inconsistently* or infrequently, may be of a *low quality* (characterized by errors and inefficiency) and may be characterized by *long latencies* (it takes the person too long to come up with the appropriate response).

3.1 Inconsistent

You may see some instances in which the repertoire appears to be present in some situations and almost completely absent in others. As mentioned in earlier chapters, some children will display repertoires in school that they don't show at home and vice-versa. Sometimes certain repertoires only occur in situations where they are *functional* for the child. As mentioned before, I've seen children who behave terribly with peers, but show very appropriate social behavior with adults. Inconsistency is really the best kind of weakness problem because the solution is achieved not by teaching new skills, but by prompting and reinforcing existing skills in a variety of settings. In essence, this is more of a motivational/support kind of prob-lem. For example, when first teaching a child how to sign, the repertoire may be consider-ably weakened if it is not prompted and reinforced in a variety of settings, and this is more often than not a problem of coordinating all the grown-ups.

3.2 Low-frequency/Low quality/Long latency

Some repertoires may show themselves only on occasion, and although they may occur across people and settings, they just don't occur very often. There can be a variety of reasons why some behaviors might occur at a low frequency. For example, there may be few oppor-tunities to engage in the behaviors and/or little need. Furthermore, if a particular behavior is difficult to perform, you might find that the less you do it, the less you do it. No, that's not a typo; I just mean that we tend to abandon things that we don't do regularly, especially if they're difficult to do. This is because we slowly become worse at doing them and, really, do you want to continue doing things when you don't improve? I don't. We have to get the frequency of these weakened repertoires up to a level that will allow the individual to become fluent. Regarding low quality behaviors, I just mean that they occur with numerous errors, require more prompting and are generally not very efficient or effective. Many times, low frequency and low quality behaviors go hand in hand as low quality behaviors are often inefficient and will tend to drop out in favor of other more efficient skills. It may be difficult to sign for what you want, especially if the skill is new, but head banging is a no-brainer. Weak repertoires are also characterized by long start up times (latency). As an example of a long latency, think of what happens when you switch on your computer. You hit the power button then wait. You go get some coffee, come back and wait. You do today's crossword puzzle, come back and wait. Sometimes the latency is so long between turning the damn thing on and being able to open up a program that you can't even remember what you wanted to do in the first place. Can you imagine how frustrating it would be if every time you wanted to write something down you had to wait for your pen to boot up? I would need to wear a Valium pump on my belt. If things take too long, they just aren't functional and we move on to other things. Can you see how low frequency behavior can result in long latency behavior and how the converse is true as well? You have to be good at something to put it to good use. If it's put to good use, you use it more. If you use it more, you become more proficient. It's an upward spiral. Remember that the problem behavior, which is always waiting in the wings, is usually very strong and can be performed quickly and easily in most cases. For replacement behaviors to *gain dominance* in the repertoire they have to be able to compete with well-established behaviors that may have been occurring for years.

SECTION 4: COMMUNICATION REPERTOIRES

This is a really short section. Partly because I'm not a verbal behavior expert and partly because most people understand the importance of communication as it pertains to behavior problems. My good friend and colleague Dr. Patrick McGreevy (who had better reference me in his book as much as I reference him in mine) is quite fond of saying, "It's all about the mands!" As a quick review for those who may have forgotten, the "mand" (from the word command) is Skinner's word for the behavior of a speaker (child) that is essentially a request to a listener (an adult in our case) who is to help the speaker obtain his or her reinforcer (the adult is the mediator) (Skinner, 1957). It's well established at this point that many problem behaviors serve the same purpose as speaking to people to control them. For children with no formal language, I would have to agree with Pat that it is indeed all about the mands. Getting people to do what you want them to do just by operating your mouth is extremely powerful. I mean really, it's like the mother of all universal remote controls. Remember, however, that teaching some form of language as a replacement behavior (although it is clearly a huge leap forward in behavioral treatment) should never be the beginning and end of your analysis and treatment. There are still other questions to be asked and answered. There are also other aspects of treatment that may need to be put into place to address what is most certainly more than a single issue (the absence of an appropriate escape response). This approach of teaching language to alleviate behavior problems is often referred to as functional communication training (FCT) (Carr and Durand, 1985).

The keyword in FCT is the "F" word! If it ain't functional it ain't gonna help. I have seen so much dysfunctional communication training that I could probably write a separate book on the topic. As I just mentioned, the terrible, evil repertoire is just waiting for a chance to leap out of the bushes again and nothing allows this to happen like a really useless communication strategy. I'm not going to go into any depth on the best communication modality to use for any particular child, and many people who have far more expertise than I have their opinions on the matter. I will say this however, if a child has to wait for someone to find or fix her communication device to be able to request things, it may not end up being very functional at all. I'm not saying it can't work, but that it will be highly inefficient and that you may see problem behaviors quickly gain dominance. *Replacement behaviors should work as quickly and easily as those behaviors they are meant to replace, even more so.* When I want something I don't have to locate my words. If a child learns to sign, he doesn't have to locate his hands, his hands aren't broken (hopefully), and his hands were not torn up in a fit of anger.[7]

I have to say at this point that although many behavior problems, especially for a nonverbal child, may serve a communication function, not all behavior problems communicate anything at all. That is, little Timmy doesn't always have a tantrum *to communicate* something to someone. When exposed to some aversives you can become very physiologically aroused. This arousal can serve as an MO for aggressive behavior. Essentially, it means that you may seek an opportunity to attack someone or something. Animals exposed to electric shock will, given the opportunity, fight with other animals even though they were not attacked by the other animal (Ulrich and Azrin, 1962). As an example, you're in your garage and you're trying to pry something open with a screwdriver and it slips and you cut your hand and you then may begin cursing and even kick something. What are you communicating? You're alone. To whom are you communicating? A child who slams the computer mouse down because Internet Explorer 9.0 is so slow isn't *necessarily* communicating a damn thing. In common parlance, she may simply be frustrated. I know people use the phrase, "The child is expressing his frustration" but you don't have to be "expressing" anything to anyone. Sometimes

---

[7]If you happen to be using a communication book or picture exchange cards or anything lose-able or destroy-able like that, you should have several duplicate sets and they should be everywhere. You might even want to affix said books/cards to the child in some manner that does not involve duct tape or superglue. Good luck if you're using an Alpha smart or one of those other highly breakable/expensive/battery operated devices that costs more than most people's cars. If it's functional for the child, great, but those devices have numerous down sides. You might want to think about an iPad (not yours) enclosed in aa protective cover such as Otterbox, Kraken, or Big Grips, but it should be kept charged and always within reach of the child.

when you get irritated you just wanna break stuff. This frustration is often a result of blocked access to reinforcement/extinction. Is it possible that the behavior might get reinforced by an adult who comes over to render assistance? Sure, but it doesn't always happen like that. There are some children whose aggression might *never* be reinforced by gaining access to a desired item, but it can still occur as a reaction to aversive stimulation—it's what we do. Similarly, self-stimulation that may also be self-injurious (skin picking) does not typically serve a communication function.

Now although I agree with my friend Dr. McGreevy on most things, I will make a departure for a moment. It isn't *always* "all about the mands." This is especially true for higher functioning children who know how to ask for just about everything. In that case the quote might be "enough with the mands already!" Some children have problems not simply because they don't know how to request things, but because they don't know how to handle it when the answer is "No!" Now Dr. McGreevy might point out (and I think he'd be correct) that when faced with a situation when your mand is met with a "no," most of us will then mand for *information* on *how and when* we can get what we want. In the worst case scenario, the child has learned to ask the dreaded "why" question, which is both a mand for information and a one-way ticket to crazy-town for the adult. After about the tenth "why" you're starting to think that the screwdriver slicing into your hand wasn't really so bad after all. Remember, knowing what to ask for is not the only thing that prevents behavior problems, but it is vitally important (it's necessary, but not sufficient). You still need to be able to... what's the scientific term? Ah yes, *keep your &@!$ together*! I'll speak more about the skills involved in "handling things" a bit later in the chapter.

SECTION 5: INDEPENDENT REPERTOIRES

OMG, there are so many kids out there who either can't or won't do something by themselves to save their lives. Good thing their lives don't depend on it! Well, in a way, their lives *do* depend on it. The consequences of not being able to do something by yourself and for yourself are significant and far-reaching. This is particularly a problem for children whose behavior is maintained at least in part by attention. There are a couple of subtypes here—children who won't do something by themselves, and those who simply can't. Those who won't don't necessarily outright refuse the request to do something independently, but they might find it difficult to stay by themselves without seeking attention from an adult. Those who can't do things by themselves are heavily prompt-dependent or simply don't have the skills necessary to complete a given task independently. These children are not necessarily running to the adults, but they will not complete the task/activity because when the adults leave the motivation to finish leaves with them! I have seen many children who can work wonderfully with adults next to them, but who completely stop working and/or fall apart when the adults move away, even just a few feet. The two big categories of independent repertoires that I look for are play (leisure) and academic repertoires.

5.1 Independent play

Especially for younger children, or those functioning at a lower level, it's important that the child can play by herself, and by play I mean something other than the simplest form of self-stimulation. That is, I don't count string twirling as independent play. Children who can't even play by themselves are a terrific drain on resources and on their parents. Some parents can't get a moment to themselves because their children can't stay engaged without the participation of an adult. I realize that we're talking about school here and that children don't really come to school to play, but usually the younger ones do get some time with toys, so it's not entirely unheard of. I'm concerned about a child's ability to play by herself because if she won't engage in independent play (something enjoyable), why on earth would she do academic work independently? Call me crazy, but that just makes sense to me.

I know some kids who won't even sit and watch a video for ten minutes, not that watching a video is really "play" any more than hand flapping is play, but at least it's something more appropriate that they can do by themselves. If you're having difficulty getting a student to work independently, see if you can get him to play independently first. For younger or lower functioning children, this means you might try having them play with with toys, while you might try having older or higher functioning students play with educational computer games. At least if a child can play independently, it's easier to fade in instructional control to make the play time a bit more academic in nature. A child with good receptive skills may be able to follow an instruction to play in a certain way, e.g., "Make me a race car with the Legos and come get me when you're done. Make sure to use all the pieces!" Now play is becoming a bit more like getting an assignment, but it's still Legos and not math.

Naturally, if someone is going to play by themselves they are going to need to know *how* to play with something properly and this may take some doing for those children with extremely impoverished repertoires. Remember that, for some children, you may need to use tangible reinforcers (food or preferred items) to even teach them to play with something appropriately unless they're absolutely fascinated with the materials that you've chosen. Puzzles are very popular and the difficulty can be changed easily according to the number of pieces and whether they fit into a frame. No, puzzles don't really "go anywhere" academically, but the idea here is independent functioning.

If you're going for independence, it's a good idea to go for something with a discrete beginning and end so that the student can see a finished product of some sort. When the student is finished, he can call an adult over who can then praise the behavior of task completion. It will also be necessary to not only fade out prompting, but to fade your *physical proximity*, which can be difficult if you're not sure how to do it. If the child can be prompted verbally, then you can begin to move away, but you can still use verbal prompting and praise to keep him going even as you move further away. Being able to keep a child on task (be it work or play) from a distance with only verbal prompts is a *huge* step in the right direction. I know many children who exist in a "prompting black hole" that is exactly four feet in diameter. When you go beyond their "event horizon" your prompts don't get sucked in, but instead go flying off into space. It's just an astrophysics way to say that stimulus control breaks down with increasing distances.

When teaching a child to do something independently, especially if her behavior is motivated by attention, it's very important to show that completing the task brings the adult back, and *not* the problem behavior. We want task completion to be reinforced by bringing an adult closer. Typically developing children with no behavior problems will quickly and easily shout out "come see what I did!" when they've finished something that they want to show off. We need to get children with special needs to do the same thing to the greatest extent possible. Initially, you might just have the child complete the last few steps of a playtime activity so that she is not doing anything by herself for too long. If you have only moved away during the last ten seconds of the activity, you can move back again the moment the child finishes. Finishing a task can quickly become a means of getting adults to come pay attention (as long as the adults are aware that the child has finished).

5.2   Independent academics

For those children who can already play by themselves, we want to get them to work by themselves to the greatest extent possible. It's a good idea to start with one of the easier academic tasks first. The fading can be done just as outlined above. The biggest difference is that the motivation to stay and complete the task might be quite a bit lower because this isn't play anymore. Therefore it will probably be necessary to increase the magnitude and immediacy of reinforcement for task completion and then fade very slowly. For example, if the child is doing handwriting, back up from his desk when he is writing the last four words of a sentence, then come closer again when he completes it. You can also crank the attention way down while you are next to the child prompting him, and then crank it way up when you return after completion of the task. Sometimes I'll suggest that the teacher avoid eye contact and just point at the assignment as a prompt and save the really good eye contact for the independent completion of the task (even if it was only independent for a matter of seconds). Many, many doors will open up for a child who can complete assignments independently and the importance of this ability should never be underestimated. You want to focus your attention on independent completion and not so much all the other behaviors that may occur during the task.

As an example, I knew a kid who would sort of work independently, but he would keep on popping up out of his seat like a Meerkat, and start walking over to the teacher to ask questions. He would also ask questions from his seat that were irrelevant or those for which he already knew the answer. This particular teacher just told him to do the ones he could do and then instructed him to call her over when he was done with those. This way she could approach after the completion of at least some of the items and give praise accordingly. Afterwards, she would assist him with the problems that were more difficult. I believe that many children have difficulty working independently because their rate of social reinforcement plummets when the teacher moves away, so they will often misbehave to boost it back up again. As mentioned, you can counteract this problem by decreasing social reinforcement in the middle of the task (when you have to come back to prompt) and then boost your interactions after task completion. Usually you see really great interactions up close when the task has *not yet* been completed and there are also great interactions during the prompting. Think about it. If a child needs a teacher to help him five times during a ten minute task, that's one interaction every two minutes. If the child completes the entire assignment, that results in just one interaction at the end so it really needs to be a damn good one!

Giving higher quality praise while right next to someone is not so much a teacher problem, as I believe that it's something *we all tend to do*. It's hard to be sincere and personal with somebody from across the room. Usually we get close and put a hand on the person's shoulder to project sincerity and concern. In this particular case, however, it may backfire and make it more difficult for the child to start completing tasks independently. Remember, you can still get close and be sincere, but save it for the task completion. Try to be more like a robot (neutral) when prompting and become human again the moment the task is completed. Does it make sense? Yeah? Later on you can get into differentially reinforcing successively longer durations of independent work. You went one minute (independently) you get one minute of computer time, you went five minutes you get five minutes of computer time, etc. Children must have a good reason to finish work independently because, for some of them, it is very difficult.

SECTION 6: OTHER KEY REPERTOIRES

6.1 Social repertoires with adults

I separate social repertoires into those with adults and those with children primarily because some children don't really orient toward other children and instead orient toward adults. As mentioned previously, many children access their reinforcers primarily through adults because, in many instances, other children do nothing but cause them grief. I have worked with many children, typically lower functioning, who just don't know what to do with a grown-up. A child who loves attention, but doesn't know how to engage an adult is going to come up with their own special interactive repertoire and it's not going to be pretty, I can assure you. There are two fundamental types of problems: Summoning adults and then engaging them once they've arrived. Many children can approach adults just fine, but those kids do not know how to (appropriately) get an adult to approach them. It's possible that some children truly don't know how, or they technically could, but the behavior has been *extinguished* or *punished*. This is partly a communication problem, especially regarding summoning the adult, but once a child knows how to get an adult to come over to him, sustaining the interactions becomes more of a *repertoire problem*. From the kid's point of view, it's like, "Okay, I've got you here, now what do I do with you?" I knew one child in particular who just loved to grab your hair. He wasn't being particularly aggressive, in fact, he was usually smiling when he did it. The adults would contort their faces and generally freak out and jump around and he seemed to think it was great fun. The big problem was not the hair pulling, although his teacher would have begged to differ I'm sure. The big problem was that he possessed exactly zero ways to engage an adult who was next to him. I believe that we had some limited success with having the teacher clip a short length of rope to her belt loop and she prompted the kid to grab the rope when he went for her hair. It helped, but then again the real problem wasn't addressed, which was the lack of a repertoire for playing with adults. He needed something that was easy and fun that produced a big reaction. Furthermore, he didn't just need one thing to do, he needed *lots of things to do*, but you have to start with something reasonably quick and easy to teach and then teach other skills later. So many very young children, typically developing children, know dozens and dozens of things to do with adults. They can talk to them, sing with them, play peek-a-boo, ask to be tickled, play simple games with them and show them things. These interactions can be either rehearsed skills or spontaneous interactions. A child with a severely impoverished repertoire like my hair-pulling buddy would need to learn very clear-cut, rehearsed, interactive kinds of skills and they would have to be carefully taught. I think that we really do take for granted the staggering number of social skills that kids learn that are not formally taught.

Many people get stumped when a child's behavior has been identified as "attention maintained" because I will hear phrases like, "I'm already giving him attention, he has my attention, then out of the blue he starts hitting me!" Now if that scenario sounds familiar, it may very well be that the child is hitting for the same reasons that another child might tell you a knock-knock joke. The main difference is that the aggressive child doesn't know any knock-knock jokes, or any other jokes, or at least the only joke he knows has no setup and the punch line actually consists of punching. Remember, attention comes in more flavors than Skittles, and even though we may have someone's attention, the child may still like to be able to *increase the magnitude* of that attention. How will a child with almost no skills increase the magnitude of adult attention? Easy. Do something that makes the adult wince. There's many ways to do that, and most of them are not very nice. My point is that children, especially those with few or no social skills, need to be taught a set of things to do with an adult that are really fun and highly interactive. These skills will most likely be chosen based on the child's developmental level and the presence or absence of language. In many instances, the child just wants to play, but he really doesn't know how to and he doesn't know what the rules are. If the child is not taught a set of skills that can be used to engage an adult, then the prognosis for the behavior problem (if it is an attention-based problem) is not good. Incidentally, my friend Steve Ward has a simply fantastic book on teaching games to children with disabilities called *What You Need to Know About Motivation and Teaching Games: An In-Depth Analysis*, and you may find it at http://www.lulu.com/shop/steven-ward/what-you-need-to-know-about-motivation-and-teaching-games-an-in-depth-analysis/paperback/product-15549283.html.

6.2 Social repertoires with other children

Depending on the skills of the child's peers, it may be best to focus only on skills with adults and then work with the peers later. Remember that the child's peers may not be very socially competent and may also exhibit significant behavior problems. Of course, we do want kids to be able to interact appropriately with other children, but if Whitney can't interact appropriately with adults who have better skills than peers and are (in most cases) well behaved, good luck getting her to interact appropriately with her peers. Once the child can have some good interactions with an adult, it should be *easier* to transfer those interactions to reasonably competent peers. First, you might want to establish that the child in question actually likes and seeks out the company of other children, because many kids don't. Typically, you can find at least one peer in the classroom who the child likes and then try to get some good interactions going with that peer. I suppose it would make sense to teach the child at least some social skills that could be used with an adult or with a peer who may have very few skills, like playing catch or taking turns manipulating a toy. What about higher functioning children who can talk? They may have gaps in their social repertoires as well. Very often the problem with older/high functioning children is not so much that they don't know how to do anything, but that they may not like their peers very much because their peers have the same kinds of behavioral excesses and deficits that they have. Remember, adults are (typically) quite civil, polite, patient, and understanding. Many kids with disabilities can be the exact opposite. Some higher functioning, verbally fluent kids *do like* to interact with their peers, but their interactions may be mostly inflammatory in nature, to put it mildly. Higher functioning children can be taught conversational skills and how to be helpful to others. They can also be taught how to give compliments to other students, how to cooperate, and how to appropriately get and then keep the attention of other children. It's critical that the child in question truly likes the other student(s). This is the basis for wanting to engage in all of these "pro-social" behaviors in the first place. I talked about some of these issues in Chapter 6 on problems with peers (pages 131–132), and those variables apply to teaching social repertoires as well.

6.3 Academic repertoires

Kids need the appropriate academic repertoires, and to know what's appropriate they need proper assessment, and that assessment has to be translated into appropriate IEP goals. Many behavior problems are (at least in part) attributable to a lack of academic skills in general or a lack of some fairly specific ones that snowball into other areas of the child's education. Many children are unsuccessful in school (special needs or otherwise) because they lack the proper repertoires or the repertoires exist but aren't strong enough to be functional. One of the biggest problems I've seen (which absolutely contributes to behavior problems) is when a child is put into an "included" classroom with such a complete lack of the academic skills needed to benefit from the curriculum that they are, in essence, in the classroom just to "be in the classroom." I'll address this educational travesty (great word if you need to sound self-righteous) in Chapter 11 on problems with inclusion.

Arguably the most fundamental academic skills are, in order of importance, communication skills and reading. True, communication is not technically an academic skill, but it's a skill that's critical for acquiring other academic skills. For children who can already communicate quite well, reading is the next hurdle in fundamentals. Except for, perhaps, math, everything else is dependent on reading skills. Although there are numerous reasons for reading difficulty, I have seen two broad subclasses of problems in reading. There is reading aloud with little or no comprehension of what's being read (which qualifies one to become a television anchor on the evening news—Walter Cronkite excluded) and reading in which the comprehension is not too bad, but the child's words per minute are so low that the reading is both very difficult and essentially nonfunctional. It's a bit of an overgeneralization perhaps, but you'll usually find more of the comprehension problems in many children with incomplete language skills, and more of the fluency problems in children who have much better overall language skills but are simply poor readers. Many children with poor or incomplete language development can decode (sound out words) quite well, but because their conversational language often suffers, their comprehension is quite often very poor. Either way, the child is going to hit a wall academically if his comprehension or reading fluency is poor. I would make the argument that if the language is good and the reading is good that everything else can be brought up to speed fairly rapidly. Still, assessment is the key. I have been in some classrooms in which I have asked teachers about the child's reading grade level and sometimes they say that they don't know. Shouldn't we know the reading level of the kids we're working with?

Regarding academic success, the skills of asking for information and answering academic types of questions are among the most important skills a child can learn. Just like the ability to read, these skills will greatly enhance all subsequent learning. I don't mean that these verbal skills are the first skills to master, but that they cannot be overlooked.

Okay—here comes the short course on Verbal Behavior. Really short. I won't go into detail because there are experts in the field who are far better than I at describing Skinner's analysis of language. I'm just going to mention three classes of "verbal operants" (language behaviors, if you will). There are mands (asking for things), tacts (naming things), and the more sophisticated, intraverbals (answering questions about things in which the words in the answer do not necessarily reflect the words in the question or any currently visible object). Mands are a "must" for children to master so that language becomes useful to them—something that they want to do and not a chore. Tacts are less useful from a "meeting your needs" perspective, but are great for some academics and if you love hearing "That's right! That *is* a giraffe!" They will only get you so far academically, however. Intraverbals are where many children fall flat. That is, when shown a picture of a bed and you say, "What's this?" the child can say, "Bed," which is a tact. However, when asked, "What do you sleep in?" The child looks at you the same way you would look at me if I asked you to describe the inner workings of the Large Hadron Collider. Children with poorly developed or absent intraverbal repertoires (and these repertoires can be vast and complex for the typically developing child) may make it through some of the simpler academic stuff (rote counting, numbers/letters/shapes/color identification, addition and subtraction and even some reading), but they will fall behind their peers at an *exponential rate* if their intraverbal repertoires are not properly built up. This intraverbal problem can be frustrating for parents because without that repertoire you can still learn quite a bit of stuff, but the longer the intraverbal repertoire remains unaddressed, the larger the educational facade that is built up around the child. Sadly, this facade comes crashing down quickly as the child progresses from pre-K to kindergarten to the first grade. Many children with a range of developmental disorders can do simple addition, but when you start into word problems you can quickly see that the emperor has no clothes, and trust me, it's not pretty. Frankly, I myself had many problems with word problems as I was too distracted by the various premises. "If Mary wants to visit her friend Jimmy and she lives twenty blocks from Jimmy and if it takes her five minutes to walk one block…." Wait a second, you mean to tell me that Mary's mom is so busy attending her spinning class that she can't take the time to drive her daughter to a friend's house? And just who is this Jimmy guy anyhow, and why isn't he out playing with the other boys? Yes, word problems contain a number of unanswered questions. Anyhow, "Intraverbals; don't leave pre-K without them." So very many academic tasks require extensive intraverbal repertoires, and these repertoires, along with the questions that prompt them, only become more complex and abstract as the child progresses through her education. What does a cow say? What do you sleep in? What is the capitol of Peru? What is the difference between the mean, median, and mode? What does it mean to *you* to be an American? What can go up a chimney down, but can't go down a chimney up?[8]

I know what you're wondering. So how exactly, Dr. Winston, do you link the lack of academic repertoires to behavior problems? First, thank you for using my correct title, and second, properly developed repertoires will make the child more successful in the classroom, and it's all about competence. I mentioned earlier that we tend to like doing things we're good at and tend to avoid things that we aren't good at. I think that everyone can agree with that sentence. Children lacking the proper repertoires cannot functionally participate in what the other children are doing and might therefore be more motivated to escape from that activity and engage in behavior that will produce at least some reinforcement. You can see this sort of problem very frequently with children labeled as "emotionally disturbed." I'm not entirely certain of which emotion is disturbing them the most, but it seems to me that they spend an inordinate amount of time disturbing the emotions of all the other children around them. I have seen numerous scenarios where the teacher asks a question, and only one or two children are able to answer. Those who can't will often make snide remarks and try to distract the teacher from the subject or even engage in more serious problem behaviors.

---

[8]An umbrella.

Very often, the child I am observing during a consultation performs academically well below his peers. Even if, for the sake of argument, he were motivated enough to attempt an answer he would most likely struggle because of skill deficits (like an almost complete inability to read). I have seen other children who would readily complete a math worksheet of simple fraction addition, but would engage in problem behavior when presented with word problems. Remember, most of us will tend to escape from or avoid things that are difficult and/or unfamiliar to us. However, we won't (typically) engage in dangerous behaviors as a result of being faced with these tasks, but children with disabilities very often will. This is why in Chapter 3 on aversives I talked about asking a number of "why" questions to understand the nature of an aversive task. As mentioned previously, there are a number of reasons why a task might acquire aversive properties, but a frequent problem is that the child is either completely lacking a key repertoire or it's very weak, which makes the task difficult at best.

6.4   Classroom readiness repertoires

This is a bit of a double-edged sword really, so I'll be mindful of where I'm wielding it. I don't believe that any parents like the thought of a professional telling them that their child isn't ready for movement to a less restrictive classroom setting. There are many skills that, believe it or not, are not measured by a standard "no child left behind" test. It's a fact that children can learn even if they are not sitting, and there is no evidence that sitting crisscross-applesauce[9] leads to higher scholastic achievement and better paying jobs. Blurting out the answer during a history lesson doesn't make you any less smart, as long as the answer is correct. Furthermore, getting mad because you couldn't be the line leader and tearing the calendar off the wall doesn't directly affect your GPA. However, like the VISA card, if you can show all the appropriate classroom readiness behaviors, you will be accepted by more people in more places. True, we don't want children who *can* essentially do the same work as their peers to have to prove themselves worthy of placement in a classroom with typically developing peers, but if a child is missing enough of these support skills there are going to be some major disruptions in the classroom. I'll talk more about this issue in the chapter on inclusion, but let me be clear that I'm not proposing that we keep children separated from their peers because of a lack of these readiness skills. We cannot neglect, however, to actively, systematically teach these readiness skills just as we teach other academics. All too often, special education teachers will accept behavior that a regular education teacher will not. Don't get me wrong, I'm not saying that special education teachers are doing something bad or wrong. I'm just saying that those teachers are *accustomed* to these kinds of disruptive behaviors and are less concerned about them on the whole because, quite frankly, they

---

[9]For the uninformed, "crisscross applesauce" is sitting with one's legs folded and crossed over and is often demanded of small children during circle-time. Long ago, when I was a child, we used to call it "Indian Style," but that term was deemed racially offensive and was changed to crisscross applesauce because apparently no one really cares about offending apple farmers.

have bigger fish to fry. Still, we cannot teach what we have not taken the time to analyze. If you don't know what support skills a child needs to be successful in a room with more peers and less teacher attention, then how can you teach those skills? Just a little something to think about. I'll give some specific examples of these classroom readiness skills (school-house survival skills) in Chapter 11 on problems with inclusion, and trust me, there are some problems....

SECTION 7: COPING AND "SELF-CONTROL" REPERTOIRES

Remember in Chapter 2 on problems with dangerous reinforcers when I said we'd talk more about self-control and coping skills? Well, here we are. There are all kinds of skills kids can learn, and certainly none of the ones I have covered are unimportant. However, in terms of behavior problems (and that's what the book is about) all those skills are, in my opinion, less important than coping and self-control skills. By coping skills, I'm talking about those skills that let you handle the curve balls that life throws at you. Except for the most fortunate among us who live charmed lives that were lifted from the pages of your most beloved fairy tale, life is a patchwork quilt of wrong turns, major disappointments, flat tires, failures, late fees, and frustrations that are all stitched together with a delicate thread of triumph, elation and the occasional hot fudge sundae; kind of like reading this book. Simply not having academic skills doesn't make children bang their heads, flip desks, and bite the teacher. Also, in some sense, getting angry isn't the problem either. We *all* get angry. The question is, "What do you do when you get angry?" Nobody gets a behavior program because they get angry. Angry alone isn't enough to be a problem. Another good question is, "What do you do *to keep from getting angry in the first place*?" Finally, "What do you do to keep from doing the things that you shouldn't do?" These last two questions get at what most people call "self-control." I put self-control in quotes because I view it as nothing more than behavior we engage in to avoid getting into trouble, which is how the brilliant Dr. Charles Catania explains it (Catania, 1975). Catania single-handedly debunked the myth of self-reinforcement as well as any other behavior that begins with the prefix "self." His main argument was that we are truly controlled by the contingencies around us, but that we learn to engage in behavior that helps us satisfy those contingencies. The point is that we don't "make ourselves" keep quiet in a meeting. It is, rather, the past consequences and the current events that control our behavior. People who can handle disappointment gracefully are generally seen as well adjusted. People who can't handle *any* disappointments are going to be seen as poorly adjusted, not to mention that they're going to be pretty miserable. Can you roll with the punches or do you try to fight every fight? I have been listening to people's descriptions of why behavior happens for nearly 25 years, and I can tell you that one of the most frequently cited reasons for behavior problems is as follows:

"HE DOESN'T LIKE IT WHEN HE CAN'T GET HIS WAY!"

No kidding? Really? He doesn't like it when he can't get his way? How dare he! I always say the following when someone tells me this, "Do you really like it when *you* can't get *your* way?" The person then laughs and says, "No." Again, the question is, "What do you *tend to do* and what do you *know how to do* when you can't get your way?" For many people with disabilities, the answer is that they have a major meltdown. Children need to know what to do when things break, when they don't get exactly what they want, when they are told "no," when they have to wait for something, and when they are so angry that they don't know what to do with themselves. We all experience these problems. We all get disappointed, we all get stymied, we all get so mad we're afraid of what we might do. Unfortunately, certain children with disabilities may not be afraid of what they might do; they are all too often busy doing it! Many behavior problems occur because of things kids want that they can't get (blocked access to reinforcement) and because of the presence of aversives that kids do not know how to respond to appropriately. First, let's look at some of the skills that can help address blocked access conditions.

7.1 Blocked access

 If, according to Harry Nilsson, "One" is the loneliest number, then "no" has got to be the most irritating word. We really don't like hearing "no" unless it is preceded by the query "do these pants make my butt look big?" Children have to understand what to do when something is denied. Many children with behavior problems will immediately resort to aggression, self-injury, or property destruction on being informed that no reinforcement this way cometh. I very frequently teach people to use the "yes but" or the "yes as soon as" strategy mentioned in Chapter 3 on aversives, but I also mentioned that *eventually* the child should learn how to deal with a "hard no." For children with good verbal skills, we can teach them to ask for information that the adult neglected to supply. We must teach them to ask questions like:

Why can't I?

When can I?

What can I do to get it?

Can I have something else until then?

Can I just have a little bit?

Can I just see it?

Can I use it for just a little while?

Can I get it in writing and can you cc: my attorney?

Okay, the last bullet is for *much* higher functioning students but you get the drift, right? Adults are typically peppered with all of those questions, and many more, from typically developing students. It's just a matter of time before you find yourself in a precarious unplanned situation where you have to say, "No!" Instead of allowing the child to be caught off guard like this, it's much better to contrive a number of "No!" situations throughout the day that quickly turn into "yes" situations. That is, purposefully create a condition (contrive it) that will make a child ask for something, deny it, and give him the opportunity to handle the denial gracefully. Naturally, you have to be very specific about what "gracefully" means, e.g., take deep breaths, sit down, and ask good questions about when and how you can get your way. You might also arrange for a small amount of reinforcement for "handling the news" appropriately. Think about it from the kid's perspective. What's in it for me for *keeping it together* when told no?

Much of this can be done by rehearsing with the child, and showing him what he should do (pre-correction), before the event ever happens. One child I know of successfully used this question asking skill after rehearsing it with his behavior analyst. He saw a muffin in a store and said, "Can I have that muffin?" and Mom gave him a "hard" no. "No, you're eating dinner soon!" Without missing a beat he said, "Can I just have a small piece?" Hallelujah! (insert sound of choir of angels singing). Mom then said, "Why yes, you certainly can have a small piece!" The other skill that falls under this section of being denied things is learning to accept reasonable alternatives.

7.2   Accepting reasonable alternatives

Stephen Stills, of Crosby, Stills, and Nash said it best. "When you can't be with the one you love, honey, love the one you're with." I'm not sure if his message was more about the inevitability of marital infidelity or that you had better learn how to lower your expectations. Children are born and there are, naturally, many things they can't do. They even have to learn how to find their own feet, which is something you might have to relearn as an adult if you can't learn to stay away from the breakfast buffet. Another thing children have to learn is how to accept alternatives. Handling disappointment well often involves accepting less desirable alternatives. Now true enough, even well adjusted adults in some circumstances are taught to never settle for less! For all of us, there are certain situations in which we will refuse to compromise. However, if you *can never* accept a lesser alternative, you're going to be pretty miserable, and those around you won't be too happy, either. I like to view accepting alternatives as a skill. At first you're not very good at it, but you can certainly get better at it given enough opportunities. Like so many skills that help prevent severe behavior problems, the opportunities to learn those skills must be *carefully contrived* so that there can be immediate successful outcomes. That said, the time to teach accepting reasonable alternatives is *not* when little Jimmy is dying for a piece of chocolate and you want him to accept pretzels. Here are some steps that I use when teaching accepting reasonable alternatives:

1. Have a *very* similar alternative ready and waiting to be given that the child doesn't know about yet. For example, if she loves a particular soda, have a soda that is almost identical, but not quite the same.

2. Give enough of the item to take the edge off. As an example, I was teaching a person to accept an alternate to coffee (not a kid), but I didn't propose an alternative until he had already had two cups (decaf) and he had calmed down quite a bit. It helps if you're using something that runs out, that is, the person needs to ask for more of it so you can offer the alternative.

3. After the individual is just partially satiated, tell him (if verbal) "I'm sorry but I can't find any more. How about some of this (alternative) until I can find some more?"

4. Reinforce acceptance of the alternative by "suddenly" finding more of the item that the child really wanted. So the child eats a piece of sub-optimal chocolate and, magically, you find more of his favorite kind.

Naturally, this may not work the first few times, but the odds can be increased based on the degree of similarity between the highly prized item and the substitute item *and* how close the child is to a satiation point. So, for example, let's say that Bobby gets tired of eating Goldfish crackers after about thirty of them. You can give him just twenty and then "run out of them." The idea here is that the child still has to want them at least a little bit, but you want to catch him when the motivation to get the item is much lower than when he first asks for it. After a long history of getting better things after accepting "less good" things you can get to the point where the less preferred of two items will be accepted when the more preferred is simply unavailable. For a child who is verbal, you can couple this strategy with teaching them how to ask for a hierarchy of alternatives, but to do this the child must be familiar with a variety of items and be able to ask for them. For example, let's take a look at the example below.

Child: "Can I have Skittles?"

Teacher: "We don't have any"

Child: "How about Nerds?"

Teacher: "Sorry"

Child: "Sour gummy worms?"

Teacher: "Nope"

Child: "What about a Jolly Rancher?"

Teacher: "Why yes I do have some of those!"

It may take time to get there, but a child who can mand can be taught to do this. The problem is that, for many children, they must be specifically taught or they may never develop the skill. Some of the other coping skills to work on are asking for help, learning how to wait, and learning how to handle reinforcer removal. There are great examples of how to approach these skills in Chapter 3 on aversives. Finally, please remember that in teaching anything that falls under the category of coping skills, you really have to teach clusters of skills and not just a single replacement behavior. If the single replacement behavior doesn't work, everyone falls back on his or her old reliable problem behavior. Teaching clusters of alternate forms of the same class of behaviors helps "bulletproof" children against multiple unsuccessful outcomes as outlined in the previous example. What if the child could only ask for Nerds and that was his only option? No Nerds + no skills at asking for and choosing alternatives = behavior problems. Everyone needs a back-up plan and children need back up behaviors, lots of them.

Chapter 8

Teaching And Curriculum Problems

Error Prevention\Correction
    Pre-Corrective Prompting
    Error Prevention
    Error Correction
Student To Teacher Ratio
    Independent Work
    One-on-One Instruction
    Small Group Instruction
    Lecture Style Large-Group Instruction

SECTION 1: INTRODUCTION

> Those who can't do, teach. Those who can't teach, teach gym. And, uh, those who couldn't do anything, I think, were assigned to our school.
>
> —Woody Allen (*Annie Hall*)

I'm not sure what people do when they can't teach gym. Maybe they become an administrator (rimshot), but the ones who *can* teach gym are most certainly really angry and looking for me. Now teachers, before you start the hate mail, I would like to remind Woody Allen that teaching IS doing, and teaching well is one of the most challenging and rewarding things a person can do. Also, I know people who know many things and can talk the talk, but still couldn't teach a starving cat to eat chicken. Teaching people with behavior problems can be very challenging, and poor teaching can make these problems worse. As I'm sure you're starting to see, many variables contribute to behavior problems, which can make treatment a tough go at best. Two of the most important contributing variables in school settings are *curriculum* and *teaching*. To the extent that one misses the mark, it can make the other more challenging.

Allow me to illustrate with what I call the "Matrix of Education" or just MOE.[1]

Matrix of Education! (MOE)		
	Right Curriculum	*Wrong Curriculum*
Good teaching	1	2
Um… not so good teaching	3	4

---

[1] In the audio book I want to get Michael Buffer to say, "Maaaaatriiiiiiix of Edu-caaaaaaaa-tion!" You know, he's the guy that says, "Let's get ready to rumble!" Either him or the racetrack guy who used to say, "Sunday! Sunday! Sunday!"

First, let me say that this is not meant to be a "teacher slam." As I said when we started this shindig, there are good behavior analysts and bad behavior analysts and there are good teachers and bad teachers. It's just the way it goes. The good news is that everyone can be better if they want to be. In this matrix, number 1 is what you're shooting for, but, for many students, number 4 is what they actually get. Numbers 2 and 3 are somewhere in the middle. I'm somewhat reluctant to say which is worse, number 2 (teaching the wrong thing really well) or number 3 (teaching the right thing poorly) as it depends on the extent of the teacher's skill and the degree of mismatch between the child's abilities and the curriculum. I imagine that in the case of number 3, if the child is very interested in the curriculum, the teaching may be a bit less critical because the motivation to learn may be fairly high. With good teaching of the wrong thing, number 2, you can only go so far, but you may get there faster if that makes any sense at all. That is, let's say that you are teaching two-digit multiplication to a child with limited verbal skills but good math skills. If the verbal skills are not addressed (wrong curriculum) the child will eventually become completely lost when it comes down to more sophisticated math that involves word problems (as mentioned in Chapter 7). I have to address both curriculum and teaching in this chapter, however, so let's start with curriculum.

SECTION 2: CURRICULUM PROBLEMS

Just in case this wasn't clear, I am not an educational curriculum specialist. In fact I would probably be the one teaching physical education to the educational curriculum specialists. I do, however, have some general understanding of the developmental progression, and which skills are more important for mastering other more complex skills. I also understand the difference between skills that are rote and those that are functional. Let me be clear that when I'm referring to curriculum. I don't really mean the type of reading program being selected like the SRA, Hooked on Phonics, or Headsprout Reading Basics. When I talk about problems with curriculum I mean problems in educational skill selection—e.g., should we be teaching Johnny how to spell when he can't communicate functionally? So I'm talking about skills to be acquired and not so much the program that arranges those skills in some kind of standardized format.

Curriculum is often taught not because the child is in any sense ready for it, but because of the state standards, what other similar-aged children are doing, what we believe that he or she could possibly learn in a year's time, or because the parents insist that certain academic skills be included in the IEP. Stated another way, especially for persons with fewer skills (including language) the issue is really one of "*why* are we teaching skill X, and is *now* the right time to be teaching it?" As mentioned in Chapter 3 on aversives, many children who are primarily nonverbal are being taught how to write their names. Why? What are they going to do with this skill? Will it truly help them acquire other academic skills? Think about it for a moment. What was your vocabulary like before you knew how to write your name? By the time you were about four, you probably had a vocabulary of somewhere around 1500 words and could put them together in sentences, but you still didn't know how to write your name. You know, there are many good ways to get bitten by children with behavior problems. One of the premier ways is to try to teach a child to write his name when he has no functional language. It would be like you moving to Japan and learning the symbols for writing your name before you learned how to ask for food, water, and where the closest bathroom could be found. Why are we spending valuable educational time teaching a child how to write her name when she has absolutely no good reason (from her point of view) to write it? Furthermore, she has not mastered the myriad of skills that typically developing children have already mastered. Remember, many of the skills that we teach typically developing children can be taught quickly and easily and we already have *willing learners*, so in most cases it really doesn't matter if the skill "makes sense" or not (discussed in Chapter 3 on Aversives). My point is that, for individuals with more severe impairments, the selection of skills to be taught at school is highly critical because of: 1) a poor learning history; and 2) the lack of what the brilliant Steve Ward refers to as " good learner repertoires."[2]

For children with more mild impairments, who have a multitude of skills, but *also* display significant behavior problems, the selection of academic skills is far less critical. This is because these children can typically learn more rapidly and already have a good base on which we can build new repertoires. Curriculum is not typically the biggest problem for these children in terms of challenging behavior. For these individuals, it's usually the lack of coping repertoires (Chapter 7) that causes problems. By far, the biggest problem I've seen is the selection of traditional academic goals for children with little or no functional language. In my opinion, job number one is the acquisition of functional language, and everything else can be put on the back burner. Is learning to read or how to write your name or how to label shapes and colors bad? No, not at all...if you already have well developed language. These aren't bad things to teach in any absolute sense, but for some children they may not be the best things to teach *right now*.

The selection of proper curriculum depends on proper assessment. Proper assessment requires the proper instruments, the proper assessor, and a cooperative student. It's not simply a matter of determining what the child can't do and then teaching those things in order of difficulty, although sometimes I believe that this is exactly what has been done. The selection of the proper curriculum is not always an easy task, but it is vitally important if a child is going to make good progress. Pertaining to children with more severe deficits, I believe that we should be focusing on the most basic skills that make teaching traditional skills possible and functional. For so many children I work with, the biggest problem goes beyond the selection of curriculum. The problem is that those children don't like the teach-

---

[2]The website is http://www.lulu.com/us/en/shop/steven-ward/the-inventory-of-good-learner-repertoires/paperback/product-5302695.html if you would like to buy his assessment.

ing *situation* at all. The selection of inappropriate academic goals makes a bad problem far worse. Remember, it isn't always the case that the behavior problem interferes with skill acquisition, but that the behavior is *produced by* the effort involved in acquiring the skill coupled with the child's inability to see the benefits of that skill. That is, there's no MO directly related to the task (nothing about it the child likes). Parents, you should be asking yourselves this question: "Is my child really better equipped to be a good learner after being taught how to _____?" You can fill in the blank with "count to 10" or "write his name" or "identify shapes." Is it better for the child to learn something out of sequence or something that has very little bang for the buck, educationally speaking (writing one's name), as opposed to learning nothing at all? Only if the child is a happy, willing participant. If the attempt to teach something is such a tremendous struggle that it turns the child off to teaching, then I would say it's better to focus on developing good rapport with the child while working on language and social development instead of traditional academics. The *rapid* mastery of a "splinter" skill (one that fails to act as an academic catapult), is much less of a problem than the r*epeated failed efforts* to teach that skill to an *unwilling learner*. In the first case the student learns a skill that may not be the best for building on later. In the second case teaching is just something that leaves a bad taste in the child's mouth. It's true enough that some kids may be unwilling learners the moment they get into a classroom. This problem will only be exacerbated by choosing the wrong curriculum. With the most severely escape motivated children, my usual recommendations are to temporarily stop all traditional academics and go back to square one and focus on functional language and reestablishing the teacher as a conditioned reinforcer (someone the child wants to run toward, not run away from, as Dr. Jim Partington likes to say). I am hesitant to use the phrase "ready to learn" because to some it may imply that the child has to graduate to a point where they are "allowed" to be educated. I guess that my three biggest questions are: 1) Can the child communicate his or her needs adequately; and 2) does the child have some basic skills that make teaching easier and more enjoyable for everyone (sitting, attending, allowing assistance, waiting, handling errors, cooperating with adults, following simple instructions, etc.); and 3) is the child generally motivated to learn? As mentioned previously, there are several behavioral curricula for language development and learner readiness skills[3] and I strongly recommend that IEP teams make use of one or more of these highly detailed inventories. The motivation to learn, can be a real sticking point and may continue to be a problem even when communication and basic skills have been addressed. If communication and basic skills are NOT taken care of, good luck with the whole motivation to learn issue—you're going to need it.

I mentioned that state standards are sometimes the driving force behind the selection of skills, and that this is less of a problem for children who learn better and faster than others.

[3]There is the Mark Sundberg's VB MAPP, Jim Partington's ABLLS-R, Steve Ward's IGLR, and an entire classroom system developed by Vicki Tucci called the Competent Learner Model (CLM) See Bibliography.

The difficulty lies in figuring out how to reconcile the needs of the state standards with the needs of a child who just isn't ready to start working on those standards. I think that the first standard that needs to be met is that *the student can be a student*. If states started to recognize the importance of placing the student in a good position to learn, then this could just become part of the educational standards for children with disabilities. I think we take for granted that there are some very good reasons why we wait for children to be of a certain age before sending them to school. If we sent them when too young, they very likely wouldn't be in a good position behaviorally or developmentally to be good students. The problem, however, is that children with special needs get sent to school because they are of the *proper age, even though* their overall development may be well behind that of their peers. Oh, I can see the angry blogs and emails now, "Dr. Winston said that children with intellectual disabilities should be kept at home until they're good and ready for school!" Everyone gets my drift though right? No, we shouldn't keep these children at home, but perhaps there needs to be better assessment of classroom readiness skills so that we can focus on those skills as opposed to traditional academics during the first few years of school. This is already done to some extent for typically developing children in pre-K and kindergarten classrooms to prepare them for the first grade. It might be important to have a parallel assessment for children with significant skill deficits and/or language impairments. My point is that putting different shaped blocks into a sorter doesn't prepare any child for *anything* (Thank you Dr. McGreevy). Learning to give up a reinforcer, follow an adult to another location, tolerate errors, wait for the delivery of a reinforcer, and allow hand-over hand prompting *does*. These kinds of skills, just to name a few, help to prepare a child to work well with teachers. The curriculum must be carefully targeted from day one. The greater the skill deficit, the more critical the specification of the curriculum.

SECTION 3: TEACHING PROBLEMS

As shown in MOE, good teaching can make the acquisition of a poorly selected skill easier and faster. Good teaching does far more than help children acquire skills quickly. Good teaching helps to create a child who loves to learn. Think about it—how many classes did you have where you weren't wild about the topic but you just loved the teacher. That person was able to transform something dry into something exciting because she was excited about it and so you got excited about it too. I, for example, got excited about behavior analysis because my very first teacher, Dr. Hank Pennypacker, was excited about behavior analysis (some might say a little too excited). By the time his first lecture was concluded I was sold. It wasn't just that it made perfect sense, which it did. It was that he was clearly excited about it and it didn't hurt that he was an excellent teacher. If you didn't have a good teacher, unless you were very good at the subject, the class may have been an educational death sentence. You may have dreaded the class because you didn't understand the significance of the subject, didn't get the material, didn't know exactly what was expected of you, and you feared failure (at least I did). I'll talk about the importance of good teachers as well when we come to the topic of inclusion in Chapter 11, but here's a sneak peek. Parents, the skills of the person who teaches your child and the skills that are taught to your child are *far more important* than the type of classroom (autism/EBD/regular ed) or the labels applied to the other children in the classroom. There. I said it. Sure there are a few caveats to add here and there, but it's just a sneak peek. Don't take it out of context yet. First read Chapter 11 and *then* take it out of context. There are numerous areas to examine when talking about good teaching, and this particular topic could be its own book or volume of books. Therefore I'm going to limit my discussion to those factors that I believe have the greatest influence on behavior problems during instruction. These factors are motivation, prompting, prompt fading, differential reinforcement, error prevention and error correction. Let's start with motivation and we'll look at other problems in the sections that follow.

3.1 Motivation

I've already talked extensively about reinforcer problems and motivation throughout the book, but here I'm not talking about the use of a specific reinforcer to strengthen a response, or the motivation to complete a certain task. Instead I'm more concerned with an overall picture of the learner. Does the child like his teacher? Does the child even want to be at school? I have seen many children, and regardless of the level of functioning, some of them just don't want to go into the classroom, don't like the teacher, and don't want to be at school. I've seen higher functioning children just sit in class and wait for it to be over. They don't want to be there and they don't want to interact with anyone; they're just waiting for the day to be over. Even if you use great teaching techniques, this can be a very difficult problem. As mentioned in earlier chapters, some kids just love being at school, and they even love their teachers, but they hate anything that smells like work. They're still better off than those students who just don't want to be at school. Anything that can be done to make school a more pleasant place will help with the general motivation to learn. I would have to say that the teacher is most likely the single greatest variable in determining how well the child likes the setting. Certainly there are other factors like the behavior of other students, the physical layout of the classroom, and even problems occurring in the home, but I would say that the relationship with the teacher carries the most weight. Let's face it, you'll put up with more things from a person you really like and your patience is very short with people you dislike. If the child likes the teacher, doesn't mind doing at least some things for the teacher, and likes pleasing the teacher, then we're halfway there. One of my first questions for teachers about a child with behavior problems is, "Does he like people?" After that I ask, "Does he like you?" Usually the kid does like his or her teacher, but not always. So let's say for the sake of argument that we have a child who, for the most part, likes being at school and likes his teacher and generally has a good relationship with him or her. The next things to look at are some components of good teaching.

SECTION 4: PROMPTING

Honestly, the biggest teaching problem I've seen in applied settings is not so much an inability to prompt. On the contrary, *it's an inability to fade prompts*, and this can be far more difficult than you might imagine. No matter what scheme you use for prompting (different folks use different schemes) learning is what we do as organisms. We learn. The question is, are you motivated to learn what *I want you to learn*? If the answer is no, I think that prompting should be the least of your worries.

Prompting is a tricky thing—almost an art form in my opinion. You are constantly striving for a balance between letting a child struggle a little bit and making her successful. If you provide full prompting, the child is in some sense successful, but if the learner doesn't have to struggle at all—that is, think hard or work for the answer—she's not likely to remember how to do a damn thing and will be hopelessly prompt-dependent. I would argue that the act of trying to answer something or remember something becomes faster and easier the more you do it, but eventually you have to be able to do it by yourself. On the other hand, if you let children struggle *too long* they may become anxious, upset, or angry, which will often make further participation difficult at best. A good teacher is constantly, gently, pushing the child's ability to come up with a solution on his own. The catch is that if you push too hard you may get escape-motivated behaviors, and if you don't push enough you may get prompt dependence (Fisher, Kodak, & Moore, 2007). The best teachers I've ever seen are really good at "reading" the child and they shift their prompting strategies on the fly based on how the child is doing. It's like shifting gears in an automobile that has a manual transmission. If you advance through the gears too quickly the engine lags and you have no power and might even stall. This is like making the work too difficult too soon before the child has "built up speed." It's a real balancing act. In teaching skills to people we use a variety of prompts including physical, modeling, gestural, and verbal prompts. I'll talk about how to fade these prompts in the next section, so not to worry.

4.1 Physical prompts

Physical prompts are required for a number of skills taught to younger children or children with more severe deficits. Physical prompts are also used when teaching complex physical movements like those that occur in sports. But let me make this perfectly clear: *physical prompting should not be turned into restraint*. What do I mean by that? Easy. If you are teaching James to write his letters and you are *guiding* his hand with his *full cooperation*, you are using a physical prompt. If James is pulling away from you because he does not want to write his letters you are now *restraining* his hand. No, I doubt you will end up writing an incident report in triplicate and sending a note home to Mommy, but don't kid yourself; it's restraint and it's *ugly teaching*. It never ceases to amaze me how we essentially force some skills physically with uncooperative learners. Sure you can do that with letter writing, but can you physically force someone to solve a quadratic equation? Not likely. We are accustomed to physically forcing very young children to do things and to stop doing things, but what happens when that child gets older and stronger? I would urge all teachers to stop doing this kind of prompting ASAP. Yes, sometimes you can force the behavior and the person will quickly give up and just accept that her lot in life is to draw letters when told to do so, but in many instances the lesson devolves into forced labor with no compensation.

Regarding prompt levels, there can be full physical prompting in which the teacher performs the entire motion or just partial physical prompting where the behavior is only initiated with a nudge in the right direction or perhaps some gross motor guidance. When appropriate for the task, physical prompting is great because you can almost guarantee a correct response immediately. Incidentally, this is one of the virtues of starting language training by teaching signs. Have you ever physically prompted the spoken word cracker? I know some speech therapists who are really quite good at doing that sort of thing to some degree, but it's pretty tough. Just about anybody can physically prompt the *sign* for cracker, even with an infant.

4.2   Modeling prompts

Modeling prompts (imitative) can be used with some children depending on how well they attend to the model and how well they can imitate what they see. This is why gross motor and fine motor imitation can be so very valuable if learning a physical skill. You can do modeling with the actual object or you can do a pantomime with no object. The pantomime is a bit more abstract, but still quite functional for some individuals. These are used quite a bit when teaching sign language to persons with language delays.

4.3   Gestural prompts

Gestural prompts are really interesting as they're the prompts that we sometimes don't even realize we're giving. The two main types of gestures are pointing and looking. I really like gestures because you can orient someone to something that should be controlling her behavior without giving away too much; it really depends on what you're pointing at, I suppose. You can make broad gestures with your arm to indicate a general area to attend to or you can point to specific items. Head movement/eye gaze is very often unintentional, and we sometimes fail to realize the extent to which some children are dependent on these subtle movements. If you want to know for certain how good a child's receptive language is (e.g., go get me the blue book on the table), give the child the verbal instruction while your hands are in your pockets and while looking only at the child and *not* at the intended items. If the receptive identification repertoire suddenly falls apart, you've got your answer. I've given these exact instructions to some staff, and they couldn't keep from looking at the item they requested even though I told them not to! That's how irresistible it can be for us to look at what we're interested in as we talk about it. If you're not sure if you're doing this or not, videotape yourself or have another teacher watch you. You might be very surprised.

4.4 Verbal prompts

Verbal prompts can be signed, written, or spoken, but typically they are spoken. Verbal prompts are great because they're easy to give and can be given from a distance and can be varied in as many ways as you can imagine, which is both a blessing and a burden. Verbal prompts may not always be appropriate for some physical skills (you would know what I mean if you have ever tried to learn a good golf swing without anyone laying their hands on you), and verbal prompts can also be problematic because they have a very short duration. Unless you know how to rehearse the prompt in your head, it's quickly gone. You know, like when you've gotten lost in one of those "convenient" automated customer support telephone directories with multiple submenus? "Please listen carefully because some of the menu items may have changed." I don't know about you guys, but I'm pressing the zero to speak to the operator.

All of these prompts can be used together or separately. If you watch people when they talk, they use a number of gestural and modeling prompts without even thinking about it. For example, when at a restaurant I will say to my server "Can I get a check please?" but I also invariably do the pantomime of scribbling on a piece of paper using my finger and my hand. One thing about verbal prompts is that because they are so easy to vary, the teacher may be unwittingly changing the prompts, which could affect student performance. Verbal prompts initially need to be very specific and the same every time until responding comes under appropriate control.

4.5 Prompts and cues

It's important to make a distinction between *prompts* and *cues*. A cue is the stimulus that is supposed to let you know that it's time to do what you do. Behavior analysts call it a discriminative stimulus or Sd. The prompt is what is given when the cue fails to control behavior. So the cue might be "touch blue!" (but don't use that singsong voice). You might give a gestural prompt (looking at the blue one) if the cue produces no response. People have varying opinions about how long to wait before giving the prompt. One of my colleagues doesn't like waiting more than about two seconds. The issue is that if you give the prompt too soon the person doesn't have to think about it at all and ultimately that's not good. If you wait too long to give the prompt the person may struggle too much, their rate of reinforcement will drop (because of the delay in answering) and they may become agitated. Also, it's important to give the same cue until responding is quite stable. Eventually, to promote generalization, it's a good idea to vary the cue to ensure that responding still occurs. For example if teaching intraverbals (fill in the blank type questions), and the cue is, "You sleep in a _____," you should keep the cue exactly the same every time until responding is perfect. Eventually, however, you will want to mix things up a bit, e.g., "What do you sleep in?" or "Can you name something you sleep in?" or "Where do you sleep?" to ensure that the skill becomes functional. In the real world people don't ask things the same way every time.

One last thing before we move on to prompt fading. Try to avoid giving the same prompt more than twice. I don't even usually give the same one twice. Giving the same prompt multiple times in a row is what I like to call "nagging." Do you like being nagged? I don't. I don't like it at all. Increase your assistance immediately. For example, when I do crisis management training I'm teaching physical skills and sometimes I can generate the correct response with a highly specific, clear verbal prompt, but sometimes I can't. You don't want to give verbal prompts over and over (e.g., "Hold at the wrist, no, the wrist... that's not the wrist, the wrist...." Now the person is angry, embarrassed, and feels like he will never be able to perform the procedure correctly. The first time someone doesn't grab the wrist with only a verbal prompt I quickly walk over to him and physically move his hand. Now he's correct in two seconds instead of fumbling for ten seconds. You can always fade your prompts again later, which is the next topic.

SECTION 5: PROMPT FADING

The inability to fade prompts is one of the *biggest teaching problems* I have ever seen in my entire career. Not just in education, but for adults with disabilities in residential centers as well. Individuals become so hopelessly prompt-dependent it's practically criminal. There are, I believe, several things responsible for this dependence. For one, it's just way easier for teachers or parents to give full prompting and get the thing done! It takes less time and no one gets frustrated. Unfortunately, it also helps to ensure that no one learns how to do anything independently. Another reason for prompt dependence is that the child may learn (sometimes rather quickly) that if she just waits long enough, *you* will do the task for her, or at least give so much assistance that the task becomes a no-brainer. Additionally, prompt dependence may occur when we just don't know the ways to fade our prompts in *small enough gradations*. So, just in case you need some ideas, here are some things you can think about trying. Incidentally, you can get crazy detailed with methods of fading prompts that get very sophisticated. My feeling on the matter is that if you have a highly motivated learner, prompt fading is not as difficult. An unmotivated learner typically becomes *more prompt dependent* as prompts make things *easier*. No prompts makes things *harder*. If you're not very motivated to begin with, what would you rather have, an easier or harder task?

5.1 Fading physical prompts

You can fade physical prompts by moving from the full movement to just a light nudge in the general direction. The classic example is going from hand-over hand with full assistance to support at the wrist, then forearm, then just a touch at the elbow. You can also fade physical prompts by doing what I like to call "stalling." This means that, for example, if you were to teach someone to feed herself using physical prompting, you get the spoon within two inches of her mouth and stop. Now you play the waiting game. How long do you wait? Typically a few seconds and the person will realize something's wrong because she isn't eating! This is particularly useful in the case of feeding because the stalling creates a slight reinforcement delay. It motivates the individual to complete the sequence. You can also fade physical prompts by making the same sort of movements you were making but without making contact. This is what you might call "shadowing." It's almost a physical prompt, but not quite. You can also fade physical prompts by simply using less force or pressure. Many times I'll go from holding someone's hand with my hand to just using two fingertips to move the hand.

5.2   Fading modeling prompts

In fading modeling prompts you can either fade pieces off of the end of the sequence (dropping the modeling prompt on the seventh of ten steps), or you can simply start the first motion of each prompt yet not complete the motion. So if you were showing someone how to draw the letter "A" then you would model drawing the two sides, but not the step of drawing the crosspiece. You might also start by modeling the action using an actual object and then move to just doing a pantomime. You can then fade the pantomime by making smaller movements. We sometimes do this naturally just because it's easier. That is, you make the same basic motions but you cover less distance in your movements.

5.3   Fading gestural prompts

With gestural prompts, I like to start with using the eyes, head, body (leaning), and pointing to provide the most information. Then you can start to fade your pointing hand so that you are still pointing, but you begin to inch your hand slowly further away from the item/object. This makes the prompt a bit more vague. Once you've faded your hand all the way out of the equation, you can start to fade your head/eye movements.

You must learn how to control your head and eye movements and be very conscious of what you're doing, as some individuals can learn to detect very subtle prompts and they become *expert prompt detectors* instead of good learners. I knew one woman who specialized in discrete trials training and was teaching receptive identification (i.e., "Touch cat" when the child was shown a picture of a dog and a cat next to each other). She had faded her gestural prompts down to a very small movement. She had her hands together and her fingers interlaced. To indicate which picture to touch, she would make an almost imperceptible movement with the tip of the index finger on one of her hands. I swear she didn't even move her finger far enough to fit a feeler gauge[4] between her fingertip and the back of her hand and this kid could still detect it. How can you solve this problem? Read on…

5.4 Fading verbal prompts

You can fade verbal prompts in a variety of ways. First you can give a partial prompt, which is a very popular method of fading. Instead of saying, "You forgot to carry the one" you can just say, "You forgot to carry…." You could lop off words or lop off syllables. "What state do you live in?" FLLLLLLLOOOORRRRR. That's right! Florida! Another way to fade your verbal prompts is to simply make them more vague—that is, they should contain less and less specific information. When I used to proofread my stepson's essays I made the mistake of telling him exactly which sentences had problems with them and exactly what the problem was. This was too easy for him, moreover it didn't teach him to scan for errors which would have been... an effort. After he knew about what kinds of things to look for, I changed my prompt to, "There's something wrong in the first paragraph." This told him that there was a problem and approximately where the problem was, but nothing more. Now he had to put in some effort and hunt for errors!

You can also fade your verbal prompts by fading the prompt volume, but of course you risk teaching someone how to get really good at detecting things at a low voice volume and how to read lips. I prefer to use the first two methods. Remember that when making prompts more vague you can make them mildly vague or wildly vague like, "There's a problem in the last sentence," "There's a problem in the last paragraph," "There's a problem on page 9," or "There's a great disturbance in the Force." These kinds of prompts really require people to think hard and will prevent them from being immediately successful so you should only make the prompts vague once the person can handle struggling for a few moments before getting things correct.

5.5 Differential reinforcement (super important)

Even if you're doing a wonderful job prompting, you may still find it difficult to completely fade your prompts. In my experience, the biggest reason for difficulty with prompt fading is that the child simply has no good reason to do things without assistance. You have to look at things from the child's perspective. Why should I (the child) struggle with figuring out what to do, when if I wait long enough the teacher will give me the answer! If the task is to point to the correct picture when asked, "Show me the cat!" and if the child gets one goldfish cracker whether he points to it by himself or points to it with your assistance, then why would he try to do it by himself if the reinforcement is the same? There MUST be differential reinforcement for better (more independent) performances! Now the traditional use

---

[4]A feeler gauge is a precision tool made of multiple paper-thin strips of steel and is used to measure very tiny gap widths of only thousandths of an inch.

of the phrase "differential reinforcement" means worse responses don't cop any reinforcement at all and better ones get the reinforcer. That's totally doable, but I prefer to use varying magnitudes of reinforcement to keep response rates at a reasonable level.

As an example, if you need a gestural prompt you get one goldfish cracker, if you perform the task given only the cue then you get *five* goldfish crackers. Remember, fewer prompts equals more work (struggling, thinking, deciding) for the child. There has to be a good reason for the child to try harder. Usually what I do is regularly shift the criteria for the big reinforcement. After you get stable responding (the child can answer correctly with a verbal prompt every time), it's time to reduce the size of the reinforcer slightly for the prompted response and then increase it for the unprompted response. As the child improves, we keep moving the mark. So if the child initially needs a full verbal prompt and gets five goldfish crackers, after the performance is stable, a response performed with a full verbal prompt now gets one goldfish instead of five. A response performed with only a partial verbal prompt now gets the five goldfish crackers. When the partially prompted responding is stable, we move the mark again. The key is to avoid changing reinforcer size (magnitude) until responding is reasonably stable. So if the cue is "What's the capitol of Florida?" and the child can reliably answer correctly (many times in a row) when given the verbal prompt "Tallahassee," then it's time to reduce the reinforcement when the full prompt is given and give bigger reinforcement when the prompt is just "Tal."

Now, *some* differential reinforcement has to be "more differential" than usual if you know what I mean. For a learner who is heavily prompt dependent, you might give one Skittle for a fully prompted response and five Skittles for the first partially prompted response. The point is that heavily prompt-dependent individuals are going to need some big-time motivation to start putting in some real effort. Naturally, you can use your praise instead of Skittles, but you have to be able to blow the roof off your praise when the person shows unprompted responding. I know what you may be thinking, and you're correct! The long-term goal is for independent task completion to become its own reinforcer. It's very common for typically developing children to volunteer to any available grown-ups "Look! I did it all by myself!" Until that happens, you might have to go through a lot of Skittles so you might want to buy in bulk.

SECTION 6:   ERROR PREVENTION\CORRECTION

It's good to try to prevent errors when you can, especially if you're working with a child who is both sensitive to making errors *and* prone to significant behavior problems. At first, preventing errors is fine and it may even be preferable to prevent all errors. It makes the teaching experience less daunting for the child and will help keep behavior problems to a minimum. Eventually though, children should be able to handle errors, whether during a teaching session or even while performing an independent skill. Errors are just a subset of a variety of minor aversives that can cause behavior problems for many children, and a child can be taught to handle errors in the same manner that we would teach him to handle any other aversive (PETCAT). Still, *preventing* excessive errors is a really good idea for the most part and knowing how to *correct errors* as quickly and painlessly as possible is helpful for those times when errors just can't be avoided.

6.1 Pre-corrective prompting

If you find you're getting numerous errors from your students you can even use pre-corrective prompting in which you give the prompt, then a moment later give the cue. So for example, you can point to the picture of the cat, then quickly say, "Show me the cat." This really falls under the category of error prevention. This kind of prompting can prevent a number of errors. You can even state the cue and model the proper response. For example you can say, "What's 2 times 3?....Six!" You would say the "six" almost immediately after the cue. Then you say the cue again immediately. Most individuals will then be able to answer correctly.

1. Teacher: "What's 2 times 3?" (wait one-second) "Six" (said by the teacher) wait 2 more seconds, then step 2.
2. Teacher: "What's 2 times 3?" (waits for the student)
3. Student: "Six!"
4. Teacher: Right!

Once you have the correct response occurring reliably after giving the cue and the answer together, you can begin to fade the pre-corrective prompt in time. That means putting a progressively longer delay between the initial pre-corrective prompt, "Six" and the second cue, "What's 2 times 3?" So using the example above you could increase the delay between steps 1 and 2 from 2 seconds to 5 seconds, then 10 seconds, etc. When the delay becomes long enough, it usually means the child can now remember the correct response with only the cue and you won't need the pre-corrective prompt anymore.

6.2 Error prevention

There was a program on Saturday mornings when I was a kid called *Multiplication Rock* and it taught you things about math using cartoons and catchy tunes. They also had *Grammar Rock* and *America Rock* and just about every other kind of rock except for maybe *Terrorist Threat Level Rock*. Anyhow, one of the multiplication rock songs was called "3 is a Magic Number." They were right. Three times is the charm, three strikes and you're out, and three errors in a row and you *get bitten*. Not only do you have to know how to correct errors, which we'll cover soon, but you have to know how to keep them to a minimum as well. It's been my experience that people who make fewer errors are happier learners and that's what we want. Also we don't want people to "practice" making errors because those behaviors can become very strong.

If you are working with students who just explode when they make an error, you may wish to adopt an errorless teaching technique (Mueller & Palkovic, 2007) until the individual can learn to handle making errors without freaking out. Pre-corrective prompts will prevent repeated errors and, as just mentioned, you can fade your second cue ("What's 2 times 3?") so that it occurs further and further away from the time of the pre-corrective prompt ("Six!"). As an example, my stepson Weston, when he was very young, would often forget his book bag in my car after getting home from school. Consequently, it was in my car when I left for work in the morning and he would be missing it all day. He made repeated errors in the presence of the cue (the cue was arriving at the house). To get errorless responding I would give a pre-corrective prompt ("Remember your book bag!") 10 seconds before we got into the drive way and he was successful. The next day it was 1 minute before we got to the driveway. The next day I gave the prompt halfway home from school and on the last day he got the pre-corrective prompt the moment I picked him up in the afternoon.

Two other ways you can prevent errors are to *physically block* the wrong response (if possible) or to *fade-in the incorrect choices* (this works really well with pigeons). So let's say that you have a picture of a dog and a picture of a cat. Unfortunately, the child repeatedly touches the picture of the cat when you say, "Show me dog." You can fix this problem by physically diverting the child's hand toward the dog when he reaches for the cat. You could alternately leave the picture of the cat on the table but move it just out of the child's reach so that the picture of the dog is the only one that can be touched and then slowly move the cat back in until the child correctly only picks the dog. If you continue having difficulty, you can try bumping up the differential reinforcement, using pictures that look more different from each other, or you can check to see if the child has developed a positional preference (favoring the left or right sides). If the child doesn't have a vision problem (which is entirely possible) you may have to enhance the differences on the pictures by circling critical areas or choose an easier discrimination (cat versus T-Rex) and then work your way back up to more difficult discriminations after mastery.

6.3 Error correction

Although you can use an errorless teaching model, someone (typically) is going to make some errors. I would also argue that it's good (in the long-term sense) for kids to be able to tolerate the errors they make. Making too many errors, however, is counterproductive and will turn children off to learning at best and at worst create tremendous behavior problems. Let's take a look at how to correct errors. When correcting errors, I just use 3 simple steps:

1. Avoid (at least initially) saying "no" or "wrong." It just isn't necessary. Students will know it's wrong because they aren't going to hear, "good job!" In fact, you can even say, "almost" or "good try" if a student is highly sensitive to making errors. Don't think of the praise as reinforcement for an incorrect response, but as reinforcement for the attempt. Also, try not to look upset; model calm behavior.

2. Immediately give the cue again and a prompt that provides more help or give an additional type of prompt (physical along with verbal) and then give a smaller than usual reinforcer when the person gets it right. (One Skittle instead of five).

3. Immediately give the cue again with the original (lower) prompt level and then a larger reinforcer when the person gets it right (the usual five Skittles, for example).

You could also correct an error with a pre-corrective prompt:

Teacher: "What's two times three?"

Student: "Eight!"

Teacher: "good try" (small reinforcer). "Two times three is six" (pre-corrective prompt) "wait...."

Teacher: "So what's two times three?" (original cue)

Student: "Six!"

Teacher: "Oh yeah, that's what I'm talkin' bout!"

Remember, if you're seeing a high rate of errors you can look at *motivation issues*. That is, is the child really into the activity you're doing? Is the child attending to the relevant parts of the task or looking around the room? If she is looking around it means that it isn't important to look in a particular place or at least look there quickly when given a cue. The other aspect to examine is the current level of prompting necessary to keep the rate of correct answers high so that the rate of reinforcement stays high.

One final thing to consider is the learner's level of physiological arousal. People don't talk about this much, but if your learner is starting to get angry or nervous, errors usually skyrocket. For example, I've found that when teaching physical skills to adults with no disabilities that there is a certain *point of no return* after which all the prompting in the world won't help. I've found that even if I just gave the verbal cue, physically prompted the movement, and waited just two seconds and gave the verbal cue again the person *could not perform correctly*. This is because, as my good friend and colleague Neal Fleisig likes to say, respondents are interfering with your operants, that is, the learner's reflexive nervousness (or anger) is disrupting his ability to perform complex purposeful movements, especially movements that are not yet fluent. What's the answer? You've got to let them calm down again or things can go very badly.

SECTION 7:   STUDENT TO TEACHER RATIO

This last section is kind of an afterthought, as it doesn't seem to fall easily under teaching or curriculum. You would think that a good teacher is a good teacher regardless of the student to teacher ratio, but because of the needs of different children, I believe that this ratio is in some instances critically important regarding behavior problems and the speed of acquisition of new skills. In most classroom settings, you may see one or more of the following: Independent work, one-on-one teaching, small group instruction or lecture-style large group instruction. Let's take a look at each one separately and how they relate to behavior problems.

7.1   Independent work

Children who require a great deal of attention are generally terrible at working independently. We talked about this a bit in Chapter 7 on repertoire problems. Granted, it's a wonderful goal to get children to work independently and I think that we should always be working toward that end. Nonetheless, the behavior of many children becomes problematic very rapidly when they are left to work by themselves. Children who are expected to work independently should be able to sit, or at least stay at their desk/table for at least ten to twenty minutes at a time, recruit attention from a distance, ask for help and know what assignment to begin after completing the current one. They also need to be able to tolerate decreased rates of reinforcement for ten to twenty minutes at a time. Independent work can be a better way to work with some students who tend to get into conflict with their peers far too often, or who just prefer to be by themselves. Working independently means doing actual work, not searching the internet for pictures of Sponge Bob Square Pants. The more students in a classroom who can work independently, the more time the teacher can spend with children individually. Incidentally, the ten-to-twenty minutes thing is pretty arbitrary, but you should be shooting for several minutes of continuous work and that can be quite a challenge for some students.

If you find it difficult to get a child to work for even a few minutes continuously, you should try thinking about things from the child's perspective. Why *should* Jeremy work without stopping? What's in it for him? Does he get the same reinforcement whether he goes continuously or stops five times? You get what you reinforce. Differential reinforcement can help with this dilemma as well:

ten minutes of uninterrupted work = ten minutes of computer time.

ten minutes of work with 1 or more interruptions = five minutes of computer time

There *has to be a reason* to work harder and that reason should be very clear to the learner.

7.2   One-on-one teaching

I'd be hard pressed to say that one-on-one teaching is inherently bad in any sense; it's just that we usually don't have the kinds of resources that allow this intensive level of instruction for very long. In many specialized classrooms, almost all the students get some one-on-one teaching, but only for a small portion of their day—not for most of it. I don't suspect you'll find many children who are worse in one-on-one teaching situations unless they just don't like being around people or don't like being prompted in any way. Individual instruction is particularly helpful for students who require high levels of attention and who are not yet independent learners. One big problem that I often see with individual instruction is that the child becomes dependent on the proximity of an adult to produce any kind of work at all.

7.3 Small group instruction

Small group instruction of about three individuals can serve as a transition between one-on-one work and large group instruction. It's also a good way to test how well a child will tolerate sharing adult attention and how well the child can tolerate periods of decreased reinforcement. Small group instruction can also serve as a good social probe to see how the child will interact with other children sitting close to him or her. I have worked with some children who can barely be productive in a one-on-one format, but when they are moved to a small group of three children their behavior deteriorates rapidly. I love small group instruction as a testing ground to see how well a child can wait his turn, work with minimal supervision, and interact with his peers. I know some children who can't even tolerate sharing attention with just one other child. If needed, you could even "fade" a child into a small group as illustrated below...

Fading a Child Into a Small Group

1. Sit the child at a table for one-on-one teaching while two other children at the same table work independently.
2. After the child gets accustomed to instruction in the presence of the other children, the teacher can slowly increase her interactions with the other two students while maintaining interactions with the child.
3. The teacher can begin to give specific instructions for brief independent assignments (finish the last two problems on your own) while she works with the other two students.
4. The child can be prompted to ask for teacher attention when he completes the brief task.

This is just an example of how you might fade in small group instruction, but if you go slowly it shouldn't prove too difficult.

7.4 Lecture-style large group instruction

In some ways, I believe this to be more difficult than just plain independent work, because with independent work the child only needs to attend to her work and little else. In a large group lecture-style format, all the students must attend to the work in front of them (on their desk), listen to other students (who are asking or answering questions), listen to the teacher, write things down that the teacher puts on the board, follow instructions from a distance, wait their turn when they wish to ask questions, and keep from interacting with the kids next to them when the teacher is relatively far away. There's really quite a lot to do in this kind of teaching format. Even typically developing children have frequent problems with this type of teaching format. When I observe children in included classrooms (to be tackled in Chapter 11), I also like to observe their typically developing peers because I often find that they may exhibit more problems than the kid that I'm observing! It takes just one child to disrupt the entire class (keystone kid) in this type of arrangement. I think that lecture-style large group instruction is primarily good for well-behaved children, sleeping children, and any combination thereof.

Chapter 9

Problems With Punishment

SECTION 1:   INTRODUCTION

1.1   Punishers

If you've ever read Dostoyevsky's timeless novel *Crime and Punishment*, then you've read one more classic piece of literature than I have. Perhaps you can email me the synopsis. Although it wasn't always this way, punishment has unquestionably become the "Darth Vader" of behavior analysis. With the appearance of "positive behavioral supports" (which

I suppose would be Luke Skywalker) people have begun to believe, quite erroneously, that punishment must be a negative procedure, as you just can't have a positive without a negative. Well, I have news for all of you, are you sitting? Punishment is reinforcement's father! Punishment is just as misunderstood as reinforcement, and trust me, reinforcement is waaaay misunderstood. So many people, including behavior analysts who should know better, eschew punishment and prefer to keep it in the basement where no one can see its hideous misshapen face. Now don't get me wrong, punishment procedures, just like reinforcement procedures, are terribly misused, and I will detail exactly how and why they are misused. I promise. There is a great misconception, propagated by people with their feet firmly planted in midair, that we can fix all the ills of society with *only* positive reinforcement. I've been on the planet for half a century now and I can state, with absolute certainty, that it just ain't gonna happen. Nope. Without punishment there would be human sacrifice, cats and dogs living together, and mass hysteria. This doesn't mean punishment *must* be part of any behavior reduction program. It means that punishment has its place, both in our general protection and in our development as social creatures, and that we should be glad that its there doing its job, 24–7 with no overtime pay.

1.2 No Life, no aversives, know life, know aversives...

Punishment involves aversive stimuli, and there is no living without aversives. It's a package deal. We experience many pleasures in life; love, marriage, sex (not necessarily in that order), pizza, beer, Lindy's Italian Ices (usually in that order) and the Matrix trilogy (absolutely in order). On the other hand, we are also subjected to grief, sadness, pain, discomfort and that awful Saturday Night Live skit that they jam in during the last three minutes of the show because it wasn't good enough to use before the musical guest plays for the first time. We are built to benefit from punishment. It keeps us alive and our exquisite sensitivity to punishing events prevents unimaginable harm.

At this point I suppose that I should provide a working definition of punishment. As with reinforcement, one can talk about the phenomenon as both a procedure (what happens in the environment) and a process (what happens to behavior over time.)

> Punishment is the delivery of a stimulus contingent on a behavior (procedure) that results in either an immediate decrease in the frequency of that behavior and/or a decrease in the probability of that behavior in the future (behavioral process).

This means that, like reinforcement, you can have two basic kinds of effects. Recall that with reinforcement you can see an immediate local effect of an increase in response rates. So if a child makes fart noises, and you do nothing, the rate may not increase at all. If you say to the child, "Ooh that's nasty!" while making a face, you will likely see an immediate increase in the frequency of the response. You might also see a global reinforcement effect over days and weeks whereby the probability of the behavior increases over many opportunities to engage in the behavior. That is, if I order a slice of pizza, and if it is delicious but also filling, I won't order another slice immediately. Over many days, however, the frequency of my patronage of a particular pizza parlor may increase as evidenced by patterns in my proclivity for pizza purchasing. That is, in an overall sense, the behavior of going to one restaurant becomes more likely. Punishment works the same way. You could get an *immediate suppression* of current responding, but you might also see a *decrease in the probability of behavior* over days and weeks given multiple opportunities for the behavior to occur when the person is properly motivated.

1.3 Naturally occurring non-socially-mediated punishers

Before proceeding, It's extremely important to understand that punishment as a procedure is not simply some programmed penance that one human being visits upon another. True, that's what most people think of when they think of punishment, usually the punisher is delivered by someone. However, punishment occurs in the natural environment just like reinforcement. If you do something stupid and dangerous, eventually the natural environment may punish that behavior. One day, my friend's young child, unbeknownst to her, was playing with her car keys, attempting to ascertain whether he could insert them into an electrical socket (ah yes, a budding young scientist). Well, the keys fit quite well, and one bright flash of light and a puff of smoke later there was one crying child, one blackened electrical outlet (Cajun style) and one very upset mommy. Needless to say, her child never put keys into sockets again. There are countless examples of naturally occurring punishers that forever eliminate or at least temporarily discourage a variety of behaviors. I'm sure you recall my motorcycle saddlebag incident from Chapter 3 on aversives. It was a naturally occurring punisher of the response-produced variety. No one did anything to me, but it was good that it happened, because I really could have been injured, but fortunately I'll never do that again. It was indeed a triumph for stupid people everywhere! I must also remind everyone that whether you get temporary suppression or banishment from the repertoire depends on a number of factors. Some of these factors *might be*: 1) the current motivating operations in effect that may compete with the punishing event[1]; 2) the history of reinforcement for the behavior that resulted in the punishing event (Bobby was stealing cookies every day for a year and finally got caught and punished *once* [losing TV for one night] but keeps stealing); and 3) the severity of the punishing event (losing a gold star or receiving a 4.2 milliamp skin shock, ouch!).

---

[1] A behavior analyst friend of mine (Kate) was working with a child on a "point" system. One day he asked Kate, "How many points do I have?" She replied "You're doing great Bobby. You have 10,000!" He then asked, "How many points do we lose for hitting?" She replied, "1000." He said, "Thanks." He then immediately proceeded to hit one of his peers really hard. She asked, "Was it worth it?" To which Bobby replied, "Yep!" Bobby actually had enough points for a good old fashion @ss-whoopin', but I guess he was saving some for a rainy day....

1.4 Naturally occurring socially-mediated punishers

There are also punishers that are naturally occurring, but socially-mediated, that is, they are delivered by people, These kinds of punishers are very common, so common you probably don't even notice them, and they're not actually planned in any programmatic sense. So if, as I stated in Chapter 3, you are at a Philadelphia Eagles game and you happen to be wearing a Dallas Cowboy jersey while shouting, "The Eagles Suck!" You will undoubtedly be subjected to some continuous high magnitude *non-programmed* socially-mediated punishers.

1.5 Programmed socially-mediated punishers

Finally, there are programmed socially-mediated punishers. They are programmed in the sense that they are prearranged, planned, or written down in some sort of organized manner. Laws and the consequences for breaking those laws are fine examples. These alleged punishers (I'll get to the alleged part later) are included in formal prearranged contingencies that are socially sanctioned. These kinds of programmed punishers, however, usually involve conditioned aversives (things that don't bother babies) that are greatly delayed from the time the behavior actually occurs. So if you get a speeding ticket, the police officer doesn't pull 100 bucks out of your wallet on the spot (maybe he should). If you get caught for tax fraud, you don't get a call from the IRS the moment you write down a bogus deduction. If you fail to make car payments, your car doesn't get repossessed the moment you tear up the bill and throw it away. Also, for these kinds of alleged punishers, the aversive isn't something painful. Speeding tickets just hurt your wallet, that's about it, and even the financial sting isn't immediate. To summarize, there are three basic categories of punishing events. Those that are naturally occurring and non socially-mediated (like the key in the socket incident), those that are naturally occurring and socially-mediated, (the Philadelphia Eagles fans) and those that are socially-mediated but programmed (speeding tickets and your mean, nasty behavior program).

SECTION 2: WHY PUNISHMENT FAILS

Man, the title of this section is so misleading, I love it! Many people will say, "Punishment doesn't work!" Guess what? People say the same thing about reinforcement and, if you truly understand these concepts, you quickly realize that neither statement makes a lick of sense. Is it possible that spankings don't work? Sure. Is it possible that even a seemingly mild punisher like a point-loss won't work? Absolutely. These things don't work as punishers in exactly the same way that M&Ms don't work as reinforcers and for the same reasons. The right aversive, under the right conditions, can stop behavior dead in its tracks, never to be seen again (motorcycle saddlebags incident). The wrong aversive, under the wrong conditions just ticks people off really badly. All things that function as punishers are by definition aversive. The converse is not necessarily true, however. Something can be highly aversive, but, depending on the behavior that produces that event, it may not function as a punisher. The recidivism rate for criminals is still very high, like 80 percent. For most criminals, the goal is to *avoid* prison, and not by giving up their life of crime forever. Not only will they avoid going to prison, but many criminals spend a lot of time trying to Shawshank their way out of prison once they are confined. By definition, things that you try to avoid or escape from are aversives. Unfortunately, going to prison is generally insufficient to punish criminal behavior, but this is more likely a function of the history of successfully committing crime and the current need to commit more crime. Career criminals don't typically straighten up and fly right. Martha Stewart, on the other hand, seems to be sticking to creating festive ironing board covers from recycled adult bladder control undergarments and has managed to steer clear of any more insider trading. Generally, smaller, more distant aversives (long after the behavior has occurred) have little if any punishing effect on well-established behaviors that have been intermittently reinforced over a long time). It's critical to understand that this whole punishment/reinforcement thing is a balancing act. Behaviors with short histories, and little motivation to perform them, can easily be snuffed out by even seemingly very small punishers. If you say something that you later realize was offensive to someone, and you didn't mean to hurt his feelings, it doesn't take much to forever squelch any subsequent similar statements. Someone might tell you, "Hey when you made that comment the other day, that was pretty cold." That is often sufficient to ensure that you never say that thing again, at least not to that person. We've all had experiences like these, and if you haven't I strongly recommend that you go out and try it so that you can identify with the other seven billion people on the planet.

Sometimes punishers merely have suppressive effects and do not by any means stomp out bad behavior forever. It doesn't mean that they shouldn't be used because their effects are only temporary. The same is true of reinforcement. Everything in life must be maintained. Everything. Ask any physicists you meet walking down the street, and they will all say the same thing. *Everything is in a state of decay!* They probably call it entropy[2]. Everything is constantly decaying. Your house, your car, the orbit of that satellite that gives you 250 crappy channels, your body, your relationships, that stuff in the bottom of the garbage disposal that just refuses to be disposed of. Everything. Are you sufficiently depressed yet? My point is not that you need to run out and get prozac (which also decays so make sure to use it up within a year), but that everything we do to produce behavior change is, in some sense, temporary. We must *maintain* our efforts until other more naturally occurring contingencies can take over and replace our highly contrived behavior program. It doesn't mean that our interventions are doomed to failure, just that some behaviors will drop out of the repertoire (at least temporarily) if they are not supported through reinforcement, whether contrived or more naturally occurring. Of course the same is true of punishment. Behavior analysts refer to this problem as one of generalization (making sure change occurs in all settings) and maintenance (ensuring that behavior change is durable). That punishers or

---

[2]Entropy is actually the second law of thermodynamics and is most easily demonstrated by a hot glass of water losing its heat to the surrounding room. Basically, anything with energy tends to "give it up" to the world.

reinforcers may only be temporary is never a good reason to avoid their use. As my colleague Dr. Ennio Cipani likes to point out, in his book *Punishment on Trial*, (Cipani, 2004) yes, speeding tickets and speed limits only suppress behavior. However, if you take away all the limits and the tickets, all hell is going to break loose. This is why we have laws, at least I think this is why we have laws.

When are punishers more likely to have a long-term elimination effect as opposed to a suppressive effect? When the behavior is still in its infancy (the behavior has not produced much reinforcement), when the motivation to engage in the behavior is low, and when the punisher is swift and large. As Jim Johnston likes to say, "Therein lies the rub!" By the time we're working with a child with behavior problems, they may have copped some big-time reinforcement hundreds or thousands or tens of thousands of times over many years. What I typically tell teachers is that they do not have a punisher big enough, bad enough, or legal enough at this stage of the game to eradicate the problem behavior. Could you have put the kibosh on the behavior with the right punisher the first time it occurred? Quite possibly yes. Does this mean that no punishers will ever be effective? No, not at all, *if* you teach the child a functional replacement behavior, *and* eliminate, (to the greatest extent possible) all sources of reinforcement for the problem behavior, *and* you crush the motivation to engage in the problem behavior in the first place, *then* the judicious use of a mild punisher might be all you need to eliminate those remnants of the problem behavior that might still occur here or there (Hanley, Piazza, Fisher & Maglieri, 2005; Hagopian, Fisher, Sullivan, Acquisto & LeBlanc, 1998). Notice that there is one big *if* and two pretty big *ands* in that last statement. If you just rush in, headlong, with your two-fisted punishers, and have not gotten all of your behavioral ducks in a row, you should expect little, if any, long-term gains.

As an example of how small changes in the behavioral economy can make a big difference in the efficacy of an alleged punisher, allow me to give the "Trucker" example. A trucker works for himself and he takes bids from companies that need their goods shipped within certain time constraints. He gets paid *a lot less money* if the goods are not delivered on time. Most likely, the trucker wants to avoid speeding tickets, but he may be more likely to speed because going too slowly will cost him money (the motivation to speed is greater). A speeding ticket would most likely only suppress his speeding behavior temporarily, especially if the fine is small in comparison to his on-time bonus. Let's say that this trucker gets a job with UPS. Let's also say that UPS drivers get safe-driver bonuses for driving the speed limit (reinforcement for safe driving). Let's also say that the routes are shorter and it's far easier to get packages to their destinations on time and the delivery window is much larger (less motivation to speed). Finally, the driver gets no additional money for early delivery (no reinforcement for speeding). Under these conditions, what are your thoughts about the efficacy of a speeding ticket as a punisher? Yep. That's what I thought. Same speeding ticket, same fine, but totally different MOs.

I mentioned that sometimes an event that we designate as a punisher is really nothing more than an aversive. What are the implications of using a mild to moderate aversive that is ineffective as a punisher? They're not good, I can tell you that. It means that you're going to subject a child to something he really hates, but only enough to escape from it or avoid it. So with my trucker example, when he worked for himself his speeding behavior may not have been suppressed at all, but his "looking out for cops behavior" may have become outstanding (stronger avoidance behavior). Also, if your "punisher" is not suppressing behavior, you really need to stop it ASAP because you may just be increasing the chances of behavior problems. Allow me to elaborate with a colorful hypothetical. If Ralphie takes Jimmy's candy-corn, and Jimmy slaps Ralphie's hand (mild aversive), there's a really good chance that Ralphie will now bite Jimmy really hard. The slap created aggression (biting) but may not punish Ralphie's stealing behavior. No doubt, you've seen this sort of thing happen between children. Now, what if the same event takes place, but this time when Ralphie takes the candy-corn, someone in a zombie costume jumps out of the bushes shouting "Must eat brains?" Result: Not only does Ralphie think twice before stealing from Jimmy again, he also now wets his pants whenever he sees candy-corn, and that's really going to put the "wee" in Halloween.

Now you can easily see why I typically tell teachers not to bother with the punishers they've arranged, at least not for longstanding behavior problems. It isn't because punishment is mean or bad or nasty or even that it's ineffective. It's just that I am reasonably certain that the teacher does not possess a functional punisher for *this* particular behavior that has been reinforced for *this* number of years with *this* level of motivation. Remember, if we could lower the motivation to engage in the behavior, *and* reinforce a competing replacement behavior the same punisher that was once ineffective may now be highly effective (like with our hypothetical trucker friend).

2.1 Why traditional "punishers" may actually cause behavior problems

You can use "traditional punishers" with typically developing children who have a long history of responding appropriately to mild punishers. That is, if a typically developing child is told that he has lost out on an opportunity to watch a movie at the end of the day, the correct response might be something like, "Aw man! That's no fair!" followed by appropriate pouting. The *incorrect* response to this kind of reinforcer loss-based punisher would be to destroy the room, threaten to kill the teacher and light the school on fire.

Many children with special needs may not be able to respond appropriately to traditional, programmed mild punishers. What would those potential punishers be? Response cost, (losing points or privileges), reinforcer removal/termination, time-out from positive reinforcement, or contingent effort (being required to do additional work). The success of these kinds of mild punishers is largely dependent on a decent self-control repertoire, a history of experiencing a variety of punishers, and the ability to tolerate a variety of aversive stimuli. One problem with many children with special needs is that they respond absolutely horribly to aversives in general, and punishment falls under that category. What happens is that traditional mild "punishers" are not truly punishers for many children, but they are most certainly aversive. What? I knew you'd say that. Aversives may be bad enough to make you really mad, but just shy of something that will make you think twice before you try that behavior again. If children can tolerate a variety of mild aversives without engaging in problem behaviors, they are well on their way to being able to tolerate punishers. If children cannot even tolerate a mild, commonplace, "non-punishment" aversive, like having to wait a few moments to get something they want, what chance do they have of tolerating a programmed punisher?

The problem is that if a child is going to be a functioning member of society, she must learn to tolerate not only common aversives, but she must also be able to tolerate mild, societally-normed, programmed punishers. Part of living a normal life means following the rules of society. Although we surely give some latitude to persons with special needs, their ultimate level of independence will depend (in large part) on their ability to handle a variety of common aversives including punishers. Just because children can't tolerate a mild punisher right now doesn't mean that they won't eventually get to the point where they could, and it doesn't mean that we shouldn't try to teach them to tolerate these events. As the highly astute Dr. Cipani has pointed out, children who can tolerate mild punishers and benefit from said punishers can, like the rest of us, avoid bigger more life-altering punishers. If you can avoid cursing at the police officer when you're given a speeding ticket, you can probably avoid a worse punisher (going to jail).

Even if we *could* create a utopian school and home setting, whereby students only learn through positive reinforcement and no one is ever exposed to any aversives including punishers, the rest of the world just doesn't work that way. Maybe it will one day, but not any time soon, I can assure you. If the child will only live within the bounds of this utopian world where all people are sweet and there are no limits set on their behavior and nothing bad ever happens, then I guess it's just fine if you don't want to teach the child how to handle adversity (which would include punishers). On the other hand, if you would like the child to live as normal a life as possible and have the same richness of experiences and the same freedoms that the rest of us enjoy, then it's probably a good idea to prepare him for what lies ahead, namely coercion, nastiness, teasing, and punishment. We were all subjected to these things as children, and we are still subjected to them as adults. Sure, many children with special needs are simply not ready to be exposed to these particular stressors. We must, nonetheless, slowly, carefully, and methodically prepare them for all of these eventualities or we are unwittingly creating for them a false life or we are setting them up for abject failure in real life. Neither option, in my opinion, is acceptable; children must be prepared. We have to teach them, the best that *we* can, how to handle these modern-day slings and arrows the best that *they* can.

SECTION 3: "HANDLING IT"

How do we teach children how to "handle" punishers?

Boy, that's a good question! I'm glad I asked it! To teach children how to handle punishers they need to be properly equipped. This is not an official "readiness for punishment checklist," but it seems to be a reasonable start. First, children need to know the "right" way to do things to get their needs met, a.k.a. replacement behaviors. This is of primary importance. If someone takes your stuff, you must be taught what to do to remedy the situation, and it has to be something effective yet appropriate and legal. Children should also be fluent with the alleged replacement behavior. Second, they should probably be able to handle typical, day-to-day mild aversives that all of us have to deal with. I've talked about these things in other chapters (waiting, being exposed to things that don't work right, being disappointed, having to give up something fun for a little while, etc.). Third, children must be taught how to respond to being overtly punished. As mentioned earlier, there are certain do's and don'ts for being punished. Higher-functioning children can be taught what they can and cannot do and say when a punisher is delivered. You can stomp your feet but you can't destroy anything. You can say, "This stinks!" but you can't curse and threaten to do harm. You can mutter under your breath, but you can't scream and disrupt the classroom. Lastly, there has to be a very good reason for displaying these "muted" versions of bad behavior. I do these things all the time. Do you have any idea how often I just wanna curse and scream and break things when I am exposed to aversives including programmed punishers? Gimme a break. How about all the time? I bite my lip, I mutter, I become sarcastic, I sigh a lot, grind my teeth, pace, and maybe vent to a friend. I do not, however, attack people, destroy rooms, threaten people with bodily injury, or pull out clumps of my own hair (and at my age, there aren't as many clumps as there used to be). Why don't I do these things? Mostly, I'm afraid of getting into worse trouble, hurting someone's feelings, and/or looking like a complete jerk. Using a discrepancy analysis, it's easy to see that children with special needs may not be concerned about the same things as you and I. I don't know very many kids with severe behavior problems who are too worried about how they will look to other students, care if they hurt the teacher's feelings, or are concerned that their aggression will become a smudge on their permanent record, forever ruining their chances of getting into an Ivy League university. In essence, they are not (in most instances) controlled by the same aversives as typically developing children. So what do we do? We have to give the child a good reason to respond appropriately to punishers. What might this look like? Here's an example (this should be done at a time when the person is calm):

Teacher: "Jimmy, if you hit someone, you know that you will lose 100 points. Right?"

Jimmy: "Yeah, I know, but that sucks!"

Teacher: "I know it does, Jimmy, but guess what?"

Jimmy: (rolling his eyes) "What?"

Teacher: "If you can handle it when I tell you that you've lost points, you will get a refund the next day of 50 points!"

Jimmy: "What does 'handle it' mean?"

Teacher: "It means that you can be grumpy if you want, but if you can do all your cursing in your head, or write it down on paper to get it out of your system, then you won't lose all 100 points."

Jimmy: "Well it still sucks, but I guess it's better than losing all my points. Okay, I'll try to handle it!"

Teacher: "OMG Dr. Winston was right!"

Class: (cheering)

Now you can see how you might stack the deck in favor of the child tolerating punishment in this blatantly pro-Dr. Winston scenario. If you prepare the child for what the punisher will look like, tell him how to behave, set limits on what he can and cannot do and explain to him the benefits of "handling it," you can greatly increase the chances that the child will be successful. I'm sure that you could figure out dozens of creative ways to do this, which will save me a lot of typing. Naturally, as stated above, several prerequisites should be in place to help ensure that the mild punisher can be tolerated. I'll review the steps now:

1. There is a replacement behavior(s) for the problem in question.
2. The child can handle typical mild aversives.
3. The child is taught what to do and what not to do when punished (they are taught how to "handle it").
4. The child has to have big-time motivation to handle the punisher.

3.1   Isn't Punishment Just Abuse? Aren't We Going to be Seen as Coercive?

Punishment does not have to be seen as "negative," it does not have to be abuse, it does not have to be coercive, and the person who arranges it does not have to be a complete bastard. Could punishment be implemented in a nasty, abusive manner that is excessively coercive and could it be set up by a complete bastard? Absolutely! It happens all the time. Why do you think that so many people are so dead set against it? Allow me to give a real life example. I was coming home from a consult at a school. I was dictating into my iPhone and was having some really great iDeas and wasn't really paying iTtention to the speed limit. I suddenly saw a cop on the side of the road and he had his radar gun in his hand and pointed at me and then pointed at the side of the road. After iCrapped my pants I pulled over, rolled down my window and said, "I'm sorry officer, I know I was going fast, I didn't even look at my speedometer (appropriate response to being punished)." He smiled and said, "I'm really sorry Mr. Winston, but I can't give you a cheaper ticket because you were more than 20 miles per hour over the speed limit. Had you been going just a little slower I could have given you a much cheaper one." He then continued to tell me how to avoid points on my license and gave me a number of options for dealing with the citation, and was generally really cool about the whole thing. As I drove off, I couldn't help thinking how cool the cop was about the whole thing. Make no mistake about it though, my behavior was punished! I *never* speed in that area anymore. Did I feel coerced by that police officer? No way. Was he nasty to me? No way. Did I harbor ill will toward him? No way. You see, like the late great Glenn Latham, the officer let the *law* do the dirty work. It wasn't personal, it was business. He was downright sympathetic to my plight. Nonetheless, I was still ticketed.

I can think of numerous examples of this kind of punishment delivery and I'm sure you can as well. This is why I positively bristle when people who know not of which they speak start bad-mouthing punishment, saying how horrible it is and how only Nazis use it, and how it destroys relationships and causes terrorism and bacne (back acne). Punishment can be implemented in a nice, clean manner, in a socially acceptable way, even in a supportive way, but it can still affect behavior. Remember, however, if the person doesn't have the skills and the motivation to handle punishment, you can be as sweet as molasses, but someone is still going to break your glasses. If you'd like to read a wonderful book on misconceptions about punishment including references showing its efficacy, look for the aforementioned Dr. Ennio Cipani's *Punishment On Trial*. Dr. Cipani relates numerous case studies involving the effective, ethical use of punishment. Naturally, he uses reinforcement as well and conducts wonderful functional assessments. His point of view is refreshing and he's a funny guy to boot. The book is free and you may obtain it by writing to me (merrill@pcma.com) and I'll send you a link. Don't read it until you're done with this book (you may as well start working on that problem of not finishing what you start right here and now).

In summary, I hope that everyone understands that I'm not recommending that people go around punishing everything in sight, only some things. I'm not so much pro-punishment as I am anti-accepting-what-politically-correct-people-tell-you-when-the-real-world-tells-you-differently. Punishment wasn't something invented by B. F. Skinner and it wasn't invented by your parents or grandparents. It exists in nature and as the wonderfully funny and astute Chris Rock might say, "Your butt is *supposed* to get punished!" Do we want children with disabilities to be subjected, without preparation, to real, full-power punishers, or should we carefully teach them how to respond effectively to planned, mild ones? I'm not going to make that decision for you. That decision is for all of you to make individually. I sometimes think that behavior analysts really never should have used the term "punishment" because it carries too much baggage. Dr. Peter Harzem at one time proposed the term "disinforcement" to replace punishment. I really think that we should have listened to Peter. I think that the new language would be refreshing. I can hear it now...."Son, I'm afraid this disinforcement is going to hurt me more than it hurts you!"

Chapter 10

Problems With Diagnosis

SECTION 1: INTRODUCTION

I'd like to kick off this chapter with a few quotes:

> In today's society, consumed with the idea that many of our problems are beyond any-one's control, we have steered away from descriptions of *how people behave* and have drifted, dangerously, towards prescriptions for *what people have...*
>
> Children once described as *being* a problem are now described as *having* a disorder...
>
> There is a disturbing trend to attribute any extreme in behavior, that could be explained by natural variation or selection through reinforcement, to something that is fundamentally (i.e., medically) wrong with the person...
>
> We are rapidly becoming a nation in which falling at either end of the bell shaped curve of human behavior is taken as evidence that we must *have* something and that only medication can return us to the safety and sanity of the middle of the distribution.
>
> —Merrill Winston, Ph.D., BCBA-D April 16, 2005

> The really great thing about quoting yourself is that it's really hard to screw it up, and even if you did, no one would know about it but you.
>
> —Merrill Winston, Ph.D., BCBA-D
> (later that day)

Stereotyping is great. There, I said it. It allows us to know what to do, what to say, and when to say it in situations that we have never experienced. Some may see this as what we call generalization of behavior, that is, behavior learned in one setting has "generalized" to a novel situation. In many ways, stereotyping can be useful, but, like anything useful, it has down sides and dangers. Diagnosis involves quite a bit of stereotyping. You can see evidence of this stereotyping in the assumptions people make about individuals with various diagnoses. Children with autism have problems with change. Children with ADHD can't sit still and/or are poorly organized and have short attention spans. Children with oppositional defiant disorder are noncompliant. The worst stereotyping I've seen by far occurs with autism as it is such a prevalent diagnosis and has attained what can only be described as a "celebrity status." Diagnoses mislead us. They cause us to be insensitive to individual differences. The diagnosis of behavioral (mental) disorders grew out of the medical model which has a longstanding tradition of using deductive reasoning to help determine what you have and subsequently what can or cannot be done about it. Disorder X is characterized by symptoms A, B, and C. You show these symptoms; therefore you, too, have Disorder X. It's really pretty neat and useful. Furthermore, we know that disorder X is readily treated by implementing protocols 1, 2, and 3. *Newsflash*: This type of reasoning isn't even completely reliable in medicine. It's quite good, but it sometimes fails because we don't yet realize that symptoms D and E can also be an indication of the disorder. Additionally, some people, because of individual differences and the presence or absence of other variables, don't respond well to protocols 1, 2, and 3. That this form of reasoning can go awry is not even the biggest problem. The biggest problem, in my estimation, comes down to the concept of "having" something.

Another thing I learned from the late Dr. Peter Harzem, is that there are all sorts of different "haves." You can have kidney stones, you can have cataracts, you can have sickle-cell anemia, and you can have high blood pressure. Clearly some of these "haves" are more "havey" than others. You can see kidney stones on an x-ray, and you certainly can feel them if you pass one (or so I'm told). Can you see your high blood pressure? Not directly, but it can be measured. Having high blood pressure is a very different sort of "have" than having kidney stones. Having autism is an even more different kind of have than high blood pressure. Certainly, physicians and researchers are always talking about the differences in the brains of children labeled autistic and those who are not, but there is *currently* no genetic marker used to diagnose most disorders as there is for Down's Syndrome, Lesch Nyhan's or Prader Willi Syndrome. With respect to autism, the diagnosis is not of something that children "have," instead it is based on what children do and do not do and the conditions under which they do the things they do. I like to explain to parents that they are far better off conceptualizing autism, or any other diagnosis for that matter, in this manner. In so doing, we can begin to focus on the *actual* problem. Really, I should say the *problems*. The problem is not the autism. The focus needs to be not on the label, but on excesses and deficits. Any child with any diagnosis is going to show excesses or deficits and typically both[3]. The problem with a diagnosis based solely on *behavior* is that we are trying to emulate the medical model and I just don't believe that it translates very well when switching from white blood cell count or liver enzyme levels to behavior. It leads to questions/assertions like:

What is the cure for autism?

Children with autism respond well to _____.

What are some good autism treatments?

Children with autism need visual schedules….

Autism is not gastroesophageal reflux! It isn't a single thing. The label is given when certain things are observed and certain other things are not observed. As one behavior analyst said to me at a conference, "If you've seen one child with autism, you've seen one child with autism." People who are easily given to phrases like "children with autism _____ " (fill in the blank with one of your own truisms), are lost before they've begun. They are

---

[3]I seriously doubt that all diagnoses can be explained solely in terms of excesses and deficits. You could also look at problems of frequency, breakdown of stimulus-control (things occurring at the wrong place/time or not occurring when they should), magnitude of response, atypical reinforcers, and atypical aversives. However, what people do and do not do is, in my estimation, the largest piece of the problem in most disorders.

hopelessly mired in the autism "if-then" swamp. If you have autism, then you are a visual learner and you need a visual schedule. Take your pick, there are countless examples strewn about the Internet and published in books. I would suggest that there are no "children with autism," they simply don't exist. There is A child with a label of autism and he or she may be completely different from another child with a label of autism. Diagnoses (of autism or other disorders) have taken on lives of their own. They have become *who a person is*, not just categorizations based on clusters of behavioral excesses and deficits. Even children with Down's Syndrome, who are arguably (at least from a genetics standpoint) a more homogeneous group than children labeled as autistic, are vastly different from one another. If any group should be subjected to the reasoning of "children with X respond well to Y," then it most certainly should be children with Down's Syndrome, yet even with these individuals you know next to nothing about them just because you know their diagnosis. As my esteemed colleague Pat McGreevy is so fond of saying, "Diagnoses allow us act as though we know a great deal about someone we really know nothing about."

SECTION 2: ARE WE ATTENDING TO BEHAVIOR OR LABELS?

How about it? Are we designing treatments based on the problem that's being presented, or are we allowing a label to be the primary determinant of treatment? What are some problems generated by labels?

2.1 Rule-governed versus contingency-shaped behavior

To get your doctoral degree, among other things, you have to write a dissertation. It's supposed to be a contribution to the field and an exercise in doing research. You don't even have to prove anything really. My dissertation was about rule-governed versus contingency-shaped behavior (Skinner, 1957). My dissertation proved, conclusively, that dissertations need not be conclusive to fulfill one's Ph.D. requirements. Whew! I did come to realize, however, that general rules, those that teach one where to look and what to look out for can be immensely helpful when problem solving, but that rules that are too specific and followed dogmatically can cause a tremendous insensitivity to real contingencies operating all around us. The whole "question authority" thing of the sixties is a testament to the value of not clinging to one's rules too dearly and learning to think outside the box. Now this certainly doesn't mean that your airline pilot should throw out his preflight checklist and just go with his gut, because wherever his gut goes yours is going to follow, and at considerable speed. The difference between the airline analogy and autism is that everyone can agree that a Boeing 737 is in fact a Boeing 737 and not a DC–10. The same is simply not true of autism. Even if ten out of ten psychiatrists come up with the same diagnosis, it doesn't mean that you need to follow the same checklist that you would for another child with autism. I may be rocking the boat here, but making assumptions about a person based on his or her diagnosis is no way to practice behavior analysis and it can easily lead to more problems than solutions. Diagnoses cause us to ask questions that are perhaps the least productive and the most misleading. Instead of asking, "What treatment is good for autism?" as though it were a rash of some sort, we should be asking, "What are the most important skills to teach *this* child *right now* and what are the best ways to teach him?" or "Which of the child's problem behaviors are causing the most harm right now?" I firmly believe that general guidelines, like the ones I'm trying to outline in this book, are far more helpful than highly specific rules like, "Give all children with autism picture schedules because they are visual learners."[4] Remember, we're talking about individual children with complex problems, not Boeing 737s. We must be sensitive to the problems and skills that each child brings us so that we can best tailor an intervention to suit each one. Does this mean that we can't start to identify similar types of problems shared by many children and keep a few tricks up our sleeves to deal with those problems? Of course not! If you have identified that a child bites the teacher when he has to give up a reinforcer, who cares what his diagnosis is? It just doesn't matter. You teach the child how to "handle" reinforcer removal. Will you teach some children differently than others? Sure, there will be slight differences based on the current repertoire and the severity of the problem. You might use slightly different strategies for a child who can talk than you would for a child who can't, but some strategies will be identical. I write similar recommendations for different kids all the time, *not* because they both have the same diagnosis, but because they both have the same kind of behavioral excess or deficit!

2.2   Children with diagnoses are seen as more different from those without

Maybe I'm wrong, (I really hate saying that, but after 15 years of marriage it keeps getting easier to do), but I like to view persons with disabilities as more similar to us than different. We all work basically the same way. We all love things and hate things and get angry and become sad and feel happy. We all get exasperated and disappointed and frustrated and we feel great and we feel awful. People who are given diagnoses do many of these things under conditions that people without these diagnoses might not and at a considerably greater intensity, but that's no reason to treat them like they're from another planet! Some children, labeled as autistic, may not like the tags in their shirts because it bothers them. Sometimes

---

[4]Are children with autism *really* visual learners, or are visual prompts easier to attend to for *everyone*? For example, could you imagine putting together a couch you purchased from IKEA by listening to the instructions through headphones? By the time you assemble the damn thing it will be out of style. When someone asks you if you are free on March 23, do you listen to a description of your calendar for the next six months? Visual stimuli are great because they are static and of a long duration (permanent). As Jim Johnston likes to say, audio information disappears at the speed of sound. If you "accommodate visual learners," isn't it *possible* that they will become even *worse* at following audible instructions as they are no longer required to? Think about it and get back to me...

my tag bothers me too and I cut the thing off with a pair of scissors. A child with a disability might just scratch himself. That child clearly doesn't like his tag either but may have a far worse reaction than the rest of us and may not know what to do about his problem. To complicate matters, some people feel compelled to come up with special words or phrases to either promote a brain abnormality hypothesis or to denote how weird and special the problem is. Merrill hates tags, but Joey with autism has "sensory issues" or is "tactile defensive." What??? Is that necessary? Is Joey so very different from me that he needs special language and special reasons for why he doesn't like things? Can't he just love some things and hate some things like the rest of us? *Some children* (labeled as autistic or with other diagnoses) don't like changes in routine. Do you? I don't. I like the status quo! I like all my stuff to stay where it's supposed to be and I don't like having new kinds of assignments at work when I'm comfortable doing what I've been doing. Sure, we like some new things now and then and so do children who are labeled as autistic, but the real issue is *not* that some of them don't like change, it's how freaked out they get by what is (to us) a very small change. Small changes can freak us out as well, but it's less typical.

It's far easier to understand others if we see them as not really all that different from ourselves. It doesn't matter if we're talking about someone who's from another culture, has different political ideologies, speaks a different language, or has a disability. Given that we understand something about why *we* do things (which is sometimes a huge assumption) it's much easier to understand why others do what they do. This is what Wilhelm Wundt (a famous introspectionist) believed, and I think that he may have been onto something. I'm not saying that we shouldn't collect and display data and observe individuals, for these are some of the hallmarks of behavior analysis. I just believe that, for any diagnosis, we can find some degree of the defining characteristics in ourselves. If you think about it, our problems are very often far more severe than those of people with disabilities. We engage in dangerous behaviors every day that put the lives of ourselves and others at considerable risk (texting while driving for example) yet we don't get saddled with a diagnosis. (Don't be surprised if the new DSM-V [Diagnostic and Statistical Manual] has HTD [hyper texting disorder] listed as one of the disorders of childhood.) Remember, all people are trying to satisfy their needs the best that they can. Everyone. The problem is that, very often, the best thing we can come up with isn't very good for us or anyone else.

2.3 Labels may relieve us of the responsibility to attempt behavior change

Oooh, I'm really gonna be an unpopular guy for this one. I included this section *not* to be purposefully inflammatory (it will be purely accidental), but because I feel very strongly about this issue. Sometimes labels allow parents, teachers, and others to abrogate their responsibilities and they may stop trying to produce behavior change altogether. "There's nothing I can do, it's the autism!" Many times I will get this question (about many disorders):

"Do you think it's a behavior or is it just the autism?"

The answer is of course, wait for it… that *it's all behavior*. What people really want to know, however, is whether the child is doing the behavior on purpose. Again, the answer is (usually) yes, but the purpose may not be the same for another child, and it's more than likely a lack of skills that's responsible and not "the autism." The difference between labels and behavior is that we cannot remove "the autism" but we can attempt to change behavior (reduce problem behavior and teach skills). I have seen too many people stop trying to change behavior and too many people setting their expectations way too low. Having poor self-control and becoming aggressive under certain conditions does not mean that *some improvement* can't be made. Might it be more difficult for one child than another? Without a doubt. Does the child's label mean we shouldn't try to teach him at all? No. Simply because children may have *great difficulty demonstrating appropriate behavior and tremendous motivation to engage in problem behavior*, does it necessarily follow that they can't help it when they engage in certain behaviors?

I really hate the phrase "can't help it" because it implies that absolutely nothing *can* be done and/or that absolutely nothing *should* be done. We don't only apply this concept of an *innate inability to change* to people with disabilities or mental health diagnoses, we also apply it to ourselves quite frequently. "I can't help it that I yell and scream and curse! It's who I am! This is who you married!" Sound familiar? It does if you're my wife. Maybe I'll never be able to keep from getting angry about certain things (just like a child with a disability might get very upset when the fire alarm sounds), but can I learn better things to do and say when I *do* get angry? Can I learn ways to become *un*-angry again? Is it even possible, regarding some things, that I could get a little less angry under the same conditions? I think that the answer to all of these questions is an emphatic "yes."

Finally, must we change all of an individual's behavior simply because it's a little bit odd? I sure hope not, because I'm going to have to change an awful lot of my own behavior. To me, anyhow, the goal is not to make children with disabilities just like everybody else, but to make them as happy, safe, and independent as they can reasonably be while giving them the best chance to live the same kind of life as everyone else.

SECTION 3: WE MUST SPECIFY THE PROBLEM

We need to spend more time specifying the problem(s) and less time specifying the diagnosis. I know Jimmy has autism (at least that's what he has today), but that doesn't tell me what the problems are. Many decisions are driven by diagnosis and not by the presenting problems. Some psychiatrists, driven by labels, may use what I like to call "tit for tat" medication regimes. You have ADHD, OCD, and bipolar disorder so you are going to get Adderal, Prozac, and Depakote. Three labels, three medications. Each medication happily doing its own thing, controlling only what it is supposed to be controlling and not at all affecting how the other medications work.... Meanwhile, back in the real world.... I have seen this kind of column A, column B diagnosis/treatment rationale countless times in behavior programs and medical records. The better psychiatrists I've worked with don't really give medicines for disorders per se, but instead deal with the presenting problems as *they see them* and as they are related to them by primary caregivers and others. As a behavior analyst, I am completely unconcerned with a child's diagnosis. I don't even ask what it is anymore, there's no point. A diagnostic label draws our attention to *alleged* problems, not *actual* problems. It's not as though the following scenario takes place: Someone tells me that: 1) a child has ADHD and then, 2) I write a behavior program based on observations and probes I conduct only to find out later on that, 3) the child was misdiagnosed and now has autism. Oh crap! Now I have to write a completely different program! Now where is my autism program book? I am frequently asked if I consider the child's diagnosis, or if I have expertise in disorder x, y, or z. I always say the same thing. I have expertise in analyzing the variables that increase the chances of problem behaviors and expertise in which skills to teach to help alleviate those behaviors. I can also help to determine the best ways to teach those skills. That is my expertise. Remember, we have to focus, like a laser beam, on the actual problems and not what the problems are *supposed* to be.

If, for example, a child has a diagnosis of OCD and becomes aggressive and self-injurious when the teacher shows up one morning wearing a new hairstyle, the OCD isn't the problem. Furthermore, that the child has difficulty when things are changed isn't the problem either. It isn't even a problem that the child gets agitated when things are changed. I don't get called out to a school because a child is simply angry. I get angry all the time but no one needs to call the police when I get angry (not yet anyhow). It's all a matter of the *behavior*, the *intensity* of that behavior, and the *context* in which it occurs. If the child just said, "I hate your hair like that, change it back right now or I'll have my attorney sue the school!" Would it be necessary to retain the services of a behavior analyst? No, you would need the services of a good attorney. As I've said before, specifying the exact problem is, in itself, a problem, one that many individuals fail to solve. It is *far easier* to say, "What label does he have?" and "Let's try treatment X, because I've heard that treatment X is good for children with that label. What could be easier? Focusing on a diagnosis is clearly the easier way to do things. It leads to non-individualized cookbook behavior programs that are easy to write. As I mentioned earlier, it doesn't mean that we have to start from square one with each individual child as though nothing we have learned from other children will be effective. No one can afford to do this. As an example, a good pediatrician relies on the experience of every child and condition she has seen over many years. This is what enables great physicians to take a quick look at a child and say, "It's whooping cough." Very often I see a kid who is doing exactly what the last kid was doing and in the same way. My recommendations have nothing to do with diagnosis, but are based on what is being presented to me at the time and my experience with similar problems.

It's *possible*, in some instances, that knowledge of a specific medical or genetic problem might alter one's *expectations* in terms of the ease or difficulty of treatment, but this knowledge doesn't necessarily help a practitioner zero in on the best treatment options. Someone with Lesch Nyhan's syndrome, a genetic disorder characterized by developmental delays and a tendency toward severe self-injury (biting) might be more behaviorally challenging than someone without the same syndrome, but it doesn't mean that the behavior analyst should just be able to open his filing cabinet and pull out a program from the "Lesch Nyhan's folder." It may mean that the motivation to bite could be much higher for that person than for someone else, but this is not *necessarily* the case. So for example, if someone told me that he had trouble treating biting in a child with Lesch Nyhan's syndrome I wouldn't be surprised at all. Still, it would not allow me to suggest a treatment based solely on the diagnosis. As mentioned earlier, even children diagnosed with Down's syndrome show tremendous individual differences even though there is a clear genetic basis for the disorder. "What??? They have Down's syndrome? Well, then that clearly rules out fading, shaping, and reinforcement as anything we can use." That is exactly what I wouldn't say. If ever there were a time to avoid judging a book by its cover, it would be during the provision of behavioral services. We simply have to take the time to *read* the individual's behavior.

Where do you start? It's really not all that difficult. You can start with a few basic questions:

1. What are the things that the child is doing that she shouldn't be doing?
2. What are the things that the child is NOT doing that she should be doing?
3. When faced with situations in which the child engages in problem behaviors, what would a typically developing child do that would be deemed appropriate for their level of development (discrepancy analysis)?
4. Is the behavior itself a problem, or is the place/time/frequency/magnitude the problem? Is screaming something that has to be eliminated? In the library[5], yes. At the soccer match, no
5. Are there problems related to atypical aversives/reinforcers?

These are just some "starter" questions. However, I have been in many situations where parents or teachers really couldn't specify *any* of the five things just outlined. They would just say things like "He doesn't listen!" or "He's noncompliant!" or "She's into everything!" We have to focus on skills. Skills skills skills. We have to stop focusing on what people "have" and begin focusing on the behaviors that people do and do not do, the magnitude of these behaviors relative to the events that occasion them, and the conditions under which they are displayed. These are most certainly not the only dimensions of behavior that we need to attend to, but they are a good start.

---

[5]For those of you who don't know what a library is or why you should be quiet in one, I blame Amazon.com and the iTunes Bookstore).

SECTION 4: ARE THERE ANY BENEFITS TO USING LABELS?

4.1 Placement and allocation of services

Well, just because I don't need labels for what I do, it doesn't necessarily mean that other people don't find labels useful. It's kind of tough to put a child into an autism classroom if he doesn't have the label. By the way, this leads to all sorts of battles. Countless times I have gone into classrooms and teachers have told me "You know Dr. Winston, I just don't think that Chucky really has autism! I think he would be better served in a _____ classroom!" You can fill in the blank with EH or EBD or VE or LD or TMR or any other two and three letter combinations you can think of because I've heard them all. Of course a "different placement" is almost always the topic about the child with the biggest behavior problems. For the longest time, I thought that "A Different Placement" was the name of some fantastic new charter school that would admit any child with any behavior problem! I even envisioned television ads for this mythical school…

> Tired of behavior problems? Is your student just not right for your classroom? Have you run out of suspension days? That child doesn't need a behavior program, that child needs…..A Different Placement! The place where everyone's welcome!

As mentioned earlier, diagnostic labels are also needed for insurance billing, and sometimes to receive special funding or services or placements. In about 29 states (currently) there are laws that mandate health insurance coverage for ABA services for autism, but not for Down's syndrome. What??? Really??? Is that right? Hell, if I were the parent of a special needs child I'd be fighting to get him an autism diagnosis too. As of the writing of this text, the DSM-V is allegedly going to have a much narrower definition of autism and parents are already freaking out about it. I don't blame them one bit. I feel that labels are more help when it comes to obtaining services (or being denied services, unfortunately) than for doing treatment. I'm not wild about it, but the "disease-i-fication" of behavior problems is most likely here to stay. I have seen parents fight to get the label of "autism" removed, and I have seen others fight to get the diagnosis, and usually it's the latter. I can't say that I blame them really, but the whole thing just seems unfair to me. People should get help because *they need help* and not because they have the right label. I can't be alone in this belief.

I think that labels also tend to be more helpful when the labeled group is incredibly homogeneous in their needs, i.e., all the children in *this class* read poorly. However, I just don't believe that a group of children have highly similar needs just because they all have the same diagnosis. Remember, even for medical patients who are diagnosed with hypertension, physicians cannot reliably predict which medication/treatment will be effective for them. Not by a long shot. Not yet anyhow. If we can't predict exactly what medicine will be effective for something as confirmable as high blood pressure, what chance do we have of knowing what treatment to use for individuals labeled with autism, or attention deficit disorder, or oppositional defiant disorder?

If you're going to group people, which may be a useful thing to do, I think that they should be grouped according to skills and deficits and not by labels. For example, If you wanted to group children because they all have major tantrums when they experience blocked access to reinforcement, well now you have my full attention! In this scenario, you have a group of children faced with the same kind of problem. Perhaps the treatment will be slightly different for each child, but in this example we are grouping individuals according to *actual* problems and not those that they are *supposed* to have. Maybe, someday, classrooms will be categorized by problems and not diagnostic labels. I can see it now... Oh you're looking for Mr. Goldberg? He's down at the end of the hall in the "blocked-access" classroom, right across the hall from Ms. Clarke in "inappropriate attention-seeking."

4.2   The knowing factor

What about the "knowing" factor? What is that? The "knowing" factor means that people tend to feel a bit better when they know what to call something. First, we are fearful because of what we see, hear, and experience. We don't know what it is or why it is happening. Then someone tells us what to call it and (allegedly) why it's happening. Now, it turns out that the "what we call it" part is much easier to pin down than the "why it's happening" part, but we'll take what we can get. Some years ago, my heart did a really weird thing one day. It scared the &@!$ out of me. My heart, instead of going thump, thump, thump, thump, was now going thump… thump thump… thump… thump thump thump. At least it was still thumping, but I thought I might be dying or something. How would I know? I drove myself to the emergency room in a panic (actually I was in a Ford Taurus), got hooked up to wires, got poked and prodded, and (naturally) they couldn't figure it out because my heart was no longer doing the cardiac conga. Eventually, I had a Holter monitor strapped to me for 24 hours. It's like an EKG Walkman. Sorry, I'm showing my age. It's like an EKG iPod Touch. The diagnosis was clear. Paroxysmal Atrial Tachycardia. Whew! I asked the doctor what it meant. He said it means that your heart sometimes goes thump… thump thump… thump… thump thump thump. I then asked my doctor, "What causes it?" He wasn't sure, so he told me it was idiopathic, which I later determined must be Latin for "I don't know why it's happening but I have to bill your insurance company for something." Thankfully, he told me it was benign. Whew! My heart still does the myocardial Macarena now and then, but it doesn't bother me because now I know what to call it. My insurance carrier calls it an increased premium, which causes other physiological problems, but that's a different story. The point of this palpitation parable is that people take solace in knowing what name to give the constellation of behaviors (and lack thereof) that their children exhibit.

Oh, I almost forgot. Last, sometimes the belief that one's child has this "thing" with a name can *relieve guilt* or *remove blame*, and this can be beneficial because it may reduce the parent's stress. I have worked with many parents over the years who both recognized and feared that their own behavior may have contributed to their child's problem. I tell all parents the same thing. As a behavior analyst I don't look for fault or blame. I look for *causes* and *solutions*. I know of no parents who are *trying* to make their children do bad things (that's a different disorder). Everyone is coping the best that they can, but the best that they can may not be "best."

4.3 Explaining a child's behavior to the general public

Parents can also explain their child's behavior more easily to other people. I know that some parents like to keep informational cards handy to explain to others about their child and his or her disorder. Kids will do things in public that some individuals don't understand, and nobody wants to get stared at like they're a bad parent (this is what parents have communicated to me). You've got to admit, it's easier to say, "My child has autism" and hand someone a card than to say, "My child lacks some of the skills and repertoires that other children have developed and my child is bothered by certain things to a much greater degree than your child, but may respond in a less socially acceptable manner."

4.4 Support

Diagnostic labels also allow parents to find support and camaraderie with other parents. Is that a bad thing? No, absolutely not. It's nice to know that someone else has faced or is facing some of the same difficulties that you face. We all like that. I just think that it's important to avoid clinging too closely to what we're told about what children are *supposed* to like and dislike and be capable or incapable of because of a given label.

4.5 Accepting that there is a problem

Fortunately, sometimes the label might just motivate parents to come to recognize/admit that their child has some serious problems that do not simply comprise a "phase" that the child is going through. Just because I don't need labels for what I do doesn't mean that children and their parents aren't suffering from some very real problems. So, if giving problems a name can cause parents to seek early intervention, then that, too, is a potential useful function of diagnostic labels.

4.6 Commercial value

This is, without a doubt, a benefit for some people. I do not believe that there has been a single diagnosis of childhood that has lead to the absolute deluge of products, services, and websites as autism. If you do a presentation at a conference, it's usually better attended if you put the word "autism" somewhere in the title. There aren't schools for children with disabilities as much as there are "autism schools." I know some behavior analysts who have just told me, straight up, that they put "autism" in the names of their schools to attract more people. I hate to say it, but autism in particular has what marketers like to call "brand recognition." When was the last time you saw an Oppositional Defiant Disorder school or a Down's Syndrome school? They may be out there, but I've never seen them.

I made a snide remark at a recent talk I gave (my talks are mostly a series of PowerPoint slides of semi-related snide remarks punctuated by the occasional gem of wisdom). I said that everything today has the word "autism" in front of it and that right now there's probably a website called www.autismfurniture.com. I'll be damned if someone didn't come up to me after the talk to inform me that there is indeed such a site. You can click the link now if you haven't already. Go ahead, I know you want to. Do they even have a link on their site to my book? No? And after all I did for them.... Anyhow, If that website doesn't prove my point I don't know what will.

I only included this subsection because some unscrupulous characters are out there selling snake oil for autism and some parents are buying it in bulk. No, I don't mean the fine folks at www.autismfurniture.com, but I think that everything changes when you start to bring money into the equation. You know, just for kicks, I did a search for ADDfurniture. com and bipolarfurniture.com and I got zilch. What are people with other diagnoses supposed to sit on? It just isn't fair.

To sum up, yes there are some ways that a diagnostic label can be of great value, not to me as a behavior analyst, but to some people. A label could have services value, placement value, peace of mind value, early intervention value, social-support value and even monetary value in the form of increased revenues for people selling goods and services that might be helpful for many people. I'm afraid that we'll have to learn to live with them, but we can at least try to avoid the pitfalls of diagnostic labels and recognize that they are not without problems and that they can, very easily, lead us away from genuine treatment gains.

SECTION 5:   EXPERTISE WITH LABELS OR BEHAVIOR?

5.1   What Is More Important? Expertise With A Particular Diagnosis Or Expertise With Particular Behaviors?

Well, if you firmly believe that a specific diagnosis has a specific treatment that is essentially the same for everyone, then I guess that expertise in a diagnostic label is what's important. If, on the other hand, you believe as I do, that we need to take a functional approach based on excesses and deficits, then perhaps teaching and behavior management skills are what's important. The reason I am writing this particular section is because some parents may believe that they need a practitioner with expertise in autism. As mentioned earlier, I don't make claims to be an autism expert. I make claims to be an expert in what to do about behavior problems. I don't get called to a school because a child has autism. I get called to a school because a child is destroying the classroom. Now, some may say, "Yes, but if you understand the intricacies of autism, then you will be better able to predict what will and won't work!" Wrong. (insert game show buzzer for incorrect answer). I'm sorry, it's just wrong. The behavior may be aggression, which can happen for many reasons across many children with many different diagnoses. It has some very similar consequences across individuals and some very similar determinants. Those exact consequences and determinants have to be specified for each child. The things that may need to be changed in the environment, or in the teacher's behavior, or in the child's own repertoire will differ from one situation to the next. Different children learn at different rates, their behavior has been occurring for varying lengths of time, and their abilities to get their needs met may vary widely, both within and across diagnostic categories. I would argue that *these* are the most important factors, not some label that is applied after looking at the child for an hour (actual observation times may vary).

Although one might argue that behavior is behavior regardless of its form, some behaviors, because of the risks they pose or their intermittent nature, might be a bit trickier than others to work with and may require that certain things be in place if treatment is going to be both safe and successful. If I were the parent of a child with significant aggression, I would want someone who has successfully treated children with aggression! Some individuals have never worked with a genuinely dangerous child and wouldn't know the first thing to do if they were attacked. Other children have severe language delays or just no language at all. In that case I would want a behavior analyst with good Verbal Behavior (VB) training, who was good at deciding which signs/words to teach first and what kind of assessment to use to help form an accurate picture of the child's current abilities. For example, I have great experience in selecting and teaching first mands (requests) but I am not equipped to set up a language program in the home for a child. It has nothing to do with my experience with a diagnosis, but with my experience with the problems of teaching specific skills. Sure, all skill acquisition involves good teaching, and a good teacher is a good teacher, no matter the skill. Still some types of skills, I would argue, might require a certain level of sophistication and knowledge that others simply do not. What I'm saying is that the selection of a behavior analyst (I'm talking to you, parents) should not be based so much on his or her experience with a diagnosis, but on experience with the kinds of problems shown by *your* child. For example, I have like zero experience in doing toilet training. I hear it isn't terribly difficult to do, and I understand the basics of it and could probably be of some assistance to parents in setting up a program. The fact remains, however, that I have never taught a single child how to use the toilet appropriately. It's just something that I haven't needed to do. I have two stepkids and they came to me pre-trained. Two opportunities missed. Damn!

The point is not just that you shouldn't call *me* if there's a toilet training problem, but that it's a good idea, as in medicine, to get a specialist. My only contention is that the specialty, when it comes to behavior problems, should be based on behavior, and not the diagnostic label that has been applied to the child. Sure, you could just take big fat reinforcers and big fat punishers and you might have some success in applying them to *any* behavior problem (and some clinicians do just that) but, in my opinion, it doesn't make you an expert in treating that kind of problem. Neils Bohr, a Danish physicist, defined an expert as follows:

> An expert is a person who has made all the mistakes that can be made in a very narrow field.

Although, in this case, I would say that the individual has made all the mistakes that can be made in treating certain kinds of behavior problems.

My suggestion to parents is to ask questions to potential behavior analysts about their experience working with *problems*, not so much with diagnoses. I think that there's also something to be said for experience working with certain populations of individuals. That is, just because someone has worked well with adults, doesn't mean that they are in any way comfortable working with children, and vice-versa. Sure, behavior is behavior, but if the therapist is going to work directly with your child don't you want her to like children? To me it just makes sense. Has the therapist worked at all with people who are completely nonverbal? There are many strategies you can use with people who talk that you just can't use with people who can't. As mentioned earlier in the chapter, one of the first things I want to know is whether the child can talk because it has implications for what I can and cannot do. You not only need knowledge, you need application experience. I have many colleagues who are excellent researchers and excellent behavior analysts, but I'm not going to call them up when I need someone to work hands on with a child who bites a lot. One of the most important things that behavior analysts can do is to inform parents about problems they're good at treating and skills that they can teach well. It's also important to disclose those areas with which they have little experience and/or direct knowledge. If I think I'm in over my head, which does happen sometimes, I'll be the first to let someone know that. I'll close this chapter with an ancient Persian apothegm...

> He who knows, and knows that he knows, is a wise man. Follow him.
>
> He who knows, and knows not that he knows, is asleep. Wake him.
>
> He who knows not, and knows that he knows not, is a student. Teach him.[6]
>
> He who knows not, and knows not that he knows not, is a fool. Avoid him.

---

[6]For graduate students only: He who knows not, and knows that he knows not, yet still acts as though he knows, is your major professor. Finally, for those of you with young children: He with nose snot, and knows not of his nose snot, needs a Kleenex. Give him one.

Chapter 11

Problems With Inclusion

SECTION 1:   INTRODUCTION

1.1   What has Inclusion got to do with behavior problems?

Good question. Why am I broaching the topic of inclusion in a book about dealing with behavior problems? Because it can, in many instances, heavily influence the acquisition of new skills and the prognosis for behavior problems. There I said it. Inclusion is not always, as Martha Stewart likes to say, "A good thing." Am I saying that we should not strive to place children with disabilities with typically developing peers? On the contrary, I believe, like many others, that there are some real benefits for a child to be educated not simply *in the same room* as their non-disabled-age-equivalent peers, but to be educated with those peers, even if perhaps the child in question doesn't have exactly the same sets of skills. Nothing under the sun, however, is all good in all circumstances. I'm not sure who coined the phrase "It's all good," but he either didn't understand what "good" means or he didn't understand what "all" means. Children with disabilities have a right to be included, but having a right to do something doesn't mean that it's always the best thing to do. It just means that no one can say, "You're not allowed to!" Some parents and advocates act as though all children *must* be placed in a classroom with their age-equivalent peers, regardless of their needs, deficits, or behavioral excesses and regardless of the impact of their behavior on the rights of their peers. The forcing of children into placements based on appearance rather than function burns my behavioral biscuits.

I am not what I would call "pro-inclusion" or "anti-inclusion." I'm more pro-let's-think-carefully-about-what-*this*-child-actually-needs. I tell parents repeatedly that they should be less concerned with *where* their child is taught and more concerned with *who* is teaching their child, *what* their child is being taught, and *how well* it is being taught. Are those the only factors that are important in a child's development? No, of course not. There are many social variables that help a child develop as well. Children can certainly benefit from incidental learning by exposure to other children, but this is not how they are educated and it certainly is not the way that they are treated behaviorally. Parents, you can't just look at the classroom where your child is placed based on the label of that classroom. Regular education, special needs, autism, varying exceptionalities (VE), etc. There are simply more important aspects of a learning environment to consider. I have seen children who are what I like to call "excluded in an included classroom." This means that the child has very few skills if any, multiple behavior problems, and has a paraprofessional working with him who constantly vultures directly overhead. The child may be prevented from going near the other students because he may grab at them or hit them. The child doesn't socialize with the other children because he has few social skills. *The child is often prompted to attempt work that is too difficult, and this can increase the number of existing behavior problems.* Is this child (and I have seen this scenario all too often) truly included, or is he included only in the physical sense of the word? Does the teacher have *any* experience with children who have learning difficulties and behavior problems? How expert is the paraprofessional? Does the child participate functionally in group assignments with the other children? My point is that if children are going to be included, *they need to be included*!

So how do we decide on what classroom a child needs? Well, it's sort of a misleading question. The child doesn't really *need* any type of classroom. At least not from a behavior analytic perspective. The child needs skills; those that all children need to be successful academically, but perhaps also *those skills that are related to their behavior problems*. The next question is, who has the skills to teach that child and what supports does that teacher have? Another question is, how free is that particular teacher to spend time doing one-on-one teaching with that child? We must also consider the skills of the other children in that classroom and if those children can help foster and support the skills that are being taught to the child. These are just a few questions that one might ask before deciding where to place a child. I'd like to take the rest of the chapter to provide a framework for how to wrangle with the decision of where to place a child and why. This analysis has nothing to do with rights, unless you believe that children have the right to learn as many functional skills as possible—skills that should also have a positive impact on their problem behaviors. If that's the case, then my analysis is *all* about rights. We'll also take a look at the notion of least restrictive environment and the pros and cons of placing a child in an included classroom. Please remember while reading this chapter that I'm talking about inclusion in terms of how it may affect behavior problems.

1.2   Least Restrictive Environment

The concept of the least restrictive environment or (LRE) has existed since 1975 with the development of the Education for all Handicapped Children Act (PL 94-142). I know that most of you reading this have already memorized it, but for those of you who haven't, here's what it says…(italics are mine)

> To the maximum extent appropriate, children with disabilities, including children in public or private institutions or other care facilities, are *educated with* children who are not disabled, and special classes, separate schooling, or other removal of children with disabilities from the regular educational environment occurs only when the *nature or severity* of the disability of a child is such that education in regular classes with the use of *supplementary aids and services* cannot be *achieved satisfactorily*.

You've just gotta love these kinds of laws. They are etched in stone with a dull chisel so that their vagueness and wiggle-room may live on in perpetuity. They empower us, with a malleable club of righteousness that conforms perfectly to the contours of whichever head we happen to be beating at the time. Of particular note in the LRE definition are the phrases: 1) supplementary aids and services; 2) nature or severity; 3) achieved satisfactorily; and 4) educated with. So, clearly the push is to have kids included. No argument from me there. Generally, I think it's great. However, when the child has severe skill deficits and severe behavior problems, that's a red flag for me. Let's examine these four phrases, because they have great bearing on our discussion. First, who defines the scope of what is "*supplementary*?" Is a supplementary aid like a support? For example, a child may have difficulty writing because of a physical impairment so we let the child type instead, but she can still, for the most part, do the work that is expected of her. What about a different scenario? What if the paraprofessional is heavily prompting (all physical) every response the child makes? The former is a support; the latter a crutch. My conception of a support or "supplementary aid" is that it is some type of *assistance* that is used to make the achievement of a task or goal easier or more likely. It is something that is used in cases where the person can almost demonstrate the skill at a functional level, but needs a little help to perform correctly. My conception of a crutch is that it's something that the person leans on so heavily, that if removed will cause the person to completely fail. I have seen some children who could only answer questions robotically, and only if heavily prompted, repeatedly. With no prompting, it's not so much that the child performed weakly or incorrectly, but not at all. I once saw a little boy, functioning at a very low level (no verbal skills, no academic skills, no eye contact) being physically prompted to look at a fourth grade text book while the teacher read aloud to the class (the paraprofessional repeatedly physically turned his head in the direction of the book). Would you say that this was an example of a supplementary aid or support? I don't even think it qualified as a crutch! I just called it "forced pretend reading." Needless to say, the parents were less than thrilled with my assessment of the situation.

I'll address the "educated with" part of the definition in a moment, but next I'd like to talk about that last part of the LRE definition. That part about the "nature and severity" of the disability preventing education from being "achieved satisfactorily." The whole nature and severity thing isn't terribly clear, but I take it to mean that the severity of the *deficits* must be taken into account. I suppose that the "satisfactorily" part refers to the quality of skills or the speed with which they are acquired, but the definition doesn't really say. Essentially, the caveat is that children should be in included classrooms unless their disability keeps them from making progress despite any supports. That's not what the law says, but that seems to be what it is implying. It seems that the wording is leaving the educational system an "out." I think it's important to consider, however, that a lack of progress is primarily a reflection of 1) the goal chosen (which may be well beyond the child's current repertoire) and 2) the expertise of the teacher, and *not* the nature or severity of the disability per se. What I mean is that if you've chosen the right goal and you're doing good teaching, what's to stop you from making progress? It's easy, however, to see a lack of progress if a child who barely possesses pre-K skills is attempting a "modified" fourth-grade curriculum.

Unfortunately, I have seen children in regular education classes being heavily prompted (on the wrong task) and making no progress, but it didn't stop them from being in the included classroom. I have also seen children in special education classrooms who had tremendous skills and I couldn't figure out why they weren't in a regular education classroom. We've got to stop blindly sticking kids in autism classrooms because they have that label or sticking them in regular education classrooms because it's the right thing to do. We have to look at each child as an individual and see what fits him or her best, and that takes time, effort, and argument (I mean discussion). The last time I checked, the "I" in IEP[1] stood for "Individualized," not "Included."

Finally, in the first part of the LRE definition it says, "Educated with" children who are not disabled. This may seem nit-picky, but I'd like to point out where people tend to provide their own interpretations of definitions. The phrase that pays is "educated with." Nowhere does the definition say, "Educated alongside of" or "Educated in the vicinity of." Does the definition mean education using the same curriculum as the other students? This is just my take on it of course, but I am inferring that it does mean the same basic curriculum, even if adjusted slightly, and even if supports are needed. If everyone in the class is working on long division and the included child is working on "How many bears are in the cup?" (I have seen even more disparate tasks) he is indeed being educated, but he is certainly not working on the same task as the rest of the class, only the same *subject*. How "included" is that? Can the child participate in a group exercise on long division? If the teacher is giving a lecture to the class on long division and the included student is only listening to his paraprofessional count out bears, how 'included" is that? On the other hand, what if the student *can do long division*, but has to work more slowly and needs the paraprofessional to help answer questions that the teacher may not have time for. That is a *very* different scenario. In that scenario the paraprofessional is (in my opinion) *supporting* the student so that he can functionally participate in the *same lesson* that the other students are receiving. Let's say that I have a disability, and I'm in an included classroom working on a curriculum that is four grade levels below my peers and 90 percent of my interactions are with my paraprofessional. Why am I in an included classroom? Maybe it makes sense to some people, but it just doesn't make sense to me. It has been my personal experience that some individuals completely ignore that section of LRE that refers to the *nature and severity*, *supports*, and *satisfactory achievement*. Some proponents of inclusion are focused solely on physical placement and I think it's just plain wrong. On what then, should we base our decision? I think it should be based on excesses and deficits that are clearly defined. Ultimately, it's a judgment call; there is no magic number on a classroom readiness scale that mandates either inclusion or a specialized classroom. However, I think that the five categories discussed in the next section will help the IEP team (including the parents) have a meaningful discussion about the child's educational needs, which has implications for placement.

---

[1]Just a matter of definitions, I understand that parents are considered to be part of the IEP team, but I am going to use the phrase "IEP team" to refer to the "school" side of the team and parents just as "parents." I am doing this not because the parents should be marginalized, but because they often will disagree (be they right or wrong) with the rest of the team members.

1.3   A Couple of Words About Discrimination and Accommodation...

I think that some people confuse discrimination and accommodation when dealing with persons with disabilities. After all, they do both end in "ation." We treat people with disabilities differently in some ways but not in others. It depends on a number of factors including age, level of functioning, and the presence of multiple physical disabilities, just to name a few. I've been working in this field for 25 plus years, and it's been my experience that if people don't value a *particular form* of discrepant treatment of a person with disabilities, then they tend to give it the label "discrimination." If they *do value* a particular form of discrepant treatment, then they tend to give it the label "accommodation." That we treat people with disabilities differently than everyone else in some important ways is not at issue. We do, because we *have to*. It would be criminal to treat them in exactly the same way in all circumstances, just as it would be criminal to treat non-disabled children exactly the same way as non-disabled adults. Treating people with disabilities differently in *specific* ways is sometimes necessary. However, we try not to treat them differently in any fundamental way. That is, they must have the same basic human rights, respect, dignity, general welfare, etc., as everyone else, right? However, to truly help them and prevent the greatest harm we must sometimes treat them differently, which is not inherently bad or a civil rights violation. If a typically developing 18-year-old hits a teacher with a chair, he's probably going to jail. If the same-aged student with a profound disability engages in the same behavior, is he going to jail? Would the teacher even press charges? Is that discrimination or accommodation? I make these points in this chapter because I believe that the issue of inclusion involves discrimination, accommodation, and treating certain populations differently in *specific ways* that are intended to decrease harm and increase success. I don't believe that included classrooms are always going to produce good educational/behavioral outcomes for all students. I also don't believe that self-contained special education classrooms are necessarily discriminatory, but they also may not be the best choice for some students. In keeping with the theme of the previous chapter about diagnoses, I'd like everyone to think seriously about the problem of blindly following general rules like "inclusion is always good." Sometimes these well-meaning rules can cause us to become insensitive to a child's specific educational needs.

Sometimes we do truly *discriminate* against children with disabilities *because we expect problems*. I was once observing a special needs child in an included classroom. The complaint was that everyone thought that the child should not be in that classroom and it was requested that I conduct an observation and then give my unbiased opinion on the matter. The child in question was functioning at a high level, good verbal skills, good academic skills, and participated in the class and answered questions appropriately. He had a couple of quirky behaviors here and there, sure, but on the whole I thought he was doing quite well. I not only observed this child, but all of his classmates. For the entire class, there was a tremendous amount of off-task behavior, talking out of turn, making noises, and a few other minor behavior problems. Honestly, this child had fewer of these problems than the rest of the class as a whole. Of course this was something that I had to point out to the teacher. One problem that I've noticed in working with all people with disabilities, not just children, is that we sometimes look for behavior problems with greater scrutiny than with other children. Also, we sometimes expect the child with disabilities to *behave better than their typically developing peers*. We sometimes overlook all the minor behavior problems of typically developing children because they have no label and their problems occur in the context of a wealth of other skills. I believe this is in keeping with what's known as the "competence-deviancy hypothesis" (Gold, 1976; Gold 1980). The hypothesis states that we will accept more deviance from people whom we see as highly competent.[2] Again, context is very important when looking at a number of behavior problems. In the context of fewer skills, deviant behavior stands out like a poodle at a pitbull fight (no animals were actually harmed in the construction of this simile).

SECTION 2: FIVE DOMAINS FOR PLACEMENT CONSIDERATION

I really didn't want to call this the "inclusion readiness checklist" or anything like that because I don't want to imply that children need to "earn" the right to be considered for inclusion. I would like the reader to consider these domains as ways of helping to predict how *smoothly* things will go. Everyone has to agree that we want things to go smoothly and that we want the child to be successful and accepted by their peers and by other teachers, right? The fit doesn't have to be perfect; I don't expect it to be, but all things considered, don't we want the child to maximize his success and as quickly as possible? These domains are not meant to be exhaustive and are somewhat arbitrary, but they are meant to give a quick overview of the child that encourages the team to focus on excesses and deficits that may affect the child's success. These domains are: 1) verbal skills; 2) traditional academics; 3) social skills; 4) schoolhouse survival skills; and 5) flat-out bad behavior (FOBB).

2.1   Verbal Skills

Without a doubt, the biggest impediment to academic progress is a lack of verbal skills. I've already talked about Verbal Behavior (VB) in Chapter 7 on repertoire problems, so I won't go into much detail here, but let me just say that for children who are completely nonverbal—that is they can't talk, can't sign, can't use an augmentive communication device, or can't use PECS (picture exchange)—their ability to learn traditional academics will be all but nonexistent. Parents, I'm talking to you now. If there are significant language deficits, your child needs to be with a teacher who has at least a rudimentary knowledge of language acquisition. One hour a day with a speech therapist is not likely to be sufficient. No other

---

[2] Thanks to Lisa Schmidt for turning me on to that hypothesis.

aspect of their education comes close to the importance of learning language. An included classroom is on the bottom rung of the ladder of educational importance. I don't even think it's *on* the ladder in this case.

A child who has no language is probably not going to learn language just because he or she is surrounded by children who can talk. This child has not learned to talk even after spending the majority of his life with talking parents and possibly also talking siblings. If being around these individuals for *years* has not produced language, don't expect a classroom of 18 kids to do it. I'll say the same thing to all of you that I have told to friends and relations; regarding children who are nonverbal, *nothing is more important than the ability of the teacher to teach language!* Nothing. Not the type of classroom, not the presence of typically developing peers, and not the paraprofessional working with him. That said, if for the sake of argument you can find a regular education teacher who also has extensive skills in teaching VB (Verbal Behavior) to children, then go for it. It's just that it would be rare to find a regular education teacher who is skilled in teaching language to children with disabilities.

Things are a bit more confusing for kids who can talk at least a little bit. As mentioned in Chapter 7, children with gaps in their language skills, particularly intraverbals (answering the question, "What is the capitol of Florida?"), will start to struggle as the curriculum gets more sophisticated and demanding. As you already know, a curriculum that is too demanding will often generate escape/avoidance behavior. A child whose skills were close to his peers in kindergarten could start to struggle in first grade. In general, a kid with good language skills, including good reading skills, will be more likely to succeed in an included classroom, even if his academics are weak in different areas.

2.2 Academics

Assuming that a child's language is good, the next thing to consider is academics. I have seen many children in included classrooms—children with some significant behavior problems—who essentially had good academics. They could do everything their peers were doing. They could answer questions about the topic in the lecture, and they had good math, spelling, and reading skills. Even though their social skills weren't great and they shouted out answers and wouldn't remain in their seats and were driving the teacher crazy, they had some great academic skills. In these cases, the problems were primarily ones of behavior management. These kids weren't really having problems *because* they couldn't do the assignments or didn't understand the assignments. In fact, some of them were so smart they could answer questions the other kids couldn't answer. They just had "acting-out," impulsive kinds of problems. I encourage the team to keep these kids in their current placements because I know that these students, for the most part, can do what is necessary to be academically successful.

In sharp contrast to the children described above, quite often I see children with almost *no* academic skills and the curriculum is "modified" for their level of functioning. As an example, one child, who was nonverbal, was in a third grade included classroom. His parents demanded that he be placed in that classroom. The other children were working on spelling. "Spelling" for this child consisted of touching the correctly spelled word 50 percent of the time, with assistance, when shown two cards; one containing the correctly spelled word and the other containing the same word spelled incorrectly. I'll let that sink in for a bit. I'm sorry, but this is not spelling. At best this is called proofreading and it's not even really that.

This is a fine example of an "adjusted curriculum" that is not even an approximation to the curriculum and is also nonfunctional. These types of curriculum adjustments are happening right now, all over the country, perhaps in your classroom if you're a teacher and perhaps with your child if you're a parent. The teacher in this example knew that the goal was nonsense, but she was directed to do it because it was in the IEP. When I asked her about it she gave me one of those "meh, what are you gonna do?" kind of looks. I don't blame her. I don't even blame the parents whose well-intentioned expectations were wildly unrealistic and damaging. I blame the system. This kind of nonsense is unacceptable as the child was receiving a sham education at best. You might think that "damaging" is perhaps too strong a word, but, for children who learn with great difficulty, time is precious and it can't be squandered on the wrong goals. If a child clearly can't perform academics then we should at least be teaching him some functional skills to enhance his quality of life. I believe the answer to this kind of problem lies in generating realistic expectations for the parents and for the IEP team and in proper assessment and evaluation. The team must also contend with the over-interpretation of state standards for education (which help generate these nonsense goals) as well as coming to grips with the fear of going through due process. These kinds of sham goals can be dealt with, but I'm afraid it's going to be painful for everyone until we can all settle on the same page. Before moving on to the next section, let me leave you with this thought: The primary goal of an IEP cannot be to make the parents happy (sorry, parents). Making the parents happy sometimes meets the goal of avoiding *litigation*. The goal of an IEP is, ultimately, to provide the correct services (things you do for the child) and to produce functional academic or functional life skills; skills that are meaningful to the child, not necessarily to the parents. Now, parents, in fairness to both of you, sometimes parents are unhappy specifically because their child isn't learning any functional skills! In that case, fixing things will help the child *and* make the parents happy.

I have nothing against happy parents. I love it when the parents are happy; I strive to make the parents happy, but not at the expense of doing the wrong thing for the child. Consequently, I really anger some parents. Certainly, what the parents feel is best for their child is sometimes at odds with what the team feels is best. It doesn't mean, however, that the team is always right either. Isn't it a shame that we are sometimes more worried about being sued and making waves than producing real, meaningful, functional skills?

2.3 Social Skills

Children who are not very social will not necessarily cause a problem in an included classroom, but neither will they be able to take advantage of all the other children with whom they can interact. So a lack of social skills alone won't necessarily cause problems if the child is more of a loner. If, on the other hand, the child has very few social skills but very much likes interacting with other children and actively seeks their attention, then he may wreak havoc with his typically developing peers. I knew one child who was not what I would call "dangerous," but he would frequently choke his little peers, not out of anger, but because he didn't know what to do with them. He caused considerable distress to the teacher and to other boys and girls. Children who love attention but have poor social skills are more often than not going to engage in very naughty behavior to get what they want. One problem of an included classroom is that instead of eight other children, there may be 18 other children! That's a lot of extra sources of reinforcement.

On the other hand, what if the child in question has really great social skills, but is currently in a special education classroom with children who have almost no social skills? Who is this child going to interact with? Most likely it will be the teacher as he or she will be the only one with equivalent skills. It kills me to see a kid with great social skills who is unable to use them because of the skill level of his peers in the current classroom. When considering placement of a student, just remember this, kids with great social skills are going to be liked more by their peers and teachers. Do our children *have* to be liked by everyone in their placement? No. Being likable has nothing to do with your right to be educated with your non-disabled peers. However, you are generally going to be more successful and happier if most people *do* like you. I know that children have a right to try to be educated in the least restrictive setting, but I think that we should try to stack the cards in the child's favor.

2.4   Schoolhouse Survival Skills

Neal Fleisig, a behavior analyst, therapist and crisis management expert likes to use the phrase "Survival Skills." These are skills that may not be absolutely necessary for success, but they greatly increase the chances of success. As an example, it's abundantly clear that children can learn whilst standing. Applying pressure to one's posterior has not been shown to increase academic success (unless the pressure is applied at high velocity, in which case academic performance might increase exponentially). Nonetheless, children will be seen in a much more favorable light if they can remain seated for 10, 20, or 30 minutes at a time. Is it absolutely *necessary* in the same way that it's necessary to be able to swim if you want to be a lifeguard? No. Will it increase the chances that a child will be more readily accepted? Absolutely. True enough, people should accept us for who we are, disability or no disability, but this is a book about things in the real world, and in the real world people judge us, have preconceived notions, show biases, and form fast first impressions that can affect their subsequent behavior for a long time.

A lack of these schoolhouse survival skills could cause problems for any child, and not just children with disabilities. Which skills are we talking about? The biggest ones are self-control skills and what I'll call independent classroom skills. I've touched on self-control skills in other chapters, but briefly, I'm talking about the impulse control types of skills that allow us to wait our turn, wait until we get permission to speak or act, stand in line patiently, remain quiet, and things like that. These are all skills that many typically developing children have already mastered by the time they leave kindergarten. I distinctly remember getting a report card in the first grade from my teacher, Miss Jackson, and it said, "Merrill has problems controlling his mouth!" She made it sound like I drooled a lot. I controlled my mouth quite well in fact. Everything I wanted to say came out correctly, but I had some impulse-control problems. Is being quiet the most important thing for a child to learn? No of course not, but all these little things can add up and it can affect someone's success. Remember, poor self-control skills can result in a child who disrupts the entire educational environment for the other children, who are also important. Remember, *all* children matter, not just the child with disabilities. Some may disagree vehemently with me, but I think that the rights of the child with disabilities should not impinge on the rights of other children, whether those other children are disabled or not.

What about independent classroom skills? Children who can function independently can certainly do well in an included classroom. As I mentioned earlier, even if they are not particularly social, they may still be able to demonstrate all the other skills that will allow them to be successful. What kinds of skills am I talking about? I've mentioned some of these in other sections, but decided to group them all together here and add a few others. These skills are not listed in any particular order, so if you like, you can start reading from number 5 and then just jump around:

1. Following instructions at a distance of greater than three feet from the teacher.
2. Being able to work independently for several consecutive minutes without prompting (15–30 minutes would be nice).
3. Knowing how to get more work materials.
4. Knowing what the next assignment is and being able to start it independently.
5. Being able to go from one area to another without prompting.
6. Being able to complete assignments independently.
7. Being able to ask for help when having problems (many higher functioning kids still don't do this).
8. Being able to wait for assistance after asking for help or wait for permission to change locations.
9. Being able to work next to other students without disrupting them.

This is *by no means* an exhaustive list, but you get the idea. I just pulled these off the top of my head based on problems I've seen. I'm certain that someone else has an entire inventory of these sorts of skills, but I would say that a child who has mastered these nine is well on her way. Children who can't do these things will absolutely slurp up an inordinate amount of teacher attention, and then what about the other students? Even if the child has a paraprofessional working directly with her, that, too, is a resource drain and often leads to prompt dependence. I strongly recommend that if a paraprofessional is needed to accomplish any or all the independence skills listed here, that there should be a plan to *fade out* that individual quickly or the child will possibly *never* learn these skills, skills that could serve that child as an adult.

2.5   Flat-out Bad Behavior

FOBB is the final area of concern when considering an included classroom. I have seen children with disabilities in included classrooms with significant behavior problems, ones that caused problems not only for those students, but for their typically developing peers as well. Even with the services of a one-on-one paraprofessional, the students still exhibited behavior problems and could still get at the other students. What kinds of behavior are we talking about? Aggression, self-injury, property destruction, major disruption of the classroom by screaming, destroying things, running around and grabbing things, cursing, and sometimes even stripping. You might think that this would be the number one consideration and even the deal breaker for getting a child into an included classroom, but this is not necessarily the case. Remember, the behavior in question may not be high-frequency, and the behavior may not always be dangerous. It's not really dangerous to strip off all your clothes, but it certainly is unacceptable. Even some of the dangerous behavior can be worked with in many instances. *Remember, typically developing children do engage in aggression and can get into fights with other students.* FOBB can often be dealt with if the child is strong in the other areas (verbal, academic, social, schoolhouse survival).

If the child can otherwise function in the classroom, but say for example, has a short fuse, then the teacher can often be taught behavior management skills to help alleviate the problem. If the skill deficits that are related to the behavior problem have been correctly identified, and if the child learns fairly quickly, then it is simply a matter of writing and implementing a plan that targets those skills. I write plans like that all the time. Of course if the nature of the behavior is such that a particular level of expertise is needed to deliver treatment, then resources may simply not be available in an included classroom. I don't want you to think, however, that some bad behavior alone should always cause the delay of an included placement. *Again, children must be considered individually and we have to look at them in the context of all sorts of skills and abilities and not just focus on their behavior problems.*

Things become more complicated when, along with FOBB, the child also has significant deficits in several other areas. Children with very poor academic skills will often behave far worse because they are being asked to do things that they aren't very good at doing. Kids who can't read generally behave worse when it's time for reading because they can't really participate. I have seen many children whose behavior problems become worse when they're placed in a situation where they must struggle to keep up with the class. If the child likes attention, he often can't get it by giving correct answers, so he gets it by acting-out during instruction. Of course if you were to put that child in a situation in which he feels confident and competent, you may get much different behavior. Any one of us can become very uncomfortable when placed in a situation where we know far less about a topic than everyone else. To sum up, don't count a child out only because of problem behavior. Very often, because of strengths in other areas, things can be turned around quickly!

2.6 How do we use these five domains to help make placement decisions?

Good question, glad I asked it. I don't currently have a rating scale and a way of calculating scores where a 70 or higher equals an included placement and a 50 or lower equals a self-contained classroom. I know some folks may want that, but I hate making major decisions based on a score from a single tool. I urge IEP teams and parents to work together and look, critically, at where each student lies regarding these general categories. Honestly, the biggest areas of importance to me as a behavior analyst are the verbal and the academic domains. If the kid can talk well (have a conversation with you including things in the past and things in the future) and has some decent academics, even if behind a grade level or two, I feel like everything else can be brought up to speed or at least improved markedly. This is because the child has a decent foundation on which to build. This is why I feel very hopeful about children who mainly strike out in the FOBB department. What about the opposite? What about a child who really has no bad behavior to speak of, but has almost zero skills. Well, these kids are not likely to interfere with the educational process of the other students, and they are not likely to take up much teacher attention, but what will they gain by being in an included classroom? I'll talk about that some more in the next section on the pros and cons of included placements. How about a third category of children? There are those who have poor skills, but they have some, *and* they have significant behavior problems. These kids may be the poorest candidates because they need expertise in teaching (because they have few or poor skills) *and* they also exhibit significant behavior problems. These kids interrupt the education of other students, take up a great deal of teacher time, usually need a one-on-one, and need a certain level of teaching expertise that is just not typically available in a regular education classroom. It seems to me that extremes at either end are less problematic. That is, the child with only FOBB is often more workable because of the presence of other significant skills and the child with no FOBB but also almost zero skills will be "accepted" by the teacher and other students (regardless of how much she will benefit from being there). I'm hoping my analysis makes some sense to all of you. Remember, I'm not saying, "Always place this child here" or "Never place that child there." I'm saying that you can expect greater or lesser probabilities of success based on strengths and weaknesses in the five domains I've outlined. I'm always trying to increase the chances of success, that's why I use these categories to help guide the decision making process and not to prove that a child belongs in one type of classroom versus another. I'd prefer that we not use our information to verbally beat up on each other. Information about a child's needs should be used as a means to generate discussion, and not as a club for pummeling people into submission.

SECTION 3: PROS AND CONS OF INCLUDED PLACEMENTS

As I mentioned already, nothing is "all good." Context, context, context. There are times where I've said to myself "What is this kid doing in this room?" Sometimes I've said it in a self-contained "autism" classroom and sometimes I've said it in a regular education classroom. So what are some pros and cons? I'll go over what I believe to be some valid reasons for one placement versus the other, and I'll try to be balanced in my review.

3.1 Pros of Included Classrooms

1. *The other kids in an included classroom are (generally) well behaved!* Why does that matter? It's really very important. It is still amazing to me that children (or adults for that matter) show any behavioral improvement while near other individuals with significant behavior problems. Some children only have problems around unreasonable and poorly behaved children. When someone is nasty to the child, the child bites the nasty person. However, put that child into a group of well-behaved children and "Boom," problem gone. Maybe not forever, but at least in that environment. Also, children will pick up each other's inappropriate behavior. Not always of course, but it does happen. Dozens of times teachers have told me about these kinds of problems. For example, I might hear, "Jermaine didn't start banging his head until Tito (who head bangs a lot) came to our classroom." God forbid that the child with behavior problems picks up some pro-social behaviors in the included classroom, right? There are (generally) good role-models for how to behave in the included classroom. Of course, if the child in question is not really an observational learner and good at imitating and/or socially aware, then it really won't matter one way or the other. He or she won't pick up any bad OR good behaviors. Remember, children with disabilities, particularly those with more severe disabilities, don't naturally pick up too many things; this is one of the reasons why they have so few skills. They have to be specifically taught very carefully and systematically over what is sometimes a very long time. I think that for some children the expectations of "good behavior osmosis" is unrealistically high given their learning histories. On the other hand, if the child is a "behavioral sponge" then an included classroom might work wonders. Incidentally, don't think for a moment that typically developing peers can't pick up nasty behavior from the children that come into their classrooms because that can happen as well. Again, we can't only be concerned with the child with disabilities. They *all* matter.

I was in an elementary school, and the kid I was seeing had a really foul mouth. Really bad. He was only about five or six, but very advanced in the curse words department. He was being escorted up to the nurse's station in the main office to get his meds. As he was being escorted up there he said, "I don't want my mother-%$#&*@! meds!" Well, I wasn't that stunned, and the teacher wasn't that stunned, and the nurse wasn't that stunned. The two first-grade girls bringing the attendance sheet up to the office turned positively white, and they were pretty white to begin with. They just stood there with their mouths hanging open for a moment. Did they go home and immediately start cursing? I don't know, but they were unnecessarily exposed to language that their parents would probably not have appreciated. My point is that any child can pick up bad behavior from any other child irrespective of diagnosis or level of functioning.

2. *Children with decent verbal skills have a verbal community of other children.* In many instances, I have seen kids in a self-contained "autism" classroom with some really great verbal skills, yet no one to talk to but the teacher and the paraprofessional. If you've got some skills that need sharpening, and these skills require other people with the same or better skill for practice, then it makes good sense to be around them most of the time. Remember, the kid already has some good skills and we want to make them better and make sure he or she keeps using them. This is not the case for a student with almost no skills. That child needs to be taught the basic verbal operants (mands, tacts, intraverbals) and there is not much chance (read no way in hell) that he is going to learn them by hanging out with typically developing peers.

3. *Typically developing children may be able to better tolerate the occasional behavior problem.* As mentioned in Chapter 4 on problems with peers, many kids with behavior problems will tend to set off their peers who also have poor self-control skills and are easily agitated. It can absolutely be easier to teach a typically developing child with no behavior problems how to ignore the occasional inappropriate behavior of a child with disabilities. Many typically developing peers can be very sympathetic and understanding about the challenges faced by a classmate with a disability. Some children can also be taught simple behavioral strategies to keep a lid on their classmate's behavior problems. Some kids do planned ignoring better than some adults I've worked with! I have also seen some typically developing kids take other classmates under their wings and form special relationships with them. No, it doesn't always happen, but it's great when it does. Of course this ability for a non-disabled peer to tolerate inappropriate behavior has its limits too. I know some kids who will tolerate taunting or weird noises or comments, but not being choked from behind.

4. *Some students are sensitive to their level of functioning and resent being with children functioning at a lower level.* I don't know how often this occurs, but it does occur. Some children with disabilities, because of school resources, may be in a special education classroom with other students who have significantly fewer skills. Some of these higher functioning children may be resentful that they are not in a room with peers who have similar skills. Of course, depending on the child's skills, she may end up feeling uncomfortable in a new placement if she now realizes that she has the fewest skills in the new classroom. Nonetheless, a child's sensitivity to her own skills and the skills of others could have a significant affect on how comfortable she feels in one placement versus another. Is this the

most important factor? I don't think that it is, but it may be much more important for some children than others.

3.2   Cons of Included Classrooms

As discussed earlier, there are plenty of reasons to avoid placements in regular education classrooms, but remember, we shouldn't focus on the child's *right* to be educated with their peers to the exclusion of all other considerations.

1. *Regular education teachers typically do not have the skills to work with children with learning difficulties and significant behavior problems.*   Sure, even special education teachers can't produce great results with all children, but in most instances, they have better skills, knowledge and experience than the typical regular education teacher. Also, I hate to say it, but special education teachers will typically tolerate more bad behavior than the average teacher because they are used to it. I know teachers who have been cursed at, threatened with death, scratched, bitten, hit, had their personal property destroyed, their front teeth knocked out, their noses broken and, incredibly, still love working with children with disabilities. These teachers have my undying respect and admiration, but most regular education teachers are not accustomed to these kinds of behaviors.

2. *Student-to-teacher ratios are much higher in regular education classrooms (more students to one teacher).*   Most regular education classrooms are roughly two to three times the size (student-wise) of self-contained classrooms. Even if the teacher has the kinds of skills that are necessary, he just can't spend the same amounts of time that he would be able to in a smaller classroom with one or two aides. Sure, the child in the included classroom might have a paraprofessional assigned to him, but that para would not typically have skills that would meet or exceed those of the primary classroom teacher. If the paraprofessional does not have some highly specialized training, then he or she often ends up becoming a "personalized inappropriate behavior reinforcer." Sure, sometimes you get some real gems, but this is the exception and not the rule. I would want to see the child get as much one-to-one teaching as possible from the most qualified person in that classroom. Along with the poorer ratio, the sheer number of students can be a problem for some individuals. The rooms may be more crowded with more commotion. If the child with behavior problems shows any attention-maintained behavior, she may be able to gain attention from a whole lot more people than in a self-contained classroom with fewer kids. Just for the sake of argument, let's say a kid curses. Really nasty cursing. Like the kind of cursing you do when your car breaks down on the worst stretch of road at the worst possible time with the worst possible cell phone signal. The impact is typically not as great in a class of six children, who are all working on different things in different areas, than in a class of 18 children during a lecture-based lesson. Can you imagine the reinforcement explosion of 18 kids laughing as a result of naughty behavior? It's potentially huge.

3. *Included classroom settings often involve multiple teachers in multiple classrooms with multiple personalities.* In an included classroom, children are changing classes five times per day (like in middle school) and every teacher interacts with the child differently. Some in good ways, some in bad ways, but all differently. It's difficult enough to stabilize behavior with just one teacher in one classroom. Imagine, if you would, trying to produce behavior change in a child's home, but instead of having two parents the child has five parents! It's not simply a matter of training more staff to implement a plan correctly—it's getting buy-in from people who may view the child's problems and the solutions to those problems very differently.

4. *The student may be "pushed" harder to attempt a curriculum that they are ill prepared for.* Students who have some academic skills (as opposed to almost none) may be pushed harder to attempt the same grade level work as their typically developing peers. Don't misunderstand, there's nothing wrong with pushing a student, but they've got to have the necessary skills to benefit from the pushing. I mentioned earlier that a child with good basic math skills, but poor verbal comprehension and a poor intraverbal repertoire will often fall apart when it comes to mathematical word problems. Yes—many of us had problems with word problems, but at least we could all talk quite well. Again, I have no problem with placing children in included classrooms, but we must set them up for success. What if a child's behavior problem is made worse because we are forcing her to learn from a curriculum that she is unprepared for? Some people may feel that either the child will learn or she won't, but they may not consider that the child's behavior could worsen. Few things make me angrier than seeing a child's behavior problem worsen because she has been forced into attempting something that is well beyond her current ability. The problem I'm describing is more typical with a student who has really good "splinter" skills. These are skills that look pretty good on their own, yet we continue to teach them with a complete disregard for other necessary academic skills and language development. These skills may include rote mathematics, tacting (labeling) and reading aloud with little or no comprehension. Students with these splinter skills are highly vulnerable to being put in over their heads, academically speaking.

Even worse than the student with some capable splinter skills is the student with essentially no academic skills who is having the curriculum "adjusted" for his developmental level. Of course by "adjusted" I mean twisted, perverted, bastardized, pureed, flambéed, homogenized, and then extruded into a paste that resembles the original curriculum in the same way that Cheez Whiz resembles a hunk of finely aged sharp cheddar. I am *so* sorry, I take that back. Cheez Whiz and finely aged sharp cheddar are much more similar than grade-level work and some of the "adjusted" curricula I have seen. Case in point. One child I saw was in a fourth-grade regular education class. The rest of the class was learning about savannas, deserts, and grasslands in earth science. This particular student, who had almost no verbal skills except for maybe several dozen tacts (labels) and a couple of mands (requests) was "participating" in the lesson. The teacher was trying to get him to color in a map and to make the land green and the water blue, or something of that nature. This particular student didn't even know his colors, but you don't need to know colors to be able to talk about different types of environments anyhow. Coloring a picture (with tremendous assistance from a para-professional) has nothing to do with becoming competent in earth science! When the teacher explained to me what she was doing (which she was mandated to do by the IEP) she just sort of looked at me and shrugged her shoulders as if to say, "I know it's crazy, but I have to do something." I felt really sorry for her because she was doing her best, but she should never have been asked to "adjust" this curriculum at all. Falderal! This child was never going to master earth science without learning to communicate and he simply could not functionally communicate. He was in the included classroom working on a fourth grade "adjusted" curriculum for other reasons. No doubt, the parent felt that this was best for the child, and who doesn't want the best for their child? Unfortunately, my understanding of what was best was far different from the parent's. Let's just say that we agreed to disagree. Asking the child to attempt this adjusted curriculum only created the illusion of education and if it wasn't a *complete* waste of time and resources it was at least 95 percent, and that's too much. This child could have been learning functional skills, language skills, self-help skills, and/or leisure skills, any of which would have been better than faux earth science. Does this example exemplify the spirit of 94–142 in an exemplary fashion? Is this what is meant by "providing supports?" Was that grade-level work? Does the law say that it has to be grade-level work? No, it definitely does not. Should a child be excluded from a regular education classroom simply because he is working one grade level lower on math or reading? I don't believe that this would prove to be much of a problem. I'm only saying that *tremendous* differences in fundamental skills sets should be a major consideration when making placement decisions.

5. *Decreased Tolerance by the regular education teacher.* This is a bit of a continuation and extension of a point made in the first "con." As mentioned, regular education teachers may have a much lower bad behavior threshold than special education teachers. One of the possible consequences is that the regular education teachers may have a bigger reaction to problem behaviors. If one teacher tends to have a bigger reaction to a child's behavior than another teacher, the chances of reinforcing attention maintained behavior is much greater. I think that this is an important point that you won't hear many people discuss in an IEP meeting. We would all like to think that all teachers will tolerate the same problems simply because a child has a disability, but this just isn't always the case. Anyone's sensitivity to behavior problems can vary regardless if they're regular or special education teachers, principals, or parents. It just depends on the person's experiences.

In summary, the point of all these pros and cons is that *nothing* is all good or all bad. We've got to stop forcing placements one way or the other without acknowledging the possible down sides of each. I feel that we also have to stop making decisions based *solely* on rights and start making them based on needs, so that we can achieve the best fit for each child.

SECTION 4: THE IEP TEAM VS. PARENTS

1.1 Can't we all just get along?

As a reminder, I know that the parents are part of the IEP team, but for our purposes here I'm referring to the IEP team as the "school side" of the inclusion equation. So, who is right about placement decisions, the IEP team or the parents? The answer is, wait for it... The side with the most attorneys! I'm just kidding. Attorneys are great, they come in really handy when you need to be protected from *other* attorneys. First, when things work properly, *we're all supposed to be on the same side; the child's side*. Everyone is fallible and anyone can have an agenda, hidden or otherwise. I have seen parents who demanded that their child be placed in an included classroom because it was the child's right, irrespective of the child's skills and behavioral issues. I have seen IEP teams recommend a special education classroom because the child had a few behavioral problems that were, in my opinion, quite fixable without having to be in a specialized class. I have seen parents who primarily wanted an included placement because, according to them, *nothing* was being done to educate their child in the specialized classroom and they simply hoped that in a regular education classroom the child would not be essentially playing with toys. I have actually heard a parent say, "Look, my kid's not gonna be a rocket scientist, but I want her to learn something useful!" He was right. She was not going to be a rocket scientist and she wasn't learning anything useful. Let me talk to both the IEP team and the parents. Mom, Dad, I know your child has the right to learn in the least restrictive environment and to not be unduly secluded from other students. However, please think about this, for just a moment, before you hit the send button on that hate mail. Why is it that we don't teach all children, grades K through 12, in the same classroom at the same time? Aren't we secluding and segregating younger students from older? Might not the kindergarten student benefit from seeing all the achievements of the 12th grader? Who knows, maybe the kindergarten student should be encouraged to attempt modified academics that are several grades above him? We already group individuals not so much by age, but by *skill*. If particularly advanced in their skills, it is not uncommon for very bright children to be skipped ahead several grades and they are placed with older students. However, age doesn't really play into placement decisions. Sure, the child might be a bit socially immature, but social maturity is not a criterion for grade-skipping. *It's all about the skills*. Yet for children with disabilities, they are sometimes placed with similar-aged peers, but not peers with similar skills. If age were the most important factor, we would never allow children to skip grades, but we do. Call me crazy (it won't be the first time), but to me it just seems logical to group children by skill level (I'm pretty sure that this is why we have grades in the first place). Why then are so many people making exceptions for children with disabilities? I believe that if the child with the disability has essentially the same skills, even if he falls into the lowest percentile academically, that he *should* be grouped with his same-skill peers, but not necessarily his *same-age* peers. Sure, the child might need assistance, or coaching, or more teacher time, or more time to complete an assignment and he *should* have those accommodations. If he has a behavior problem that does not flat out endanger all the other children or disrupt *their* rights to a free public education, then he *should* have his problem treated in that classroom if possible. I think that this is really the spirit of PL94–142.

For the IEP team members, I would encourage you all to ask the parents, politely of course, about their expectations regarding what their child will gain in an included classroom that cannot be gained in a special education classroom. Ask the parents about what they fear might happen if their child continues to stay in a special education classroom. I have worked with parents who confided in me things that they would not bring up in a team meeting. You know, that box of Kleenex in the middle of the conference table is not typically used by the school staff I can tell you that much. Parents, IEP teams most certainly aren't always right. Although the team is composed of professionals, being a professional doesn't necessarily make you right (this includes behavior analysts too). Everyone has to remember, however, that these meetings are about the children. They are not about egos and rights and advocates and attorneys. At least they're not *supposed* to be about those things. They aren't even about what's best for children with disabilities. These meetings are about this child, right now. They are about working from an accurate assessment of what this child can do and where we could expect to see him or her in a year's time. They are about planning for how to teach this child as many functional skills as possible in the best ways possible by the best people. These meetings should not be about *where* the child will learn best, but *what and how* the child will learn best. If we really understand the child's needs, and put aside our assumptions and our pride, we can craft a plan that makes sense. One that will help us achieve as many outcomes as possible with as few problems as possible. This should be the focus of everyone's attention. Parents, you should be asking the following kinds of questions:

Which skills will my child learn?

Why is she learning these skills first, and not others?

How long will it take to teach my child these skills?

How long will the IEP team wait if there is no progress before making a substantive change?

Where are these skills going, what will they lead to, how do they relate to what my child will do next year?

What are the qualifications of the teacher who will teach my child?

How many minutes of direct instruction per day can I expect in one setting versus another?

If most of the direct contact is by a classroom assistant, what are that person's qualifications?

These are the questions I would like to see parents asking. I think that these questions are much harder to answer than "What kind of classroom will my child be placed in?" I believe that these kinds of questions are particularly important if a child has very few skills, academic or otherwise. Remember, higher functioning children with good language skills can be taught almost anything. This may not be the case for those children with very few skills.

4.2 Does inclusion have to be all or none?

No, of course not! If there is any hesitance by the parents or the IEP team to place a child in an included classroom, just start with a brief trial in the intended placement. Many IEP teams do just that. I think it's a great way to see what sorts of problems may arise before there is any kind of a major blowout. I was once called in to look at a child who honestly had some very good academic skills and was in an included classroom with about 17 or 18 other kids. He was also lacking in some schoolhouse survival skills and had some minor behavior problems. His parents wanted him in that room, but the IEP team really didn't seem to be leaning that way. In this particular case, the parents were insistent, but also reasonable. It's a tough balance to strike, but they did it. We settled on a compromise that would help ensure success. For example, this particular child had great difficulty working independently and following instructions from a distance. I suggested that we work on these skills (for they are skills) in the smaller self-contained classroom and then conduct probes in the included classroom specifically looking for these skills in action. That is, the child wasn't simply to be brought into the regular education classroom to "be there" but to accomplish a particular goal while in the classroom. It can be difficult to teach certain skills in the same setting where the child needs to demonstrate them and at the time he needs to show them. That is, sometimes you can do on the job training and it's okay because if there are some errors it's no big deal. In other situations, however, errors can cause huge problems, and it is for this reason that we train first and place later. In other situations, where errors really aren't such a big deal or easily prevented, we can place first and then train. It's probably okay for some on the job training at McDonalds when it comes to the intricacies of operating the Fry-o-Lator 2000. On the other hand, I really don't think that you want your airline pilot, who has never even used a flight simulator, to just waltz on into the flight deck and try to fly the plane while Captain Skywalker gives him verbal prompts. My point is that sometimes it's best to have a plan that outlines how to increase the chances of success in an included classroom and that this plan should be implemented well before the decision is made to change classrooms. I'm not saying that a child who doesn't have all of their classroom readiness skills should *never* be considered for placement in an included classroom, but I do like to increase the odds of the child being successful the first time.

4.3 Are we there yet?

Don't you hate it when kids keep asking that on long trips? My stepson, Weston, used to do that. Finally I got tired of it so I gave him my watch to wear (he could tell time at the time) and I gave him an ETA for our destination. Every so often I would ask him, "Are we there yet?" He would say, "No, we have another hour left." I guess the moral of that story is to give people what they need and maybe they'll leave you alone for a while. Well, we don't want children with special needs to leave us alone necessarily, but we do want them to be independent to the greatest extent possible and we do want to give them what they need to be successful. For every professional reading this and for every parent of a child with disabilities, I would urge you all to focus on what the child needs and not what Mom, Dad, the IEP team, and the Department of Education needs. I realize that all of those needs cannot be ignored entirely, nor should they be. I do think, however, that they should play second fiddle to the child's needs. Unfortunately, I think that the biggest obstacle is getting all the grown-ups to agree on exactly what those needs are. During your meetings (and some of them may be more like hostage negotiations than meetings) please try to avoid any arguments that begin with "children with disabilities need _____" or "children with autism need _____." Limit your discussion to *this* child. What does she know, what doesn't she know? What is going to increase her chances of learning more skills more quickly? The presence of typically developing peers or the presence of a highly skilled and motivating teacher? What is more important, socialization or education? They aren't necessarily mutually exclusive, but remember that the ability to play nicely with other students doesn't get you a diploma; academic skills do that. Also, if the student is allegedly being placed in an included classroom for socialization reasons then there should be some clear, objective, quantifiable skills that are being worked on and mastered. Just being in the same room with typically developing peers doesn't count as socialization any more than sitting in that chair in the corner at the high school prom. I have seen wonderful examples of carefully targeted socialization skills in which children were being taught how to ask each other questions and answer them in a conversational format and they were quite skilled, but I'm sure it didn't start that way. Also, this was done in a special education classroom and not in an included classroom. Is that kind of skill-oriented group socialization going to occur in an included classroom? I don't think so. Furthermore, children can socialize in school in a number of ways and in a number of places, not just in their primary classroom. So parents, if you're going to insist that your child be placed in an included classroom, make your expectations clear to yourselves and the IEP team regarding how the included room will increase your child's actual, functional skills. Also, carefully consider, as laid out earlier, the down sides of an included classroom just as you no doubt have already considered the downsides of the special education classroom. There is nothing under the sun with only up sides. If there were I would have found it, bottled it, and would be selling it on my website. IEP teams, if you're quite certain that a child *should not* be in an included classroom, why? You can't just say, "We think it's not an appropriate placement." Uh uh. Nope. Why isn't it an appropriate placement? Talk about the probability of the child attaining grade-level functional skills. Also be ready to demonstrate that the current specialized classroom is good for the child by being able to show skill acquisition. Earlier I mentioned that I have seen "sham" educations in included classrooms. Well, I've seen the same thing in special education classrooms and so have many angry parents and I don't blame them for being angry. If there is no significant functional skill acquisition in a specialized classroom or an included classroom, what are we doing? Think about it.

Chapter 12

Problems With Restraint

What's Inside:

SECTION 1: PREAMBLE

This is the time for all the disclaimers. First, I am currently the Director of Program Development for the Professional Crisis Management Association (PCMA) and, among other services, we provide crisis management training (which involves teaching restraint) both nationally and internationally. This chapter is not about promoting our system, but to discuss issues that cut across all systems. Of course I believe that our system is the best, but then again, why wouldn't I? Knowing that different schools use different systems, I want this chapter to help both parents and professionals understand some very important issues regarding the use of restraint in schools. I'm not going to tell anyone that restraint in schools is necessary in any *absolute* sense, but then again, whom do you wish to attend public school? When I was a child, there were zero restraints in schools. There were no seclusion time-out rooms. There were no behavior programs. There were no children with disabilities, at least not at my elementary school. Even when there were children with disabilities in my middle school there were no behavior problems. The police never got called to the school. If you were bad you went to the principal's office. As you all know from the previous chapter, PL 94-142 changed all that. I'm not saying it's a bad thing. I think it's a good thing, but every decision we make has consequences, some foreseeable, others mmm… not so much. I have spent nearly a quarter of a century working with adults with disabilities in residential settings, and can say with complete confidence that we have been dealing with restraint issues in developmental services much longer than the schools. Regarding the development of policies, safeguards, and general experience with restraint, the schools are still in their infancy. We must concede that the public schools, once charged only with the education of students, are now charged with both the education and *behavioral treatment* of students, and some of those schools still can't even get the education part right. Hey, I'm not writing this to pull punches. Things are broken all over the place. Here's (essentially) how the argument has been going lately:

Parents: "There should be no restraint in schools!"

Legislators: "We need to stop restraint in schools!"

Schools: "We need kids and teachers to be safe!"

Legislators: "They need kids and teachers to be safe!"

Parents: "Restraint means treatment has failed!"

Legislators: "Yes! Treatment has failed!"

Schools: "Give us funds for more behavioral services!"

Legislators: (pretend their cell phones are ringing)

Legislators: "Okay! No more restraint!" Well, okay some restraint, but only when it's an emergency.

Parents: "But who decides when an emergency exists? Also, you didn't get rid of the restraints that we wanted you to get rid of!"

Legislators: (pretend their cell phones are ringing)

It's exasperating, and it is making some forward movement, but the real issues are being drowned in an undertow of sensationalism and cases of outright abuse that have more to do with the reluctance/inability to fire abusive teachers than the issue of whether or not to restrain. For the parents reading now, I would *also* like to see a reduction in restraint, but I don't focus on restraint reduction. *The focus must be on fixing behavior problems and fixing the things that prevent fixing behavior problems.* I have heard the phrase "restraint is evidence of treatment failure" so many times I'm ready to start hand biting. I would like to clarify that phrase. The use of restraint, on the whole, does not necessarily reflect treatment failure. Repeated restraint for an individual child for extended periods may indicate a treatment failure, but restraint use, occurring at any particular school, may reflect a number of problems. When you get a new student with severe behavior problems you might need to use some restraint initially, but I would expect that, eventually, some adequate treatment takes place. You may still continue to have restraint at *a school* because of the admission of new students, even though current students may no longer require any. That is, there is a big difference between eliminating restraint *for the school* and for an *individual child.* Also, restraints may be necessary during treatment, but they should become less restrictive, shorter in duration and fewer in frequency. Still, restraint may happen during treatment as treatment effects are rarely instantaneous and treatments do not always reduce all behavior problems to zero. Furthermore, there is a big difference between treatment *failure* and *no treatment at all.* Many times I'll see no treatment at all. Incidentally, treatment failure occurs as well and for a number of reasons. People can't figure out all problems all the time, and even when they do there may be systems failures that prevent treatment effects. So for the parents in the room, I would recommend the following: Stop demanding that restraint be stopped, and start demanding competent behavioral services and properly supported and trained teachers in the schools. Demand that those teachers have enough staff and a manageable number of students. Demand it. Address my child's behavior problems! Why is my child's behavior continuing? This is what I ask when I see continued behavior problems, restraint or no restraint. Write your legislators and instead of asking them to limit restraint, ask them to give schools enough money to hire enough competent behavior analysts. Who is doing that? That would be a great start.

I have written this chapter because, as far as I can see, restraint in schools isn't going away anytime soon because severe behavior problems aren't going away anytime soon. With proper treatment, problems may be resolved or at least greatly improved for *individual students*, but for the population of special needs kids, as a whole, there will always be behavior problems as new kids are constantly filing into the system. I don't have the power to ban things or the power to release monies to schools. I do however have a great deal of expertise in the use of restraint and in treating severe behavior problems and I'd like to share that expertise with parents, teachers, behavior analysts and others. I can tell you this much right now. It isn't a simple issue and it won't be handled effectively by banning things as much as it will be by ensuring that more things happen the way they should; and this is far more difficult, expensive, and unpleasant than issuing decrees that ban[1] things.

SECTION 2: AMBLE

Probably more of a ramble than an amble, but here goes. Yes, I am one of the principals in a company (Professional Crisis Management Association: PCMA) that does crisis management training, so I like to think I know a thing or two about the use of restraint and seclusion. Restraint and Seclusion are often lumped into the same category, and I'll talk about both here, but let's take them one at a time, shall we?

First things first, what is restraint? You can find numerous definitions with slight variations in various bits of legislation, bills, policies, state guidelines and local policies, but common to most of these definitions is the idea of the deliberate restriction of movement of the person or some part of the person which causes the individual to resist in some manner. This is what restraint is at its heart. People twist this fundamental definition to their liking and they call it different things for different reasons, and some restraint is better than others, safer than others and may accomplish more than just momentary safety. This is such a large (and controversial) topic that there have been many books written on the topic which you could find easily with a simple Internet search. I am going to limit my treatment of the topic to how restraint can be used properly, what increases its safety, potential benefits, potential risks, the questions parents should be asking about its use with their children, and how to minimize/eliminate its use in clinically meaningful ways.

Regarding the definition, exceptions to the term "restraint" are often allowed when it is for a medical reason. Boy, it's good to be the doctor. In residential facilities and hospitals, if a child or adult is severely aggressive or injuring himself the physician can order the use of mechanical restraints. No one questions it. There are no committee meetings and no one calls the local news station to complain about it. Even in legislative language "medical" restraints are exempt from the definitions. News flash… *it's restraint*!!! Restraint is not some

---

[1]In the history of man, no solutions to human problems have ever been easier (seemingly) than banning useful things because some people have used them carelessly or abusively. What? Telling people to stop using restraint doesn't pass the dead man test. What should they do? How should they do it? Who is going to help them? It's far easier and more cost-effective to complain about how bad things are than it is to determine what's broken and fix it. It's also easier to pass legislative language that outright bans procedures than it is to analyze and correct fundamental problems. Banning things doesn't stop them from happening completely. It will stop some people, but others will simply hide what they do. Banning all restraints or various types of restraints will cause people to make up their own restraints and hide their usage. I already know of schools that are "hands off" but after you probe a bit you find that staff do indeed put their hands on children, but do so in an unplanned, untrained, undocumented manner.

nefarious tool invented by behavior analysts to torture children. If you've raised children, you've restrained them. This bears repeating.

If you've raised children, you've restrained them, most likely multiple times.

Were you certified to use a specific procedure learned in a crisis intervention seminar? Most likely you were not, but I know many parents who have been. Have you ever grabbed your toddler by the hand and pulled her away from something dangerous? Have you ever picked your child up off the ground and transported her *against her will* while she struggled, unable to break free from your evil clutches? Then you used restraint. She didn't want to be picked up. She didn't want to be held. She didn't want to be transported away. She wanted to escape and may have screamed and caused quite a scene at the Walmart. It is a commonplace occurrence. Do parents suppress their child's movement for twenty minutes? Not likely, but whether it's five minutes or twenty minutes, it's still restraint. My point is that restraint, like most things in life, can be described on a continuum from less safe to more safe, from least restrictive to most restrictive, from brief to extended in duration and from totally justified and humane to totally unjustified and abusive. Those that are more restrictive, of the longest durations and abusive are the ones that make it into the papers. The nightly news doesn't talk about the brief, less restrictive justified restraints carried out by non-abusive, caring teachers who put themselves at risk physically and legally by protecting students from themselves and keeping their peers safe. I will say this however; some form of restraint at some point in an individual's life is going to be needed to protect him from harm and/or set limits on his behavior. For non-disabled children this usually happens when they are too young to be controlled through words, or they may be slightly older but the words just don't work.

Many advocates for persons with disabilities are pushing for a complete ban on all restraint in schools. Most then say that it is acceptable to use restraint in an emergency, but then that isn't a ban on its use. Some schools ban it, some schools don't. Some ban only certain types (horizontal floor holds), some don't ban any forms. I think that its use will never go away and it shouldn't go away (be banned) for the population in general. Get ready for another truth bomb...

If a small segment of the population is not permitted to arrest the movement of another small segment of the population... you have anarchy!

Much of what the police do is not just enforce laws and protect citizens from evildoers; they also have to *arrest people*. This involves a severe restriction of the individual's movement against his will (restraint) and transportation of the individual. Now don't be mad at me for telling you that your reality check just bounced. It's the way things are. It's not that people with disabilities are the same as criminals. They're not. Nonetheless, there will be times when their movement will have to be arrested for their own safety and the safety of others. There is some good news, however. Although restraint will always be needed in *some form* for persons with disabilities *as a population*, just like it will always be needed for the general population (police), we can *in most cases* move beyond the need for restraint with *an individual*. That is, it can be expected that restraint might be needed on occasion, initially, for an out-of-control child who arrives at a new school. If treatment is provided in a timely, competent manner, then any need for restraint will be rapidly reduced because the child's behavior will be rapidly improved as new, more functional, acceptable skills are learned. Right? I have no problem with the appropriate use of restraint, either to provide safety while a behavior program is being developed or as part of its implementation when things go awry (which is mostly what things do). *I have a big problem with the* continued *use of restraint with the same child when there is no evidence of any progress whatsoever*. This should be a problem for everyone else as well.

SECTION 3: PROPER/IMPROPER USE OF RESTRAINT

By *proper use* I am not talking about the exact method, but the *criteria* for its use. In our system of crisis management we give some criteria for when to use restraint, which exists in a hierarchy from least to most restrictive, and staff are always taught to use the least restrictive means that will get the job done. We give a guideline that dictates that the behaviors in question be continuous in nature and for severe aggressive/destructive behaviors (crisis behaviors). Ours is only a general guideline and cannot possibly cover all eventualities. This is why personalized criteria, based on an assessment of the individual, will always be superior to generalized criteria. As an example, if a child throws a single chair and makes no immediate attempt at grabbing a second chair, we do not consider this a crisis. We consider this to be a single dangerous behavior that has stopped on its own. It doesn't mean that the teacher should do nothing, but it means that there is no need for restraint, because the episode is already over. If the same child throws a chair across the room and runs to the next chair to grab it, this is something different. Do you wait to see if the child throws the second chair or do you intervene? You get the point. Of course intervening does *not* necessarily mean that you use the most restrictive procedure possible. You might just remove the chair and transport the child out of the room.

What about the child who has his head down on the desk and is sleeping and refuses to do work? Should this result in restraint? Absolutely not, because there is no crisis. Now some people will create a crisis by demanding that the child leave the room and/or yanking on the child. This is a very different scenario than continuous chair throwing, is it not? I have been involved as an expert witness in legal cases during which the main issue was whether the use of restraint was appropriate. The issue was not one of "restraint is evil and these people used restraint" but the legal complaint was that the use of restraint was *unwarranted*.

What about a child who is restrained, even lightly in a chair, to force the completion of a task? I'm not a fan of this particular methodology, as reluctance to work is not a crisis, but it may become one shortly. As stated before, it's not that a battle of wills can't work, but I just prefer other methods. I have also seen people forcibly prompting a student to write when the student was clearly resisting. I'm sorry, but to me that's restraint, not as a reaction to dangerous behavior but as a means of forcing desired behavior. If you are making the child write and the child is pulling his hand away from you, it's restraint. You're also creating an angry learner, not to mention that you're making teaching an ugly, unpleasant experience and it doesn't have to be.

What about having a customized definition of when to intervene with a particular child instead of a generalized definition? Doesn't that sound better? Don't you want people to intervene *only* when it's indicated? Do you want some staff to restrain a child for one behavior and other staff to restrain that child for a completely different behavior? How would they know what to do? This is why I recommend making customized criteria for restraint use, to prevent over-utilization and under-utilization. So many people are opposed to having any mention of restraint written into an IEP or behavior plan because they believe it will give people license to use it whenever they like. This is not the case if the criteria for its use and termination are written properly. People can't just say, "If Johnny is aggressive use restraint." That's worthless. Let me give you a real life example. I worked with a young man with severe self-injury. He had hit himself in the head/neck area so many times over so many years that he had detached both retinas and was now completely blind. He had developed a form of SIB in which he would cry out, then bring his open hand way back and then slam it down on the back of his neck as hard as he could. You could hear it 100 feet away; it was really hard. He also showed the same topography (form), but it was very light when he was happy, excited, and smiling. We found out the staff were restraining him even with the light hits. We created a customized definition that clearly stated what light hits looked like (smiling, laughing, arm comes back only halfway) and that also stated what staff should do when there were light hits (how to redirect the behavior). This reduced a number of his restraints. Some children are aggressive, but they only pinch, not break your nose (which some kids do). Some kids do tremendous damage because staff don't intervene quickly enough. Some kids go into a fully blown crisis because staff attempt to use restraint when they should not be doing anything. A clear definition of when to intervene, and when not to intervene, and what to do when the behavior in question is borderline, will greatly reduce and/or eliminate false positives (restraining when it wasn't warranted) and it will also help to prevent false negatives (failing to intervene when it was necessary). If it were my child in school I would *demand* that specific criteria for physical restraint be written into the IEP. I would also want to verify that the proper documentation exists that clearly specifies who has been trained to implement the procedures. Although there are certainly times when staff may have to use their best judgment, I would prefer to reduce uncertainty by providing clear, individualized criteria for restraint use whenever possible. Using generalized criteria is good to do when you know almost nothing about the person or their behavior; you've got to have some standard to guide your decisions. As we gain more information about a child, however, we *can* and *should* craft individualized criteria that clearly describe when to intervene, when not to intervene, and what to do when we are uncertain. Parents, if restraint is to be used at your child's school, the criteria for its use should be clear. If the school policies say, "Danger to self or others," then ask the IEP team to give specific examples and non-examples of when staff are to intervene.

SECTION 4   RISKS/BENEFITS OF RESTRAINT

4.1   The potential benefits of restraint

Restraint can be used in a number of ways. Some people are comfortable with some of its use, but not all uses. Some people are not comfortable with any use whatsoever. Some are only comfortable in its use as an emergency procedure. Some believe it should *not* be part of any behavior support plan or IEP in any manner. Others (like me) believe that it *should be* part of a plan if the dangerous behaviors are predictable, and I stated some additional reasons why in the previous section. Before looking at the risks, let's look at some of the potential benefits of restraint. The benefits of restraint go well beyond the immediate safety of the child and those around him. That is, there are additional benefits to help offset the risks involved. So then, what are the potential benefits? I believe that they are as follows (and this is not every possible benefit, just some big ones):

1. Providing immediate safety.
2. Allowing the parent/teacher/caregiver to effectively set limits.
3. Providing a condition during which previously reinforced problem behaviors are not accessible.
4. Severely curtailing the potential reinforcement available for problem behavior.
5. Allowing for the development of "self-control."
6. Decreasing the need for psychotropic medications that are used specifically to reduce aggression.
7. Preventing intervention by law enforcement.
8. Allowing a child to remain in his or her current placement.

   1. *Immediate safety*   Now most people agree with this one. Clearly, if a child is biting herself, now is not the time to reaffirm your positive relationship. Does it mean that the individual must be restrained using the most restrictive procedure you can find? No, only what is needed to stop the behavior. Isn't it possible that touching the child at all may escalate her behavior? Quite right you are, but the behavior should have already met the criteria for restraint. It's not as though the child was simply upset and then restraint was used and the child exploded. There is no need to lay hands on children who are merely upset and/or noncompliant.

If a student is already hitting the teacher, his behavior may escalate, true, but this is no reason to fail to stop him. That a child who is biting himself may get even more agitated during restraint is not a reason to let him continue biting; it is, however, a reason to intervene in a manner that will provide the necessary restriction of movement. This will in turn make it (temporarily) impossible to engage in the behavior. I think that most regulations and guidelines reflect an understanding of the need for using restraint in this manner with some individuals.

2. *Allowing the parent/teacher/caregiver to effectively set limits*   I don't necessarily mean that we are setting limits by doing restraint; I mean that when setting limits, even in a mild way, e.g., "I'm sorry Timothy, but no one can have computer time until we have finished the lesson," you may see tremendous behavior problems, especially when no one has set *any* limits before. If you know how to safely stop a child who explodes, you don't have to be so freaked-out about a possible exploding child. Some parents, teachers, and others are so afraid of starting a behavior problem that they won't even set reasonable limits, limits that *must* be set if one intends to be a functioning member of society. What's that? You don't care if *your child* is a functioning member of society? You just want them to be happy and never be upset and always get what they want when they want it? God bless you, and I wish you the best in your endeavor. I mean it. I'm not going to be telling parents what kind of life they should want for their child. It's their child, not mine. I know some parents who subscribe to this philosophy and it does indeed "manage" the problem, but I prefer to call it "prolonging" the problem, indefinitely. I have run into many teachers, parents, advocates, behavior analysts and others who tell me that if the child has gotten to the point of anger you've done something wrong! Sometimes you have. Sometimes you haven't. *I would suggest that it is not our job to engineer the perfect world with the perfect responses and the perfect staff where nothing ever goes wrong.* We all need limits; humane, reasonable, age-appropriate limits, and we need to know how to respond to those limits. Those of you who don't subscribe to this philosophy may skip to the next section, and I'll meet up with you all there. For the rest of you, if you live in the real world where stuff happens and things go wrong and you can't have everything you want, then you need to be prepared for the wrath of someone who isn't allowed to eat the one-pound bag of Skittles or stick his hand down his own or someone else's pants. It's not as though we're running around ticking people off on purpose so we can restrain them. Most of the teachers I know would prefer *not* to restrain anyone, trust me. Unfortunately, limits *must* be set. Many behavior analysts use a procedure called "escape extinction" and I mentioned it in Chapter 2. This is when a child tries to escape from a task and you essentially don't let him. Sometimes it involves holding the child in his seat or physically returning him to his seat. It might mean tolerating having your hair pulled, and being bitten, scratched, etc. The point is that you are most clearly setting limits on the child's behavior. In so doing, the child could go into a fully blown crisis and you must be prepared for that. Now I'm not the biggest fan of the escape extinction procedure (Ahearn, Kerwin, Eicher, Shantz & Swearingin, 1996), but the fact is that, when done properly, it can

work very quickly. It isn't particularly elegant or very analytic in my opinion. It's more of a battle of wills. Like I mentioned, most people are not looking to "go to war" with the child, but I have seen simple, reasonable, nicely worded requests produce aggression, and I'm not the only one.

3. *Providing a condition during which previously reinforced problem behaviors are not accessible*   As most of you know, in many instances, children will use their self-injury and/or aggression as a means of controlling their environments or communicating their needs. Everybody's on board with that, right? Furthermore, some of these behaviors have been intermittently reinforced over many years. That means that they're really strong and resistant to change. Also, as mentioned in Chapter 2, some children under certain conditions specifically seek out the ability to injure others (signs of damage). During restraint, those behaviors are *temporarily inaccessible.* Let me explain. For most children who are aggressive, hitting does not immediately result in a condition during which no hitting can occur. Usually a child who hits continues to hit if allowed to do so. Many of them will chase you down to injure you. If they can't get *you*, they may go after another more defenseless student, it's quite common. Applying appropriate restraint, even briefly, creates, if you will, a "time-out" from the ability to engage in subsequent aggression. Furthermore, any behaviors occurring during restraint may extinguish rapidly because they may produce very little reinforcement. If the application of appropriate restraint, *during an emergency,* is coupled with functional communication training (when behavior is stable) or any other *functional* replacement behavior or repertoire, you can get a very rapid improvement in behavior. Even when teaching a replacement behavior, if other reinforcers can still be produced by the problem behavior, the replacement behavior may be learned, but it will not necessarily be performed to the exclusion of all the problem behaviors. There are several studies that have validated the use of restraint and some form of replacement behavior in which both procedures together resulted in a much greater decrease in problem behaviors than the replacement behavior alone (Hanley, Piazza, Fisher, & Maglieri 2005; Hagopian, Fisher, Sullivan, Acquisto, && Lebanc 1998). Time for another example. You're on a diet (really, who isn't?). You're very hungry and there are two refrigerators in front of you. One is filled with things you love but *should not eat* (mmm). The other is filled with *healthy alternatives* (blech). When you reach for the naughty food, both refrigerators snap shut and are locked for 10 minutes. When you reach for the healthy food, the door opens and allows access. How long will it take you to stop reaching for the naughty food? Now, what if you are allowed access to both refrigerators? True, I am giving an example where one type of food reinforcement is more potent than another, but in fairness, many replacement behaviors do not produce the same quality of reinforcement as the problem behavior. Couple this with an understanding that people are not so keen on just giving up old behaviors in favor of new ones or "shifting" reinforcers like we talked about in Chapter 2. In other words, because the old behavior *can occur*, it can contact some reinforcement (like the ability to open the naughty fridge). Restraint can provide this temporary inability to engage in the problem behavior. Remember, I'm not saying that

this is what people are planning to do when they use restraint in an emergency, but it is one possible benefit. Now would this be of any benefit if there were no programming in place to teach functional replacements? Probably not. The possibility of providing a temporary condition during which certain behaviors are inaccessible leads to the fourth potential benefit.

4. *Severely curtailing the potential reinforcement available for problem behavior* I have seen children destroy entire classrooms because no one intervened. I have seen children hit, slap, bite, tear clothing, and pull hair freely. I have seen children go from one student to another attacking each one along the way. For many children, the consequences of their behavior are varied, big, and exciting. Things smash, people yell, faces contort, and they gain access to many things they may not otherwise get. Sometimes a child can clear out an entire classroom of children and adults. We call this a "room clear." Do you all have any idea how powerful it is to be able to empty out a room full of people? Wouldn't you love to be able to do that during an IEP meeting that has gone way too long? Using proper restraint methods, at appropriate times (which I'll address shortly) removes almost all the functionality of these dangerous behaviors. When restraint is used properly, the only thing that happens as a result of severe, dangerous problem behavior is that it is stopped. No one leaves the room, nothing smashes, people aren't running and screaming, and everyone still has all their hair. What is the behavior good for? Very little. Perhaps it isn't accurate to state that the child's behavior does nothing, because there are always consequences (I don't mean punitive consequences, I mean environmental changes). The behavior will still control the adults. It's good for making someone stop you, and it's also good for getting out of doing math. That's about it. Now for some children, this is a consequence that is significant enough to maintain the behavior. I have consulted with countless behavior analysts about children who appear to like the restraint. That is a distinct possibility and there are journal articles that verify that a restraint can even function as a reinforcer for some individuals with particularly intractable SIB (Favell, McGimsey, & Jones, 1978; Favell, McGimsey, Jones, & Cannon, 1981). In the cases where it is suspected that either the restraint is functioning as a reinforcer or some aspect of the restraint is functioning as a reinforcer (one-on-one attention from multiple staff, escape from/avoidance of tasks, disrupting the class, etc.), then you need to look for competing reinforcers and for things that are motivating the child to seek restraint. The way I explain it is that if being restrained is the most fun thing the kid can think of, you've got some serious reinforcement problems going on.

So, are there still consequences of the aggressive/self-injurious/dangerous behavior? Yes, absolutely. Many things happen when someone is restrained, those all count as changes in the environment that occur as a direct result of the behavior. However, in most cases, it may not be the change that the child was looking for. Also, if done properly, it will be a *consistent and predictable* change. As I always tell people, anytime you try to *interrupt or redirect* a behavior you are *automatically* providing a consequence. There's no way around it unless you attempt an extinction procedure, and this is generally NOT what you want to do when there is a crisis. Sometimes the best you can do is to provide *the same predictable reaction* and do your best to ensure that the primary maintaining consequences (if they have been identified) do not occur anymore (escape from the room, access to tangibles, destruction of property). If this is coupled with huge, important reinforcers for replacement behavior, then you are well on your way to solving the problem.

5. *Allowing for the development of self-control*   Based on my experience, I would tell you that most children would prefer not to be restrained. Furthermore, although restraint as used in an emergency is not *intended* to be aversive, it often is, at least somewhat. Don't misunderstand, I don't mean painful, and if it's done properly it isn't. Think about the chat we had in Chapter 3 on what it means for something to be aversive. If restraint is aversive, it may only mean that the child will try to minimize, avoid it and/or escape from it, and this is typically what you will see. Now remember, especially those of you who eschew restraint and positively balk at the idea that it could ever be a part of treatment, it nonetheless can provide substantial benefits. Now, doing restraint alone, and not providing alternative behaviors, teaching new skills, making antecedent manipulations, etc., will not generally create any long-term clinical gains, particularly regarding longstanding behavior problems. So when people say that restraint is not effective, I agree with them, but only regarding the likelihood of restraint being effective *as a treatment* by itself. I'm glad that children don't like to be restrained. *You have to learn to engage in some form of self control behavior if you wish to be a functioning member of society.* Now there are plenty of people with disabilities who have practically no self-control and their ability to access the things we access are severely restricted as a result. I've already talked about this in Chapter 3 on aversives when I discussed tolerating, so I won't go into much detail here. Essentially, if some type of warning signal is given, reliably, before restraint, then there is a very good chance that the warning alone will be sufficient to stop the behavior. This *is* the essence of self-control. It is control by others in which said control is usually preceded by a warning to "get one's self together." Recall that in Chapter 2, I spoke about Dr. Glenn Latham's categories of control (direct, indirect, influence). Initially, because the behavior of typically developing children is *not* well controlled verbally—i.e., they don't listen to warnings—we *must* control them physically to prevent harm. If a child reaches for a hot stove and you say, "Stop!" but she doesn't stop, you *must* restrict her movement to protect her, even if only momentarily. Eventually, a verbal warning to stop is usually sufficient, but many children with disabilities never develop the self-control repertoires to benefit from verbal warnings. The mistake most practitioners make is that they give no reliable information about an impending restraint and they do not give a clear instruction for what the child *should do*. For example, if the child had practiced deep breathing as a means of calming himself, then the teacher could prompt the child to take some deep breaths after the first act of non-continuous aggression *before* ever doing any restraint. Eventually the child should be able to learn to take a few breaths, when prompted, and *avoid the restraint entirely*. This is especially likely if the prompts to breathe take place *before* the child's behavior escalates to the point of crisis. Before I leave this particular section, let me be clear. I am not promoting restraint as a therapy for teach-

ing self-control. There are many ways to teach self-control. I am saying that if you have to restrain anyway, for safety, that there is this possible extra benefit if you carefully consider what you do *before restraining*, and if you are simultaneously teaching calming strategies as part of a behavior program. You can also provide ample reinforcement for a child who initiates a self-control behavior (like sitting down with only verbal prompts).

6. *Decreasing the need for psychotropic medications*   Very often, psychotropic medications, allegedly given for a "disorder," are specifically given to reduce aggression and/ or self-injury. Psychotropic medications are much more accepted by society than the use of restraint yet they can be far more dangerous. Medications almost go unnoticed (unlike restraints) as they are softened by a veil of medical legitimacy. Unfortunately, many children with severe behavior problems are taking antipsychotic medications and there is not a single antipsychotic medication on the market today that does not include Neuroleptic Malignant Syndrome (NMS) as one of the potentially lethal serious reactions.[2] In many instances, psychotropic medications may reduce the need for restraint or eliminate them entirely. Unfortunately, like restraint, they teach the child no adaptive skills. On the contrary, they very often make skill acquisition impossible because they may render certain aversives neutral. Recall the disruption to conditioned avoidance responding described at the end of Chapter 3. You can't learn how to cope with things that no longer bother you. Unlike medications, which may take considerable time to become clinically effective (sometimes weeks) and then must be carefully tapered for discontinuation over days or weeks, *restraints can be started and stopped instantly*. Finally, antipsychotic medications (not psychotropics in general) can have permanent side effects like TD (Tardive Dyskinesia).

7. *The prevention of intervention by law enforcement*   As I mentioned earlier in the chapter on inclusion, the police don't just visit schools for "Say No to Drugs!" day anymore. Most middle and high schools have full time police officers at the school. The police do not have to use any particular kind of restraint. They can, for the most part, do whatever they feel is necessary to protect themselves and others. A teacher will tolerate hits from a child. The police will not. Although not terribly common, children have been pepper-sprayed, shot with a taser and handcuffed. My point is that what a police officer chooses to do in any given instance may be highly idiosyncratic and is not typically subject to school board policies.

8. *Allowing a child to remain in his or her current placement*   Some school districts use little restraint because they farm out their children to specialized schools and residential facilities outside of the district. Even schools within the same district will fight tooth and nail to get a child moved to a more restrictive placement. The proper use of restraint allows

---

[2]Neuroleptic Malignant Syndrome is a rare but serious, sometimes life-threatening side-effect that can occur while taking a variety of medications classed as antipsychotics (Haldol, Thorazine, Ablify, Risperda, Melleril). It is characterized by "leadpipe" muscle rigidity and a severe sudden fever. If not caught quickly, this condition can be fatal.

students to stay at their home schools with teachers, students, and surroundings with which they are familiar and comfortable. A new placement that allows the use of restraint, although arguably safer for the child and his peers, is not necessarily a better *school*. New placements, especially residential placements, can disrupt the child's routine, uproot families, and cost states hundreds of thousands of dollars. The ability to stabilize even a highly aggressive child in the least restrictive setting can be accomplished through a combination of the judicious use of restraint and proper behavioral supports.

I've spent quite a bit of time talking about some of the benefits of restraint that may go well beyond the immediate safety of the child, his teacher and his peers. Now let's turn to a candid discussion about some of the risks of restraint. I'll try to address the issues of both physical and psychological risk.

4.2   Risks of Restraint: Physical risks

Most books, articles, stories, and blogs you see on restraint only emphasize the risks of restraint, so I'm not going to spend much time on this. Children have received bruises, rug burns, cuts, broken bones, and have even died during restraint. Let me say this, however, as this is not stated clearly anywhere. Regarding fatalities, the worst possible risk factor, there are *two terms* that are very important if you're going to have any sort of reasonable discussion. Oh by the way, if you subscribe to the line of reasoning that even a single death means that something should be deemed dangerous and then banned, then you should just skip this section. You should also stop riding in cars effective immediately. These terms that we must understand (which are often confused) are *prevalence* and *incidence*. Both terms are used in medicine to describe, respectively, how widespread something is and new occurrences. Incidence means the number of new cases of something that occurs in a given period. Let's say that, hypothetically, over the last 10 years there were approximately 20 restraint-related deaths. Then the incidence would be, on average, 2 per year. Incidence is the only information that can be garnered in stories about restraint-related fatalities in newspapers, broadcasts, websites and blogs, and this is what grabs most people's attention. Prevalence, on the other hand, is expressed as a ratio of occurrences per targeted population. The *prevalence* for the diagnosis of ASD (autism spectrum disorder) is now (2012) about 1 out of 88 children or about 1 percent. Do you know what the prevalence is for restraint-related deaths for children in public schools? I'll save you the trouble, the answer is no. No one does, not yet anyhow. Here is a quote from an article by the Council for Children with Behavioral Disorders in their position summary entitled "The Use of Physical Restraint Procedures in School Settings" (CCBD 2009):

> The Government Accounting Office in 1999 stated that an accurate estimate of deaths or injuries due to restraint was impossible since only 15 U.S. states have established reporting procedures for such incidents (U.S. Government Accounting Office, 1999 p. 5).

Let's take a look at how we *might* calculate the *prevalence* of restraint-related deaths in public schools. According to the Coalition Against Institutionalized Child Abuse (CAICA), as many as 75 children have died in some form of restraint from 1988 to 2006, which is an 18-year span. Taken out of context this seems like a large number, because we are just looking at the number 75. For the sake of our purposes here, let's say that this is accurate. Of those deaths, *only 3 occurred in public schools*. The rest were in residential facilities, specialized treatment schools and hospitals. Now first we must obtain the deaths per year, which is 3 divided by 18 years, which is .16 children per year with a disability in a restraint-related death in a public school. This is our *incidence*. To get the *prevalence*, however, we need to know the total population of children in public schools with disabilities. As of 2009 (so it's presumably more now) there were 6.4 million students with disabilities ages 3 to 21.So, in a simple ratio it is .16 children for every 6.4 million, which equals a mortality rate of .0000026 percent per year. That would be the prevalence of restraint-related death for the entire population of children with disabilities in public school. Sure, this did not include the other 72 children who died in restraint, but if you included them, then the population sample would also have to be increased above the 6.4 million students to include the population of all the children being treated in nonpublic school settings in the United States. The more important question to be answered is, how many restraints are performed every year in the United States for that population of students? That way you could derive a mortality rate for restraint. That is, to determine the *actual risk* you need to have a ratio of incidents to the total number of procedures performed. Clearly, the ratio I calculated above would be much, much lower because the denominator would not consist of all children served in special education, but instead would consist of *all restraints performed* in all special education settings in a year's time. Although the CCBD claimed that this number is currently unknown (because there is no national school restraint database), the United States Department of Education (ED) reported that out of 72,000 public schools[3] there were 131,990 instances of physical restraint in a single year (Shah, 2012). This number was for all students although, as I would expect, the number was disproportionately high for students with disabilities. To calculate a mortality rate (prevalence of fatalities) for a single child, we have to multiply both numbers (.16 children per year and 131,990 restraints) by 6. This would yield a mortality rate of approximately 1 child per 791,940 restraints, which gives a rate of .00012 percent per year. Now this is only an example of *how* one would go about obtaining *the prevalence* for restraint-related fatalities in schools based on an estimate of 3 fatalities over an 18-year period (from CAICA's website) and based on the Department of Education's report of the total number of restraints in 85 percent of schools in a year's time. Given that these numbers are even reasonably accurate, this is the closest to an actual mortality rate that I've seen yet. No fatality of a child is ever acceptable, no matter how small the chances. Still, it would be valuable to know the specific circumstances of these fatalities so that we may learn from

---

[3]There are currently about 98,000 public schools in the United States. Of those, the information presented here was collected from 72,000 of these schools.

them. Of those fatalities occurring at three schools listed on the CAICA website, one child was restrained by a staff member who was *sitting* on top of him. Another child was being restrained by a staff member who was bending over the child with his arms wrapped around him and then several other students jumped on the staff member and they all fell on the child. A third child was suffocated by being rolled in a weighted blanket that was used to restrain him. Were *any* of these restraint methods appropriate? No. Were *any* of these methods specifically taught to certified staff trained in any of a dozen different nationally recognized crisis management systems? No. Without the senseless deaths of these children by untrained staff, would there even *be* a mortality rate in public schools? It doesn't seem likely.

The Florida Department of Education now has a statewide database, so if other states follow suit we will soon be able to obtain an even better estimate of actual risk instead of relying on *perceived risk.*[4]

What about other risks? Certainly there are risks of injuries. I do not know either the prevalence or incidence of injuries related to restraint, but they certainly do happen. On the other hand, I also don't know the prevalence or incidence of injuries to students or their peers/teachers that are a direct result of problem behavior that has not been stopped. I know for certain that children injure themselves and others because they *have not* been stopped; I have witnessed it numerous times. The American Association of School Administrators (AASA) has just written a paper entitled *Keeping Schools Safe: How Seclusion and Restraint Protects Students and School Personnel* (Pudelski, 2012). The AASA conducted a randomized survey of school administrators across the United States regarding seclusion, restraint, and staff injuries. Here is what they found:

1. 10 percent of respondents used seclusion and restraint more than 5 percent of the time in a single year.

2. 97 percent of respondents said staff who perform seclusion and restraint are trained/certified.

3. 95 percent of personnel are trained in de-escalation or positive behavioral interventions.

---

[4]In the book *Freakonomics*, (Levitt and Dubner, 2005) The authors wrote a section on actual versus perceived risk. They cited Peter Sandman, a risk communications consultant who talked about what affects perceived risk. According to Sandman, risks you control are seen as less risky than those you don't (parents and advocates cannot directly control restraint). He also talked about "outrage" which has to do with unfamiliarity and sensationalism. Regardless of the actual risk, perceived risk is off the charts when outrage is high. Outrage is high with restraints. Incredibly high. The outrage isn't as high for the eight teens who die every day in car crashes because we are *accustomed* to these numbers, *and* we control our own cars, therefore we perceive the risk as lower, i.e., "That will never happen to my child, he's a safe driver!" I would go one step further than Sandman though, and say that things that are not valued *and* produce a visceral reaction also contribute to perceived risk. Those who see little or no value in restraint, and who see it as little more than modern-day barbarism will perceive the highest possible risk of harm. For individuals who feel this way about restraint, any actual risk is irrelevant.

4. 25 percent of districts reported that staff were threatened or attacked by students at least 20 times for the year.

5. 30 percent of districts reported that there were at least five hospitalizations of staff over five years due to behavioral outbursts.

So there are physical risks from using restraints and physical risks from not using them. I wish I could say conclusively which were more dangerous but I don't know that those data exist. I feel confident in saying that non-lethal minor injury is much more common than restraint-related death, which is actually quite rare. Later, I will talk about things that make procedures more safe or less safe. The most we can ever hope for is continuing on a path toward increased safety. There is no absolute perfect. How can you eliminate the *most* risk? Eliminate behavior problems.

4.3   Psychological risks

Okay, so we know that there can be physical damages, but what about psychological? This is a sticky wicket. It usually falls under the rubric of "trauma." Unfortunately, this label is often bandied about with reckless disregard for any proof and/or the application of diagnostic criteria. People like to use the phrase "potentially traumatizing" when they talk about the risks of restraint. Is it possible to be traumatized by being restrained? Sure, it's *possible*. First, however, we have to look at the definition of trauma. There is a wonderful article all about trauma, and for those interested in the topic, you can find it by visiting http://vcoy.virginia.gov/documents/collection/trauma0513.pdf. It was released by The Commonwealth of Virginia Commission on Youth. The authors give a thorough overview of the definitions of trauma, post-traumatic stress disorder, and DSM-IV TR definitions of trauma. The definition ranges from actual or threatened death to a threat to one's "physical integrity" (American Psychological Association, 2000). According to those definitions, not only can you experience trauma by actual events or threats that have happened to you, but you can also experience trauma by witnessing an event that happened to someone else or *by simply learning about a close friend's traumatic experience*. It is currently a *very broad* definition. According to this definition, seeing an aggressive classmate injure himself, attack the teacher, or attack another peer could potentially traumatize a child. Incidentally, the word restraint doesn't even appear in the article. There are also no data, anywhere, regarding either the incidence or prevalence of trauma that has been demonstrated to be the direct result of a single restraint or series of restraints. There is at least one study showing the prevalence of PTSD for a population of children exposed to extreme traumatic events, and those rates are 2 percent for natural disasters (like a tornado), 28 percent after an act of terrorism (mass shooting) and 29 percent after a plane crash (Smith, North, & Spitznagel, 1993). These are *very different* circumstances than being restrained and physically unharmed by people who know you. Even in these extreme catastrophic events, *most* children *did not* develop PTSD. If most children exposed to a mass shooting do not develop PTSD, why would anyone expect the rates of PTSD to be high for restraint?

Am I saying that it's not possible to be traumatized by restraint? No, of course not. I think that it most likely *has happened* to someone somewhere, especially if the restraint was abusive, excessive and painful. I am saying, however, that there are just no numbers out there. That a child doesn't like restraint, or screams and cries while in restraint or tries to avoid restraint, or whose behavior escalates during restraint is not evidence of trauma. Children will cry and scream and try to escape and avoid going to the doctor to get a painful injection. Doubtless you have seen parents carrying children away who were also crying and screaming horribly because they didn't want to leave something or some place but were being forced to do so. Are those things traumatizing? I wish I could give parents definitive numbers like, "1 out of 300 students will develop PTSD because of restraint," but I can't and neither can anyone else. All that anyone can say is that there is the *potential* for trauma—that is, there is a *possibility*. No one can say that there is a high probability, for they would have no data on which to base that claim. Is there the potential for trauma? Yes, undeniably, there is the *potential*, but that's as definitive as anyone can get unless they're making wildly unsupported assumptions.

Could children be *re-traumatized* by being restrained? Yes, I believe that it's a possibility, especially for a child who was physically or sexually abused in the past. These are things that everyone has to consider. However, because trauma can occur in a variety of ways, it is possible for the child to be traumatized not only by what is done to him, but by what he has done to others as well. Being the victim of violence is not the only thing that can traumatize a police officer or a soldier. They can also be traumatized by violent acts that they commit against others in the line of duty, or by acts that they have witnessed. Why can't an aggressive child become traumatized by seeing what he has done to another child? I would argue that he could be, but I would not expect it to be highly likely. Could restraint protect someone from the trauma of self-injury? I would argue that it could and it has.

In summary, I would say that there is nothing more than the *potential* for trauma during restraint but first consider this; a child who is endangering himself or others, and has done so before, is *highly likely* to do it again if not stopped. There may be the remote possibility that the child could become traumatized, but he is either injuring himself or others *right now* or is engaging in behavior that, if not stopped immediately, has a *very high probability* of causing injury. This is called weighing the risks and benefits. Unfortunately, the *actual risk* of restraint-induced trauma is completely unknown, but the benefits of restraint in an emergency are clear. To give an example that you might better relate to, let's look at the risks versus benefits of driving one's child to the hospital when she is suffering a high fever. High fever carries with it many risks and may indicate a number of serious medical conditions, and there are clear benefits of taking the child to a hospital, including but not limited to ruling out life-threatening conditions. Unfortunately, there are risks in driving. In the United States alone, there are approximately 30,000 deaths each year in automobile accidents. There are also approximately 190,000,000 licensed drivers in the US. That means that there is approximately a .015 percent chance of dying in a car accident. That is, about 1 in 6,000 people will die in a car crash every year. Now of course, the actual risk could be higher or lower depending on a number of factors including how often you drive, where you drive, time of day, your driving habits, etc. There is, however, a very real risk and (unlike restraint-induced trauma) that risk can be expressed as a percentage and is *extremely well documented*. Given this remote chance of a fatality, do you then decide *not* to drive your sick child to the hospital because of the minute possibility of dying in an automobile accident? I don't know of a *single parent* who would keep her child at home because of the risk of death, however remote, from driving a car.

Unfortunately, because so many individuals are opposed to restraint on a visceral level, *any risk at all* is often seen as too great and any benefit too little or nonexistent. The decision to restrain is made more difficult because no one can quote statistics, as is the case with many surgical procedures.

Before moving on to the next section, I'd like to remind everyone that there will always be risks for *any* child who continues to display dangerous aggressive or self-injurious behavior or property destruction at a level that could easily cause harm. It seems to me that no one, and I mean no one, acknowledges the possibility of trauma for a child who bites himself until he bleeds or severely injures another person. Why is destroying your own body or seriously harming another *never suspected* of producing trauma, yet not being allowed to move freely is *highly suspected* of producing trauma? I'm not talking about the act of injuring or abusing someone—those are different things. If simply not being able to move freely when angry or upset were sufficient to cause *trauma* (not just emotional outbursts, but clinical trauma), then there would be millions of traumatized children in the general population *including yours*. Are small children restrained in the same way as highly aggressive older children and teenagers with disabilities? No, of course not. They are much smaller, weaker, and much less dangerous. Nonetheless, small children are *routinely* held by parents *against their will* and are *not allowed to escape* until the parents decide to put them down. The way that children *cry, scream, and struggle* makes it *appear that* they are suffering, frightened, or in pain. Are these children frightened or just angry? Do they perceive that the integrity of their bodies is being threatened or are they having a tantrum? Is being restrained by the parent traumatizing or just unpleasant? Parents place small children in cribs and leave them screaming and crying in isolation from which they cannot escape. Parents even use mechanical restraint by placing small children in high chairs from which they cannot escape. Sometimes it's done for convenience of the parent and sometimes it's done for the child's own safety. Yes, it's very different from what happens in schools, but it's different in specific ways (older children who are more dangerous, implemented by teachers instead of parents, and in some cases done for different reasons). It is, however, *fundamentally* the same phenomenon. Just a few things to think about.

SECTION 5: WHAT AFFECTS THE SAFETY OF RESTRAINT?

5.1 Seven factors that affect the safety of restraint

As mentioned earlier, there is no perfect "safe." There is safer and less safe. At some tipping point, when the safety falls below a certain standard, either codified in official documents or perhaps only in the vagueness of our own consciousness, we start to call things dangerous. If we feel comfortable we call them safe. I prefer to think of things as more dangerous/less dangerous and safer/less safe. Given the assumption that perfect safe is an unattainable ideal, what might make restraints safer? I co-authored a position paper on the matter with Neal Fleisig and we outlined seven areas that should be addressed to increase the safety of any restraint used in any system of crisis management. They are:

1. Design
2. Training
3. Skill retention
4. Utilization criteria
5. Oversight
6. Medical evaluation
7. Existing treatment programs

  1. *Design.*   Design refers to the actual form of the restraint and the body mechanics involved. Design involves both the position of the child and the position of the staff and whether safety equipment is used during the procedure (we use a mat in our system). Procedural design should be such that the holding does not cause pain or discomfort, awkward or unnatural body positioning, or any restriction of breathing. Restraints should just provide momentary immobilization. The design should be such that small deviations in the implementation of the procedure (drift) do not produce catastrophic results. Neal Fleisig, one of the foremost authorities on crisis management and physical holding, refers to procedures as "robust" if they can withstand small deviations in their implementation yet still retain a high margin of safety. Many injuries that occur as a result of restraint have no identifiable crisis management system associated with them. That is, many staff who intervene are completely untrained. One problem with untrained staff is that there is no procedural design because they are not implementing a procedure—they are just holding. Parents should ask to see procedures that are being used with their children, and highly involved parents do just that.

2. *Training.* Regardless of the system being used (and of course we think everyone should use ours), staff must be properly trained. Important questions to ask about the crisis management system used at your child's school include, whichever system is being used, were staff properly trained? Did they pass the course? Are they certified? Did the certification lapse or have they reliably re-certified annually? Was the training fluency-based or attendance-based? Have *all staff* working with your child been trained or only some of them? How long did the training last? You should be very suspicious if it was only a 6–hour training, for very little can be taught in that amount of time. Is there a mechanism for checking to see if staff are truly certified? What is the content of the training? Are staff shown how to avoid the use of restraints during the training? Does the training cover which appropriate behaviors to focus on? These are the questions I would want answered if I were a parent of a child who might need to be restrained at some point.

3. *Skill retention.* Staff may have demonstrated a skill properly during training, but are they still doing it correctly one month later? Six months? A year? I mentioned the notion of drift earlier and drift can occur with any behavior. In some cases, the staff performance may slowly deteriorate until a procedure is almost unrecognizable. Sure, drift happens to a greater degree with some people, but eventually it happens to some extent with everyone. How often are staff re-certified? Although most companies require at least annual recertification, people's skills can deteriorate sooner than one year. Staff who are given frequent refreshers by qualified on-site instructors can keep their skills razor sharp from one month to the next. Sometimes refreshers aren't even necessary, but at least spot-checking by a qualified instructor can be a great hedge against procedural drift.

4. *Utilization criteria.* I talked about this briefly earlier in the chapter under the section about the proper use of restraint. Remember that it must be clear to everyone when restraint should be started and, just as importantly, when it should be ended. Ideally, we want to prevent over- and under-utilization. Frankly, the bigger problem is over-utilization. It's not that under-utilization doesn't occur, but most people are more worried about the use of restraint when it is not called for. Most folks have no problem with events that fall at the extreme ends of the continuum. That is, if a child is sleeping, duh, you don't use restraint. If a child calls you a "&@!$-head," it's not very nice, but you don't use restraint. If a child gets really mad and rips up his own exam, you don't use restraint. If a child continuously starts throwing chairs at other children, some form of restraint (even an escort) may be necessary. Most people have difficulty with behaviors that occur in the gray area. What if the child has not yet engaged in a dangerous behavior, but is about to? What if the child is not throwing chairs *at* people, but *near* them? What if the child hits once, drops, waits one minute and then repeats the same action, and this goes on for an hour? What then? In the gray areas, staff will need support from the behavior analyst or other team members. This is why I so strongly advocate for the inclusion of utilization criteria into an IEP.

People have to make judgement calls. Things are not so black and white as some would lead you to believe. When you're in the middle of being attacked and all hell is breaking loose it can be challenging to do the right thing. It's easy to say in hindsight what people *should* have done when you weren't there experiencing it too.

5. *Oversight.* Oversight is so incredibly important. I just can't stress it enough. You can take the best staff, who are the most well meaning people on the planet, train them thoroughly and then stick them in a classroom off on their own with no supervision from anyone, and bad things can happen. Bad things don't always happen because the staff are bad people, but because there is not someone checking in on them to ensure that all questions have been answered and all problems resolved. Good staff, with proper oversight, become great staff. Who is checking on the teachers and giving constructive feedback, corrections, and praise for correct behavior? Is there a person at the school with an instructor-level understanding of the crisis management system? Does the principal go into the classrooms? Is the principal trained as well? I know many who are. Good oversight keeps good staff on track and stops bad staff before something terrible happens. My question as a parent would be, "Who checks up on the classroom staff to ensure that everything is being done correctly, and how often?

Did you ever hear one of those (true) stories about a teacher who tied a child to a chair or duct taped someone? Do you honestly believe that there was good oversight in those cases? Highly doubtful. Good oversight is *critical* in determining the safety of *any* restraint procedure. I know some principals who are in classrooms either during a crisis or immediately after it's over. The teacher knows to expect the principal and that questions will be asked. It isn't necessarily punitive in nature, but it is expected. We need to know that someone is looking over our shoulders, it keeps us "on our game."

6. *Medical evaluation.* Children should be evaluated to rule out any medical contraindications for restraint of any kind. A child would not be able to join the football team without first undergoing a medical evaluation to rule out any possible preexisting conditions. During any restraint a child may exert themselves at levels that are comparable to weightlifting or competitive sports. Whenever I teach a crisis management course, I always go over some of the possible medical contraindications to look out for. Instructors frequently ask me about the safety of restraint when a child has this condition or that condition, and I tell everyone the same thing. I'm not a physician, and even if I were, I'm not your client's physician. Tell it to the doctor (the child's doctor). Most physicians will want to know how the child will be held (standing, face up, face down, seated) and may want to see what the procedure looks like before making any judgments. Typically, physicians don't sign things that say, "I approve of restraints for this child" but they may indicate that they "see no clear medical contraindication for the use of restraint." If a determination is made that all restraints should be avoided, or that some restraints should be avoided, then everyone has to agree on what will be done when the child's behavior must be stopped.

7. *Existing treatment programs.*   Existing treatment programs don't technically make restraint safer, but they make it less likely to occur because behavior problems are less likely to occur. Anytime you can do fewer, less intrusive, or shorter restraints, it's a good thing. Again, I see benefits to restraint that others may not see or agree with, and that's fine with me, but still, restraints are not treatment. Treatment is treatment. Restraints can assist in a number of ways, but if the child has to be restrained multiple times, then the IEP team should consider the need for proper evaluation and treatment. Now this doesn't mean, as I mentioned before, that just because a plan is in place that all bad behaviors are going to stop immediately, but if the plan is a good one and implemented properly, then some dimension of restraint use should decrease sharply.

5.2   A word about seclusion

Seclusion and restraint are often lumped together whenever anyone talks about restraint, and they really shouldn't be because seclusion is becoming increasingly prohibited in schools. Seclusion typically involves moving the child to a space void of other children or adults. There is closed-door seclusion, locked seclusion, open door seclusion, seclusion with one adult in the room with the child and just about any other kind of variation you can think of. There is even "reverse seclusion" as I like to call it, which is when everyone clears out of the room and lets the child trash it. That is, instead of bringing the child to seclusion, you bring seclusion to the child. Oddly enough, my personal experience is that as much as people hate restraint, they seem to hate seclusion even more! My honest opinion on the matter is that, for children who can be secluded safely, (they are not self-injurious) in a proper seclusion room (proper door, padded, ventilated, well lit, observation window, etc.) there are many fewer risk factors. Any person can overreact in a crisis. Anyone. Once the child is in a seclusion room those risk factors are removed. Also, for those children whose behavior may be reinforced by physical contact, or the ability to fight staff, seclusion makes perfect sense. Remember when I talked about restraint providing a brief period during which the child doesn't have access to their aggressive behavior? Seclusion does a great job at removing targets of aggression. It's not that children can't be injured in seclusion, they can be. It's not that children can't be injured *on the way into seclusion*. They can be. Everything has risks. Unfortunately, the elimination of seclusion rooms in schools is on the rise. I say unfortunately because it is absolutely appropriate for some children. It's also unfortunate because those children whose crisis could have been managed by using seclusion are now going to require physical restraint because there's simply no other option during an emergency. I fear that restraint rates will rise because seclusion rooms are being banned, and I believe that it may already be happening.

5.3   Restraints don't work!

I am so tired of hearing people say that. They don't work in what regard? Emergency restraints are designed to stop people, not punish them. It's not that a punishment "effect" cannot be obtained—it could happen, but it just typically does not. If I have to restrain any-one, I'm not doing it with the expectation that it will necessarily cause an overall behavioral improvement. I am doing it to stop the behavior now, even though it is *possible* that there are some additional beneficial effects for a particular child. If the question is, "Can restraints stop dangerous behavior that is occurring right now?" then the answer is "Yes they can." The only time restraints aren't effective for stopping behavior is when they are poorly designed, poorly implemented, or the individual is freaky strong relative to staff (which happens more often than you realize). People often ask me if the procedures that I teach are effective. I ask them, effective at doing what? Usually, when they ask that question they mean effective at decreasing the future probability of the behavior that made the restraints necessary. They are asking about a punishment effect. We cannot predict if the restraint will function as a punisher or not. It's odd because some of the same people who say restraints don't work also say that restraints are nothing but "punishers." They obviously have a misunderstanding of a behavioral definition of punishment. Most people may mean that restraint is "punitive" in the common sense of the word, and not technically a punisher. If restraints were "universal" punishers, then you would get an immediate suppression in behavior. If the behavior were brand new, never having occurred before, then restraint may never be needed again. If the behavior were well established, then restraints would most likely not eliminate it forever but only suppress it for some indeterminate amount of time. My point is that the intended use is to stop dangerous behavior now, and that there may also be other effects that go beyond the immediate cessation of behavior. Also, please keep in mind that a restraint is stopping behavior, immediately, in a mechanical sense. That is, restraints are not necessarily stop-ping behavior because of their possible aversive nature, but because it is simply physically impossible to run around the room and attack people during restraint. Electric shock, which *does not* make behavior physically impossible, will often suppress behavior long after it (the shock) has stopped. The same is not necessarily true of restraint. Although most legislative language specifies that emergency restraint is not to be used as a punisher, it may nonethe-less function as one. Even if restraint is not used in a "programmatic" way, we cannot predict whether or how it will affect behavior other than providing for immediate safety. Restraints *may*: 1) punish behavior; 2) allow extinction to take place by reducing the efficacy of strug-gling; 3) serve as a time-out from the opportunity to injure people or break things; 4) fail to cause any changes in the future probability of behavior; or 5) restraints may even serve as a reinforcer (Favell et al., 1978; Favell et al., 1981). Asking a child to write his or her name wasn't *designed* to be an aversive, but it sure as &@!$ can be one. I hope everyone realizes that things are just not so black and white, especially when it comes to restraint. Unfortunately, when you show people gray areas some of them become very uncomfortable. If you think in absolutes, *and* if you think that restraints are evil, then they *must* be evil and no data can change that. Of course only some people show this extreme rigid thinking, but this type of rhetoric can be very dangerous and may, ultimately, harm the very people that it was designed to protect.

SECTION 6: QUESTIONS ABOUT RESTRAINT

6.1   What questions should parents be asking?

If your child's school uses some form of restraint, it's good to ask lots of questions. I've outlined some of them already, but let me summarize them here.

1.   *What system is being used?*   There should be a formal system of crisis management and not simply a handful of procedures.

2.   *Who can I contact if I have a question about how the system is being used with my child?*   There should be someone to contact at the crisis management organization who can explain things to parents should they have questions that are not addressed by the school.

3.   *Am I going to be notified after a restraint is used? How long after?*   Parents are not usually happy when their child has been restrained. Why would they be? When parents find out that their child has been restrained multiple times and they have never been contacted about it they are (understandably) livid. The better schools I've been to notify the parents the same day that a restraint occurs.

4.   *When and how will my child be restrained? How long might it go on? What are the criteria for release?*   It's important to know which procedures are being used with your child. Are they being escorted or immobilized? If they are being immobilized is it in a vertical position, prone (downward facing), supine (upward facing), seated in a chair, or seated on the floor? Is there a recommended maximum time limit for restraint? Are there clear criteria for when restraints will be implemented and when they will be stopped?

5.   *What is being done to prevent the use of restraint?*   Has the school at least conducted a functional assessment? Is there a behavior plan? Are there new skills targeted for acquisition? Do they make sense? Is your child learning the new skills? Given that three basic things to look for regarding restraint reduction/elimination are; 1) changing the behavior of the child (teaching new skills, not reinforcing inappropriate behavior); 2) changing the behavior of staff; and 3) changing the environment, are any of these things being done?

6.   *How will my child's behavior be managed if I do not approve the use of restraint?*   If you do not wish to have restraints used with your child, I would suggest that you find out exactly what the school plans to do when your child is in crisis. Don't find out *afterward* that the police were called to intervene. Find out up front what will be done, how, why, and by whom. I believe that restraints have an appropriate place in schools as long as those schools are serving children who exhibit dangerous behaviors. However, I also recognize that they can be misused. It's the same way I feel about giving children psychotropic medications. If you don't allow people to safely stop your child, there are risks. If people say that they are hands off, there is still risk involved because they have never been shown what to do and

what not to do. Also, if your child puts hands on them, the staff will *most definitely not be hands off.* For those parents who are uncomfortable with the use of restraint, what do you expect the school to do with your child when he or she is crisis? Have your expectations been communicated to the school? If you're not comfortable with certain procedures (prone holding, for example) does the school know what to do when less restrictive forms cannot stop the child? I understand fully that some parents don't want their children held at all, but failing to talk about what *should* be done leaves the door open for unplanned, untrained tactics, and those are *never* a good idea.

6.2 How do we reduce/eliminate restraint?

Again, you've missed out because you don't have the iPad version of the book. Never fear! You can still view the powerpoint presentation by going to www.pcma.com and going to the public downloads section to find the presentation on meaningful restraint elimination and reduction.

The presentation explains how some methods of reducing restraint may not produce meaningful clinical outcomes for individuals, but simply reduce the restraint numbers. The presentation also contains an examination of six categories of problems that lead to the increased use of restraints and some ways to reduce restraints in ways that still produce meaningful clinical gains.

6.3 The Principal with principles…

I knew a behavior analyst working at a school serving a child with a high frequency of restraints—more than any other child at the school. A directive came from the school's upper administrative levels to reduce restraints. The principal was specifically told by his superiors to omit the child's data from the database because those data would skew the school's numbers. The principal refused, saying that this child needed help and that these high restraint numbers showed that the child needed more supports. I don't know what kind of trouble this principal got himself into, but I admire him for what he did. The pressure put on this principal to omit data is exactly why restraint reduction, although a great outcome (when it results from proper treatment) is a horrible goal.

6.4 Conclusions

Everyone's expectations need to be clarified before anyone does anything regarding restraint. The schools and the parents both have responsibilities in this regard. Some of the biggest problems I have seen resulted from a lack of communication from both parties. Also, parents, please remember that *risks to your child do not start with restraint.* Risks to your child start with *severe behavior problems that have not been adequately addressed.* No one wants restraint. Many of the teachers I know want absolutely nothing to do with it. Everyone is afraid of hurting someone and everyone is also afraid of being sued, and trust me, the United States is a great place to be worried about being sued. Try to focus on fixing behavior problems and/or fixing those things that prevent people from fixing behavior problems. Try not to demand that restraints be stopped. Instead, demand that your child's teachers get the training and support they need to change behavior.

Chapter 13

Problems With The Players

1.1 Behavior Analysts

First, let me talk *to* behavior analysts, then I'm going to talk *about* behavior analysts. As most of you may already know, you can't do much without the cooperation of others. I take that back: you can, as Ogden Lindsley used to say, "Play with pencils" (thank you, Dr. McGreevy). Dr. Lindsley (Og) whom I have only met once briefly in an elevator, meant that you can write behavior plans or do your fancy-schmancy functional assessment, or write a stupid book that probably won't sell very well, but if you don't actually *change behavior*, then it's just writing things down on paper for billable hours. Of course this book isn't even billable hours, so I'm really hoping it will directly change your behavior and indirectly the behavior of your students. Anyhow, if you want to do more than just write a report that gets stuck in a student's binder, you need help from others. Even if you perform a wonderful magical demonstration in which you get a child to sign, or come to the table, or complete an assignment with no prompts, it's all for naught if everyone isn't on board. Not only does the teacher have to be on board, but the assistant teachers as well. I have seen countless instances where each person in the classroom thinks that he or she knows better than the others and chaos quickly ensues. I've seen teachers doing the right thing, and paraprofessionals undo it. I've seen paraprofessionals get it right and watch the teachers cause a crisis. Parents can also play a huge role in improving the behavior of their children. Other professionals can also have a tremendous affect on the child's progress (Speech Therapist, Occupational Therapist, Physical Therapist, the school psychologist, etc.). Even the principal can contribute to behavior change. I'll try to make some observations and suggestions based on my experience with all the players. Also, please remember that no one group of people is any better than the others, including behavior analysts. I do not wish to portray all teachers, teacher's assistants, behavior analysts or parents as making a bad thing worse, because only some of them do that, and although *they* may not know who they are, everyone else *does*.

Now it's time to talk *about* behavior analysts (BAs), and, being one myself, I know the problems that can occur with behavior analysts. There are good BAs and bad BAs and then there are those in between, just like in any other profession. Of course these are just my opinions, but it's the end of the book, why break with tradition now? Beware of BAs who use too much jargon, alienate people, make the teacher feel like he or she is worse off after the consult, and use what appear to be "canned" programs. Also, beware of those BAs who will not demonstrate the procedures that they are recommending. Except for the canned programs, I have been guilty of many of these shortcomings myself. A good BA should be able to explain, in simple, everyday terms, why the child is doing what he's doing and what is going to be done about it. Although most behavior plans look very formal and technical and are littered with jargon, this is kind of the standard. There's nothing necessarily wrong with that. However, when it comes down to what staff are supposed to do, the steps need to be incredibly clear and they should be void of jargon and generalities to the greatest extent possible. That is, the program shouldn't say, "Reinforce Bobby's appropriate social interactions." Reinforce them how? With what? What are the social interactions? Does it mean anything other than punching? The recommendations need to be very specific, e.g., "verbally prompt Joey to share part of his soda with Ryan, and then tell him that he is a good friend because he shares." Is the behavior analyst telling you pretty much what you already know, or has she given you some insight and direction for what to do?

A good BA should also be sensitive to a teacher's concerns about his or her ability to implement a behavior plan given the number of students in the class and the amount of support the teacher has. The teacher should not feel worse off after the BA is done with the consult than she was before it was started. In essence, do the recommendations given make sense? If they don't, does the BA do a good job of explaining the logic behind the recommendations? A good behavioral intervention should *make sense*. If it doesn't, it needs to be explained well enough so that it does make sense. If things don't make sense, it's hard to get buy in from all the concerned parties.

Finally, with any BAs, there is sometimes an expectation that they will just wave their magic wands and bad behavior will disappear. Interventions are often hard work and they don't always change behavior rapidly. Sure, there are times when I'll make a simple recommendation that requires little work and produces quick changes, but that isn't the norm. Everyone needs to remember that the BA helps with behavior change, but that, ultimately, the behavior change is produced by the teacher and the teacher's assistants, and *not* by the BA. I always tell teachers and parents that when children get better it's not directly because of my efforts, it's because of *their* efforts. Teachers *should* claim most of the credit, but then again they have to do most of the work.

1.2 Teachers

If I had to rank order the players according to importance, the teacher would easily come out on top. In my (relatively) short ten years working in the schools I have met some incredibly talented and patient teachers. Some had no special training, but they just knew how to influence behavior and how to make learning fun. The really good ones are typically a joy to work with. They are positive, confident and typically very thankful for any assistance. They listen to the consultant, they ask good questions, and they demonstrate a detailed knowledge of the child—not just of the child's bad behavior, but also of the good things and the funny things and the touching things the child does, and that's refreshing. These folks usually just need a fresh set of eyeballs to pick up on some things that were less than obvious. Typically, when given reasonable recommendations based on a sound assessment and good probes, these teachers can usually take the ball and run with it. In many instances, they have already made progress with the child even before I become involved. They just may reach an impasse with certain behavior problems.

What about other teachers? Everyone simply can't have the same skills and the same attitude. Most teachers are very well meaning but may not have received the proper training. It happens. Frankly, the *attitude* toward behavior change is more important. Skills can be taught to anyone who is willing to be open-minded and who doesn't feel angry, threatened, or unsupported. Some teachers just need some help. They're trying to work with the child but they are, very often, a bit negative about the child by the time the behavior analyst shows up. This is particularly problematic when the teacher has been injured by a child in some manner or has seen the child attack other children. This sort of thing can be very trying on a daily basis and it might wear down just about any of us. I try to keep this in mind whenever I'm consulting, and I make an effort to be as sympathetic and supportive as possible. Even if the teacher is frustrated, she may still be open to a different perspective.

Okay, I'm mostly talking to behavior analysts now, but teachers you can listen in too. There are two basic kinds of problems that I have encountered with teachers. There are those who are a bit frustrated, yet reasonable and still willing to try some new things as long as those things make sense. Then there are those who are almost "oppositional defiant" teachers. That is, they have already come to the conclusion that the child needs a different placement. These are often the first words out of the teacher's mouth. Now it doesn't mean that this is a bad person, or even a bad teacher necessarily, but it usually means that the teacher is, despite her best efforts, done with the child. It seems that these folks always have a reason at the ready to explain why every one of my suggestions won't work. Teachers who have already decided that certain children don't belong in their classrooms are not likely to implement anything you write. Why would they? They already know that it will be a huge waste of time and they don't have time to do it anyhow! You see the same sorts of problems in homes with parents and in residential facilities with direct-care staff. Same problem, different venue. It could be burn out. It could be feeling unsupported. It could be just 46 more days until retirement. Either way, this can be a real roadblock to behavior change. Remember, no one likes to feel that they haven't done the best that they could, but some can accept this unpalatable possibility gracefully, and others will deny it till the very end. Good teachers make all the difference in the world, nothing else comes close. I know I'm repeating myself, and admitting that I have a problem is the first step to recovery. Hello, my name is Merrill, and I can't stop beating dead horses. Sorry, back to good teachers. If you see something good that they're doing, unleash the praise. When working with teachers, be sympathetic, be encouraging, be realistic and be patient. It really pays off.

1.3 Paraprofessionals (Teacher's Aides)

Teachers need to provide leadership in their classrooms. When people say, "Too many cooks spoil the soup," they don't mean that many people working together like a well-oiled machine is a bad thing. They mean that several people, each with his or her own philosophy and agenda will bring down a classroom quickly. Is the paraprofessional kind of doing his own thing, or is he working in concert with the classroom teacher? Is the teacher abrogating his or her responsibility and just using the paraprofessional to keep a watchful eye on the child? Is the teacher ensuring that the paraprofessional is implementing the behavior plan correctly? If not, is the teacher giving corrective feedback? Are the paraprofessionals getting the training they need to be able to manage behavior and teach new skills? Who is spending the most teaching time with the child, the teacher or the paraprofessional?

1.4 Parents

Although parents are not (typically) in the classroom, they can still greatly affect what happens in the classroom. Getting the full cooperation of the parents can be very important in getting a behavior problem under control. Don't misunderstand; children can still improve even if the parents do very little. I've seen it happen before. The kid's behavior improves in class but he is still terrible at home. Some children can figure out, pretty quickly, that there are two different sets of rules for home and school and their behavior changes accordingly. Still, things generally go much better when the parents are following up on what is being done in the classroom. There are so many things parents can do to improve behavior problems at school. I have known parents who send in meticulous notes with the child explaining what has been happening at home and whether the child is sleeping/eating properly. Some of them send in special reinforcers so the teacher doesn't have to buy them with his or her own money (yes teachers frequently spend their own money to buy reinforcers). Still other parents follow up on what was accomplished at school and arrange powerful reinforcers at home contingent on behavior at school. I have seen parents and teachers cooperate wonderfully and I have seen them at odds with each other (and that's putting it mildly). Behavior change is just one of those things where you get out of it what you put into it. What else, what else… oh yes, Meds! I've mentioned it before in Chapter 4 on intermittent behavior problems, but it bears repeating. Ever-changing meds and a *failure to communicate* these changes is one monkey wrench that should have stayed in the toolbox. Medications seldom fix behavior problems, but they can at times alleviate them or at least render the child a bit more workable. It's very difficult for a child's behavior to stabilize if her neurochemical makeup is constantly being rewritten. Parents, if you're reading this, please get the school to collect data on target behaviors and graph those data so that trends can be seen over weeks and months and across medication changes. Furthermore, try not to change things in the middle of a trend—let the behavior stabilize and give the behavior plan a chance to do its work. Generally, it's best to change one variable at a time so that we can tell what did what.

1.5   IEP teams

The IEP team is usually made up of an Exceptional Student Education coordinator, classroom teacher, parents, and other professionals as necessary who support the child (Speech Therapist/Physical Therapist/Occupational Therapist/Behavior Analyst services). Each individual contributes to goal setting, along with input from the parents. If the wrong behavioral goals are specified, the child is not going to make progress. The behavior analyst should be trying to work the behavioral goals into the IEP such that any functional replacement behaviors are clearly stated in the IEP and not just in a behavior program. It's up to the team to ensure that the current assessment of a child's skills is accurate and is reflected in the setting of reasonable goals. The parents sometimes contribute to the goal setting process as well and, frankly, sometimes I think the goals are too numerous and too heavy on academics in cases where the behavior problems have not yet been adequately addressed. I don't want parents to believe for a moment that the IEP determines what gets done on a moment-to-moment basis. It's just a road map; it's not a guarantee of anything. It is an educated guess as to where the child should be (hopefully) in a year's time. It's critical to avoid choosing the wrong behavioral goals (failing to specify actual, doable behaviors that pass the dead man test) and to avoid setting academic goals that just don't make sense right now or are too numerous.

1.6 Principals

The principal can play an important role in behavior change and may be very active in the education of a particular child. Or, leave everything up to the teacher. Some principals may be very understanding of a child's behavior problem and willingly accept even very difficult students and support their teachers accordingly. Some may spend more of their time trying to get a kid moved to a different placement, regardless if the other placement is truly better for the child. Some principals do an outstanding job of supporting their teachers and still others may be at odds with them. The same things happen in residential settings between administrators and direct care staff. I suppose that, in large part, it comes down to one's management style. Teachers, particularly those who work with children with challenging behavior have very difficult jobs. I've been in more than my share of classrooms with upset and/or crying teachers. Those who feel supported and valued tend to be less stressed-out. Those who don't feel that way end up feeling like they're constantly behind the eight ball. I know this much, when I see a teacher doing a good job I march myself up to the principal's office and make it clear to her that she has a really great teacher. The principals are usually very appreciative and they typically agree with me.

1.7 Summary

I once saw a presentation by the late great Don Baer, a giant in the behavior analysis world, whose shoulders we all stand on. It was at a conference in Florida and I'll never forget one of the things he said "When all the grown-ups agree, the kids tend to get better." Now this doesn't mean that just agreeing is sufficient to get behavior change. Everyone agreeing on the same wrong thing just means that everybody isn't going to blame each other when things don't go well. I think, however, that all the adults agreeing goes a long way because it means that they're working as a team and everybody understands where everyone else is coming from. When all the adults agree, it means that everyone has their eyes on the same prize.

I've been to my fair share of IEP meetings where everybody was "lawyering up." Things rarely go very well when parent/school relations have gotten to this point. I'm not saying that the parents are necessarily wrong for threatening to go the due process route—perhaps they see it as the only way to get people to listen. My point is that in such situations, people typically start coercing each other, and in a fairly big way. These kinds of meetings are clearly adversarial, usually unproductive, and just plain nasty. The parents aren't always right and the IEP team isn't always wrong in these cases and vice-versa. Everyone has to start doing some self-examination, self-doubting, self-correction, and all the players have to start showing some genuine concern about each other's problems if the child is going to truly make progress.

The process can work well. I swear it can. I remember one particular meeting where the parents were very vocal about their wishes, but also reasonable and flexible, and the school was flexible as well. As a result, everyone agreed on a reasonable course of action for getting the child, slowly, into a full-time included classroom and everyone felt comfortable with the plan. It was almost magical. I wish I had video of the event because it demonstrated how well things can go if everyone unclenches a little bit and listens to each other.

I know that working with all of these players, some of whom may have very different priorities, can be challenging but we all have to work together or the child will suffer. I can almost guarantee it, and I really don't think that anyone wants that. Incidentally, when I've felt strongly about something, I have gone head to head (at considerable speed) with just about every one of the players and one thing is for certain; you pay a price if people feel like you've coerced them. I know that I'm guilty of doing this in the past. So take it from me, you don't want to get your way on paper or get a "yes" to your face when things just go back to what they were after you leave. You just can't *force* a teacher to reverse his belief that a child is inappropriately placed in his class. You might be able to gently convince him, but you can't really force a new perspective. The same goes for all the other players. The trick is not to make people do what you tell them to, but to make people think *that it's a good idea* to do the kinds of things that you would like them to do. This is how I approach behavior change in children, and there's no reason why it shouldn't work for adults!

References

Abbott, B. The Matching Law (2009) http://users.ipfw.edu/abbott/314/MatchingLaw.html.

Ahearn, W. H., Kerwin, M. L., Eicher, P. S., Shantz, J., & Swearingin, W. (1996). An alternating treatments comparison of two intensive interventions for food refusal. *Journal of Applied Behavior Analysis*, 29, 321–332.

American Psychological Association. (2008). Children and trauma: update for mental health professionals. 2008 Presidential Task Force on Posttraumatic Stress Disorder and Trauma in Children and Adolescents. [Online]. Available: http://www.apa.org/pi/familiies/resources/update.pdf. [March 2010].

Athens, E.S., & Vollmer, T. R. (2010) An investigation of differential reinforcement of alternative behavior without extinction. *Journal of Applied Behavior Analysis,* 43, 569–589.

Azrin, N.H., Hutchinson, R. R., & McLaughlin, R. (1965) The opportunity for aggression as an operant reinforcer during aversive stimulation. *Journal of the Experimental Analysis of Behavior*, Volume 8, Number 3, 171–180.

Baillargeon, R. & DeVos, J., (2008) Object permanence in young infants: Further evidence. *Child Development*, Volume 62, Issue 6. http://onelinelibrary.wiley.com/journal/10.1111/(ISSN)1467-8624.

Behar, D.; Hunt, J.; Ricciuti, A.; Stoff, D.; Vitiello, B. (1990). "Subtyping Aggression in Children and Adolescents". *The Journal of Neuropsychiatry & Clinical Neurosciences* 2 (2): 189–192.

Binder, C. (1996) Behavioral fluency: Evolution of a new paradigm. *The Behavior Analyst*. 19, 163–197.

Blakely, E. (2009) Signs of Damage http://www.fitaba.com/page11/.

Bosch, S. & Fuqua, R. W., (2001) Behavioral Cusps: A model for selecting target behaviors. *Journal of Applied Behavior Analysis*, 34, 123–125.

Carr, E. G., & Durand, V. M., (1985) Reducing behavior problems through functional communication training. *Journal of Applied Behavior Analysis*. 18, 111–126.

Carter, S. L., (2010) A comparison of various forms of reinforcement with and without extinction as treatment for escape-maintained problem behavior. *Journal of Applied Behavior Analysis* 43, 543–546.

Catania, A. C. (1975) The myth of Self-reinforcement. *Behaviorism* vol. 3, 192–199.

Cipani, E., & Schock, K. (2007) *Functional behavioral assessment, diagnosis and treatment: A complete system for education and mental health settings*. New York: Springer Publishing Company.

Cipani, E., (2004) *Punishment on trial.* Reno: Context Press.

Cooper, J. O., Heron, T. E., & Heward, W. L., (2007) *Applied Behavior Analysis. Second Edition.* New Jersey: Pearson Education.

Courtney, K., & Perone, M., (1992) Reductions in shock frequency and response effort as factors in reinforcement by timeout from avoidance. *Journal of the Experimental Analysis of Behavior.* 58, 485–496.

CCBD *The Council for Children with Behavioral Disorders: The Use of Physical Restraint Procedures in School Settings 2009.* http://www.cec.sped.org/AM/Template.cfm?Section=Content_Folders&TEMPLATE+/CM/ContentDisplay.cfm&CONTENTID=12385.

DeGrandpre, R., (2000) *Ritalin Nation: Rapid fire culture and the transformation of human consciousness.* New York: W.W. Norton & Company, Inc.

Faber, A., & Mazlish, E. (1980) *How To Talk So Kids Will Listen & Listen So Kids Will Talk.* New York: Scribner.

Favell, J. E., McGimsey, J. F., & Jones, M. L. (1978) The use of physical restraint in the treatment of self-injury and as positive reinforcement. *Journal of Applied Behavior Analysis*, 11, 225–241.

Favell, J. E., McGimsey, J. F., Jones, M. L., & Cannon, P. R. (1981) Physical restraint as positive reinforcement. *American Journal of Mental Deficiency, 85*, 425–432.

Fisher, W. W., Kodak, T., & Moore, J. W., (2007) Embedding an identity-matching task within a prompting hierarchy to facilitate acquisition of conditional discriminations in children with autism. *Journal of Applied Behavior Analysis.* 40, 489–499.

Fleisig, N. (2005) *Professional crisis management practitioner manual.*

Friman, P. C., Wilson, K. G., & Hayes, S. C. (1998) Behavior analysis of private events is possible, progressive, and nondualistic: A response to Lamal. *Journal of Applied Behavior Analysis*, 707–708.

Gold, M. (1976). *Try Another Way.* Training film produced by Glenn Roberts. Indianapolis: Film Productions of Indianapolis.

Gold, M. (1980). *"Did I say that?" Articles and commentary on the Try Another Way system.* Champaign, IL: Research Press Company.

Hagopian, L. P., Fisher, W. W., Sullivan, M. T., Acquisto, J., & LeBlanc, L. A. (1998) Effectiveness of functional communication training with and without extinction and punishment: A summary of 21 Inpatient cases. *Journal of Applied Behavior Analysis.* 31, 211–235.

Hanley, G. P., Iwata, B. A., Roscoe, E. M., Thompson, R. H., & Lindberg, J. S. (2003) Response-restriction analysis II. Alteration of activity preferences. *Journal of Applied Behavior Analysis. 36,* 59–76.

Hanley, G. P., Piazza, C. C., Fisher, W. W. & Maglieri, K. A. (2005) On the effectiveness of and preference for punishment and extinction components of function-based interventions. *Journal of Applied Behavior Analysis.* 38, 51–65.

Herrnstein, R. J. (1961). Relative and absolute strength of response as a function of frequency of reinforcement. *Journal of the Experimental Analysis of Behavior*, 4, 267–272.

Iwata B. A., Dorsey, M. F., Slifer, K. J., Bauman, K. E., & Richman, G. S. (1994) Toward a functional analysis of self-injury. *Journal of Applied Behavior Analysis.* 27, 197–209.

Jacobson, E. (1964) *Anxiety and tension control: A physiologic approach.* Philadelphia: J. B. Lippincott, 1964.

Kupfer, A. S., Allen, R., & Malagodi, E. F. (2008) Induced attack during fixed-ratio and matched-time schedules of food presentation. *Journal of the Experimental Analysis of Behavior.* 89(1): 31–48.

Laraway, S., Snycerski, S., Michael, J., & Poling, A. (2003) Motivating operations and therms to describe them: Some further refinements. *Journal of Applied Behavior Analysis, 36*, 407–414.

Latham, G. (1994) *The Power of Positive Parenting : A Wonderful Way to Raise Children.* P&T Inc.

Levitt, Steven D. (2005) *Freakonomics; a rogue economist explores the hidden side of everything.* Steven D. Levitt and Stephen J. Dubner. Harper Collins

Lewis, T. J., Colvin, G. & Sugai, G. (2000). The Effects of Pre-Correction and Active Supervision on the Recess Behavior of Elementary Students. *Education and Treatment of Children. Vol. 23,* Issue 2.

Li, M., He, W., & Mead, A. (2009) Olanzapine and Risperidone Disrupt Conditioned Avoidance Responding in Phencyclidine- Pretreated or Amphetamine-Pretreated Rats by Selectively Weakening Motivational Salience of Conditioned Stimulus. *Faculty Publications, Department of Psychology. Paper 413.* http://digi-talcommons.unl.edu/psychfacpub/413.

MacFarlane, C. A. (1998). Assessment: The key to appropriate curriculum and instruction. In A. Hilton, D. Finn, & R. Ringlaben (Eds.) *Best and effective practices in educating students with developmental disabilities.* Council for Exceptional Children, Division on Mental Retardation and Developmental Disabilities. Austin, TX: Pro-Ed.

Mager, R.F. (1968). Developing Attitude Toward Learning. Palo Alto: Fearon Publishers.

Mayer, Roy, B. Sulzer-Azaroff, & M. Wallace, Behavior Analysis for Lasting Change, 3rd Ed. (2014). Cornwall on Hudson, NY: Sloan Publishing.

Michael, J. (1975) Positive and negative reinforcement: A distinction that is no longer necessary; or a better way to talk about bad things. *Behaviorism*, 3, 33-44.

Mueller, M. M., Palkovic C. M., & Maynard, C. S. (2007) Errorless learning: Review and practical application for teaching children with pervasive developmental disorders. *Psychology in the Schools, 44*(7), 691–700.

Piazza, C. C., Fisher, W. W., Hagopian, L. P., & Toole, L. (1998) Using a choice assessment to predict reinforcer effectiveness. *Journal of Applied Behavior Analysis. 29,* 1–9.

Perone, M. (2003). Negative effects of positive reinforcement. *The Behavior Analyst.* 26, 1–14.

Premack, D. (1959). Toward empirical behavioral laws: Instrumental positive reinforcement. *Psychological Review*, 66, 219–233.

Premack, D. (1962). Reversibility of the reinforcement relation. *Science,* 136, 255–257.

Pudelski, S. Keeping Schools Safe: How Seclusion and Restraint Protects Students and School Personnel (2012) http://www.asa.org/uploadedFiles/Resources/Tool_Kits/AASA-Keeping-Schools-Safe.pdf,

Rosales-Ruiz, J., & Baer, D. M. (1997) Behavioral cusps: A developmental and pragmatic concept for behavior analysis. *Journal of Applied Behavior Analysis, 30,* 533–544.

Shah, N. (2012) Federal Data show disproportionate use of seclusion and restraint. Source: *Education Week* 3/13/12.

Siegel, G. M., Lenske, J., & Broen, P. (1969) *Journal of Applied Behavior Analysis.* 2, 265–276.

Skinner, B. F. (1984). The operational analysis of psychological terms (and commentaries). *Behavioral and Brain Sciences*, 7, 547–582.

Skinner, B. F. (1957). *Verbal behavior.* Englewood Cliffs, NJ: Prentice Hall.

Skinner, B.F., (1948) Superstition in the Pigeon. *Journal of Experimental Psychology, 38,* 168–172.

Smith, E. M., North C. S., & Spitznagel, E. L., Post-traumatic stress in survivors of three disasters. *Journal of Social Behavior and Personality*, 8(5): 353–368, 1993

Tranter, R. & Healy, D. (1998) Neuroleptic discontinuation syndromes. *Journal of Psychopharmacology.* 12: 401

Valenstein, E. S. (1998) Blaming the brain: The truth about drugs and mental health. New York: The Free Press

Vollmer, T. R. (1999). Noncontingent reinforcement: Some additional comments. *Journal of Applied Behavior Analysis, 32,* 239–240.

Vollmer, T. R., Iwata, B. A., Zarcone, J. R., Smith, R. G., & Mazaleski, J. L. (1993). The role of attention in the treatment of attention-maintained self-injurious behavior: Noncontingent reinforcement and differential reinforcement of other behavior. *Journal of Applied Behavior Analysis, 26,* 9–21.

Woods, T. S. (1987) On diversity in the terminology concerning inhibitory stimulus control: Implications for practitioners of applied behavior analysis. *The Analysis of Verbal Behavior*, 5, 77–79.

Zhou, L., Geoff, G., & Iwata, B. A. (2000) Effects of icnreased response effort on self-injury and object manipulation as competing reinforcers. *Journal of Applied Behavior Analysis, 33,* 29–40.